LET'S STUDY
ACTS

Let's Study

ACTS

Dennis E. Johnson

THE BANNER OF TRUTH TRUST

THE BANNER OF TRUTH TRUST
3 Murrayfield Road, Edinburgh EH12 6EL, UK
P.O. Box 621, Carlisle, PA 17013, USA

*

© Dennis E. Johnson 2003
First Published 2003
ISBN 0 85151 834 6

*

Typeset in 11/12.5 pt Ehrhardt MT at the
Banner of Truth Trust, Edinburgh

Printed in Great Britain by
Bell & Bain Ltd.,
Glasgow

Contents

PART 2: THE LORD'S WORD DISPERSED TO JUDEA AND SAMARIA (8:1–12:25)

PART 3: THE LORD'S WORD TO THE END OF THE EARTH

I: ASIA AND GREECE (13:1–20:38)

Contents

Publisher's Preface

*L*et's *Study Acts* is part of a series of books which explain and apply the message of Scripture. The series is designed to meet a specific and important need in the church. While not technical commentaries, the volumes comment on the text of a biblical book; and, without being merely lists of practical applications, they are concerned with the ways in which the teaching of Scripture can affect and transform our lives today. Understanding the Bible's message and applying its teaching are the aims.

Like other volumes in the series, *Let's Study Acts* seeks to combine explanation and application. Its concern is to be helpful to ordinary Christian people by encouraging them to understand the message of the Bible and apply it to their own lives. The reader in view is not the person who is interested in all the detailed questions which fascinate the scholar, although behind the writing of each study lies an appreciation for careful and detailed scholarship. The aim is exposition of Scripture written in the language of a friend, seated alongside you with an open Bible.

Let's Study Acts is designed to be used in various contexts. It can be used simply as an aid for individual Bible study. Some may find it helpful to use in their devotions with husband or wife, or to read in the context of the whole family.

In order to make these studies more useful, not only for individual use but also for group study in Sunday School classes and home, church or college, study guide material will be found on pp. 351–70. Sometimes we come away frustrated rather than helped by group discussions. Frequently that is because we have been encouraged to discuss a passage of Scripture which we do not understand very well in the first place. Understanding must

[ix]

always be the foundation for enriching discussion and for thoughtful, practical application. Thus, in addition to the exposition of Acts, the additional material provides questions to encourage personal thought and study, or to be used as discussion starters. The Group Study Guide divides the material into thirteen sections and provides direction for leading and participating in group study and discussion.

Acknowledgements
and Dedication

It has been my privilege to teach the Acts of the Apostles at Westminster Theological Seminary in California for twenty years. I thank the trustees of the seminary for this delightful task, and for granting me a study leave during the 2002 winter term and spring semester, during which this study was written.

It has been my joy to be married to Jane for over thirty-two years. I am always amazed by and thankful for her love. On this project, as on others, I am grateful as well for her proofreading skill and editorial wisdom: always just the right blend of encouragement and incisive suggestions for improvement.

Recently Jane and I have given thanks to the Lord for the births of our first two grandsons, Jonathan David Jones and Simeon Nathanael Johnson. Several hours after his birth Jonathan joined the martyr Stephen in the presence of the Son of Man. His parents, grandparents, uncles, and aunts miss him; but we rejoice in the assurance that God's promise is for us and for our children (*Acts* 2:39), and we confess our hope in the resurrection of the dead (23:6).

Simeon, whose namesake welcomed Jesus as 'a light for revelation to the Gentiles' (*Luke* 2:32), is moving to 'the end of the earth' with his parents, who have heeded God's call to bring the Word to people who will, we pray, some day say, 'We hear . . . in our own tongues the mighty works of God' (*Acts* 2:11). This study is offered to the Lord in gratitude for these two little boys.

Introduction

The Acts of the Apostles is unique among the books of the New Testament. Four early Christian leaders (two of them apostles, according to reliable tradition) wrote accounts of Jesus' ministry, death, and resurrection. Only one, Luke, continued the story into the events of the following decades. Paul and a handful of others wrote epistles to newly established churches throughout the Graeco-Roman world, most of the churches composed predominantly of Gentiles. Only Luke's book of Acts provides us with the historical context that enables us to understand so much in those letters.

Consider what we would *not* know if we did not have Acts to 'fill the blanks' between the resurrection of Jesus (recorded in the four Gospels) and the composition of Paul's epistles. As the Gospels close, a small band of Jewish people – eleven men whom Jesus had named apostles, some women, perhaps others (only from Acts do we learn that they number 120) – are still reeling from the double shock, first of Jesus' crucifixion and then of his resurrection. They expected neither event, though he had foretold both. They abandoned him when his enemies closed in, and after his execution they hid behind locked doors for fear that those enemies should come after them as well. Even when he stood among them in the tangible body that bore the scars of his suffering and radiated the vitality of a new creation, still some doubted (*Matt.* 28:17, *Luke* 24:37, 41). Yet he commissioned this motley crew to take his message to the ends of the earth, to recruit all nations to his cause (*Matt.* 28:18–20, *Luke* 24:46–48). He promised that he would be with them, that the Spirit of truth would come, and that the

Father's promise would clothe them with power (*Matt.* 28:20, *John* 16:13–14, *Luke* 24:49). John the Baptist had promised a Coming One who would baptize with the Spirit, but as the Gospels close that promise awaits fulfilment (*Luke* 3:16). The disciples' bewilderment and doubt were giving way to joy, but the next step is unclear.

Now if we had no book of Acts we would pass in our New Testaments from the last page of John, chapter 21, to the beginning of the Epistle to the Romans, and countless questions would crop up. Who is this Paul, who claims to have been called by Jesus as an apostle? He was not one of the Twelve, nor was he mentioned at all in the Gospels. His autobiographical comments here and there make it clear that he once persecuted people who believed the message that he now propounds with joyful abandon (*Gal.* 1:23, *Phil.* 3:6, *1 Tim.* 1:13). What turned his life around? From the Gospels we learn that Jesus foresaw the geographical and demographic expansion of his movement. But how did there come to be a group of 'saints' loyal to him in Rome itself, the capital of that Empire that dominated the world, subjugated the Jewish people, and authorized Jesus' execution? Thumbing through Paul's epistles we discover that 'churches' (a term used only twice by Jesus in the Gospels) have sprung up in Asia Minor, Macedonia, Achaia, and Crete. Paul seems to have started many of them – what happened to the Eleven who stayed true after Judas' treachery?

We find Paul's epistles addressed primarily to Gentiles who apparently entered the church *not* in the manner of proselytes entering Judaism, that is via circumcision, but simply through faith, sealed in baptism. This rankles with some of those whom Paul opposes. Who made the decision to drop the covenant sign that had distinguished God's people since Abraham's day? The promised Spirit has arrived: indeed, anyone who lacks the Spirit does not belong to Christ (*Rom.* 8:9), for the Spirit incorporates Jews and Greeks, slave and free, into one body, enabling them to serve each other in love (*1 Cor.* 12:13). When did the Spirit come? How did the Spirit come?

Of course, God gave us the book of Acts to do more than satisfy our historical curiosity. Like all Scripture, its purpose is to inform and deepen our faith in Jesus Christ. Acts does this in a special way, by letting us view how Jesus kept his promise to be with his church and build his church through the personal presence and power of the Holy Spirit. We watch as the risen Lord uses apostles and prophets to lay the foundation of the church in its new covenant form (its 'last days' phase, as Peter affirmed, *Acts* 2:17), and we discover the contours and priorities that must shape the church in our time as well. In some ways, the foundational period was unique. Not every age has apostles who having walked with Jesus before his death now give eyewitness testimony to his resurrection. But the foundation determines the shape of that edifice that is still, today, being raised up to the glory of God.

AUTHOR: 'LUKE, THE BELOVED PHYSICIAN' (*Col.* 4:14)

Like the Gospels, the text of Acts does not name its author. Nevertheless the book reveals that its author was proficient in literary Greek, well acquainted with Hellenistic historical conventions, and deeply influenced by the Old Testament Scriptures in Greek translation – that is, the Septuagint. He also composed the Third Gospel and addressed it to the same recipient, Theophilus (*Luke* 1:3, *Acts* 1:1). Moreover, in several sections describing Paul's travels, the author quietly implies his own presence by switching the pronouns referring to Paul's entourage from 'they' to 'we'. The first of these so-called 'We' sections indicates that on Paul's second journey the author joined the apostle's company at Troas and travelled to Macedonia, remaining at Philippi when Paul moved west (16:10–40). On Paul's third journey the author rejoined the team in Macedonia, and intermittent references suggest that he accompanied the apostle to Jerusalem (20:5–15; 21:1–18). After Paul's Roman protectors secretly spirited him from Jerusalem to Caesarea, the author apparently joined him there. With Aristarchus of Thessalonica, the author shared the perils of the apostle's voyage to Rome (27:1–28:16). Our author had not only his first-hand experience of Paul's ministry but also access to eyewitnesses of other events, including Philip the evangelist (21:8) and some of the original apostles in Jerusalem (*Luke* 1:2).

Acts itself thus reveals its author as a highly educated colleague of Paul, who travelled with the apostle and observed significant portions of his ministry. To this internal evidence from the book, early and unanimous church tradition adds a name: Luke the physician, a dear friend of Paul's who was with him in Rome (*Col.* 4:14, see also *2 Tim.* 4:11, *Philem.* 24). Paul's greetings in Colossians distinguish his Jewish Christian co-workers (verses 10–11) from those who were Gentiles, placing Luke in the latter category (verses 12–14). This accords with our author's interest in the gospel's spread to the Gentiles, ranging from the God-fearers on the margins of synagogues to superstitious pagans and sophisticated philosophers. The *Muratorian Canon*, a list of New Testament books recognized by the church at Rome in the mid-second century, attributes the Third Gospel and Acts to Luke. Church fathers Eusebius and Jerome concur. In fact, these books are attributed to no other early Christian leader – a noteworthy point that confirms the tradition. Since Luke is not among Paul's more prominent colleagues, mere speculation would not have brought his name to the top of the list.

His designation as author must have arisen from the knowledge of earlier generations. Since the rise of historical criticism, the ancient and unanimous tradition supporting Luke's authorship of the Third Gospel and Acts has been challenged. Some scholars have found the Paul of Acts more 'heroic' than Paul's self-presentation in 2 Corinthians, or more appreciative of Jewish heritage and customs than the Paul of Galatians and Philippians. They overlook, however, the record of Paul's sufferings and hints of his fears in Acts, as well as the reminders in his letters of the miracles that attest his authority (*2 Cor.* 12:12, *Gal.* 3:5). They forget that the same Paul who resisted the requirement for Gentiles to be circumcised was ready to comply with the Mosaic Law in order to reach his fellow-Jews (*1 Cor.* 9:20). Others suspect that Acts paints too sanguine a picture of the ease and peace with which Gentiles were welcomed into the church, believing that a second-century author retold the story of Peter and Paul, casting all in a rosy glow. Such suspicions minimize the frank description in Acts of the ongoing tensions both within the church and with Judaism over the Gentile mission (*Acts* 11:3; 13:45; 15:1, 5; 17:5;

21:21, 28–29). In short, no modern misgivings are substantial enough to overthrow the conviction of those closest in time, that both the Third Gospel and Acts are the work of Paul's friend and co-worker, Luke the doctor.

Consider the significance of Luke's identity and background with respect to the dominant theme of Acts: through the Spirit's power the salvation accomplished by Jesus comes not only to the Jews but to all the nations, to the Gentiles who live at the ends of the earth. Luke, a Gentile, builds a bridge between two worlds. On the one hand, he writes articulate, literary Greek and reflects the standards and style of the Hellenistic historians. On the other, his mind has been steeped in the Old Testament Scriptures, which he not only quotes but also imitates in his own narrative approach. Luke's thorough knowledge of the Scriptures suggests that, even before he believed in Jesus, he may have been a God-fearer like Cornelius (see chapters 27–31 below), standing on the margins of a Jewish synagogue, attracted by Israel's God but excluded when he would not undergo circumcision. How Luke's heart must have soared when he heard from Paul that Israel's God welcomes all comers, even Gentiles, who trust in the Lord Jesus Christ! How his heart must have soared as he researched and recorded his account of how Christ threw open the floodgates of divine grace to all nations! Think of it: God gave a Gentile, once 'alienated from the commonwealth of Israel' (*Eph.* 2:12), the privilege of writing more words of the New Testament than any other author. That's right: Luke's Gospel and Acts are longer than all of Paul's letters put together, and longer than John's Gospel, Epistles, and Revelation combined. As he penned his record of God's salvation in Christ, Luke was himself an exhibit and a proof that God's light now shone on all the peoples of the earth.

AUDIENCE: 'MOST EXCELLENT THEOPHILUS' (*Luke* 1:4, *Acts* 1:1)

In the introduction to his Gospel Luke addresses the recipient of his two-volume work as 'most excellent Theophilus'. The title 'most excellent' is not merely flattery, but the appropriate form of address for members of the equestrian class – not the highest tier of Roman society, but close to it. In Acts the title reappears in a letter and in speeches addressed to the Governors Felix and Festus (23:26; 24:3; 26:25). Perhaps Theophilus had a governmental office of comparable authority. It has been suggested that Theophilus was Luke's literary patron who funded the (hand-copied!) publication of the Gospel and Acts, in that the Jewish historian Josephus calls his patron 'most excellent Epaphroditus' at the beginning of his polemic *Against Apion*. This suggestion is possible, but speculative.

Others have proposed that Theophilus was an official at the imperial court who could influence the outcome of Paul's hearing before Caesar. This theory is based not only on the 'most excellent' title but also on the perception that Paul's appeal had not been heard when Acts was written. The opinions of the tribune Claudius Lysias, Governor Festus, and King Agrippa, affirming Paul's innocence are cited as evidence that Luke was writing a 'friend of the court' brief to persuade a sympathetic Roman official that Paul should be exonerated. Both the Gospel and Acts, however, contain so much material that would be irrelevant to Roman legal issues and of interest only to Christians. This hypothesis therefore is unlikely.

What Luke makes clear is that Theophilus had been 'taught' (literally, 'catechized') the message of Christ, but that he needed the reassurance that a carefully researched, orderly account of Jesus' deeds and words would provide (*Luke* 1:3–4). The attention given in Acts to Gentile God-fearers, who believed in Israel's God but declined circumcision, may suggest that Theophilus himself was a God–fearer who attended synagogue services. That would explain why Luke not only quoted many Old Testament Scriptures but also referred to others, expecting his audience to recognize the connections between the ancient promises and their fulfilment in Jesus. As a Gentile accustomed, like Luke, to being treated by Jews as a 'second-class citizen' on the outskirts of Israel, Theophilus would need the assurance that Luke's history affords, that God himself had authorized the church's welcome of Gentiles by faith alone. Moreover, as a member of the upper classes, he would need reassurance that he had not become involved in a movement devoted to disrupting the peace and order of Roman society.

PURPOSE: 'CERTAINTY CONCERNING THE THINGS YOU HAVE BEEN TAUGHT' (*Luke* 1:4)

Luke wrote his two volumes, therefore, to provide a carefully researched, orderly narrative of 'the things that have been accomplished' – the long-promised establishment of God's kingdom now fulfilled – in the Christian community (*Luke* 1:1). The prologue to his Gospel has reference to the book of Acts as well. Others were setting their hands to this assignment, at least with respect to the earthly life and ministry of Jesus, but Luke carried his narrative beyond the resurrection into the early decades of the church's mission after Jesus ascended to heaven. Luke's record would substitute for the apostles' preaching in person, giving Theophilus access to the testimony of 'those who from the beginning were eyewitnesses and ministers of the word' (verse 2). He therefore wrote, in part, to impart confident faith to educated, upper-class Gentiles who were well acquainted with the ancient Scriptures and newly converted to faith in Jesus, Israel's Messiah and the Saviour of the nations.

Acts is a work of theological history. True to his stated purpose, Luke records accurately the events of early Christian history. Unlike some modern historians, however, he does not pretend to be 'objective' or attempt to be exhaustive. The scenes that he describes and the angles from which he views them are carefully selected to achieve his theological and pastoral objectives. He stands squarely in the tradition of the covenantal history of the Old Testament. For ancient Israel, history was never a dispassionate record of bare facts or academic speculation about causes and effects. It was the account of God's intervention to make Israel his own; of Israel's failures and infidelities; and of the just discipline and patient faithfulness of the Lord of the covenant. Luke carries the Israelite tradition of covenantal history forward into fulfilment in Christ the Lord.

Acts is not simply a blueprint for ministry or a book of church order in story form, although its narratives often illustrate the principles for church life and leadership that the New Testament epistles teach directly. As the opening paragraph of Acts implies, this book is, first and foremost, the record of what Jesus continued to do and teach after his ascension through the power of the Holy Spirit.

STRUCTURE: 'JERUSALEM . . . ALL JUDEA AND SAMARIA . . . THE END OF THE EARTH' (*Acts* 1:8)

Acts traces the expansion of the kingdom of God through the growth of the Word both geographically and demographically. The overarching structure (see the following outline) is geographic, following the contours of Jesus' promise and commission (*Acts* 1:8): 'But you will receive power when the Holy Spirit has come upon you, and you will be my witnesses in Jerusalem and in all Judea and Samaria, and to the end of the earth.'

The witness in Jerusalem begins with Peter's sermon on the Day of Pentecost and concludes with Stephen's defence speech and martyrdom (chapters 1–7). The church is then dispersed by persecution throughout Judea and Samaria (8:1; 9:31) and even reaches Damascus and Antioch in Syria (8–12). Finally, from the church at Antioch Paul is sent out with various partners to bring the gospel to the Jewish Dispersion and to Gentiles at 'the end of the earth', beginning with Cyprus and Asia Minor, including Macedonia and Greece, and finally reaching Rome itself (13–28).

In each section Peter has a significant role, although his prominence progressively diminishes. In Jerusalem, he is the prominent preacher and the spokesman before the Sanhedrin. In Judea and Samaria, he (with John) confirms God's salvation of the Samaritans and proclaims the gospel to uncircumcised Gentiles in the home of Cornelius. In the book's third section, he stands to defend Paul's Gentile mission at the apostolic council in Jerusalem.

In each section Paul has a significant role, and his prominence increases. In Jerusalem, he approves the violence of those who martyr Stephen. In Judea and Samaria, he actively pursues the scattered believers in his zeal to eradicate Jesus' name, until the risen Lord confronts him on the road to Damascus. In the third section, he embarks with Barnabas, and later with Silas, Timothy, and others, on the work to which the Holy Spirit separates him, proclaiming salvation to the Gentiles at the earth's end.

A further hint of the contents of the third section, which focuses on Paul's worldwide ministry, is given in Jesus' words to the pious Ananias, who was to heal Paul's blindness and tell him the good news of grace. Jesus said that Paul was 'a chosen instrument of mine to carry my name before the Gentiles and kings and the children of Israel' (9:15). Thus in Acts 13–28 we hear Paul's testimony before Gentiles (13–20), kings (and other rulers, climaxing in King Agrippa, 24–26), and the people of Israel (22–23, 28).

Coinciding with the geographical expansion is the kingdom's invasion of new demographic groups, bringing saving grace to new categories of people. The catalogue of nationalities present on the Day of Pentecost to hear the Word, each 'in his own native language', provides a preview of the church's impending ethnic explosion, but the audience that day is limited to Israelites and Gentile proselytes to Judaism (2:8–11). It is in the second phase of its expansion that the gospel bursts through religious and ethnic barriers. In Jewish eyes, the Samaritans occupied an ambiguous status on the boundary between God's people and the pagan nations, but God welcomes them, as Philip preaches and Peter and John pray for them. During this phase the Ethiopian eunuch and Cornelius, both pious God-fearers yet uncircumcised, come to faith as the first-fruits of the Gentiles, and the church at Antioch reaches out to Gentiles in large numbers. In carrying the gospel 'to the end of the earth', Paul's ministry typically began in the Dispersion synagogues but was redirected to the Gentiles – and not only to God-fearers, but also to pagans enmeshed in idolatry, philosophy, and occult arts.

Because Christ's kingdom advances through the power of the gospel, each of the three sections is dominated by sermons and speeches. In these we hear how the apostles presented the gospel to Jewish audiences in the temple, to mixed audiences in the synagogues, and to Gentile audiences ranging from the superstitious to the sophisticated. We hear the Jewish ruling council rebuked for its rebellious unbelief (by Stephen, *Acts* 7) and a Jewish king boldly challenged to believe the prophets' promises (by Paul, *Acts* 26). Each phase includes a summary that describes the growth of the church as the growth of the Word:

PHASE ONE: 'And the Word of God was growing and the number of the disciples was multiplying exceedingly . . . ' (6:7).

PHASE TWO: 'But the Word of God was growing and multiplying' (12:24).

PHASE THREE: 'Thus with might the Lord's Word was growing and exerting strength' (19:20; Author's translations).

By filling Acts with sermons Luke enables us to hear the eyewitnesses' proclamation of what they had seen and heard in Jesus, and of the life-changing significance of those events for all peoples.

Outline of the Book of Acts

III. THE LORD'S WORD TO THE END OF THE
EARTH, PART 1: ASIA AND GREECE (13–20)

A. The First Mission to the Nations (13–14)
   Sermons: Paul at Pisidian Antioch
   and Lystra (Asia Minor)
B. The Reception of the Nations into the church
   (15:1–35)
C. The Second Mission to the Nations
   (15:36–18:22)
   Sermon: Paul at Athens (Achaia)
D. The Third Mission to the Nations (18:23–20:38)
   Sermon: Paul's farewell to the Ephesian
   elders

IV. THE LORD'S WORD TO THE END OF THE
EARTH, PART 2: ROME (21–28)

A. Paul Attacked and Arrested in Jerusalem
   (21:1–23:11)
   Sermon: Paul's defence to the Jerusalem crowd
B. Paul Tried before Felix in Caesarea (23:12–24:27)
C. Paul Tried before Festus and Herod Agrippa II
   (25–26)
   Sermon: Paul's defence to Agrippa
   Paul Appeals to Caesar (25:11)
D. Paul's Voyage to Rome (27:1–28:10)
E. Paul Preaches the Word of the Lord in Rome
   (28:11–31)
   Sermon: Paul's to the Jewish Leaders
   at Rome.

The Risen Lord
Commissions His Witnesses

In the first book, O Theophilus, I have dealt with all that Jesus began to do and teach, ² until the day when he was taken up, after he had given commands through the Holy Spirit to the apostles whom he had chosen. ³ To them he presented himself alive after his suffering by many proofs, appearing to them during forty days and speaking about the kingdom of God.

⁴ And while staying with them he ordered them not to depart from Jerusalem, but to wait for the promise of the Father, which, he said, "you heard from me; ⁵ for John baptized with water, but you will be baptized with the Holy Spirit not many days from now."

⁶ So when they had come together, they asked him, "Lord, will you at this time restore the kingdom to Israel?" ⁷ He said to them, "It is not for you to know times or seasons that the Father has fixed by his own authority. ⁸ But you will receive power when the Holy Spirit has come upon you, and you will be my witnesses in Jerusalem and in all Judea and Samaria, and to the end of the earth." ⁹ And when he had said these things, as they were looking on, he was lifted up, and a cloud took him out of their sight. ¹⁰ And while they were gazing into heaven as he went, behold, two men stood by them in white robes, ¹¹ and said, "Men of Galilee, why do you stand looking into heaven? This Jesus, who was taken up from you into heaven, will come in the same way as you saw him go into heaven" (Acts 1:1–11).

The opening paragraphs of the book of Acts turn our eyes back to Jesus' deeds and words during his earthly ministry, as told in Luke's 'first book', the Third Gospel. The risen Jesus also points his disciples' eyes forward to the future, to the outpouring of the Spirit prophesied by John the Baptist and the worldwide expansion of God's kingdom by the Spirit's power. This opening section of Acts and the closing paragraphs of Luke's Gospel (24:36–53) interlock like the two sides of a hinge, connecting the two phases of Jesus' actions and teachings. The first was the period of his ministry on earth (through sufferings to resurrection glory) and the second his present heavenly enthronement, from where he pours out his Spirit to empower his church for its mission.

LOOKING BACK AND FORWARD

The two-verse prologue of Acts recalls the more detailed introduction to Luke's Gospel. Luke introduced his Gospel by announcing his intention to record an accurate and orderly account of 'the things that have been accomplished among us, just as those who from the beginning were eyewitnesses and ministers of the word have delivered them to us' (*Luke* 1:1–2). Luke stands in the tradition of redemptive history, stressing that God's promises spoken through ancient prophets have now reached their fulfilment in Jesus. But he also stands in the tradition of Hellenistic history, which, in its best expression, stressed that careful investigation and accurate reporting are necessary for the credible narration of real events. Luke's pastoral purpose is that Theophilus may have certainty regarding the things he has been taught. Theophilus represents readers who have not had direct contact with the apostolic eyewitnesses and need to hear their testimony through Luke's careful account. The same redemptive viewpoint, historical method, and pastoral purpose control Luke's approach to his second volume: Acts.

In characterizing the contents of his Gospel as that which Jesus *began to do and teach*, Luke implies that the book of Acts will continue the story of Jesus' deeds and words, though the mode of Jesus' action and instruction undergoes a radical change because of his ascent to heaven. The change is foreshadowed in the forty-day period between his resurrection and his ascension. During this period it is *through the Holy Spirit* that Jesus instructs his apostles. Luke's Gospel underscored the physical nature of Jesus' resurrection body, evidenced in such convincing *proofs* as his invitation to feel his flesh and bones and his eating of a meal (*Luke* 24:39–43). Yet his physical body now has powers unknown to the old creation (*John* 20:19). As the last Adam and first-fruits of the resurrection, Jesus had 'become a life-giving spirit' (*1 Cor.* 15:45, see also *Rom.* 1:4), the first burst of life in the new creation. So his every appearance and every word were expressions of his new vitality in the power of the Spirit – the Spirit through whom Jesus would continue to speak and act in his apostles, after taking his seat at God's right hand in heaven. The convincing proofs that Jesus showed to the *apostles* look forward to their special role as witnesses to his resurrection (*Acts* 1:22; 2:32). Luke mentions that Jesus himself had *chosen* his apostles (*Luke* 6:12–16) to prepare us for his selection of a replacement for Judas the traitor in the days preceding Pentecost (1:24–26).

THE TIMING, DIMENSIONS, AND POWER OF THE KINGDOM

The message preached previously by John the Baptist and Jesus himself could be summed up, 'The kingdom of heaven is at hand' (*Matt.* 3:2; 4:17). Now, after his suffering, Jesus spoke again of God's *kingdom*. As had often happened before, his disciples mistook his meaning, trying to force his promise into the mould of their own expectations. Their misunderstanding was threefold, having to do with the timing of the kingdom's coming, its dimensions, and the power that would establish it.

With respect to timing, they had forgotten Jesus' observation that mere humans cannot pry into God's hidden timeline for history (*Matt.* 24:36). In fact, only recently Jesus had told the parable of the *minas* to disabuse his followers of the illusion that the kingdom of God (in its final form) was about to appear (*Luke* 19:11).

Their question about restoring *Israel* to royal power drew the boundaries of the kingdom too narrowly, constricting its dimensions. The realm to be reached by God's saving dominion would go far beyond Israel. The Lord had commissioned his Servant to do more than restore Jacob's tribes: 'I will make you as a light for the nations, that my salvation may reach to the end of the earth' (*Isa.* 49:6). Jesus the glorified Servant refers here to this promise by defining the expanding dimensions of God's reign: *Jerusalem, all Judea and Samaria*, and finally the Gentiles at *the ends of the earth*.

The sphere of God's rule to be exercised by Jesus from his throne at God's right hand would not only be broader than they imagined. It would also be deeper. The only power strong enough to invade and enliven dead, rebel hearts is the Holy Spirit, the gift promised by the Father. When the Spirit would come, the apostles would receive 'power from on high' (*Luke* 24:49, see also *Isa*. 32:15; 44:3–5) and fulfil Israel's calling as the Lord's *witnesses* to the nations, testifying that he alone bestows salvation (*Isa*. 43:10; 44:8).

DEPARTURE AND PROMISED RETURN

Jesus ascended to heaven as our priest and our king. In his Gospel Luke notes that Jesus lifted his hands in blessing as he was taken into heaven (*Luke* 24:50–51), just as Aaron lifted his hands to bless the Israelites when he entered the tabernacle as their high priest (*Lev*. 9:22–24). The Epistle to the Hebrews shows the confidence we can derive from the fact that Jesus our high priest now represents us in God's heavenly sanctuary (*Heb*. 8:1–2; 9:11–14; 10:19–23).

In Acts the emphasis is on the royal significance of Jesus' entrance into heaven. He was hidden by a *cloud*, reminding us of the clouds on which the Son of Man approached the Ancient of Days to receive his eternal and worldwide kingdom (*Dan*. 7:13–14; *Mark* 14:62). Peter would soon declare that God had fulfilled his promise to enthrone David's heir forever by seating Jesus at his right hand (*Acts* 2:33–36). In heaven Jesus always prays for us; from heaven Jesus always rules us.

Two men dressed in white – their sudden appearance and white clothing show that they are angels – chided the disciples' stunned amazement. Jesus will return from heaven *in the same way* in which the apostles watched him depart. Even now, before his second coming, Jesus would keep his promise, 'I am with you always, to the end of the age' (*Matt*. 28:20) through the Holy Spirit. Having the certainty of Christ's eventual return and the promise of his Spirit's imminent arrival, the disciples' wistful gaze into the sky was distracting them from the mission at hand.

It is not ours to know the date of that great day of the Lord. It is ours, rather, to carry on the apostles' witness in our generation, confident that his Spirit uses his Word to draw dead rebels into true life and glad submission to Christ's rule.

[4]

2

The Apostolic Number Restored

Then they returned to Jerusalem from the mount called Olivet, which is near Jerusalem, a Sabbath day's journey away. [13] *And when they had entered, they went up to the upper room, where they were staying, Peter and John and James and Andrew, Philip and Thomas, Bartholomew and Matthew, James the son of Alphaeus and Simon the Zealot and Judas the son of James.* [14] *All these with one accord were devoting themselves to prayer, together with the women and Mary the mother of Jesus, and his brothers.*

[15] *In those days Peter stood up among the brothers (the company of persons was in all about 120) and said,* [16] *"Brothers, the Scripture had to be fulfilled, which the Holy Spirit spoke beforehand by the mouth of David concerning Judas, who became a guide to those who arrested Jesus.* [17] *For he was numbered among us and was allotted his share in this ministry."* [18] *(Now this man bought a field with the reward of his wickedness, and falling headlong he burst open in the middle and all his bowels gushed out.* [19] *And it became known to all the inhabitants of Jerusalem, so that the field was called in their own language Akeldama, that is, Field of Blood.)* [20] *"For it is written in the Book of Psalms,*

" 'May his camp become desolate,
    and let there be no one to dwell in it';
and
" 'Let another take his office.'
[21] *So one of the men who have accompanied us during all the time that the Lord Jesus went in and out among us,* [22] *beginning*

from the baptism of John until the day when he was taken up from us – one of these men must become with us a witness to his resurrection." ²³ And they put forward two, Joseph called Barsabbas, who was also called Justus, and Matthias. ²⁴ And they prayed and said, "You, Lord, who know the hearts of all, show which one of these two you have chosen ²⁵ to take the place in this ministry and apostleship from which Judas turned aside to go to his own place." ²⁶ And they cast lots for them, and the lot fell on Matthias, and he was numbered with the eleven apostles (Acts 1:12–26).

With their Lord's promise to baptize them with the Holy Spirit 'not many days from now' ringing in their ears (1:5), the eleven apostles returned to Jerusalem to await the Father's gift. As they joined with other believers in expectant prayer, their ascended Lord continued to teach them by showing Peter from Scripture that a replacement for Judas the traitor must be chosen. Then through the casting of lots Christ revealed his choice of Matthias to fill the apostolic vacancy. Because Pentecost would fulfil God's promises to ancient Israel and usher the people of God into a new era, the gap created by Judas' defection must be filled. The leadership of the new Israel must be at full strength as the new epoch dawns.

PREPARING IN PRAYER

From the Mount of Olives the Eleven returned to the city of Jerusalem, to the upstairs room where they were staying. This may have been the same room in which they had observed the Passover with Jesus on the night of his betrayal (*Luke* 22:12). If so, it held a host of bitter-sweet memories: Jesus' puzzling identification of himself during the meal with the Passover lamb and the suffering servant; their own confusion and cowardice when he was arrested later that evening; his astonishing appearances to them after his crucifixion, alive from the dead and risen from the tomb. Now they gathered, at his command, to wait.

Luke lists the Eleven by name, calling attention to their number, since Peter's speech to the expectant congregation will stress that the apostolic *number* must be restored to completeness: twelve apostles, corresponding to Jacob's twelve sons, the heads of Israel's tribes. The names are identical to those in Luke 6:13–16, which recorded Jesus' first selection of the Twelve (after a night spent in prayer), except for the omission of Judas the traitor. The order has changed slightly. James and John now follow Peter at the top of the list, since these three had emerged as Jesus' closest intimates (*Luke* 9:28). Peter still comes first, despite his denials of Jesus. Jesus had prayed for Peter's restoration (*Luke* 22:31–34) and designated him to take the lead in preaching the gospel.

These eleven apostles gathered with the women who had supported Jesus and his disciples (*Luke* 8:2; 23:49; 24:1, 10), with his mother Mary, and with his brothers. Luke's Gospel revealed Mary's submission to God's plan, her pondering of the mysteries surrounding her Son, and her anxious misunderstanding of him (*Luke* 1:38, 46–55; 2:19, 48–51). Later she and his brothers had tried to draw Jesus away from the crowds that surrounded him – 'to seize him', as Mark says, thinking him mad (*Mark* 3:21, 31–35, Luke 8:19–21). At that point Jesus' own brothers did not believe in him (*John* 7:5). Now, however, their doubt and confusion dispelled by Jesus' resurrection, Mary and her sons belonged to the church that prayerfully anticipated the outpouring of the Spirit.

As they awaited the Father's gift, they prayed with single-minded persistence and passionate devotion. Their persistence was 'with one accord', for Luke emphasizes the early Christians' perseverance and unity in prayer both here and elsewhere (2:42, 46; 4:24; 5:12; 6:4). Jesus had taught them to pray confidently. After all, even evil human fathers give good gifts to their children, 'how much more will the heavenly Father give the Holy Spirit to those who ask him!' (*Luke* 11:13). They confronted a great task, for which they needed a great gift. This Spirit is the gift for which they persistently petitioned their Father. Do our prayers lack fire and persistence because we doubt the Father's generosity or because we underestimate our need – or both?

REPLACING THE TRAITOR

In the context of this expectant prayer we hear the first speech of Acts, in which we see that Jesus' post-resurrection instruction on how the Scriptures find their fulfilment in himself has borne good fruit. Peter now realized what Jesus had been teaching his disciples both before his death (*Luke* 9:22; 17:25; 18:31–34; 22:37) and after his resurrection (*Luke* 24:25–27, 44–49), that *the Scripture*, in which God announced that his Messiah would suffer rejection and death, *had to be fulfilled*. Specifically, Peter saw in Psalms 69:25 and 109:8 the dark treachery of one who repaid the friendship extended by God's king with hatred and harm (see *Psa*. 109:4–5). Such betrayal demanded a judgement that included the desolation of an inheritance and the removal from a position of influence.

The desolation was fulfilled in Judas' gory death in a field purchased with the proceeds of his betrayal. His blood defiled the land, making it unfit for the living to dwell there and so it became a cemetery for aliens (*Matt*. 27:7–8). Judas' untimely death also removed him from his apostolic office, and Scripture required that *another take his office*. Since Judas was *numbered among us* (1:17, see also *Luke* 22:3), his fall created a vacancy on one of the twelve thrones from which the apostles would judge Israel's twelve tribes (*Matt*. 19:28, *Luke* 22:30). Therefore Judas must be replaced as well as removed. The company of apostles must be complete.

Whereas Psalm 109 spoke generally of a *place of leadership* (or 'position of oversight', as in 1 Tim. 3:1), Peter defined those qualifications and that role which identify the uniqueness of the apostolic office. The replacement must come from those men who had travelled with Jesus throughout his ministry, *from the baptism of John* until Jesus' ascension. This extensive and intensive association would qualify him to accomplish the apostles' unique calling as a witness *with us* of his resurrection. To apostles and prophets in the New Testament church God revealed mysteries previously concealed; this enabled them together to form the church's foundation, of which Christ is cornerstone (*Eph*. 3:4–5; 2:20). But the apostles, as eyewitnesses to Jesus' resurrection, are of more importance even than the prophets (*Luke* 1:2, *Acts* 2:32; 4:20; 10:39–41; 13:30–31).

For this reason apostles must be appointed directly by Jesus himself (see *Acts* 1:2). Later the whole congregation would recognize leaders to oversee mercy ministry (6:3), and Paul and Barnabas would appoint elders to shepherd new churches (14:23). But here, having narrowed the field to two men who met the criterion announced by Peter, the church turned to her Lord in prayer, asking him to reveal the man he had chosen. They then cast lots, to remove the human factor from the decision and to seek an indication of God's will (*Prov.* 16:33, *Jon.* 1:7). Although Christ gives other leaders to his church through our discernment of the appropriate gifts and graces, apostles are appointed 'not from men nor through man, but by Jesus Christ and God the Father, who raised him from the dead' (*Gal.* 1:1). Once Matthias was numbered with the Eleven, the new Israel stood ready to receive the Father's great 'last days' gift, the Spirit who would set their tongues on fire in testimony to his wonderful deeds in Jesus.

Judas' defection was planned by God and predicted in ancient Scriptures. It had to occur because it was an integral component of God's surprising strategy to redeem believers through the suffering of his Messiah. Yet Judas was responsible, and his treachery is a solemn warning to us. Paul would later call upon the church elders in Ephesus to stand guard over each other, since some of their own number would distort the truth in order to attract a following for themselves (20:30–31). Church leadership is not a refuge from spiritual attack, but a place of exposure and vulnerability. Pray for your leaders. If you are a leader, seek spiritual safety where it can be found: close to Jesus in the words of his gospel and in urgent prayer, and in ongoing accountability to your brothers.

3

The Lord Comes to His Temple

When the day of Pentecost arrived, they were all together in one place. ² And suddenly there came from heaven a sound like a mighty rushing wind, and it filled the entire house where they were sitting. ³ And divided tongues as of fire appeared to them and rested on each one of them. ⁴ And they were all filled with the Holy Spirit and began to speak in other tongues as the Spirit gave them utterance.

⁵ Now there were dwelling in Jerusalem Jews, devout men from every nation under heaven. ⁶ And at this sound the multitude came together, and they were bewildered, because each one was hearing them speak in his own language. ⁷ And they were amazed and astonished, saying, "Are not all these who are speaking Galileans? ⁸ And how is it that we hear, each of us in his own native language? ⁹ Parthians and Medes and Elamites and residents of Mesopotamia, Judea and Cappadocia, Pontus and Asia, ¹⁰ Phrygia and Pamphylia, Egypt and the parts of Libya belonging to Cyrene, and visitors from Rome, ¹¹ both Jews and proselytes, Cretans and Arabians—we hear them telling in our own tongues the mighty works of God." ¹² And all were amazed and perplexed, saying to one another, "What does this mean?" ¹³ But others mocking said, "They are filled with new wine" (Acts 2:1–13).

In Luke's Gospel the descent of the Spirit on Jesus in his baptism was followed and interpreted by Jesus' sermon at Nazareth (*Luke* 3:21–22; 4:14–19). Likewise in Acts, Luke first recounts the event of the Spirit's descent on the church, and then Peter's sermon explains this watershed event. The event is illustrated by audible and visible signs which emphasize that Pentecost parallels and fulfils God's descent upon Mount Sinai to make his covenant with Israel.

WIND AND FLAMES

In writing that the day of Pentecost *arrived* Luke uses an unusual Greek word, better translated 'was fulfilled', in order to emphasize the epoch-defining importance of this day. Elsewhere this word refers to the arrival of a promised event at the completion of a specific time period (*Jer.* 25:12, *Luke* 9:51). Pentecost was the day on which Jesus would fulfil his promise to baptize his followers with the Holy Spirit.

Falling fifty days after the Passover, Pentecost is called the Feast of Weeks in the Old Testament (*Lev.* 23:15–21, *Deut.* 16:9–12) and is sometimes associated with the first-fruits of the wheat harvest (*Exod.* 34:22, *Num.* 28:26). Since it fell in the third month after Passover, the rabbis also came to associate it with the giving of the Law to Moses at Sinai (*Exod.* 19:1).

The Spirit's coming was accompanied by three observable wonders: (1) a *sound like a mighty rushing wind* descending from heaven and filling the house, (2) what seemed to be *tongues of fire* distributing themselves and resting on each believer, and (3) the Christians' ability to *speak in other tongues.*

(1) Both the Hebrew and the Greek words for *Spirit* can also mean *wind* or breath, and the Spirit's life-imparting power is portrayed in the imagery of filling lungs with the breath of life (*Ezek.* 37:9–10, 14, *John* 3:6–8; 20:22, *Rev.* 11:11, see also *Gen.* 2:7). Here the church's spiritual lungs were filled to declare God's mighty deeds. The sound of the Spirit filled the whole house where they were sitting, just as the glory of the Lord had filled the tabernacle and temple long ago (*Exod.* 40:35, *1 Kings* 8:10–11). The Spirit was consecrating a new sanctuary, in which God would dwell among his people.

(2) The visible phenomena that seemed to be *tongues of fire* were miniaturized pillars of fire, like the cloud of glory over the tent of meeting in the wilderness, designating it the Lord's residence in the

centre of Israel's camp (*Exod.* 40:36–38). These flames marked each believer as a sanctuary on whom the Spirit of God rested (*1 Cor.* 6:19, see also *1 Pet.* 4:14). The fact that the flames were *divided* to rest on each of them implies that, even when Jesus' followers were dispersed from Jerusalem, the site of Israel's temple, God's Spirit would accompany them, making their community, wherever they gathered, 'a holy temple in the Lord' (*Eph.* 2:21–22).

GOD'S WONDERS IN THE TONGUES OF THE NATIONS

(3) A wordplay links the visible *tongues* (flames) of fire with the audible tongues (languages) of the nations, in which Jesus' servants spoke the wonders of God. These spoken tongues were the native languages (or 'dialects', *Acts* 2:8) spoken in the Roman Empire's far-flung corners and beyond, as the audience from the Jewish Dispersion recognized.

Luke's catalogue of regions and nationalities sweeps from east (*Parthians*) to west (*Rome*), from north (*Asia*) to south (*Egypt* and *Libya*), from island peoples in the centre of the sea (*Cretans*) to desert peoples on the outskirts of the Empire (*Arabs*). The crowd included not only those born of Jewish parents but also Gentile proselytes who had converted to serve the God of Israel. To the amazement of all, unlettered Galileans proclaimed God's achievements in the world's diverse dialects.

This list of nationalities echoes the table of nations in Genesis 10, which leads up to the account of the confusion of languages at Babel (*Gen.* 11:1–9). At Babel God judged human pride, thwarting the plans of those who sought to control deity and gain fame. He divided the rebels by disrupting communication, scattering them over the earth (*Gen.* 11:8–9; 10:32). At Pentecost God's grace in Jesus began to reunite divided people so that God might be glorified and not man. God spoke his good news directly to the nations, in the languages of their hearts. The instantaneous, miraculous gift at Pentecost foreshadowed the labours of preachers, Bible translators, and others through the centuries, through whom the Spirit still spreads Jesus' fame through all the earth.

THE DEAFNESS OF UNBELIEF

The Gospel always provokes two responses, joyful faith and angry rejection. Even though the news of Jesus is unimaginably good and its messengers strive to make it as plain as day, still the aroma of Christ is the fragrance of life to some and the stench of death to others (*2 Cor.* 2:15–16). Jesus' parables revealed God's kingdom to his disciples while obscuring it to outsiders (*Mark* 4:10–12). In the same way, at Pentecost, the gift that made God's wonders clear to so many, simultaneously garbled the message to others, who dismissed the Spirit-given speech as a symptom of drunkenness (*Acts* 2:13, see *1 Cor.* 14:20–25). To native Judeans the church's preaching sounded like Babel revisited. But even when the form is no obstacle to understanding, the content of the gospel – Christ crucified and risen – attracts some while repelling others.

Does it thrill you to think that God is preaching the gospel of his Son today in languages you do not know, to people you have never met? How do you – or how may you – participate in this ongoing mission to speak the wonders of God in the tongues of the world?

4

The Rejected, Risen Christ
Pours Out the Spirit

*But Peter, standing with the eleven, lifted up his voice and
addressed them, "Men of Judea and all who dwell in Jerusalem,
let this be known to you, and give ear to my words. ¹⁵ For these*
men are not drunk, as you suppose, since it is only the third hour
of the day. ¹⁶ But this is what was uttered through the prophet
Joel:*
> ¹⁷ *" 'And in the last days it shall be, God declares,*
> *that I will pour out my Spirit on all flesh,*
>   *and your sons and your daughters shall prophesy,*
> *and your young men shall see visions,*
>   *and your old men shall dream dreams;*
> ¹⁸ *even on my male servants and female servants*
>   *in those days I will pour out my Spirit, and they shall*
> *prophesy.*
> ¹⁹ *And I will show wonders in the heavens above*
>   *and signs on the earth below,*
>   *blood, and fire, and vapour of smoke;*
> ²⁰ *the sun shall be turned to darkness*
>   *and the moon to blood,*
>   *before the day of the Lord comes, the great and magnificent*
> *day.*
> ²¹ *And it shall come to pass that everyone who calls upon the*
> *name of the Lord shall be saved.'*

²² *"Men of Israel, hear these words: Jesus of Nazareth, a man
attested to you by God with mighty works and wonders and signs
that God did through him in your midst, as you yourselves know
— ²³ this Jesus, delivered up according to the definite plan and*

foreknowledge of God, you crucified and killed by the hands of lawless men. ²⁴ God raised him up, loosing the pangs of death, because it was not possible for him to be held by it. ²⁵ For David says concerning him,

> *" 'I saw the Lord always before me,*
> *for he is at my right hand that I may not be shaken;*
> *²⁶ therefore my heart was glad, and my tongue rejoiced;*
> *my flesh also will dwell in hope.*
> *²⁷ For you will not abandon my soul to Hades,*
> *or let your Holy One see corruption.*
> *²⁸ You have made known to me the paths of life;*
> *you will make me full of gladness with your presence.'*

²⁹ "Brothers, I may say to you with confidence about the patriarch David that he both died and was buried, and his tomb is with us to this day. ³⁰ Being therefore a prophet, and knowing that God had sworn with an oath to him that he would set one of his descendants on his throne, ³¹ he foresaw and spoke about the resurrection of the Christ, that he was not abandoned to Hades, nor did his flesh see corruption. ³² This Jesus God raised up, and of that we all are witnesses. ³³ Being therefore exalted at the right hand of God, and having received from the Father the promise of the Holy Spirit, he has poured out this that you yourselves are seeing and hearing. ³⁴ For David did not ascend into the heavens, but he himself says,

> *" 'The Lord said to my Lord,*
> *Sit at my right hand,*
> *³⁵ until I make your enemies your footstool.'*

³⁶ Let all the house of Israel therefore know for certain that God has made him both Lord and Christ, this Jesus whom you crucified" (Acts 2:14–36).

Peter's sermon interpreted the meaning of the Spirit's coming, affirming that the strange phenomena that amazed and confused the crowd were the work of Jesus, whom they rejected but whom God raised to life and exalted to rule in heaven. Woven into the fabric of Peter's message were three Old Testament texts (*Joel* 2, *Psalm* 16, *Psalm* 110), for the risen Lord's instruction and the Spirit's illumination had opened Peter's eyes to see the Scriptures fulfilled in Christ's sufferings and subsequent glories (*Luke* 24:25–27, 45–49, see *1 Pet.* 1:10–12).

THE SPIRIT POURED OUT ON A PROPHETIC PEOPLE

Peter deflected the detractors' dismissive charge of drunkenness by pointing instead to God's ancient promise, spoken through the prophet Joel, to pour out his Spirit on all his servants, men and women, enabling them to prophesy. This outpouring means that *the last days* – foretold by the prophets as the time in which the Lord would bring salvation and judgement – have come.

In describing the Spirit as *the promise of the Father* (1:4), Jesus invited his disciples to remember the many promises delivered by prophets such as Joel (*Joel* 2:28–32). God's promise through Joel to *pour out my Spirit* on Israel's sons and daughters, so that all – male and female, young and old – *shall prophesy* confirmed a wistful desire of Moses generations earlier. God had distributed the Spirit on seventy of Israel's elders, so that they might share Moses' burden of leadership. Two of the seventy were not near Moses, yet they received the Spirit like the rest, provoking objection from Joshua, Moses' loyal aide. Moses, however, responded, 'Are you jealous for my sake? would that all the LORD's people were prophets, that the LORD would put his Spirit on them!' (*Num.* 11:29).

Just as the elders in Moses' day prophesied only once but afterwards continued to exercise the Spirit's wisdom (*Num.*11:25), so also in the apostolic church not all continually prophesied or spoke in tongues, yet every believer received from the Spirit some gift for service (*1 Cor.* 12:4, 28–30). The initial outpouring of the Spirit at Pentecost fulfilled Joel's prophecy that the whole people of God would 'prophesy', as they spoke God's wonders in the ancient world's diverse dialects. The New Testament gift of speaking in tongues is a special form of prophecy.

Wonders in the heavens and *signs on the earth* would precede the Lord's arrival to judge and to save. Jesus' miraculous wonders and signs on earth had attested to his Messianic authority (2:22). The darkening of the sun had shown that on the cross the Messiah was enduring the Last Judgment for his people (*Luke* 23:44–45). Now from heaven come the roar of a *mighty wind* and the visible sign of *tongues of fire*, testimonies to Jesus' resurrection and enthronement at God's right hand. The crisis of the *great and magnificent* day of the Lord now brings salvation to everyone who calls on the name of the Lord – on the name of Jesus, who has been made *both Lord and Christ*.

REJECTED BY MEN, EXALTED BY GOD

After quoting the prophecy of Joel, Peter's sermon seemed suddenly to shift directions. His hearers needed to understand that Jesus, whom they had rejected but whom God had raised to life and exalted to heaven, was the one responsible for the Spirit's outpouring and the amazing signs that accompanied his arrival. Drawing terms from Joel's prediction, Peter reminded them that the wonders and signs performed by Jesus throughout his ministry were God's seal of authenticity, confirming Jesus' authority. Nevertheless God's own people had done away with Jesus, using the cross and the hands of Gentiles who lived outside the covenant and Law given through Moses (as to their being 'lawless', see also *1 Cor.* 9:21). The conflict between God's accreditation of Jesus and their repudiation of him revealed their complicity in this travesty of justice; yet their crime could not thwart God's plan. God's *definite plan and foreknowledge* decreed and guaranteed Jesus' undeserved death, without exonerating his murderers.

But death could not have final victory. When Peter said that God freed Jesus from *the pangs of death*, he used an expression from Psalm 18:4–5, which pictures death's cords entangling their victim like seaweed, to drown him in the depths. Death could not keep its grip on Jesus, for he is the Holy One who spoke through David in Psalm 16. Jesus, not David, is the One was not abandoned to the grave and did not see decay. David's tomb, still standing as Peter spoke, bore mute but irrefutable testimony that David had not been delivered from the grave before decay set in. But David had received God's oath as king. David's descendant would rule on his throne forever (*Psa.* 132:11). And David had received God's Spirit as prophet, to peer down the centuries and foresee the resurrection of the Messiah.

This Messiah, who saw the Lord at his right hand and rejoiced in that security, had now been exalted to God's right hand in heaven. This also David had foreseen, announcing the enthronement edict that the Lord addressed to *my Lord*: 'Sit at my right hand until I make your enemies your footstool' (*Psa.* 110:1). Jesus had silenced his opponents earlier (*Luke* 20:41–44) with the conundrum of this Messianic text: How can the Messiah be both David's son (subordinate to David, as a son ought to be) and David's Lord (superior to David, as a Lord ought to be)? Jesus' resurrection and ascension – fulfilling God's oath to put a descendant on David's throne forever – lift the veil on this mystery. Jesus is not only David's descendant, born in the last days to reign on David's throne, he is also David's Sovereign, rightly called 'Everlasting Father' (*Isa.* 9:6–7, see *Mic.* 5:2). The resurrection and ascension constitute God's public declaration that the Jesus who was crucified in weakness and rejection has been installed as Lord over all and as Christ, the anointed King (2:36).

From his heavenly throne, the Son, to whom the Father gives the Spirit in limitless supply (*John* 3:34), has *poured out* this Spirit on his expectant disciples, with the attendant miraculous signs of wind, flames, and tongues. If the Lord himself promised through Joel that he would *pour out* the Spirit, and if Jesus has now poured out the Spirit on his followers, only one conclusion can be drawn: Jesus is the Lord on whose name we must call for salvation.

5

Showers of the Spirit Bear Fruit

Now when they heard this they were cut to the heart, and said to Peter and the rest of the apostles, "Brothers, what shall we do?" 38 And Peter said to them, "Repent and be baptized every one of you in the name of Jesus Christ for the forgiveness of your sins, and you will receive the gift of the Holy Spirit. 39 For the promise is for you and for your children and for all who are far off, everyone whom the Lord our God calls to himself." 40 And with many other words he bore witness and continued to exhort them, saying, "Save yourselves from this crooked generation." 41 So those who received his word were baptized, and there were added that day about three thousand souls.
42 And they devoted themselves to the apostles' teaching and fellowship, to the breaking of bread and the prayers. 43 And awe came upon every soul, and many wonders and signs were being done through the apostles. 44 And all who believed were together and had all things in common. 45 And they were selling their possessions and belongings and distributing the proceeds to all, as any had need. 46 And day by day, attending the temple together and breaking bread in their homes, they received their food with glad and generous hearts, 47 praising God and having favour with all the people. And the Lord added to their number day by day those who were being saved (Acts 2:37–47).

The prophet Isaiah pictured the outpouring of the Spirit as showers of rain falling on thirsty ground, causing grass and trees to spring up in new life (*Isa.* 44:3–4). He also portrayed God's

Word as rain that waters the earth and makes it fruitful (*Isa.* 55: 10–11). The response of the crowd to Peter's sermon fulfilled these prophetic portraits of refreshment and productivity. God's Word, preached in the power of God's Spirit, pierces and softens hard hearts producing repentance, trust in God's promises, and a community of joy and compassion.

PIERCED HEARTS AND GOD'S PROMISES

Peter's message reached a convicting climax: 'God has made him both Lord and Christ, this Jesus whom *you crucified*.' The clash between God's vindication of Jesus and the crowd's repudiation of him overwhelmed their conscience with the enormity of their guilt and of the divine judgement that loomed over them. The result was intense inner pain: they were *cut to the heart*, feeling the anguish and despair of 'the brokenhearted' (*Psa.* 109:16). Understandably, they begged for direction. Could anything be done to avert the vengeance that God would surely bring on people who so shamefully mistreated his Messiah?

Peter's answer was straightforward, 'Repent and be baptized . . . in the name of Jesus Christ.' Repentance is a change of mind and heart, a turning of our allegiance away from sin, self, and God-substitutes (*Luke* 3:3). Repentance reaches deeper than regret over sin's unpleasant consequences. It registers pain over the offence that we have given to God. Repentance also includes turning toward the living God and his saving grace (*1 Thess.* 1:9–10). In this sense it includes faith in Christ and his promises, as we see elsewhere in Acts (15:9; 16:31) and the epistles of Paul. So radical a turning away from ourselves and towards God bears fruit in changed behaviour (*Luke* 3:8–14). Peter's hearers, who had publicly repudiated the Messiah, would need to acknowledge publicly their dependence on Jesus by undergoing baptism in his Name. Elsewhere we learn that in Christian baptism the name of the triune God is placed upon us (*Matt.* 28:19, see *James* 2:7, *Num.* 6:23–27). Here the focus is on Jesus' Name, for baptism in his Name would signal a Copernican revolution in their relationship to him.

Peter added a reassuring twofold promise: those who turn from their high-handed opposition to Jesus and acknowledge him as the exalted Lord would receive both forgiveness of their sins and the gift of the Holy Spirit. Peter did not explain here, as he would elsewhere, how Jesus' sacrifice provided our forgiveness (*1 Pet.* 1:18–19; 2:24). It was enough that Peter's hearers acknowledge their guilt by submitting to baptism in Jesus' name. Their grief showed that the Holy Spirit was already at work in them, convicting them of their sin, of Jesus' righteousness, and of impending judgement (*John* 16:8–11). As they identified with Jesus in repentant faith, the Spirit whom the baptismal waters symbolized would unite them with the new people of God, the body in which the Spirit enables every member to serve others (*1 Cor.* 12:13).

Although they had broken covenant with God by rejecting his Redeemer, the promise of forgiveness and of the Spirit's presence still stood open, to be received by faith not only by Peter's hearers but also by their *children*. This was in keeping with God's covenantal faithfulness through generations (*Gen.* 17:7; 18:19, *Isa.* 44:3). Moreover, the promise now includes *all who are far off*, a phrase from Isaiah 57:19 applied to the Gentiles in the New Testament (*Acts* 22:21, *Eph.* 2:17). Now the *Lord our God will call* all the peoples to find deliverance on Mount Zion (*Joel* 2:32).

A COMMUNITY OF JOY AND COMPASSION

The three thousand who received baptism at Pentecost at once entered a new family, defined not by genetics but by allegiance to Jesus. In his first transition summary Luke lists four activities in which believers were continually absorbed – the *apostles' teaching*, the *fellowship*, the *breaking of bread*, and *prayers*.

The *apostles' teaching*, as we see from Peter's sermon, focused on Jesus as the fulfilment of God's promise to redeem and renew his people. Though they once demanded Jesus' death, these new believers now became absorbed in learning all that the apostles could teach about him. Just as Jesus' ministry had been attested by miracles, so also awe-producing signs confirmed the testimony of his witnesses.

The *fellowship* was primarily the pooling of material resources, having everything in common (2:44–45). (The Greek words translated *fellowship* and *common* are derived from the same root word.) In gratitude for God's gift, confidence in his care, and compassion for their spiritual brothers and sisters, believers sold their excess possessions to meet the needs of others. This sharing of resources will be explained more fully in the second summary (4:32–35).

Their *prayers* they offered daily in the temple courts. The next scene will show Peter and John entering the temple at the time of prayer, the time of the evening sacrifice (3:1). They also prayed in their own gatherings, apart from the institutions of Judaism, asking the Lord to show his choice of an apostle (1:24) and to give boldness (4:24–30).

The *breaking of bread* no doubt took place in the setting of shared meals as believers gathered in homes for encouragement, instruction, and worship. Luke's reference, however, seems to be more specific: the original reads 'the breaking of the bread'. This is the Lord's Supper, which Jesus instituted when he broke the bread with the Twelve on the eve of his death (*Luke* 22:19; see also *Luke* 24:30). Breaking the bread to commemorate Jesus' sacrifice was a central element of early Christian worship each Lord's day (*Acts* 20:7, 11).

Does the Word of God, carried by the Spirit of God, descend like life-giving, life-transforming rain on your heart, on your church? Although signs and wonders marked the uniqueness of the apostles' time and ministry, yet the Spirit still pursues his mighty work of piercing hearts, convicting consciences, evoking faith, and creating churches in which God's truth reigns, God's love is expressed in generosity, and God's praises are sung with joy.

6

The Lame Leaps

Now Peter and John were going up to the temple at the hour of prayer, the ninth hour. ² And a man lame from birth was being carried, whom they laid daily at the gate of the temple that is called the Beautiful Gate to ask alms of those entering the temple. ³ Seeing Peter and John about to go into the temple, he asked to receive alms. ⁴ And Peter directed his gaze at him, as did John, and said, "Look at us." ⁵ And he fixed his attention on them, expecting to receive something from them. ⁶ But Peter said, "I have no silver and gold, but what I do have I give to you. In the name of Jesus Christ of Nazareth, rise up and walk!" ⁷ And he took him by the right hand and raised him up, and immediately his feet and ankles were made strong. ⁸ And leaping up he stood and began to walk, and entered the temple with them, walking and leaping and praising God. ⁹ And all the people saw him walking and praising God, ¹⁰ and recognized him as the one who sat at the Beautiful Gate of the temple, asking for alms. And they were filled with wonder and amazement at what had happened to him (Acts 3:1–10).

In his summary of the vibrant life of the church after Pentecost, Luke mentioned both the miraculous signs that had confirmed the apostles' preaching and the worship of the believers at the temple (2:42–47). He next records an incident that began as two apostles entered the temple for prayer, unfolded with an astounding miracle of healing, and issued in Peter's bold proclamation of the power of Jesus' name. Boldness was needed for their preaching about Jesus and the resurrection would be opposed by the Sadducean authorities. These were the men who controlled the temple and who had condemned Jesus a few months earlier. Overnight incarceration and vague threats would be the first of an escalating series of persecutions to be endured by Jesus' witnesses.

THE LORD'S NAME COMES TO THE TEMPLE

The prophet Malachi had predicted the sudden appearance of the Lord in his temple, purifying Israel's defiled sanctuary and compromised priests by his fiery holiness (*Mal.* 3:1–4). The Lord Jesus had come to the Jerusalem temple as an infant, destined to divide Israel (*Luke* 2:25–35); he had come as the zealous defender of the temple's sanctity as a house of prayer (*Luke* 19:45–46); and as the invincible teacher of God's truth (*Luke* 19:47–48). Now through Peter and John, Christ came to the temple in the saving power of his Name.

Jesus' death had rendered the temple and its sacrifices obsolete as means of atonement before God. In the bright light of the cross these shadows had no further purpose. In fact, the flames resting on Jesus' followers had marked them as God's new temple, composed of living stones. Yet in God's plan the new does not obliterate the old; rather, it affirms even as it fulfils, transforms, and transcends. Therefore Peter and John continued to frequent the temple with their fellow-Jews, entering the gate called *Beautiful* (probably the Nicanor gate with massive doors of Corinthian bronze) *at the hour of prayer, the ninth hour* since daybreak. According to the Jewish historian Josephus, the ninth hour was the time of the evening sacrifice (*Exod.* 29:38–39), an especially appropriate time to offer petitions to God.

A man *lame* from his mother's womb asked them for a donation, an act of mercy. His ankles and legs had been useless since birth, so others carried him daily to a spot outside the temple gate to beg alms from worshippers as they entered. The rabbis taught that gifts to the destitute please God, so what better time and place to appeal to the Jews' pity and piety than when they are entering God's temple?

Others would view his disability and humiliating dependency as signs of God's disfavour, like blindness (*John* 9:1–2, 8) and the woes of Job (*Job* 4:7–8). After all, the Psalmist had never seen a righteous man's children begging bread (*Psa.* 37:25). The blind and the lame in Aaron's line were barred from priestly service (*Lev.* 21:17–23).

Perhaps the gate was the closest to God's sanctuary that this man was allowed to come. Peter and John, however, serve a Master who reaches out to the untouchable, welcomes the unacceptable, and cares for the insignificant. So Peter awakened the beggar from his mindless mantra for alms with the arresting words: '*Look at us.*'

THE POWER OF THE NAME

The rare gift of eye contact from Peter raised expectations that a generous contribution was forthcoming; but the apostles, though they co-ordinated the church's care for its needy (2:45; see also 4:34–35), had no silver or gold to fulfil his expectations. The gift that they could bestow, however, was of infinitely greater value: they bore the name of the Messiah and authorization from the King to initiate the restoration of the creation's wholeness by calling broken people to believe. When Peter commanded the lame to walk *in the name of Jesus Christ of Nazareth*, he was not invoking Jesus' name in a magical incantation, as the misguided sons of Sceva would try to do (19:13–16). Rather, he was inviting faith in Jesus' Person (3:16). The Lord's Name often stands for his personal presence (*Exod.* 23:21, *Deut.* 12:5, 11). So now by his Name Jesus revealed himself and drew near to heal, eliciting trust and imparting strength.

THE LAME LEAPS LIKE A DEER

Peter's grip raised the beggar to stand on ankles that had never borne his weight before but were instantly made strong. Suddenly he not only stood, but also walked and jumped for joy. No longer the epitome of defective helplessness, in an instant he became living, leaping, praising proof of God's power to keep his promise: 'Your God will come . . . Then the eyes of the blind shall be opened, and the ears of the deaf unstopped; then shall the lame man leap like a deer, and the tongue of the mute sing for joy' (*Isa.* 35:4–6). When John the Baptist asked from prison, 'Are you the one who was to come, or should we expect someone else?' Jesus answered with this prophecy (*Luke* 7:20–23). Jesus' miracles of healing were confirming his identity as the promised Saviour, whereas his judgment of the wicked, which John also predicted, awaits his return.

Since defective limbs no longer excluded him from God's sanctuary, the man accompanied Peter and John into the temple courts, mingling his praises with those of Israel's psalms. People who recognized him from his years at the gate were amazed, just as the witnesses to Jesus' raising of a paralysed man had been (*Luke* 5:26).

Are you equally astonished at the power of Jesus' name to cure the disabilities of the human heart? Isaiah's prediction that the lame would leap symbolized a healing deeper than the physical: 'Strengthen the weak hands, and make firm the feeble knees. Say to those who have an anxious heart, "Be strong; fear not! Behold, your God will come"' (*Isa.* 35:3–4). This healing was a sign, pointing to the strengthening of hearts paralysed by fear. Still today his life giving Spirit imparts faith in his Name, empowering timid people to leap in praise to God.

7

The Glorified Servant Bestows Blessing

While he clung to Peter and John, all the people ran together to them in the portico called Solomon's, astounded. ¹²*And when Peter saw it he addressed the people: "Men of Israel, why do you wonder at this, or why do you stare at us, as though by our own power or piety we have made him walk?* ¹³ *The God of Abraham, the God of Isaac, and the God of Jacob, the God of our fathers, glorified his servant Jesus, whom you delivered over and denied in the presence of Pilate, when he had decided to release him.* ¹⁴ *But you denied the Holy and Righteous One, and asked for a murderer to be granted to you,* ¹⁵ *and you killed the Author of life, whom God raised from the dead. To this we are witnesses.* ¹⁶ *And his name – by faith in his name – has made this man strong whom you see and know, and the faith that is through Jesus has given the man this perfect health in the presence of you all.*

¹⁷ *"And now, brothers, I know that you acted in ignorance, as did also your rulers.* ¹⁸ *But what God foretold by the mouth of all the prophets, that his Christ would suffer, he thus fulfilled.* ¹⁹ *Repent therefore, and turn again, that your sins may be blotted out,* ²⁰ *that times of refreshing may come from the presence of the Lord, and that he may send the Christ appointed for you, Jesus,* ²¹ *whom heaven must receive until the time for restoring all the things about which God spoke by the mouth of his holy prophets long ago.* ²² *Moses said, 'The Lord God will raise up for you a prophet like me from your brothers. You shall listen to him in whatever he tells you.* ²³ *And it shall be that every soul who does not listen to that prophet shall be destroyed from the*

people.' ²⁴ And all the prophets who have spoken, from Samuel and those who came after him, also proclaimed these days. ²⁵ You are the sons of the prophets and of the covenant that God made with your fathers, saying to Abraham, 'And in your offspring shall all the families of the earth be blessed.' ²⁶ God, having raised up his servant, sent him to you first, to bless you by turning every one of you from your wickedness" (Acts 3:11–26).

The leaps of joy and shouts of praise of the once-lame man, combined with the fact that many recognized him as the well-known cripple who used to beg outside the temple, gathered a curious crowd around the two apostles. Behind their rapt stares lay an unspoken question, 'Who are these men who wield such power, to raise the lame to walk and leap?' In answer Peter pointed away from himself and John to another, to the Messiah Jesus whom God had raised from the dead to heavenly glory.

As on the day of Pentecost, the apostolic Word interpreted the miraculous sign: the rejected but risen Jesus is the source of salvation, both physical and spiritual. Just as Peter and John here deflected attention from themselves to the Lord who called them as his witnesses (3:15), Paul and Silas would do likewise when another lame man was healed in the pagan city of Lystra (14:8–18). Peter's explanation of the healing also turned a searchlight on to his hearers, revealing their guilt for repudiating the Messiah promised and provided for them, and their need for the forgiveness and change of heart that he alone can give.

NOT OUR POWER OR PIETY, BUT JESUS' NAME

Pagan legends spoke of 'divine men' who had supernatural powers to heal. Jewish traditions spoke of teachers so pious that God was obligated to answer their prayers. Peter and John, however, would permit neither of these explanations for the miraculous healing that had taken place through them. Peter's rhetorical question makes clear that it is not 'by our own power or piety' that the lame man has gained use of his feet for the first time in his forty years of life (3:12; 4:22).

Rather, this healing has occurred because the God of Abraham, Isaac, and Jacob, *the God of our fathers* has glorified his servant Jesus. When the Lord identified himself to Moses at the burning bush as the God of the patriarchs, he was emphasizing that he would set Israel free from slavery because he was faithful to the promises he made to Abraham, Isaac, and Jacob (*Exod.* 3:6). Jesus had cited this passage to show the Sadducees (who accepted only the books of Moses and rejected the resurrection) that even in Moses' day God's covenant faithfulness guaranteed victory over death through the resurrection of the body (*Luke* 20:37). Now Peter announced that God had given the ultimate demonstration of his faithfulness to the fathers: he glorified his dead Servant by raising him from the dead, fulfilling the promise of Isaiah 52:13.

But the Servant Song of Isaiah 52:13 – 53:12 also spoke of the Servant's suffering as one repudiated by the very people whose punishment he would bear. This too was fulfilled in Jesus. The honour that he received from God stood in sharpest contrast to the contempt with which his own people treated him. God judged him *Holy and Righteous* (see the expression, 'the righteous one, my servant', *Isa.* 53:11); and even the Roman governor Pilate wanted to release him as innocent (*Luke* 23:4, 14–16, 22).

Peter's hearers, however, handed him over to pagan authorities, disowned him, and so killed *the author of life*, obtaining in the bargain the freedom of the *murderer* Barabbas (*Luke* 23:18–19, 23–25). The word that is translated *author* refers elsewhere to a trail-blazer or commander who leads others, and that meaning fits well here (*Heb.* 2:10; 12:2, *Acts* 5:31). God raised Jesus from the dead to make him the One who leads others to life, and from his resurrection healing flows to others. Thus the healing of the lame man is itself a sign of resurrection, for the same Greek verb describes Peter's action toward the lame man ('he raised him up') and God's raising of Jesus. It is not the apostles but the risen Jesus himself, evoking trust by revealing himself in his Name, who has given this complete healing to the man. Jesus is not only the object of the trust that brings rescue from disability and even death itself; he is also the initiator of our faith, for faith comes *through him.*

YOUR SINFUL IGNORANCE, BUT GOD'S SOVEREIGN GRACE

By this point the crowd's curious question, 'Who are these men to exercise such healing power?' had been replaced by a more sobering and more personal question: 'How shall we escape the wrath of the God whose Holy and Righteous One we hounded to death?' Peter therefore changed his tone from blunt indictment to passionate invitation. His hearers and their leaders had *acted in ignorance* when they rejected Jesus (see also *1 Cor.* 2:8). Their ignorance did not remove their culpability, but it left the door open for God's mercy and their repentance (*1 Tim.* 1:13). Paradoxically, their hope of rescue from the judgement they deserved lay in the fact that the bloodshed which they had committed in guilty ignorance, was in fact planned in God's sovereign grace and predicted through his holy prophets. On the road to Emmaus Jesus had shown downcast disciples that the prophets foretold that the Christ had to suffer before entering his glory (*Luke* 24:25–27). Now Peter linked the Messiah's travails to the Servant's sufferings foretold by Isaiah (see *Acts* 8:32–35).

Peter supported his call to repentance – to turn from their rejection of God's righteous Servant Jesus and cast themselves instead on God's mercy – with strong motivations. Those who turn to God by faith in Jesus' name will have their sins *blotted out*, erased from God's record book (*Rev.* 20:12, see also *Col.* 2:14). Moreover, forgiveness of their sins opens a hopeful future, a coming age that Peter described both as *times of refreshing* and as the time for God to restore everything (3:19, 21).

Jesus, whom they rejected, is nevertheless still *the Christ appointed for you*, and his return from heaven at the time chosen by the Father will effect the restoration of all things. Before his ascension Jesus' disciples had asked about 'the kingdom,' which they understood in terms of the restoration to Israel of political independence and dominance amongst the nations (1:6). Jesus' answer had then lifted their sights to the nations at 'the ends of the earth.' Now with this expanded angle of vision Peter foresaw a re-creation of the entire cosmos, a new heavens and earth in which the brokenness caused by sin is erased (*2 Pet.* 3:13).

The fulfilment of prophetic promise in Jesus confronted Peter's hearers with a crisis, in which two alternative destinies stood before them. To the rich portrait of Jesus that he had already presented – the Holy and Righteous Servant, the author of life, the Christ – Peter now added two more themes: the prophet like Moses and the offspring of Abraham. Moses was the unique fountain-head of Old Testament prophecy, but he had promised that the Lord would raise up a prophet like himself, about whom he commanded, 'To him you shall listen – whatever he speaks to you' (*Deut.* 18:15–20). Other prophets followed in Moses' train, but none matched the face-to-face intimacy of the revelation that Moses had received (*Num.* 12:6–8). Now, however, the chosen Son had come, and on the Mount of Transfiguration Peter heard God's voice echo the command of Deuteronomy 18: 'Listen to him!' (*Luke* 9:35). The consequences of refusing to hear and heed the voice of this last Spokesman from the Father would be dire: he will be completely cut off from among his people (see *Lev.* 23:29).

On the other hand, the threat of covenant curse was accompanied by the promise of covenant blessing. Despite their wickedness Peter's listeners were *sons of the prophets and of the covenant*. The promise extends back beyond Moses to Abraham, and it is a promise of blessing for all earth's peoples through Abraham's seed (ESV: *offspring*; citing *Gen.* 22:18; 26:4). Although 'Abraham's seed' sometimes refers collectively to Abraham's descendants or heirs (*Gal.* 3:29), here the seed identifies a single individual (as in *Gal.* 3:16). This is clear from Peter's conclusion in verse 26, which brings together Jesus' role as prophet ('raised up' echoes verse 22), as servant (echoing verse 13), and as seed of Abraham ('to bless you' echoes verse 25). Jesus himself is the promised offspring who brings blessing to Jews first, and then to the other clans of the earth.

The blessing begins with the gift of repentance, *turning every one of you from your wickedness*, for even though the hearers were responsible to turn to God (verse 19), they could not do so unless the Christ whom they had spurned mercifully turned them around. Soon the Gospel would spread to the Gentiles, and to them also the Lord would give repentance leading to life (11:18).

As we consider the exalted titles of Jesus we do well to ask ourselves if we are responding appropriately to who he is and to what he has done and is doing: 'Do I eagerly hear him as he, the final prophet, speaks in his Word, written and preached? Do I readily repent of the ways in which I still repudiate or ignore the Servant King whom God sent to bring us blessing, and who will come again to set everything right?'

8

The Name That Saves

And as they were speaking to the people, the priests and the captain of the temple and the Sadducees came upon them, ²*greatly annoyed because they were teaching the people and proclaiming in Jesus the resurrection from the dead.* ³ *And they arrested them and put them in custody until the next day, for it was already evening.* ⁴ *But many of those who had heard the word believed, and the number of the men came to about five thousand.*

⁵ *On the next day their rulers and elders and scribes gathered together in Jerusalem,* ⁶ *with Annas the high priest and Caiaphas and John and Alexander, and all who were of the high-priestly family.* ⁷ *And when they had set them in the midst, they inquired, "By what power or by what name did you do this?"* ⁸ *Then Peter, filled with the Holy Spirit, said to them, "Rulers of the people and elders,* ⁹ *if we are being examined today concerning a good deed done to a crippled man, by what means this man has been healed,* ¹⁰ *let it be known to all of you and to all the people of Israel that by the name of Jesus Christ of Nazareth, whom you crucified, whom God raised from the dead—by him this man is standing before you well.* ¹¹ *This Jesus is the stone that was rejected by you, the builders, which has become the cornerstone.* ¹² *And there is salvation in no one else, for there is no other name under heaven given among men by which we must be saved."*

¹³ *Now when they saw the boldness of Peter and John, and perceived that they were uneducated, common men, they were astonished. And they recognized that they had been with Jesus.* ¹⁴ *But seeing the man who was healed standing beside them, they had nothing to say in opposition.* ¹⁵ *But when they had commanded them to leave the council, they conferred with one another,* ¹⁶ *saying, "What shall we do with these men? For that*

*a notable sign has been performed through them is evident to all the inhabitants of Jerusalem, and we cannot deny it. *[17]* But in order that it may spread no further among the people, let us warn them to speak no more to anyone in this name." *[18]* So they called them and charged them not to speak or teach at all in the name of Jesus. *[19]* But Peter and John answered them, "Whether it is right in the sight of God to listen to you rather than to God, you must judge, *[20]* for we cannot but speak of what we have seen and heard." *[21]* And when they had further threatened them, they let them go, finding no way to punish them, because of the people, for all were praising God for what had happened. *[22]* For the man on whom this sign of healing was performed was more than forty years old* (Acts 4:1–22).

The gospel of Christ always evokes sharply contrasting responses. On the day of Pentecost, the believers' ability to proclaim the mighty deeds of God in Jesus in the diverse languages of the nations moved some to awed wonder and others to derisive dismissal (2:11–13). The growing numbers of believers in Jesus and the public preaching of Peter and John in Jesus' name now moved the Sadducean authorities, who controlled the temple precincts, to take forceful action to oppose the spreading name of Jesus.

The name of Jesus, which elicited the lame man's faith and brought him physical and spiritual salvation, was the point at issue when the apostles were arraigned before the Sanhedrin, Judaism's highest court. The high priestly circle challenged them: *By what power or by what name* did this healing take place? Peter answered that the man's salvation from lameness had been effected *by the name of Jesus Christ of Nazareth*, and he affirmed that there is *no other name under heaven given among men by which we must be saved*. Unable to refute the evidence of the healing, the council in the end feebly charged the apostles no longer to speak or teach *in the name of Jesus* – a command that had to be respectfully refused. As we will see in our next study, the church in response to the report by Peter and John of the Sanhedrin's threats turned to God in prayer, begging for boldness and further signs and wonders through *the name of your holy servant Jesus*, to confirm their message (4:30).

OPPOSITION AND HARVEST

Peter and John were addressing the sizeable crowd in Solomon's portico. (Conversions from this sermon would swell the church's numbers by several thousand, 4:4.) To stop them a group composed of priests and other Sadducees, and commanded by the captain of the temple guard, approached to take the apostles into custody for a hearing the next day. The captain, who was second in command to the high priest, had charge of temple security and order. To that end he commanded a 'police force' of Levites trained and armed to quell disturbances. His force had participated in the arrest of Jesus in the Garden of Gethsemane a few months earlier (*Luke* 22:52). In fact, the apostles' arrest and 'trial' resembles that of their Lord in several ways, including the inability of their accusers to lodge any credible charge against them.

The party affiliation of this group as *Sadducees* is significant. Though not genealogically descended from Zadok, the high priest during the reigns of David and Solomon (*2 Sam.* 8:17, *1 Kings* 1:34), the Sadducees probably derived their name as a party from his. They recognized only the five books of Moses as divine Scripture. In Moses' writings they saw no doctrine of the resurrection of the body, nor of the survival of the soul after death, so the Sadducees denied these doctrines and dismissed the Pharisees' belief in them as an illegitimate later innovation (*Acts* 23:6–8). The high priestly dynasty of Annas and Caiaphas, who controlled the temple and its profitable concessions in money-changing and the sale of sacrificial animals, were Sadducees. When they put to Jesus a 'test case' that exposed (as they thought) the absurdity of resurrection, Jesus had silenced them by appeal to Exodus, which even they recognized as normative (*Luke* 20:27–40). It is no wonder, then, that the leading priests and other Sadducees should be upset that the apostles were preaching the power of Jesus (whose execution they had engineered), now risen from the dead! In their view the Pharisees' belief in a resurrection of the righteous at history's end was bad enough, but to proclaim that a crucified Messianic pretender had come back from the dead in their own time – unthinkable!

Peter and John spent the night in the custody of the temple guard, awaiting a hearing before Judaism's high council in the morning; but

Luke notes the expanding harvest of the word of Jesus that they had preached. The message that brought many to faith, increasing the number of men to about five thousand, is 'the word' – Luke's watchword for the Christ-centred gospel that grows in strength, extending its life-giving influence to more and more people, and eventually to all the peoples of the world (*Luke* 1:2, *Acts* 6:7; 12:24; 19:20).

THE REJECTED AND RESURRECTED STONE

The rulers, elders (heads of prominent Jerusalem families), teachers of the law (or 'scribes'), and those belonging to the high priestly family constituted the Sanhedrin of Jerusalem, the highest court in Judaism (4:15). This body had condemned Jesus and turned him over to the Roman governor for execution (*Luke* 22:66–23:2). They opened the hearing with a question focused on the power or name (that is, authority) by which the apostles had done this – a conveniently vague reference to an extraordinary miracle.

Peter, however, would not let them hide behind this ambiguity. He neatly noted the irony that Israel's leaders were interrogating men for having performed a *good deed* by healing a cripple. By inquiring how this man was healed they were raising a much larger question about salvation in general, both physical and spiritual. *Has been healed* in verse 9 is literally, 'was saved', the verb that reappears with a broader meaning in verse 12. Various terms for healing appear in this narrative, but the most important is 'save' and 'salvation'. Just as the man's lameness symbolized a deeper disability also shared by those of sound body, so also his cure represented a rescue more radical than mere physical restoration. The name that authorized and empowered this healing, this salvation – let not only the rulers, but also *all the people of Israel* take note – is that of Jesus the Messiah, the Nazarene.

The stark contrast between the leaders' mistreatment of Jesus (*whom you crucified*) and God's vindication of him (*whom God raised from the dead*) has become a frequent theme in Acts (2:23–24; 3:13–15). Like other aspects of Jesus' suffering, his rejection by the leaders of his chosen people was planned by God and foretold in Scripture. Peter cited Psalm 118, which had been chanted by the crowd at Jesus'

[36]

triumphal entry (*Luke* 19:38) and quoted by Jesus himself as a commentary on his rejection by Israel's leaders and his vindication by God (*Luke* 20:9–17). In his first epistle Peter would cite Psalm 118:22 again to draw the same contrast (*1 Pet.* 2:4, 7–8). The psalmist offers praise that, though people opposed him, the LORD helped and strengthened him against his foes (*Psa.* 118:10–14). The imagery of the enemies as *builders* implies that the psalmist's enemies had authority and expertise, making it all the more amazing that the LORD reversed their judgement, exalting the rejected stone to the place of prominence.

This, said Peter, is what has happened to Jesus: though rejected by those in authority within Judaism, he has been vindicated and exalted by God himself. In fact, Jesus' name is the only one in the whole world in which salvation is to be found (4:12). Not even Israel's law, given by God to Moses, was intended as a means of redemption and rescue from our spiritual paralysis; much less the gods whom the Gentile nations serve. With one sentence Christ's apostle sweeps away the sophisticated follies of post-modern relativism and religious pluralism. There are not many paths to salvation; there is one, and his Name is Jesus.

PERPLEXITY AND COURAGE

Astonished at the courage, the open boldness, of Peter and John despite their lack of rabbinical training, the members of the Sanhedrin recognized the impact that Jesus' presence and teaching had had on his disciples (verse 13). The leaders were perplexed: the lame man stood with the apostles, constituting undeniable evidence of the saving power of Jesus' name to reverse a disabling condition well known to have existed for over forty years. Moreover, the people were praising God for his saving deed. The only solution that they could think of to contain this 'infection' was raw power and intimidation: they commanded the apostles not to speak or teach at all in the name of Jesus, reinforcing their prohibition with threats. Though the people's celebration of God's saving power in Jesus' name kept them from following through on their threats for the moment (see also *Mark* 14:2), the leaders' opposition to the gospel would escalate to flogging (5:40) and even killing Jesus' witnesses (7:54–60).

Peter's *boldness* had replaced his cowardly denials on the night of Jesus' arrest (*Luke* 22:54–62). Such boldness is not a natural human trait. Nor is it the product of will power or self-directed 'pep talks'. Rather, it is the gift of the risen Lord through his Spirit's transforming power, in response to his people's prayers (4:29, 31, see also *Eph.* 6:20). Being with Jesus, listening to Jesus' word, and praying in Jesus' name impart supernatural boldness to bear witness for Jesus; and this boldness is a hallmark of the church in the after-glow of Pentecost (9:27–28; 13:46; 14:3; 18:26; 19:8; 28:31).

Knowing that all human authorities depend for their legitimacy on God (*Rom.* 13:1–2, 1 Pet. 2:13–17), Peter posed a dilemma for the Sanhedrin. Let the rulers themselves judge whether God would consider it right for the apostles to heed their prohibition instead of his command to bear witness concerning 'what we have seen and heard', namely, the arrival of God's saving power in Jesus' Name and Spirit. Only one of these alternatives is even thinkable, of course, as the apostles would state bluntly in a later inquest (5:29). God's clear command trumps every human instruction that contradicts it.

If your testimony to Jesus' grace is stifled by intimidation from people around you or over you, seek the boldness that the Holy Spirit alone can give: spend time with Jesus in his Word, and in urgent prayer ask him for the courage to be faithful to your calling as his witness.

9

Scripture-Formed, Christ-Centred Prayer

*When they were released, they went to their friends and reported
what the chief priests and the elders had said to them.* ^{24} *And
when they heard it, they lifted their voices together to God and
said, "Sovereign Lord, who made the heaven and the earth and
the sea and everything in them,* ^{25} *who through the mouth of our
father David, your servant, said by the Holy Spirit,*

" *'Why did the Gentiles rage,
and the peoples plot in vain?*
^{26} *The kings of the earth set themselves,
and the rulers were gathered together,
against the Lord and against his Anointed'—*
^{27} *for truly in this city there were gathered together against your
holy servant Jesus, whom you anointed, both Herod and Pontius
Pilate, along with the Gentiles and the peoples of Israel,* ^{28} *to do
whatever your hand and your plan had predestined to take place.*
^{29} *And now, Lord, look upon their threats and grant to your
servants to continue to speak your word with all boldness,* ^{30} *while
you stretch out your hand to heal, and signs and wonders are
performed through the name of your holy servant Jesus."* ^{31}*And
when they had prayed, the place in which they were gathered
together was shaken, and they were all filled with the Holy Spirit
and continued to speak the word of God with boldness* (Acts
4:23–31).

The church's prayer in response to the threats of the Sanhedrin
concludes the sequence of events that began with the healing
of the lame man. The theme of Jesus' Name has been woven through

this entire section, so it is appropriate that at this conclusion we hear Christians asking God to continue to exert the saving power of *the name of your holy servant Jesus* (4:30).

Several things about the prayer of these early Christians may strike us as unusual, in view of the Sanhedrin's threats that provoked their prayer. Everything that they said to God was shaped by what God had said to them in Scripture, those divine words brought to focus and fulfilment in Jesus. They mentioned the crisis only at the end of the prayer, almost as an afterthought. Their petition was completely God-centred: they asked not for personal safety but for the courage to persevere in their Christ-glorifying mission.

In significant respects their prayer echoes that offered by King Hezekiah at a time when Jerusalem was being threatened by Sennacherib's army (*2 Kings* 19:14–19, *Isa.* 37:14–20). Both prayers open with praise to God as creator of heaven and earth, and both call his attention to the enemies' threats. In both, petitions are introduced by 'and now.' Yet the petitions differ markedly: Hezekiah asked the Lord to deliver Judah so that all earth's peoples may know that the Lord alone is God (*Isa.* 37:20). These Christians requested not deliverance but boldness to continue speaking, threats notwithstanding. The ultimate goal, the Lord's fame among the nations, is the same.

LORD OF CREATION

Peter and John returned and reported to *their friends* – to the church, which is now the people of God. Jesus had come to 'his own people,' Israel, but they had refused him welcome – except those who believed, the children born of God (*John* 1:11–13). The believers' immediate and unanimous response to the Sanhedrin's threats was to pray *together*, as they had prayed with one accord for the gift of the Spirit (1:14).

Their confidence in the Lord's control of the situation was expressed when they addressed him as *Sovereign Lord* (a rarer word than the name most frequently found in the New Testament and typically translated 'Lord'). This title, addressed to God also in Luke 2:29 and Revelation 6:10 and in Old Testament prayers (*Jer.* 4:10, *Dan.* 9), implies that God exerts absolute control over his universe, including the present adverse circumstances. He is sovereign as

Creator of the heaven and the earth and the sea, and everything in them. Here the prayer echoes Psalm 146:6, which warns against trusting mortal men and promises blessing to those who look for help to the LORD their God. The psalm even extols God as the champion who 'sets prisoners free' (as he had Peter and John). By confessing to the Lord his supremacy over his creatures, the believers bolstered their own confidence in his control over the enemies that threatened their safety and freedom.

LORD OF REVELATION

Their risen Lord had given them the key that unlocks the Old Testament: the law, the prophets, and the psalms, all foretold of Jesus (*Luke* 24:25–27; 44–47). This insight transformed their praying as well as their preaching. As Scripture's divine author, *the Holy Spirit*, spoke the second Psalm through the human author, the mouth of *your servant, our father David*, they together foretold that the *Anointed*, descended from David, would be targeted by an international conspiracy and yet emerge victorious, enthroned as God's royal Son on God's holy hill, to rule all nations to the ends of the earth.

In their prayer, these disciples quoted exactly the opening two verses of Psalm 2, which describe the conspiracy of nations and peoples, of kings and rulers against the Lord and his Anointed One. Then the prayer traced, point by point, how this prediction had been fulfilled in the sufferings of Jesus, God's holy and anointed servant (4:27). The rebels were *the Gentiles* (the same Greek word appears in verses 25 and 27), but they also included *the peoples*, namely the peoples of Israel (Luke's Greek in verse 27 echoes the plural 'peoples' referring to Israel's tribes). Technically Herod Antipas was not a king but a tetrarch (*Luke* 3:1), yet he was of royal blood. The procurator Pontius Pilate was the ruler prophesied in the Psalm, if only by his passivity in handing over Jesus, whom he knew to be innocent, into the hands of his enemies (see *Luke* 23:6–25).

This bizarre alliance *gathered together*, as the Psalm foretold (the same Greek verb appears in verses 26 and 27). The title *servant* recalls Jesus' sufferings as prophesied in Isaiah 53, to which Peter had alluded in his earlier sermon (3:13–14, 26). It also links Jesus to his ancestor David, God's servant and the mouthpiece employed by the

Holy Spirit to write the Psalm (4:25, see *Isa.* 37:35). The fact that God had *anointed* Jesus highlights his royal qualification as Messiah or Christ.

LORD OF PROVIDENCE AND REDEMPTION

The one-to-one correspondences between the Psalm and its fulfilment showed that God's enemies, though expressing their own rebellious impulses, were doing what God's power and will had decided beforehand should happen. Luke's metaphor, '*your hand*', has Old Testament roots (*Exod.* 13:3, 14, 16) and reappears in the petition to stretch out *your hand* to confirm their witness through miracles (4:30; see also 11:21).

In trying to break the chains of God's reign, the conspirators had only accomplished his predetermined purpose (compare 2:23). At the cross of Jesus, where it seemed that Satan and his cohorts had gained the upper hand, the Messiah's weakness and defeat proved to be God's secret weapons for the redemption of his guilty people. This world-transforming proof that God rules supreme not only in Eden's pristine perfection but also in the horrors of Calvary banished from the believer's minds any fears for their personal safety, freeing them to focus on the mission that the Lord had given them.

LORD OF THE CHURCH AND ITS MISSION

Having adored God as Creator, Revealer, Ruler, and Redeemer, the believers called his attention to the problem at hand, the Sanhedrin's threats. They requested boldness to speak his words, and confirming signs worked by God's outstretched hand '*through the name of your holy servant Jesus*'. The cripple's restoration had been a '*sign of healing*' (4:22). Jesus' healing miracles were not mute bursts of power, but revelatory illustrations of God's redemptive truth.

Their prayer is answered with an earthquake, signifying the awesome presence of God in their midst as at Sinai and in Isaiah's call (*Exod.* 19:18, *Isa.* 6:4) and with a fresh filling by the Holy Spirit. *Filled with the Holy Spirit* refers to a special enabling to speak God's Word (*Luke* 1:15, 41–45, 67; *Acts* 2:4; 13:9). Here it brings no gift of tongues, as at Pentecost, rather, the focus is on the boldness needed to go on speaking in the face of threats. Are your prayers to God moulded by God's words to us? Is your assessment of your situation transformed by confidence in his sovereignty over its dangers? Are your desires conformed to his purpose to extend his kingdom of grace through the Name of Jesus his Servant?

IO

Witness in Word and Deed

Now the full number of those who believed were of one heart and soul, and no one said that any of the things that belonged to him was his own, but they had everything in common. [33] And with great power the apostles were giving their testimony to the resurrection of the Lord Jesus, and great grace was upon them all. [34] There was not a needy person among them, for as many as were owners of lands or houses sold them and brought the proceeds of what was sold [35] and laid it at the apostles' feet, and it was distributed to each as any had need (Acts 4:32–35).

A second summary (see *Acts* 2:42–47) of the ongoing life of the church forms a bridge between the events that precede it and those that follow. The apostles' powerful testimony recalls Peter and John at the temple (3:1–26) and before the Sanhedrin (4:8–20), and the church's boldness in declaring God's Word (4:31). The believers' openhearted generosity in sharing resources looks ahead to the gift of Barnabas (4:36–37) and the counterfeit contribution of Ananias and Sapphira (5:1–11).

As in the earlier summary, Luke emphasizes the impact of the Spirit on the everyday life and relationships of people set free by faith in the mighty Name of Jesus. That their hearts were knit together in love showed in their sacrificial sharing, and the source of their unity was the resurrection power of Jesus to which the apostles bore witness.

POWERFUL WITNESS IN WORDS

The apostles continued to fulfil their mission as witnesses of Jesus' resurrection (1:22; 2:32), and they did so *with great power.* As Peter hastened to make clear to the curious crowds in the temple (3:12) and to their leaders (4:12), the power was not their own. Jesus the risen Lord had promised power with the outpouring of the Spirit (1:8), and he had kept his word. When the whole church had prayed for boldness, the Holy Spirit had answered with earth-shaking suddenness (4:29, 31). The Holy Spirit, the divine Witness to Jesus' resurrection, is given not only to the apostles but to all who heed God's call to repentance and faith (5:32). Here Luke focuses again on the apostles' unique calling and qualification to bear eyewitness testimony to the fact that Jesus had been raised from the dead.

As well as the Spirit's *great power* at work in the apostles, God's *great grace* rested on all the believers. As the Father's favour had rested on Jesus while he was growing up (*Luke* 2:40; see also verse 52), so now the Father's grace rests on the youthful church, creating a community of mutual compassion that surpasses anything that human societies can achieve.

SACRIFICIAL GENEROSITY IN DEEDS

The Spirit-produced unity, love, and compassion among believers found tangible expression in their readiness to part with their property in order to relieve others' needs. Thus this summary expands upon the first one, even repeating the expression to each *as any had need* (2:45 and 4:35). The fact that *the full number of those who believed* (literally, 'the multitude of the disciples', emphasizing the increasing numbers, 5:14; 6:1, 5, 7) were one in heart and mind is impressive in view of the economic spectrum represented in the burgeoning movement. They varied from those who were affluent enough to own extra property to those in deep financial need, dependent on fellow-believers for life's necessities.

Such spiritual solidarity and deep empathy was a social ideal admired by Greek and Roman writers. Aristotle, for example, had described friends as 'one soul in two bodies' and spoke of friends having all things in common, just as these Christians had 'one heart and soul' and 'they had everything in common' (or shared everything they had).

This community formed by grace, expressing gratitude in generosity, was also a fulfilment of God's ancient promise to Israel. The observation that there was *not a needy person among them* echoes the promise of Deuteronomy 15:4: When Israel heeds God's law – particularly his command to lend generously and forgive debts – 'there will be no poor among you'.

This sharing of possessions was not required for church membership, but it was a reflex of love toward God's family. No one was forced to pool resources into a common fund controlled by the apostles. Rather, as needs arose, Christian landowners would sell excess properties and place the proceeds at the apostles' feet as an offering to the Lord, whose authority the apostles represented. Peter's rebuke to Ananias makes clear that such gifts were not mandatory (*Acts* 5:4). Such open-handed generosity is, however, symptomatic of hearts set free from the tyranny of Mammon (*Luke* 16:13) – freed to convey God's gracious provision towards brothers and sisters in need, near or far. Does your heart know this freedom, or does money and the fear of its loss still hold you in chains?

II

The Spirit's Dangerous
Holiness

*Thus Joseph, who was also called by the apostles Barnabas
(which means son of encouragement), a Levite, a native of
Cyprus, ³⁷ sold a field that belonged to him and brought the money
and laid it at the apostles' feet.*

*¹ But a man named Ananias, with his wife Sapphira, sold a
piece of property, ² and with his wife's knowledge he kept back
for himself some of the proceeds and brought only a part of it
and laid it at the apostles' feet. ³ But Peter said, "Ananias, why
has Satan filled your heart to lie to the Holy Spirit and to keep
back for yourself part of the proceeds of the land? ⁴ While it
remained unsold, did it not remain your own? And after it was
sold, was it not at your disposal? Why is it that you have
contrived this deed in your heart? You have not lied to men but
to God." ⁵ When Ananias heard these words, he fell down and
breathed his last. And great fear came upon all who heard of it.
⁶ The young men rose and wrapped him up and carried him out
and buried him.*

*⁷ After an interval of about three hours his wife came in, not
knowing what had happened. ⁸ And Peter said to her, "Tell me
whether you sold the land for so much." And she said, "Yes, for
so much." ⁹ But Peter said to her, "How is it that you have agreed
together to test the Spirit of the Lord? Behold, the feet of those
who have buried your husband are at the door, and they will
carry you out." ¹⁰ Immediately she fell down at his feet and
breathed her last. When the young men came in they found her
dead, and they carried her out and buried her beside her husband.*

[11] And great fear came upon the whole church and upon all who heard of these things (Acts 4:36–5:11).

L uke's description of the gift brought by Joseph of Cyprus, nicknamed Barnabas by the apostles, provides a concrete illustration of the ongoing practice of open-hearted family sharing mentioned in the preceding summary. It also introduces a Christian leader who would play a key role in the Gentile church of Antioch in Syria and in the life of Saul of Tarsus, a persecutor who became Christ's apostle to the Gentiles. Finally, Barnabas' sincere generosity serves as a counterfoil to the troubling account of the hypocritical 'generosity' of Ananias and Sapphira. Thus these twin stories about two gifts portray both 'the kindness and the severity of God' (*Rom.* 11:22).

SON OF ENCOURAGEMENT

At verse 36 a change of Greek tenses, from the *imperfect* (ongoing or repeated past actions) to the *aorist* (a simple reference to past action) marks the transition from the summary description of the church's pattern of life to the next set of specific events. The first event seems unremarkable: a man named Joseph did precisely what Luke had just described many wealthy Christians doing: *he sold a field that belonged to him and brought the money and laid it at the apostles' feet.* The significance of his gift, however, lies in who he is and in the reaction it evokes from two other affluent members of the church, Ananias and Sapphira.

Three identifying features set Joseph apart as a man who will have an important role in the unfolding story of the book of Acts. First, the apostles had named him Barnabas (meaning Son of Encouragement). To be singled out by the church's leaders for this special name was an honour, showing that they had seen in Joseph the spirit of servanthood that distinguishes those whom Jesus calls to leadership (*Mark* 10:42–45). Of course, Jesus had renamed Simon as Peter long before Simon exhibited the solidity of the 'rock' that he would become (*Matt.* 16:18, *John* 1:42), and the Lord's nickname for James and John, 'Sons of Thunder', was ironic and reproving rather than honorific (*Mark* 3:17, *Luke* 7:54–56). Joseph, however, received his nickname because he was well known for encouraging others and for furthering their spiritual growth. The Aramaic name Barnabas can mean 'son of prophecy' – a prophetic teacher who brings verbal encouragement. He would show the appropriateness of his name by welcoming Saul into the church at Jerusalem; by encouraging and teaching the young church at Antioch; by teaming up with Paul on his first mission to Asia Minor; and by patiently extending to Mark another opportunity to prove faithful after failure.

Second, Joseph 'Barnabas' was a *Levite*. The Mosaic Law stipulated that the Levites were not to inherit a region of the Promised Land with the other tribes. Rather, Israel's tithes were the Levites' inheritance, supporting their ministry in the sanctuary (*Num.* 18:21–24). Levites were also to be given towns throughout the land (*Num.* 35:1–5, *Lev.* 25:32–34), so perhaps Joseph's property was a house in one of the Levitical towns. As a Levite, he would empathize with those who depended on donations for their daily needs and gladly part with his excess to provide for them.

Finally, Joseph had been born on *Cyprus*, an island in the eastern Mediterranean. As a member of the Jewish Dispersion, he was fluent in Greek and well acquainted with Hellenistic culture and with people of diverse ethnic groups. God's providence had prepared him to minister to the multi-ethnic church planted in Antioch by Christians from Cyprus and Cyrene (*Acts* 11:20). His background prepared him also to take the lead in the gospel's advance beyond Palestine, beginning with his native Cyprus.

LYING TO THE HOLY SPIRIT

Luke's portrait of the early church up to now has been idyllic. His commitment to truth compels him, however, to place alongside the beautiful fruit of the Holy Spirit the disturbing evidence that serious sin persisted within the Christian community. In the Old Testament Israel had witnessed God's hand extended in rescue through judgement (the plagues on Egypt, the drowning of Pharaoh's forces, the destruction of Korah). The miracles that Jesus had performed during his earthly ministry, heralding the kingdom's coming, expressed God's mercy through restoration and protection (healing, feeding, exorcising, stilling a storm), with the exception of the fig tree that he cursed to signal judgement to come on unbelieving Israel. In Acts, along with healing and rescue from prison, we see four miracles of judgement: two of them inflicting blindness (Saul, Elymas) and two inflicting death (Ananias and Sapphira, King Herod). These miracles remind us of the pervasive biblical truth that God is not only abundantly gracious but also jealously holy. The Lord of all the earth is not one to be trifled with. If we respond to his kindness with complacent indifference rather than awe, gratitude, and repentance, we have misjudged him!

Ananias' donation seemed superficially to follow the pattern set by other wealthy believers (4:34–36). Just like Barnabas, Ananias sold a piece of property, brought money, and put it at the apostles' feet. He had, however, secretly *kept back* some of the purchase price *for himself.* The verb *kept back* means to embezzle from one's master and appears only twice elsewhere in the Greek Bible (*Titus* 2:10, *Josh.* 7:1). Chapter 7 of the book of Joshua describes the sin of Achan, who secretly (as he thought) seized plunder from Jericho, which the LORD had claimed for himself. For despising the LORD's omniscience and defiling the LORD's assembly, Achan's sin of stealing his Master's booty was punished by death.

Ananias' sin (and Sapphira's, since she had full knowledge of his plot) was not, however, his refusal to give the whole price that he had received for his property. It was not required that he sell the land at all. Peter confronted Ananias and made clear that Ananias had been free to keep the property or sell it, free to bring all or part or none of the proceeds. The problem was that Ananias, in bringing part of the purchase price but claiming to have brought the whole, had *lied to the Holy Spirit.* In trying to deceive the church's leaders, he had *not lied to men but to God* (see *Josh.* 7:11). Later, when Peter quoted the amount of their gift to Sapphira, she confirmed her husband's lie, revealing her complicity in the deceit. Like the ancient Israelites who doubted God's presence in the desert, Ananias and Sapphira had conspired to *test the Spirit of the Lord* (see *Exod.* 17:7, *Num.* 20:12–13). They had overlooked the Holy Spirit's divine omniscience and his zeal for integrity in his church. (The title *church* is applied to Jesus' followers for the first time in Acts 5:11.)

Peter himself did not inflict the judgement. He simply confronted their sin and, in the case of Sapphira, predicted that she would fare no better at God's hands than her husband and co-conspirator: the men who had just buried Ananias would carry her out for burial as well. *Immediately she fell down at his feet* – the apostolic feet at which Ananias had placed their deceptive donation – *and breathed her last.*

Fear of losing the security that money promises held their hearts captive. They were not free to express oneness of heart by giving all to help others, nor did they trust God to provide for their own needs through the gifts of others. Yet a fear of losing face kept them from acknowledging that they were not Barnabas-calibre givers. What they lacked was the one fear they needed: fear of the Spirit of God, who searches hearts. This *great fear* was instilled in all who heard of their judgement (5:5, 11). Is your confidence in God's grace mingled with a healthy fear of his holiness? Have the twin truths that he searches hearts and forgives the guilty set you free to drop the masks by which you have tried to enhance your image?

12

The Terrifying Power
That Makes Us Whole

*Now many signs and wonders were regularly done among the
people by the hands of the apostles. And they were all together
in Solomon's Portico. ¹³ None of the rest dared join them, but
the people held them in high esteem. ¹⁴ And more than ever
believers were added to the Lord, multitudes of both men and
women, ¹⁵ so that they even carried out the sick into the streets
and laid them on cots and mats, that as Peter came by at least
his shadow might fall on some of them. ¹⁶ The people also gathered
from the towns around Jerusalem, bringing the sick and those
afflicted with unclean spirits, and they were all healed* (Acts
5:12–16).

Instead of focusing on the church's life together as the first and
second summaries did, this third summary dwells exclusively on
the impact that the apostles were having on those outside the fold.
That impact was directly related to what had transpired within the
fellowship, for people who were not prepared to surrender to Jesus'
heart-searching holiness now kept a respectful distance from this
community, in which wonderful and terrifying powers were
obviously at work.

POWER AND UNITY
In response to the threats of the Sanhedrin, the church had prayed
for boldness to speak God's Word and for God to extend his hand
to confirm his gospel through healing, signs, and wonders (4:29–30).
God's answer came immediately in the sign of an earthquake and

the prophetic filling of the Spirit, emboldening their speaking (4:31). The apostles continued to bear bold witness about Jesus' resurrection (4:33) and the sudden deaths of Ananias and Sapphira were sobering signs of God's presence. Now many more miraculous *signs and wonders* – particularly the healing of disease and liberation from the spiritual torment of unclean spirits – were flowing through the apostles' hands. Luke's Greek, 'through the hands of the apostles many signs and wonders were happening', expresses more clearly than most translations that the apostles were not the source of healing power, but only its means (see 3:12).

Since Luke's original does not specify that it was the believers who met regularly in Solomon's Portico (5:12), some scholars conclude that the apostles alone took their public stand there, because *none of the rest* of their fellow-believers dared to join them. It is more correct, however, to interpret verse 12 as referring to a public gathering, not just of the twelve apostles, but of all the believers in Jesus. They continued their meetings for worship in the temple (2:46), despite the Sanhedrin's threats. '*The rest*' who did not dare to join them were those outside the church, who admired its joy, power, and grace but shied away from its call to commitment and life-threatening holiness.

CONFLICTING REACTIONS

At first glance Luke seems to contradict himself when he states first that no one dared join the church, and then that increasing numbers of believers were added to it. Could both dynamics occur at the same time? Yes! These conflicting reactions to the Spirit's presence in the church replicate the responses that Jesus evoked during his earthly ministry. After Jesus expelled the legion of demons from the local demoniac, the people of Gerasa, overcome with fear, asked Jesus to leave, while the man himself begged to go with Jesus (*Luke* 8:37–38). At times even Jesus' disciples did not dare to be near him, for his consuming holiness was dangerous to their sinful selves (*Luke* 5:8).

Nor is it unusual that they were held in high esteem by the people, just as their Lord was. Nicodemus spoke for at least some of Israel's leaders when he called Jesus a teacher sent from God (*John* 3:2). Another teacher of the law admired Jesus' wisdom in identifying the

Law's pre-eminent commands. To him Jesus responded, 'You are not far from the kingdom of God' (*Mark* 12:32–34).

The messengers of the gospel are both 'the smell of death' to the perishing and 'the fragrance of life' to those being saved through faith (*2 Cor.* 2:15–16). It is no surprise, then, that many, having heard of the death of Ananias and Sapphira, kept their distance, even as more and more men and women, irresistibly drawn by grace, believed in the Lord and were added by him to his church.

WIDESPREAD HEALING

Finally, Luke focuses on the healing power at work through the apostles. People carried their sick on beds and mats into the street, in case Peter should pass by, even as four men had carried their paralyzed friend to Jesus (*Luke* 5:18–19). To look to Peter's shadow as a means of healing sounds superstitious. Yet it differs little from the hopes of those who tried to touch Jesus 'for power came out from him and healed them all' (*Luke* 6:19, see also *Acts* 19:11–12). When a woman reached out to the hem of Jesus' robe, he welcomed and blessed her faith, even in its confused expression (*Mark* 5:27–28, 34). Faith in Jesus' name is the key to healing of body and soul (*Acts* 3:16).

The saving power of God encompassed afflictions which were spiritual as well as physical, for not only the sick but also those afflicted by unclean (defiling) spirits were set free. In his Gospel Luke told how people flocked to Jesus from Judea, Jerusalem, and even Tyre and Sidon, seeking deliverance (*Luke* 6:17–18). As Jesus' fame then spread beyond Israel's borders, so now his power to heal through his apostles attracted crowds from beyond Jerusalem. Although the second wave of witness, into Judea and Samaria, had not yet broken, God's kingdom was spilling over Jerusalem's walls.

As Christ's representatives before a watching world, Christians today should emulate his gracious welcome to anyone and everyone who needs his healing touch. We should strive to adorn the gospel by our behaviour, 'being well thought of by outsiders' (*1 Tim.* 3:7, *Titus* 2:5, 10). At the same time, we will not be surprised that Christ's sweet grace, which attracts God's elect, frightens and threatens those who desperately cling to their independence.

13

Obey God Rather Than Men

But the high priest rose up, and all who were with him (that is, the party of the Sadducees), and filled with jealousy [18] *they arrested the apostles and put them in the public prison.* [19] *But during the night an angel of the Lord opened the prison doors and brought them out, and said,* [20] *"Go and stand in the temple and speak to the people all the words of this Life."* [21] *And when they heard this, they entered the temple at daybreak and began to teach.*

Now when the high priest came, and those who were with him, they called together the council and all the senate of Israel and sent to the prison to have them brought. [22] *But when the officers came, they did not find them in the prison, so they returned and reported,* [23] *"We found the prison securely locked and the guards standing at the doors, but when we opened them we found no one inside."* [24] *Now when the captain of the temple and the chief priests heard these words, they were greatly perplexed about them, wondering what this would come to.* [25] *And someone came and told them, "Look! The men whom you put in prison are standing in the temple and teaching the people."* [26] *Then the captain with the officers went and brought them, but not by force, for they were afraid of being stoned by the people.*

[27] *And when they had brought them, they set them before the council. And the high priest questioned them,* [28] *saying, "We strictly charged you not to teach in this name, yet here you have filled Jerusalem with your teaching, and you intend to bring this man's blood upon us."* [29] *But Peter and the apostles answered, "We must obey God rather than men.* [30] *The God of our fathers raised Jesus, whom you killed by hanging him on a tree.* [31] *God*

exalted him at his right hand as Leader and Saviour, to give repentance to Israel and forgiveness of sins. ³² And we are witnesses to these things, and so is the Holy Spirit, whom God has given to those who obey him" (Acts 5:17–32).

The apostles' second encounter with the high priest and the Sanhedrin shows that the Jewish leaders' opposition to the gospel was escalating. After the lame man was healed, only Peter and John were jailed and questioned. Now all the apostles were included in the arrest and interrogation. Having warned Peter and John not to preach in Jesus' name on the earlier occasion (4:18; 5:28), the Sanhedrin now followed through on its threats with a flogging. For their part, the apostles make even more explicit their responsibility to obey God rather than human authorities, when the latter forbid what God commands (compare 4:19–20 with 5:29, 32). As the persecution intensified, so also did the joy of Jesus' witnesses at the privilege of suffering for his sake and their resolution to persevere in their calling as his witnesses. The officials' confusion, frustration, and fear in handling the apostles, illustrates the wisdom of Gamaliel's observation that human efforts to thwart a work of God are doomed to failure (see the next study for verses 38–39).

THE FREEDOM OF OBEYING GOD

Luke again mentions that the high priest and his associates belonged to *the party of the Sadducees*, which rejected both the doctrine of final resurrection and the existence of angels (4:2; 23:8). One of several ironies in this text is that *an angel of the Lord* acts to thwart and confuse these Sadducees. No longer simply disturbed because the apostles were preaching resurrection, the high priest and his colleagues were now *filled with jealousy* over the impact that Jesus' witnesses were having on the hearts and minds of the people of Jerusalem. The word jealousy sometimes refers to zeal, that is, jealousy for God's honour (*John* 2:17), but too often our self-centred jealousy often disguises itself as God-centred zeal (*Phil.* 3:6, *Rom.* 10:2). Here, the temple officials' true motive was resentment at the apostles' expanding influence, as would happen again in the synagogue of Pisidian Antioch (Acts 13:44–45). To counteract the apostles' popularity, the temple guard locked them overnight in *the public prison* – a highly visible humiliation, like the public beating that Paul and Silas would receive in Philippi (16:37) – to await a hearing before the Sanhedrin. The public nature of this arrest however was to be a means of compounding the officials' embarrassment.

In the middle of the night an angel of the Lord opened the doors of the jail and released them, not to enjoy personal safety but to engage in even riskier obedience. The Lord loves to rescue his servants in the darkest hour of the night. The Lord's angel would lead Peter out of Herod Agrippa's prison by night (12:1–11). At night God's earthquake would shake prison cell doors open at Philippi, but instead of escaping Paul and Silas would stay to speak good news to their jailer (16:25–34). God can and sometimes does deliver his servants from chains and death, but he often sends them right back into danger, to advance the cause of Christ's kingdom.

Therefore the angel told the apostles to *go and stand in the temple* – very publicly, in the arena ruled by the high priest's party – and to tell the people *all the words of this life*. This venue would invite re-arrest, and inflame the authorities' hostility. The angel summarizes the gospel as a message of *life*, and rightly so. Before Jesus' death Peter had rightly confessed: 'You have the words of eternal life' (*John* 6:68). In Solomon's Portico, Peter had rightly called Jesus 'the Author of life' (3:15). The gospel's call to repentance opens the doorway to eternal life (11:18). The apostles obeyed the command readily: *at daybreak*, as soon as the doors of the temple courtyard opened in preparation for the morning sacrifice, they took their stand and began to teach the people the truth about Jesus.

THE FRUSTRATION OF OPPOSING GOD

When the high priest and his associates arrived at the temple complex, they summoned *the council and all the senate of Israel*. This description of the Sanhedrin emphasizes its august authority and the high visibility of the legal process that was about to begin. Mysteriously, the defendants could not be found. The officers sent to retrieve them found the jail securely locked, with the guards standing at the doors (not sleeping on their watch), but the holding cell was empty. This inexplicable work of God perplexed both the chief priests and the captain of the temple guard, who was responsible for the security of both the jail and the temple precincts.

The question of the apostles' whereabouts (though not their means of escape) was soon answered by a report from the temple courts, where Jesus' witnesses were boldly testifying in his name. The captain of the guard and his forces effected a second arrest, no doubt with little relish for doing so publicly this time, and with gentle persuasion rather than force. Popular admiration for the apostles was so high that their opponents feared harm – even stoning – at the hands of the populace, if they were seen treating the apostles roughly. The same fear had dictated their strategy when seizing Jesus (*Luke* 20:19; 22:2, *Matt.* 26:5).

THE INDICTMENT AND INVITATION OF THE GOSPEL

When the apostles compliantly accompanied the temple guard to the Sanhedrin's chambers, the high priest launched his interrogation. Conveniently overlooking the mystery of their escape, the high priest charged the apostles with flagrant disobedience of the strict orders that the Council had given them *not to teach in this name* (see 4:18). Although he referred to Jesus twice, he never mentioned Jesus' name (this name, this man's blood). Not only had the apostles filled Jerusalem with the message of life in Jesus' name, but also their preaching portrayed the high priest and the Sanhedrin as guilty of Jesus' blood. From the dawn of biblical history the blood of an innocent victim was said to cry out against his murderer (*Gen.* 4:10, *2 Sam.* 1:15–16). The crowds of Jerusalem, inflamed by their leaders, had overcome Pilate's protest by accepting responsibility for Jesus' death: 'Let his blood be on us and on our children!' (*Matt.* 27:25, *Acts* 3:13–15). Now, however, the high priest objected to being held responsible for Jesus' death, as was being done by the apostles, both publicly and to the Sanhedrin directly (3:17; 4:10–11).

Peter took the lead in answering the high priest's charge. His answer is all about obedience, as the original word order shows clearly: 'to obey God is necessary' are the first three words (in Greek), and 'those who obey him' are the last three (5:29, 32). The apostles do not put their personal preference above the commands of duly constituted ecclesiastical or political authority, as so many do today. Peter would exhort persecuted Christians to 'submit for the Lord's sake to every authority instituted among men,' whether in the state, the workplace, or the home, both to just and kind leaders and to harsh ones (*1 Pet.* 2:13 – 3:6, see also *Rom.* 13:1–7). Jesus also called people to submit to scribes who 'sit in Moses' seat', despite the inconsistency of their behaviour (*Matt.* 23:2–3), and sent lepers to priests to certify their cleansing (*Luke* 5:14). Here, however, the apostles were confronted with a human authority that set itself against the divine Authenticator of all authority. When men forbid what God has commanded or command what God has forbidden, we have only one option: 'We must obey God rather than men!'

The apostles summarized the message that God had commanded them to declare. Their summary echoes earlier sermons: *the God of our fathers* (3:13) *raised Jesus* from the dead, whom you had killed (3:15; 4:10), and exalted him at his own right hand (2:33–34) as Leader (3:15 – there translated Author) and Saviour (see 4:12), that he might give repentance (3:26) and forgiveness of sins to Israel (2:38; 3:19). To all these truths the apostles bore testimony (2:32; 3:15; 4:20; see also 4:33). Although the Sanhedrin shared the guilt for Jesus' execution, the apostles invited Israel's elders to receive repentance and forgiveness from Jesus.

Two new features join these familiar themes. First, the detail that Jesus was killed by being hanged *on a tree* echoes the wording of Deuteronomy 21:22–23, which required that the flagrant lawbreaker, when executed, be hanged on a tree to symbolize God's curse. Israel's leaders treated Jesus as deserving God's curse, but Peter and Paul would later recall 'the tree' as the place where Jesus bore our sins (*1 Pet.* 2:24) and where he became a curse in our place (*Gal.* 3:13).

Second, *the Holy Spirit*, who is given not just to the apostles but to all who obey God, joins his divine witness to that of the apostles. Jesus had promised that the Counsellor, the Spirit of truth, would testify about him, as would the apostles (*John* 15:26–27, see also *Isa.* 59:21). The signs and wonders performed by the Spirit's power confirmed the apostles' testimony to Jesus' resurrection (4:29–30, *Heb.* 2:3–4). But the Spirit's mission as Jesus' witness is by no means confined to the apostles, as his coming to all the believers at Pentecost showed (2:1–4, 11; see also 4:31). He opens every believer's heart and mouth to 'declare the praises of him who called you out of darkness into his wonderful light' (*1 Pet.* 2:9).

Are you ready to obey God rather than men, confident that his love holds you fast, even if his command leads you into conflict and danger?

14

Worthy to Suffer Dishonour

When they heard this, they were enraged and wanted to kill them.
³⁴ But a Pharisee in the council named Gamaliel, a teacher of
the law held in honour by all the people, stood up and gave orders
to put the men outside for a little while. ³⁵ And he said to them,
"Men of Israel, take care what you are about to do with these
men. ³⁶ For before these days Theudas rose up, claiming to be
somebody, and a number of men, about four hundred, joined him.
He was killed, and all who followed him were dispersed and came
to nothing. ³⁷ After him Judas the Galilean rose up in the days
of the census and drew away some of the people after him. He
too perished, and all who followed him were scattered. ³⁸ So in
the present case I tell you, keep away from these men and let them
alone, for if this plan or this undertaking is of man, it will fail;
³⁹ but if it is of God, you will not be able to overthrow them. You
might even be found opposing God!" So they took his advice,
⁴⁰ and when they had called in the apostles, they beat them and
charged them not to speak in the name of Jesus, and let them go.
⁴¹ Then they left the presence of the council, rejoicing that they
were counted worthy to suffer dishonour for the name. ⁴² And
every day, in the temple and from house to house, they did not
cease teaching and preaching Jesus as the Christ (Acts 5:33–42).

The apostles, not intimidated by the Sanhedrin's power, had
answered the high priest calmly, affirming that the chief priests
and elders indeed shared responsibility for Jesus' death but holding
out also an implicit promise. Jesus, risen from the dead in order to
rule and to save, gives to his enemies repentance – a humbling change

of heart – which brings forgiveness and renewal by the Holy Spirit. The reaction of the Sanhedrin was anything but repentant, however. Their rage was so intense that bloodshed was averted only by the wise, moderating counsel of a respected teacher of the law. Adopting the 'wait and see' attitude that Gamaliel recommended, the officials limited their violent reaction to flogging the apostles. The apostles responded to this first physical persecution with joy, considering disgrace for Jesus' name to be an honour for which God deemed them worthy.

THE WISDOM OF WAITING AND WATCHING

The apostles' words evoked a hostile reaction in their hearers. In Acts 2:37 Luke used a vividly pictorial verb to describe the convicting effect that Peter's Pentecost sermon had on the crowd gathered at Pentecost: 'They were cut (literally, pierced) to the heart.' Here he employs a different but no less vivid term: 'They were sawn through.' (ESV: *They were enraged*). This term will reappear again, describing the mob's murderous rage in reaction to Stephen's speech (7:54). At this earlier point also the prevailing sentiment in the Sanhedrin favoured putting all the apostles to death.

A wiser mind prevailed, however. The Pharisees and Jesus had disagreed strongly regarding the Law and oral tradition (*Luke* 11:37–54). Nevertheless, unlike the Sadducees, the Pharisees believed in the resurrection of the dead in the age to come. Therefore Gamaliel, successor to the revered Hillel, did not share the Sadducean chief priests' antipathy to the resurrection theme in the apostles' message. His advice, however, did not hinge on that point of theological difference between Pharisees and Sadducees.

Instead he observed that history had shown that movements set in motion by messianic pretenders quickly dissipated after the death of their founders. He cited two examples, *Theudas*, who had attracted four hundred followers, and, after him, *Judas the Galilean*, who led a revolt in the days of the census. The Jewish historian Josephus, in his *Antiquities of the Jews* (20.97–98), describes an uprising led by a self-styled prophet named Theudas, who was captured before he could miraculously part the Jordan River (as he had predicted he would) and was beheaded by the troops of Fadus, Roman governor of Judea. Because Fadus governed Judea from 44 to 46 AD, at least a decade after the events of Acts 5, Gamaliel must have had a different Theudas in mind. This conclusion is confirmed by the fact that Judas, who came *after* Theudas, led his revolt in response to a census (a prelude to higher taxes) ordered by Quirinius in 6 AD (Josephus, *Antiquities* 18.4–10, 23).

Gamaliel's point is clear and convincing: the violent deaths of these leaders at the hands of the Romans quickly dispersed their followers, because God was not in these movements. Now that Jesus has died a violent death at the hands of the Romans, his followers will be scattered without the Sanhedrin having to resort to violence – unless this movement is *of God*. In that case, not only will violence be ineffective in stopping the movement, but also Israel's elders will be waging war against God himself! Implicit in his logic is the assumption that nothing less than the resurrection of Jesus from the dead (unlike Theudas and Judas) could sustain the Christian movement after his crucifixion. The vitality and growth of the church is itself testimony to the fact that Jesus is not the dead leader of a failed movement.

When we ask how Luke, using historical research, could have learned what Gamaliel said in this closed-doors session of the Sanhedrin, the most plausible source is Saul of Tarsus, a young Pharisee trained by Gamaliel (22:3) who also had access to the high priest (9:1–2). It is ironic, then, that Gamaliel's disciple completely disregarded his mentor's counsel, ravaging the church in Jerusalem and elsewhere (8:3; 9:1–2; 22:4–5). Saul, later called Paul, would look back on his persecution of the church, which he thought at the time expressed his zeal for God (*Phil.* 3:6), and would in retrospect recognize it as the worst display of his hostility to God (*1 Cor.* 15:9, *1 Tim.* 1:13–15).

THE HONOUR OF DISHONOUR FOR THE NAME

Though persuaded by Gamaliel not to act according to their murderous desires, the Sanhedrin escalated the pressure on the apostles by reinforcing further threats with a flogging or beating. Paul's catalogue of sufferings would include five occasions on which he received from the Jews 'the forty lashes minus one' (*2 Cor.* 11:24). The Law capped the number of lashes at forty to shield the offender from excessive humiliation (*Deut.* 25:3). Very possibly the Sanhedrin exacted this maximum penalty to reinforce their prohibition against speaking in the name of Jesus.

The apostles, however, responded to the *dishonour* of the beating as though it were an honour of which they had been counted worthy by God. What transformed pain into joy and disgrace into glory was the Name for which they suffered – the Name of Jesus, which the Sanhedrin wanted to silence. Jesus called his followers to rejoice when mistreated 'because of the Son of Man' (*Luke* 6:22–23), and he promised that those who would lose their lives for his sake would save them (*Luke* 9:24). (Although Gamaliel's caution averted lethal violence on this occasion, death was quickly approaching for Stephen, the first of Jesus' witnesses to prove his promise true.) Peter would summon suffering Christians throughout Asia Minor to rejoice in their share in Christ's sufferings, the insults and harsh treatment they were receiving for the name of Christ (*1 Pet.* 4:13–16). The blows of the enemies' rods engraved God's promise on the apostles' hearts and, without pausing, they pursued the task that their Lord had given them. All the time (*every day*) and everywhere (*in the temple and from house to house*) they incessantly proclaimed the good news that Jesus is the Christ, who gives repentance, forgiveness, and eternal life to those who believe.

In our experience 'dishonour for the name' may entail condescending insults, social exclusion, discrimination in school or workplace, or worse. Has the glory of bearing Jesus' name so gripped our hearts that we too rejoice in the honour of that shame and boldly, constantly convey the good news of his grace?

15

Ministry of the Word
and of Tables

*Now in these days when the disciples were increasing in number,
a complaint by the Hellenists arose against the Hebrews because
their widows were being neglected in the daily distribution. ² And
the twelve summoned the full number of the disciples and said,
"It is not right that we should give up preaching the word of God
to serve tables. ³ Therefore, brothers, pick out from among you
seven men of good repute, full of the Spirit and of wisdom, whom
we will appoint to this duty. ⁴ But we will devote ourselves to
prayer and to the ministry of the word." ⁵ And what they said
pleased the whole gathering, and they chose Stephen, a man full
of faith and of the Holy Spirit, and Philip, and Prochorus, and
Nicanor, and Timon, and Parmenas, and Nicolaus, a proselyte
of Antioch. ⁶ These they set before the apostles, and they prayed
and laid their hands on them.*

*⁷ And the word of God continued to increase, and the number
of the disciples multiplied greatly in Jerusalem, and a great many
of the priests became obedient to the faith* (Acts 6:1–7).

The growth of the church not only provoked external
opposition but also produced internal strains. Increasing
numbers led to a disparity in the distribution of material support
to the poor, with widows in the Greek-speaking portion of the
church suffering neglect. Diversity of cultures and needs
overburdened the apostles, who consequently recognized the need
for a diversity of ministries and ministers. So that the apostles could
pursue the ministry of the Word to which Jesus had called them,
others must oversee the ministry of tables, to express Christ's

compassion toward his own. The seven appointed to this task would open the door for the Gospel's spread to Judea and Samaria, and to the ends of the earth.

DIVERSITY OF LANGUAGE AND NEEDS

From the start the church in Jerusalem had reflected the many cultures and spoken the many languages of the nations into which the Jews had been dispersed (2:8–11). Hebraic Jews, raised in Palestine, spoke Aramaic, a Semitic language akin to Hebrew. Grecian Jews, who had resettled in Jerusalem from other nations, preferred Greek, the *lingua franca* throughout the Empire. Christians met in homes to share food and fellowship, and it is likely that either Aramaic or Greek predominated in each of these home gatherings (2:46). Presumably through these home groups the apostles administered the distribution of relief for needy widows and orphans (2:45; 4:35).

As the number of disciples was increasing the home fellowships no doubt multiplied, and their role in maintaining the church's unity and expressing its compassion expanded. In this proliferation of groups the widows in Greek-speaking house churches were being neglected in the daily distribution of food. The result was the Grecian Jews' complaint against the apostles, expressing a discontent that could have degenerated into distrust.

DIVERSITY OF MINISTRIES

The apostles did not dismiss the Greek-speaking Christians as malcontents. Instead they addressed the problem seriously and promptly. During Jesus' earthly ministry they had observed, often with little sympathy, his patient compassion toward those whom society considered insignificant: the poor, the disabled, and the scandalous. Now, however, the transforming grace of his Spirit bore sweet fruit in their non–defensive, compassionate response to the criticism of their leadership. They *summoned the full number of the disciples* together to propose a solution.

The apostles first observed that it would not be right – that is, not pleasing to God – for them to neglect the Word of God in order to serve tables. Their vocation was to be Jesus' witnesses concerning his resurrection (1:8, 22; 4:33). Serving tables was not a demeaning task. Its dignity is shown in the high qualifications that it demands: an abundance of the Spirit and wisdom. Moreover, in contrast to their pride and competitive spirit before Jesus' suffering (*Mark* 10:35–45), the apostles now saw their call to preach as a call to ministry, to service (using the same word for ministry of the Word in 6:4 as they had used for service to tables). Serving material needs, however, was not the apostles' primary calling, and once a choice had to be made between distributing food and preaching the gospel, their Lord would be displeased if they gave urgent material needs a higher priority than eternal spiritual needs.

The apostles, as servants of the Word, set out the high qualifications of those to be entrusted with the ministry of tables, but they did not select these new leaders. Rather, since the congregation's trust in these men was essential, the believers themselves must identify those men who fulfilled the criteria. These servants must be men who are of good repute, full of the Spirit and of wisdom. The expression 'of good repute' means that others bear witness to their integrity and wisdom. *Full of the Spirit* in Luke and Acts describes people whose characters are distinguished by the sanctifying presence of the Holy Spirit – for example, Jesus himself (*Luke* 4:1), Stephen (*Acts* 6:5, 55), and Barnabas (*Acts* 11:24). The Spirit would impart the *wisdom* that they would need to handle the distribution equitably (see also *Isa.* 11:2).

The Greek verb rendered *pick out* in the apostles' proposal more often means 'visit' (7:23; 15:36) or 'show concern' (15:14). In the Greek translation of Numbers 27:16, however, it appears in a prayer of Moses for the LORD to 'appoint' his successor. This prayer God answered by commanding Moses to lay hands on his aide Joshua – exactly the same method as that used by the apostles in setting these seven servants apart. These parallels suggest that through the congregation's discernment God set apart these men, whose ministry extended beyond that of the apostles into new territory, just as Joshua's extended beyond that of Moses. Stephen and Philip, whose ministries are described in some depth, would proclaim the Word powerfully, working miracles to attest their message, like the apostles (6:8; 8:6–7).

With the widows' needs in the trustworthy and capable hands of others, the apostles would be able to devote themselves to prayer and the ministry of the Word. Few if any preachers would deny that prayer is integral to the ministry of the Word. Do our practice and time priorities, however, reflect this unbreakable bond between speaking to God for people and speaking to people for God?

Stephen and his colleagues are not called deacons, and the recorded ministries of Stephen and Philip extended beyond serving tables. Nevertheless the general distinction drawn here between Word ministry and table ministry (also called mercy ministry) would be worked out later in the distinction between the offices of *elder* (overseer) and *deacon* (*Phil* 1:1, *1 Tim.* 3). Some minister God's manifold grace by speaking God's words, while others use the strength that God supplies to serve (*1 Pet.* 4:10–11).

SPIRIT–FILLED SERVANTS

Pleased with the proposed solution, the *whole gathering* selected seven Spirit-filled, wisdom-filled men, whose names are all Greek. Perhaps, to reassure the Greek–speaking portion of the church, all the leaders appointed to oversee the food ministry were from their numbers. Of Stephen and Philip, the first two, Luke will say more in the coming chapters. At this point, he calls attention to Stephen and Nicolaus, the first and the last, by describing them more fully. Stephen was full of faith and of the Holy Spirit, and will later be described as 'full of grace and power' (6:8). Although we read nothing more about Nicolaus, he is significant because he is from Antioch, and a proselyte, a convert to Judaism. Proselytes as well as Jews heard the gospel in their own dialects at Pentecost (2:11). Nicolaus' Gentile background anticipates the inclusion even of Gentiles who, unlike Nicolaus, had not submitted to Israel's Law. His home town, Antioch in Syria, would become the site of a vibrant multi-ethnic church, from which the Word would spread to distant lands (11:19–26; 13:1–3).

THE WORD GROWS

In a brief summary Luke characterizes the growth of the church for the first time as the growth of the Word (see also *Acts* 12:24; 19:20,

Col. 1:5–6). As Christian widows were cared for and apostles freed to focus on teaching, the number of the disciples in Jerusalem increased rapidly. The power of the Spirit working through the Word about Jesus made the church grow. The large number of priests who became obedient to the faith were probably not the Sadducean chief priests but men of a humbler class, who identified with the needy and saw in the church's care for its widows the compassion to which the Lord had called Israel (*Deut.* 14:28–29).

Does your congregation exhibit this blend and balance of Word and mercy ministries, each overseen by officers qualified by the Lord with maturity to serve? Pray for those who minister the Word, and for those who minister mercy in action, 'that in everything God may be glorified through Jesus Christ' (*1 Pet.* 4:11).

16

Witness in the Wisdom of the Spirit

And Stephen, full of grace and power, was doing great wonders and signs among the people. ⁹ Then some of those who belonged to the synagogue of the Freedmen (as it was called), and of the Cyrenians, and of the Alexandrians, and of those from Cilicia and Asia, rose up and disputed with Stephen. ¹⁰ But they could not withstand the wisdom and the Spirit with which he was speaking. ¹¹ Then they secretly instigated men who said, "We have heard him speak blasphemous words against Moses and God." ¹² And they stirred up the people and the elders and the scribes, and they came upon him and seized him and brought him before the council, ¹³ and they set up false witnesses who said, "This man never ceases to speak words against this holy place and the law, ¹⁴ for we have heard him say that this Jesus of Nazareth will destroy this place and will change the customs that Moses delivered to us." ¹⁵ And gazing at him, all who sat in the council saw that his face was like the face of an angel (Acts 6:8–15).

Luke drew our attention to Stephen by placing him at the head of the list of servants called to care for the church's widows, and by describing him as 'a man full of faith and of the Holy Spirit' (6:5). Now the spotlight is focused more directly on Stephen and his invincible gospel witness, which leads to his death and to the dispersion of the church to regions beyond Jerusalem. The ministry and martyrdom of Stephen thus mark the transition from the first phase of apostolic witness 'in Jerusalem' to the second phase 'in all Judea and Samaria' (1:8).

Opposition to the gospel of Jesus had escalated from the first hearing of Peter and John before the Sanhedrin, which had ended in threats, to the apostles' second appearance, which ended in flogging. In those confrontations the chief priests' reaction was restrained by the fear of the people, who held the apostles in awe. Stephen's opponents, however, would be Hellenistic Jews from the Dispersion, and they would stir up not only the Sanhedrin, but also the people as a whole. This time the result would be death.

STRONG TESTIMONY AND IMPOTENT OPPOSITION

For a third time Stephen is described as full of gifts from God. Along with his fellow servants he was 'full of the Spirit and of wisdom' (6:3), and he was distinguished among them as 'full of faith and of the Holy Spirit' (verse 5). Now we see him as a man full of God's *grace and power*, which are exhibited in the great wonders and miraculous signs that he performed as well as his persuasive preaching. In Stephen we see the reality implied in Acts 5:32, namely that since the Holy Spirit who is given to all believers, testifies together with the apostles, all believers participate in the church's witness about Jesus. Until now miracles occurred only through Jesus and the apostles, to attest their word (2:22, 43; 4:30; 5:12). Through Stephen, God gave wonders and signs to confirm the witness of a non-apostle, who had been ordained not to a ministry of the Word, but to a ministry of compassion. Yet the fullness of the Spirit enabled him to speak Christ's message with irresistible power.

Although Stephen was called to serve Greek-speaking Christian widows, his opponents were also Greek-speaking Jews belonging to the *synagogue of the Freedmen*. In the original the word *freedmen* is a Latin word transposed into Greek letters. Apparently this synagogue was founded by freed Jewish slaves from Italy (where Latin was spoken) and later included Jews from elsewhere in the Dispersion: Cyrene and Alexandria in North Africa and Cilicia and Asia in Asia Minor. Having lived as a minority in a decadent Hellenistic culture, these Dispersion Jews were fiercely loyal to the Law of Moses and the Temple. Saul, who was born in Cilicia, boasted of his early devotion to his ancestral traditions (*Gal.* 1:14). When his family moved from Tarsus to Jerusalem, they may have associated with this very synagogue. He certainly sympathized with the members of this synagogue who took the lead in accusing and executing Stephen (7:58; 8:1). Later, however, he would take Stephen's place as a witness for Jesus, arguing for faith in Jesus with the same circle of Greek-speaking Jews (9:29; 22:15, 20).

In Stephen's message these opponents heard threats to historic Judaism, so they began to argue with Stephen. The wisdom and the Spirit by whom he spoke, however, belonged to the invincible Lord Jesus, who had silenced his debating opponents (*Luke* 20:40) and had promised his followers, 'I will give you a mouth and wisdom which none of your adversaries will be able to withstand' (*Luke* 21:15). Stephen's witness was unanswerable, as Jesus had promised.

FRAMED BY FALSE WITNESSES

Unable to best Stephen in open debate, his enemies resorted to perjury. They *secretly instigated* men – the verb implies bribing witnesses to lie – to charge Stephen with speaking words of blasphemy against Moses and against God, in violation of Exodus 22:28: 'Do not blaspheme God or curse the ruler of your people.' The blasphemy against Moses did not consist in slanderous comments about Moses, whom Stephen honoured highly (7:17–44). Rather, his accusers claimed that Stephen spoke against the law, claiming that Jesus would '*change the customs that Moses delivered to us*'. Jesus' inauguration of the new covenant did change customs handed down in the Mosaic law (and even more the oral traditions, which the rabbis attributed to Moses). Whether Stephen announced these implications Luke does not tell us. If Stephen did speak of changes to the law, his words would not in any way have been a slander of Moses, for Moses' role was to point ahead to the Christ (*Heb.* 3:5, *John* 5:45–47).

The blasphemy against God did not entail frivolous use of the divine Name. Rather, it apparently had to do with teaching that the temple's indispensable role as the meeting place of God with Israel was ending. Possibly Stephen repeated Jesus' prophecy that the temple would be destroyed (*Luke* 21:6). At Jesus' trial false witnesses had accused him of claiming that he could destroy the temple and rebuild it in three days (*Matt.* 26:60–61) – garbling his metaphorical prediction of his resurrection (*John* 2:19) with his prophecy of

Jerusalem's fall at Roman hands (*Mark* 13:2). Stephen was a victim of the same false accusation as was his Lord, whom he would also imitate by forgiving his murderers (*Acts* 7:60, *Luke* 23:34). Moreover, if Stephen predicted the temple's destruction, he stood squarely in the tradition of faithful prophets such as Micah and Jeremiah, who at God's command foretold the desolation of the first temple (*Mic.* 3:12, *Jer.* 26:1–19).

Whatever the way the false witnesses may have twisted the facts, they were no doubt correct in reporting that Stephen's constant theme was the difference that Jesus of Nazareth makes.

THE FACE OF AN ANGEL

Luke prefaces Stephen's answer with the intriguing comment that those sitting in the Sanhedrin – the chief priests, elders, and experts in the law – fixing their gaze on Stephen, beheld his face *like the face of an angel*. Similar descriptions appear in the Apocrypha and in later Christian descriptions of martyrs (the latter probably in imitation of our text), but none clarify how Stephen's appearance changed. It was noticeable to his judges, yet it did not avert their rage when he concluded his 'defence' by accusing them of showing contempt for Moses and for God (7:54).

Whatever visible feature made Stephen's face resemble that of an angel, the significance of his transfiguration was to reveal his intimacy with God (*Exod.* 34:29–35). Stephen would speak as a prophet, carrying a convicting message from God's heavenly court. As he died, he would see God's glory and Jesus, standing at God's right hand, as his advocate (7:55–56).

God does not promise that testifying about his truth will be risk free, nor that our witness will be welcomed with open minds. He assures us, however, that his Word accomplishes the mission on which he sends it and that, when witnessing brings us suffering, his strength shines through our weakness.

17

Promise, Rejection, and Deliverance

And the high priest said, "Are these things so?" ² *And Stephen said:*

"*Brothers and fathers, hear me. The God of glory appeared to our father Abraham when he was in Mesopotamia, before he lived in Haran,* ³ *and said to him, 'Go out from your land and from your kindred and go into the land that I will show you.'* ⁴ *Then he went out from the land of the Chaldeans and lived in Haran. And after his father died, God removed him from there into this land in which you are now living.* ⁵ *Yet he gave him no inheritance in it, not even a foot's length, but promised to give it to him as a possession and to his offspring after him, though he had no child.* ⁶ *And God spoke to this effect – that his offspring would be sojourners in a land belonging to others, who would enslave them and afflict them four hundred years.* ⁷ *'But I will judge the nation that they serve,' said God, 'and after that they shall come out and worship me in this place.'* ⁸ *And he gave him the covenant of circumcision. And so Abraham became the father of Isaac, and circumcised him on the eighth day, and Isaac became the father of Jacob, and Jacob of the twelve patriarchs.*

⁹ *"And the patriarchs, jealous of Joseph, sold him into Egypt; but God was with him* ¹⁰ *and rescued him out of all his afflictions and gave him favour and wisdom before Pharaoh, king of Egypt, who made him ruler over Egypt and over all his household.* ¹¹ *Now there came a famine throughout all Egypt and Canaan, and great affliction, and our fathers could find no food.* ¹² *But when Jacob heard that there was grain in Egypt, he sent out our fathers on their first visit.* ¹³ *And on the second visit Joseph made*

himself known to his brothers, and Joseph's family became known to Pharaoh. ¹⁴ And Joseph sent and summoned Jacob his father and all his kindred, seventy-five persons in all. ¹⁵ And Jacob went down into Egypt, and he died, he and our fathers, ¹⁶ and they were carried back to Shechem and laid in the tomb that Abraham had bought for a sum of silver from the sons of Hamor in Shechem (Acts 7:1–16).

W hen the high priest, who presided over the Sanhedrin, gave Stephen opportunity to answer his accusers, Stephen delivered the longest, most unusual, and one of the most significant addresses found in Acts. By recording Stephen's remarks at length Luke stresses their importance, and they indeed form a watershed in the progress of God's Word. To do it justice we will devote three chapters to this address.

The contents and tone of Stephen's speech are unexpected and exceptional. We would have expected the defendant to take up the charges against him and refute them explicitly. Instead Stephen embarked on a narrative of Israel's history in which themes related to the charges – the location of God's presence and the treatment of God's servants – were subtly interwoven. His purpose seems not so much to defend himself as to put his opponents on the defensive, showing how they have despised and mistreated Moses and other deliverers sent by God.

When compared to the other messages in Acts, Stephen's speech is the exception in several respects. (1) *It does not mention Jesus by name,* and alludes to him only twice by other titles: the promised prophet like Moses (7:37; see also 3:22, *Deut.* 18:15) and the suffering Righteous One (7:52; see also 3:14, *Isa.* 53:11). (2) *It never mentions Jesus' resurrection,* a central feature in all the evangelistic preaching in Acts, whether to Jews or to Gentiles. (3) *Its tone is one of indictment without a call to repentance or promise of forgiveness.* It sounds like the oracles of judgement that Old Testament prophets pronounced against Israel and Judah for breaking the Lord's covenant. Like a prophet pressing charges against God's unfaithful people, Stephen was not only a witness for Jesus but also a witness against Jewish unbelief. Stephen's speech functions for Jerusalem much as Paul's words would function for the leaders of the synagogue of Antioch in Pisidia when they insulted the gospel: 'It was necessary that the word of God be spoken first to you. Since you thrust it aside and judge yourselves unworthy of eternal life, behold, we are turning to the Gentiles' (13:46). At the end of Acts Paul would warn the Jewish leaders at Rome against responding to the gospel with calloused hearts, deaf ears and closed eyes, declaring, 'This salvation of God has been sent to the Gentiles. They will listen' (28:28). In Stephen, Jesus says to Jerusalem, 'You have had your opportunity to hear. Now I am sending my light to the nations.'

Stephen started, however, not on the negative note of accusation but on the positive note of God's promise to Abraham, a promise that he, his accusers, and his judges all treasured.

A PROMISED LAND FOR ABRAHAM, THE WANDERER

A lifetime of movement and resettlement began for Abraham when the God of glory appeared to him while he was still in Mesopotamia (*Gen.* 12:1–3). Stephen drew his description of God from Psalm 29:3 to underscore that the God whose glory had filled the tabernacle and temple (*Exod.* 40:34–35, *1 Kings* 8:10–11) cannot be confined to man-made structures. Throughout his selective history of Israel, Stephen noted God's presence with his servants in all sorts of places, not only outside the temple and Jerusalem but even outside the land of promise. This theme would be established finally by his quotation from Isaiah 66:1–2 (7:48–50).

In response to God's call Abraham left the land of the Chaldeans, settling for a time in Haran, a great distance northwest of Ur, and finally pressing on, as Stephen said, to this land where you are now living. This was the land that the Lord had promised to show him when he was still in Mesopotamia, yet God gave him no inheritance in it, not even sufficient territory for the sole of his foot to cover. Although Abraham was childless, God promised that after four hundred years of sojourn and slavery as strangers in a country not their own, Abraham's descendants would return and worship him in this place. Stephen here summarized God's solemn covenant promise, sealed to Abraham as God's flaming glory passed through the sacrificial animals (*Gen.* 15:9–21), but he added to it (with modification) God's later promise to Moses that, after the Exodus,

Israel would 'worship God on this mountain' (*Exod.* 3:12). 'This mountain' was Horeb in the Sinai Desert, where Moses saw the burning bush and would later receive the law, but Stephen stressed that God's intention was that Abraham's children would worship in the land of promise – *in this place*, which Stephen had been accused of dishonouring (6:13).

Stephen had not forgotten the significance of place: the place that God had promised to wandering Abraham, the place where God would cause his Name to dwell (*Deut.* 12:5). Yet God appeared and spoke to Abraham when there was no temple, nor any descendants to worship in it. Instead of seeking security in what he could see in the present, Abraham looked forward in faith and, in due time, passed on the covenant of circumcision to his son Isaac, and Isaac to his son Jacob, and Jacob to the twelve patriarchs (see *Heb.* 11:13–16).

SALVATION THROUGH JOSEPH, THE REJECTED

The story of Joseph continues the motif of God's presence with his servants apart from the temple, and it adds a second theme: the Israelites consistently repudiated the men whom God sent to rescue them. Stephen opened the next part of his discourse with this theme: because the patriarchs were *jealous of Joseph*, they sold their brother as a slave into Egypt (*Gen.* 37:17–36). Jealousy motivated the Sadducees to arrest the apostles (5:17) and would later motivate synagogue leaders to oppose Paul's gospel (13:45; 17:5). It is symptomatic of a heart that resents God's sovereignty and resists his Spirit, and it lay behind the Israelites' subsequent rejection of Moses, of the prophets, and finally of the Righteous One whom the prophets foretold (7:27, 35, 39, 51–53).

But God was with Joseph (a theme repeated in *Gen.* 39:2, 3, 21, 23) and rescued him from all his troubles: being falsely accused by Potiphar's wife, unjustly imprisoned, and forgotten by Pharaoh's cupbearer. While his treacherous brothers remained in the promised land, God was with Joseph – in Egypt! Joseph's wisdom won Pharaoh's favour, so Egypt's king made him ruler over Egypt and all his palace (*Gen.* 41:16–40). When famine struck both Egypt and Canaan, his position of power enabled Joseph not only to feed Pharaoh's subjects but also to save from starvation the brothers who had sold him into slavery, his father Jacob, and his whole family. On the brothers' second trip to buy Egyptian grain, when Joseph told his brothers who he was, he calmed their fears with his recognition of God's wise purpose: 'God sent me before you to preserve for you a remnant on earth, and to keep alive for you many survivors' (*Gen.* 45:7).

Stephen concluded the story of Joseph and his brothers with their deaths in Egypt and burials in the promised land, *in the tomb that Abraham had bought*. Though they did not live to see the fulfilment of God's promise that Abraham's descendants would inherit the land, their bodies were laid to rest there. Here Stephen employed a respected narrative technique to make a point. He telescoped the purchases of two burial plots: Abraham's purchase of the cave of Machpelah in Hebron, in which Jacob was buried (*Gen.* 23:17–20; 50:12–13), and Jacob's purchase from the sons of Hamor of a parcel at Shechem, in which Joseph was buried (*Gen.* 33:19, *Josh.* 24:32). Hebron lay in Judean territory south of Jerusalem, but Shechem was in the north, within the promised land but in the region once occupied by the northern Israelite tribes and near Mount Gerizim, where in Stephen's day Samaritans worshipped in their rival temple. The body of Joseph, the honoured patriarch through whom the Lord saved his people from starvation, rested not near '*this holy place*' about which Stephen's accusers were so exercised, but in the north, among the despised Samaritans.

Do we, like Abraham and Joseph, place more confidence in God's promises for the future than in the present circumstances that we see? Are we ready for God to uproot us from the trappings of material security, prepared to live as pilgrims and endure affliction until we reach the inheritance that he has promised?

18

Moses, the Rejected Redeemer

"But as the time of the promise drew near, which God had granted to Abraham, the people increased and multiplied in Egypt [18] until there arose over Egypt another king who did not know Joseph. [19] He dealt shrewdly with our race and forced our fathers to expose their infants, so that they would not be kept alive. [20] At this time Moses was born; and he was beautiful in God's sight. And he was brought up for three months in his father's house, [21] and when he was exposed, Pharaoh's daughter adopted him and brought him up as her own son. [22] And Moses was instructed in all the wisdom of the Egyptians, and he was mighty in his words and deeds.

[23] "When he was forty years old, it came into his heart to visit his brothers, the children of Israel. [24] And seeing one of them being wronged, he defended the oppressed man and avenged him by striking down the Egyptian. [25] He supposed that his brothers would understand that God was giving them salvation by his hand, but they did not understand. [26] And on the following day he appeared to them as they were quarrelling and tried to reconcile them, saying, 'Men, you are brothers. Why do you wrong each other?' [27] But the man who was wronging his neighbour thrust him aside, saying, 'Who made you a ruler and a judge over us? [28] Do you want to kill me as you killed the Egyptian yesterday?' [29] At this retort Moses fled and became an exile in the land of Midian, where he became the father of two sons.

[30] "Now when forty years had passed, an angel appeared to him in the wilderness of Mount Sinai, in a flame of fire in a bush. [31] When Moses saw it, he was amazed at the sight, and as he drew near to look, there came the voice of the Lord: [32] 'I am the

God of your fathers, the God of Abraham and of Isaac and of Jacob.' And Moses trembled and did not dare to look. ³³ Then the Lord said to him, 'Take off the sandals from your feet, for the place where you are standing is holy ground. ³⁴ I have surely seen the affliction of my people who are in Egypt, and have heard their groaning, and I have come down to deliver them. And now come, I will send you to Egypt.'

³⁵ "This Moses, whom they rejected, saying, 'Who made you a ruler and a judge?' – this man God sent as both ruler and redeemer by the hand of the angel who appeared to him in the bush. ³⁶ This man led them out, performing wonders and signs in Egypt and at the Red Sea and in the wilderness for forty years. ³⁷ This is the Moses who said to the Israelites, 'God will raise up for you a prophet like me from your brothers.' ³⁸ This is the one who was in the congregation in the wilderness with the angel who spoke to him at Mount Sinai, and with our fathers. He received living oracles to give to us. ³⁹ Our fathers refused to obey him, but thrust him aside, and in their hearts they turned to Egypt, ⁴⁰ saying to Aaron, 'Make for us gods who will go before us. As for this Moses who led us out from the land of Egypt, we do not know what has become of him.' ⁴¹ And they made a calf in those days, and offered a sacrifice to the idol and were rejoicing in the works of their hands. ⁴² But God turned away and gave them over to worship the host of heaven, as it is written in the book of the prophets:

" 'Did you bring to me slain beasts and sacrifices,
during the forty years in the wilderness, O house of Israel?
⁴³ You took up the tent of Moloch
and the star of your god Rephan,
the images that you made to worship;
and I will send you into exile beyond Babylon'

(Acts 7:17–43).

S tephen's narration about Moses is the longest section of his speech: twenty-four verses (excluding the introduction in verses 17–19) in comparison to seven on Abraham and eight on Joseph. Moreover, in this section Stephen spared no praises in his exaltation of Moses as the ruler and redeemer of Israel. Both the length and the laudatory contents show the absurdity of the charge that Stephen had spoken against Moses (6:11). More importantly, Moses' life and work illustrated the two themes that Stephen was tracing through the history of Israel: God has been present with his people without a temple, and God's people have rejected the deliverers whom he has sent.

A brief transition sets the scene, linking Moses to both Abraham and Joseph. Moses was born as the time drew near for God to fulfil his promise to Abraham, that after four hundred years of mistreatment Abraham's descendants would inherit the land and worship God 'in this place' (see verses 6–7). The mistreatment took place at the hands of another king, who knew nothing about Joseph – nothing of the respect and power that Pharaoh had accorded Joseph (see verse 10). This later king fulfilled God's prophecy to Abraham when he dealt treacherously with Israel, oppressing them by forcing them to expose their newborn babies to the elements. Yet *the people increased and multiplied in Egypt*. Here Stephen paraphrased Exodus 1:7, but Luke's readers are also reminded of the Word's growth and the church's multiplication in the days after Stephen and the six others were appointed: 'And the word of God continued to increase, and the number of the disciples multiplied greatly in Jerusalem' (6:7). In Stephen's day and ours God is still fulfilling his promise to Abraham, multiplying his descendants like the stars of the sky (see also 3:25).

Stephen presented Moses' life in three blocks of forty years each. The conclusions of the first two stages are closely linked in the original: *When [Moses] was forty years old* is, literally, 'when a forty-year time period was fulfilled for him' (verse 23), just as *When forty years had passed* is more literally 'after forty years had been fulfilled' (verse 30). In his first forty years Moses grew to maturity, well prepared to rule and rescue his people (verses 20–22). His second forty years, which began with his flight from Egypt (his first rejection by his brothers) and concluded with his call at the burning bush, Moses spent as a foreigner in Midian (verses 23–29). Finally, *for forty years* (verse 36) he led Israel through the wilderness, enduring further rejection despite the fact that he had led them to freedom.

THE IDEAL RULER

At birth it was evident that Moses was no ordinary child. The ESV translates the Greek words used as 'beautiful in God's sight'. From his infancy Moses' mother recognized his special destiny and shielded him for three months from the king's edict that Israelite infant boys be thrown out to die. When he was *exposed* (verse 21 echoes verse 19), it was in the tiny boat fashioned by his mother. Pharaoh's daughter *adopted him* and brought him up as her own son.

Moses' preparation for leadership included his education as a member of Egypt's royal family. As Joseph's wisdom gained notice among the Egyptians (verse 10), so Moses was instructed in all the wisdom of the Egyptians (see also *Dan.* 1:4, 17–20). Moreover, Moses was *'mighty in his words and deeds'*, foreshadowing Jesus, described in Luke's Gospel as 'a prophet, mighty in deed and word' (*Luke* 24:19). In Exodus Moses, in response to God's call, protested that he was an inept speaker (*Exod.* 4:10), but Stephen focused on what Moses would become when God had fulfilled his promise, 'I will be with your mouth and teach you what you shall speak' (verse 12).

THE REJECTED RULER

The second phase of Moses' life began when, at the age of forty, he decided to visit his fellow Israelites. The word *visit* is significant, meaning not just 'go to spend time with' someone, but also 'intervene on behalf of' someone. It appears in Joseph's deathbed promise of the Exodus: 'God will visit you and bring you up out of this land' (*Gen.* 50:24). At the burning bush the LORD used this term, assuring Israel through Moses, 'I have oberved you and have seen what has been done to you in Egypt' (*Exod.* 3:16). Moses expected his brothers to see in his visit – especially in his defending a mistreated Israelite from an Egyptian oppressor – the beginning of the LORD's redemptive visitation to rescue his people (see also *Luke* 1:68, 78; 19:44). But they did not.

Rather, the next day, when Moses tried to reconcile two Israelites who were fighting, the aggressor thrust Moses aside with the taunt, 'Who made you a prince and a judge over us?' (*Exod.* 2:14) This thrusting aside (not explicitly mentioned in Exodus) was Israel's typical response to Moses, as Stephen would show by recalling the taunt in verse 35 and repeating *thrust aside* in verse 39. As the patriarchs in jealousy sold Joseph, who was to save them from starvation, so the Israelites would resist, resent, and disregard Moses whom God had sent to be their ruler and deliverer (verse 35).

Realizing that his killing of the Egyptian had become public, Moses fled to Midian, where he settled as an exile, emphasizing his alienness by naming the first of his two sons Gershom, 'a sojourner there' (*Exod. 2:22*). Just as Abraham sojourned in Canaan without possessing even a footstep of it, and just as the generations between Joseph and Moses had been strangers in Egypt, 'a land belonging to others', so Moses spent forty years as an alien. Yet living outside the promised land did not exclude him from God's presence and care.

THE REJECTED REDEEMER

In that strange setting, far from the site where the temple would be built, an angel appeared to Moses in the flames of a burning bush and the Lord himself spoke to Moses. The fiery messenger was the Lord himself, for when he spoke, it was the Lord's voice that Moses heard, declaring his own identity (*I am the God of your fathers, the God of Abraham, Isaac and Jacob*), the plight of his people, and the liberation that he would accomplish for them. Stephen recounted the meeting at the burning bush in detail, following Exodus 3–4. His purpose is twofold.

First, God's sending of Moses to deliver the Israelites answers the derisive question, *Who made you a ruler and a judge?* which precedes and follows (verses 27, 35). Echoing the question but incorporating the 'sending' term that he had just quoted from Exodus 3:10, Stephen drew the obvious conclusion: Moses was sent to be their ruler and redeemer by God himself. Stephen replaced *judge* with *redeemer*. The role of the judges in Israel involved deliverance from enemies, and not merely legal adjudication only, and this is what Stephen now stressed, showing that Moses fitted the pattern that included Joseph before him and Jesus, the promised prophet like Moses who was to come.

Second, the Lord's description of the place where Moses was standing – in the desert near Mount Sinai – demonstrates undeniably that God was with his servants outside of the land and apart from the temple. Where God was, there was holy ground. The very adjective that Stephen's accusers applied to the temple, *this holy place* (6:13), God had applied to the Sinai desert, requiring Moses to remove his sandals in reverent awe.

At verse 35 Stephen launched into a list of descriptions of Moses, each introduced by 'this Moses' or 'this man': 'This Moses whom they rejected . . . This man God sent as both ruler and redeemer . . . This man led them out . . . This is the Moses who said to the Israelites . . . This is the one who was in the congregation in the wilderness . . . '. Stephen's accusers had used the pronoun 'this' scornfully in referring to Jesus (*this Jesus of Nazareth*, 6:14), as the Israelites would do in dismissing Moses: *As for this Moses who led us out from the land of Egypt, we do not know what has become of him* (7:40). Stephen uses the pronoun for the opposite purpose, to say: 'Look at the achievements of the deliverer whom God sent, and realize the impudence of our fathers, who rejected him!'

As Moses had been sent to be their deliverer, so Jesus was the one who was to redeem Israel (*Luke* 24:21). Just as Moses in Egypt had been attested by wonders and miraculous signs, so also had Jesus (2:22). Just as Moses had *received living oracles to give to us*, so Jesus brings '*all the words of this life*' (5:20, see also *John* 6:68). Moses had predicted, *God will raise up for you a prophet like me from among you, from your brothers* (*Deut.* 18:15), and Peter had already declared that Jesus was that prophet (3:22–23).

But – sad commentary! – '*Our fathers refused to obey him.*' Later generations would kill the prophets, and Stephen's contemporaries would follow in their fathers' footsteps, betraying and murdering the Righteous One whom the prophets foretold (7:52). When the fathers rejected (pushed aside) Moses, they were turning away from God, back to the idols of Egypt, serving and celebrating what their hands had made. To dismiss God's Redeemer is to reject God himself. As their hearts turned back from God and his promises, so God turned away from them and gave them over to the worship of *the heavenly host* (*Deut.* 4:19, *Jer.* 8:2; 19:13). He judged them by handing them over to the gods they preferred (see also *Rom.* 1:24, 26, 28).

Stephen quoted Amos 5:25–27 to show that the pattern begun in the wilderness – Israel's sacrifice not to the Lord but to his rivals, Molech, Rephan, and others – continued in the land of promise, from which the Lord eventually sent Judah into exile beyond Babylon.

(*Babylon* replaces Amos' 'Damascus' because the idolatry that led Amos' audience, the northern kingdom, into captivity in Assyria beyond Damascus later sent the southern kingdom – with which Stephen's hearers identified – into exile in Babylon.)

Freed from slavery but confronted with the challenges of a wilderness, the Israelites turned their hearts back to Egypt, trusting the familiar gods of the surrounding culture. Which idols exercise lordship over your heart? Or do you trust the living God and submit to Jesus, the Prophet who is like Moses but greater than Moses – Jesus, the Son who radiates God's glory and rules God's house (*Heb.* 1:2–3; 3:1–6)?

19

Murderers of the Righteous One

"Our fathers had the tent of witness in the wilderness, just as he who spoke to Moses directed him to make it, according to the pattern that he had seen. ⁴⁵ Our fathers in turn brought it in with Joshua when they dispossessed the nations that God drove out before our fathers. So it was until the days of David, ⁴⁶ who found favour in the sight of God and asked to find a dwelling place for the God of Jacob. ⁴⁷ But it was Solomon who built a house for him. ⁴⁸ Yet the Most High does not dwell in houses made by hands, as the prophet says,

⁴⁹ *" 'Heaven is my throne,*
    and the earth is my footstool.
What kind of house will you build for me, says the Lord,
    or what is the place of my rest?
    ⁵⁰ *Did not my hand make all these things?'*

⁵¹ *"You stiff-necked people, uncircumcised in heart and ears, you always resist the Holy Spirit. As your fathers did, so do you.* ⁵² *Which of the prophets did not your fathers persecute? And they killed those who announced beforehand the coming of the Righteous One, whom you have now betrayed and murdered,* ⁵³ *you who received the law as delivered by angels and did not keep it"* (Acts 7:44–53).

As Stephen concluded, his survey of Israelite history moved briskly from wilderness wandering under Moses to Joshua's conquest of the land, and then on to the reigns of David and Solomon. The theme also shifted from Moses' role as leader, redeemer, and lawgiver, to the issue of the temple as God's dwelling place among his people. Wrapping up his historical survey and argument with a quotation from Isaiah 66:1–2, Stephen in closing applied directly to his hearers the sobering lessons of their ancestors' shameful history of hostility to God's messengers.

FROM TABERNACLE TO TEMPLE

Israel's treachery in turning from the Lord to sacrifice to the products of their own hands, the idols they made to worship in the tent of Moloch (7:41–43), was all the more wicked because they had the tent of witness with them in the desert. The contrast is sharp between the tent of a pagan god and the tent that sheltered the ark, which contained the stone tablets of testimony to the LORD's covenant with Israel. The construction of the tabernacle was initiated and directed by God himself, and its design revealed in the heavenly prototype shown to Moses on Mount Sinai (*Exod.* 25:40, see also *Heb.* 8:5).

Likewise when Joshua led the Israelites into Canaan, to take possession of the land that God had promised to Abraham, the tabernacle came with them. It was the central sanctuary, the place that the LORD their God had chosen 'to put his name and make his habitation there' (*Deut.* 12:5). This tent fulfilled that role until the time of David. Here Stephen's treatment of the sanctuary theme took an interesting turn. Whereas the tabernacle was the Lord's idea, the temple was David's (*2 Sam.* 7:2, 6–7).

It was not necessarily a bad idea in itself. After all, David enjoyed God's favour and his request to provide a dwelling place for the God of Jacob received commendation in Psalm 132:5, to which Stephen alluded. But it was an idea fraught with potential for dangerous confusion, as Solomon, who built the house for God acknowledged: 'But will God indeed dwell on the earth? Behold, heaven and the highest heaven cannot contain you; how much less this house that I have built! . . . Listen to the plea of your servant and of your people Israel, when they pray toward this place. And listen in heaven your dwelling place, and when you hear, forgive' (*1 Kings* 8:27, 30).

NO HAND-MADE HOUSE FOR THE MOST HIGH

Solomon's prayer stands behind Stephen's assertion that the Most High does not live in houses made by men. He selected the Old Testament title *Most High* (*Gen.* 14:18–20, 22, see also *Luke* 1:32, 35, 76) to emphasize how far God's heavenly throne is exalted above his earthly footstool. In describing the temple as a house made by hands (literally, 'hand-made things'), Stephen stated the obvious: both the tabernacle and the temple were constructed by human artisans (*Exod.* 31:1–11, 2 *Chron.* 2:7, 13–14, see also *Heb.* 9:11). But the term is also associated with idols in the Old Testament (*Lev.* 26:1, *Isa.* 2:18, compare verse 8; *Psa.* 115:4). Stephen himself had described the golden calf as 'the work of their hands' (7:41). The temple was not a hand-made idol, certainly, but it had been treated as such by Israelites who had ignored Solomon's humble assessment of the house he had built for the LORD's Name.

The distinction drawn by Stephen and, long ago, by Solomon finds definitive confirmation in the voice of God himself, recorded in Isaiah 66:1–2. Since God affirms, *Heaven is my throne, and the earth is my footstool,* how dare his creatures think that their hands could build a house or resting place to contain him? How dared Stephen's accusers so equate the temple with the God who stooped to meet his people there, that they mistook a prediction of its destruction for blasphemy against God himself?

The Lord's hand was already building a new kind of temple, not limited to Jerusalem but soon to spring up in Judea and Samaria, in Antioch (*Acts* 11:21), and elsewhere. It was and is a 'spiritual house' composed of 'living stones,' people called out of darkness into his wonderful light, united to Christ the life–giving Stone, rejected by men (as Stephen would be) but precious to God (*1 Pet.* 2:4–10).

LIKE FATHERS, LIKE SONS

Stephen's speech suddenly switched from historical narrative to sharp, direct address: *You stiff-necked people, uncircumcised in hearts and ears!* In the words and the spirit of ancient prophets, Stephen prosecuted the LORD's lawsuit against his wayward people. The LORD called Israel stiff-necked, when they rejected Moses and turned away from their God to worship the golden calf (*Exod.* 33:3,

5; *Deut.* 9:13). Jeremiah spoke of Israel's 'uncircumcised' ears, which refused to hear God's Word (*Jer.* 6:10). Moses and later prophets even categorized Israel with the pagan nations, all of whom were 'uncircumcised in heart', defiled and resistant to the Lord's commands (*Lev.* 26:41, *Jer.* 4:4; 9:25, see also *Deut.* 10:16; 30:6, *Ezek.* 44:7, 9, *Rom.* 2:25, 28–29).

Stephen's hearers fit the pattern set by their ancestors. Israel's earlier generations grieved the Holy Spirit, 'the angel of his presence' who had delivered them in Moses' days (*Isa.* 61:9–12). Now their children carried on the tradition: *You always resist the Holy Spirit.* Earlier generations persecuted the prophets, and even killed those who predicted the coming of the Righteous One. This persecution of the messengers whom God sent, out of pity for his people and his dwelling place, contributed to Jerusalem's fall and the exile: 'They kept mocking the messengers of God, despising his words and scoffing at his prophets, until the wrath of the LORD rose against his people, until there was no remedy' (*2 Chron.* 36:16). Jesus promised blessing to his followers, who would suffer rejection as the prophets had (*Luke* 6:22–23). He foretold the woe to come on Israel's teachers who, in building tombs for the prophets, were not honouring the prophets but celebrating their murder (*Luke* 11:47–51). He predicted in parable the treachery of Israel's leaders, who would bring past abuse of God's servants to a gruesome climax in the assassination of the beloved Son (*Luke* 20:9–19).

Stephen recalled that event, when the Sanhedrin had betrayed into Gentile hands, and thereby murdered, the Righteous One promised by the prophets, as seen especially in Isaiah's portrait of the suffering Servant (*Isa.* 53:11, see also *Acts* 3:14; 22:14). The actions of these leaders revealed that, although they acknowledged that the angels who delivered the law to Moses established its inviolable glory, their own uncircumcised hearts were far from obeying it. The role of the angels who conveyed the law to Israel is hinted in the Old Testament (*Deut.* 33:2), mentioned in the New Testament (*Gal.* 3:19, *Heb.* 2:2), and discussed more fully in Jewish sources. This tradition should have produced a reverence for God's law, yet the chief priests, elders, and scribes had conspired to destroy the world's one righteous man, the Moses-like prophet whom Moses promised. They, not Stephen, were Moses' enemies.

Stephen's courageous conclusion challenges our hearts, as it did the hearts of the Sanhedrin. The issue of life and death is not whether we have God's Word in our possession, or where and when we gather for worship. The issue is whether our hearts are circumcised, our deep uncleanness cut out by the scalpel of the Spirit.

20

A Witness to the Death

Now when they heard these things they were enraged, and they ground their teeth at him. ⁵⁵ *But he, full of the Holy Spirit, gazed into heaven and saw the glory of God, and Jesus standing at the right hand of God.* ⁵⁶ *And he said, "Behold, I see the heavens opened, and the Son of Man standing at the right hand of God."* ⁵⁷ *But they cried out with a loud voice and stopped their ears and rushed together at him.* ⁵⁸ *Then they cast him out of the city and stoned him. And the witnesses laid down their garments at the feet of a young man named Saul.* ⁵⁹ *And as they were stoning Stephen, he called out, "Lord Jesus, receive my spirit."* ⁶⁰ *And falling to his knees he cried out with a loud voice, "Lord, do not hold this sin against them." And when he had said this, he fell asleep* (Acts 7:54–60).

The Greek word from which we get 'martyr' did not originally refer to one who died for his or her faith. It meant simply 'witness', a person who bears testimony in a court of law. With this word the risen Jesus commissioned his disciples: 'You will be my witnesses in Jerusalem, and in all Judea and Samaria, and to the end of the earth' (1:8). Now, as Luke's account of their testimony to Jerusalem draws to a close, Stephen seals his testimony with his blood – as would countless other Christian witnesses down through history (see *Rev.* 2:13; 17:6; 12:11). Ironically, the title 'witness/martyr' would first be applied to Stephen by Saul, who makes his entrance here as a wholehearted supporter of those who killed Stephen (22:20).

Stephen's demeanour shows us the calm hope and kindness that faith in Jesus imparts to those who rest in his grace. In Stephen we see the fruit of the Spirit's fulness, conforming the believer to his Lord in his death. Moreover, through Stephen's eyes we see Jesus, the triumphant Son of Man, standing at God's right hand to defend those who hold fast their testimony to his truth.

THE REBELS' RAGE

Stephen had turned the tables on his accusers, accusing them of violating the law that angels had delivered to Moses. They precisely fit the pattern set by their ancestors, rejecting God's deliverers and turning from their God to become fixated on things made by human hands.

Brushing aside the opportunity for self–examination that Stephen's indictment presented, Stephen's accusers and his judges were filled with rage. They were enraged – literally, 'sawed through in their hearts' – as the Sanhedrin members had been when Peter proclaimed Jesus as Leader and Saviour (5:31). They were so outraged that they gnashed their teeth at him, expressing hostility (*Job* 16:9, *Psa.* 35:17, 37:12) and frustration (*Psa.* 112:10, Luke 13:28). Stephen was about to taste the bitter-sweet blessing that Jesus promised to those whom men hate for his sake (*Luke* 6:22).

THE MARTYR'S ADVOCATE

Bloodshed might still have been averted, as it had been by Gamaliel's prudent counsel earlier (5:34–40). But Stephen had one more word of witness to declare, a testimony that would push his enemies 'over the top'. At that crucial moment God granted him a revelatory vision to confirm all that he had declared. Stephen became *full of the Holy Spirit*, not only because the Spirit was constantly moulding his character (6:3, 5; see also 11:24) but also, now, as a recipient of prophetic revelation (see 4:8; 13:9). He saw heaven open, just as at Jesus' baptism (*Luke* 3:21), at Peter's vision of the sheet of animals (*Acts* 10:11), and at John's visions in the Book of Revelation (*Rev.* 4:1; 19:11). As he gazed into heaven he saw the glory of God, as had Abraham in Mesopotamia (*Acts* 7:2) and Moses in the desert (7:31–32, 35).

Moreover, he saw Jesus standing at the right hand of God. The apostles had announced that Jesus, risen from the dead, was exalted to sit at the right hand of God, fulfilling Psalm 110:1 (*Acts* 2:33–35; 5:31). The right hand is the position of highest authority in the presence of the Sovereign, and a seated posture implies enthronement. In Stephen's vision, however, Jesus was *standing* at God's right hand. The departure from Psalm 110 is significant. In the Sanhedrin's earthly court opponents had (literally) 'made false witnesses stand' to speak their slanderous accusations (6:13; ESV: *set up false witnesses*). Stephen now beheld the heavenly court, where another Witness stood to give testimony, as he had promised: 'I tell you, whoever acknowledges me before men, the Son of Man will also acknowledge him before the angels of God' (*Luke* 12:8).

Reporting his vision, Stephen called Jesus *the Son of Man*, the title that Jesus himself had used so often. Daniel had seen the Ancient of Days in his heavenly court, and 'one like a son of man' approaching the throne to receive authority, glory, sovereign power, and everlasting dominion over all peoples, nations, and languages (*Dan.* 7). The Sanhedrin had heard Jesus himself link Daniel's vision with the enthronement in Psalm 110: 'You will see the Son of Man seated at the right hand of the Power, and coming with the clouds of heaven' (*Mark* 14:62). Stephen was testifying that Jesus' prophecy had come true: the innocent man that Israel's leaders had tried to eliminate, had been exalted by God as Lord over all.

THE REBELS' RAGE TURNS VIOLENT

Stephen's testimony about Jesus, the Son of Man, was more than they could bear: to allege that a man condemned by Israel's high court now occupied so supreme a place in heaven they considered blasphemy against God. To silence it they stopped their ears and yelled at the top of their voices. Rushing him, they dragged him out of the city and began to stone him. Presumably they considered Stephen guilty of blasphemy, and therefore liable to death by stoning (*Lev.* 24:10–23, *Deut.* 17:2–7). They complied with Mosaic requirements that the execution take place outside the community and the witnesses take the lead in casting stones. Yet not even the semblance of an orderly procedure was followed: no weighing of evidence, reaching of a verdict, pronouncement of sentence. In fact, under Roman occupation, the Sanhedrin was painfully aware that it lacked authority to enforce capital punishment (*John* 18:31). Instead of justice and order, mob violence ruled.

Almost casually Luke introduces *a young man named Saul*, at whose feet the false witnesses laid their cloaks as they took up stones to wound Stephen. As Barnabas was introduced by his generosity (4:36–37), so the first thing to learn about Saul is that he approved of the mob's murder of Stephen (8:1; 22:20). He would take the lead in scattering and hunting down the church (8:3; 9:1–2). But Jesus had other plans for him!

THE MARTYR'S PRAYER

The tumult of the angry mob contrasted with the calm confidence and compassion of their victim. As the stones struck him, two brief prayers formed on Stephen's lips. Both echoed the Lord Jesus' prayers from the cross. First, a prayer of confident trust: 'Lord Jesus, receive my spirit.' David had prayed to God, 'Into your hands I commit my spirit; you have redeemed me, O LORD, faithful God' (*Psa*. 31:5). Quoting his royal ancestor, Jesus entrusted himself to his Father's safekeeping: 'Father, into your hands I commit my spirit' (*Luke* 23:46). Now Stephen, his faith ablaze with the glory of the Son of Man, placed himself in Jesus' strong hands.

Then, Stephen cried out in a loud voice to overcome the mob's roar (the Greek references to the crowd's yelling and Stephen's cry are identical), pleading for mercy on his murderers: 'Lord, do not hold this sin against them.' Jesus' prayer, 'Father, forgive them, for they know not what they do' (*Luke* 23:34), though absent from some early manuscripts, conveys the compassion of the Saviour, who was crushed for the iniquities of those who despised him. Jesus calls us to 'pray for those who abuse you' (Luke 6:28). He himself had led the way, and Stephen followed in his steps (see *1 Pet*. 2:21–25; 3:9). So Stephen fell asleep. The New Testament often refers to death as sleep (*John* 11:11, *Acts* 13:36, *1 Cor*. 15:6, 18, 51, *1 Thess*. 4:14–18). The sleep metaphor does not erase the painful separation that death inflicts, but it affirms that death will not have the last word for those who trust in Jesus, the resurrection and the life (*John* 11:23–26).

In order to face our adversity with calm trust and treat our enemies with compassion, we too need to see that the Son of Man is at God's right hand, invested with all authority in heaven and on earth. What Stephen experienced in prophetic vision God conveys to us in the sure words of Scripture.

21

The Word Scattered as Seed

And Saul approved of his execution. And there arose on that day a great persecution against the church in Jerusalem, and they were all scattered throughout the regions of Judea and Samaria, except the apostles. ² Devout men buried Stephen and made great lamentation over him. ³ But Saul was ravaging the church, and entering house after house, he dragged off men and women and committed them to prison.

⁴ Now those who were scattered went about preaching the word. ⁵ Philip went down to the city of Samaria and proclaimed to them the Christ. ⁶ And the crowds with one accord paid attention to what was being said by Philip when they heard him and saw the signs that he did. ⁷ For unclean spirits came out of many who were possessed, crying with a loud voice, and many who were paralyzed or lame were healed. ⁸ So there was much joy in that city.

⁹ But there was a man named Simon, who had previously practised magic in the city and amazed the people of Samaria, saying that he himself was somebody great. ¹⁰ They all paid attention to him, from the least to the greatest, saying, "This man is the power of God that is called Great." ¹¹ And they paid attention to him because for a long time he had amazed them with his magic. ¹² But when they believed Philip as he preached good news about the kingdom of God and the name of Jesus Christ, they were baptized, both men and women. ¹³ Even Simon himself believed, and after being baptized he continued with Philip. And seeing signs and great miracles performed, he was amazed (Acts 8:1–13).

The Word Scattered as Seed

The aftermath of Stephen's martyrdom was a great persecution against the church at Jerusalem, leading to the dispersion of the church throughout Judea and Samaria. Thus the second wave of witness predicted by Jesus in Acts 1:8 – *'in Jerusalem, and in all Judea and Samaria, and to the end of the earth'* – began through the ordeal of suffering. Saul, who had approved the killing of Stephen, now took the initiative, violently trying to destroy the church through house-to-house searches and arrests. Yet dispersed Christians, fleeing from the city into the surrounding region of Judea and north into Samaria, spread the good news about Jesus wherever they travelled. Philip's preaching to Samaritans is one example of the scattered believers' witness. Through Philip the Word crossed a significant ethnic and religious frontier with saving power, on its way to the Gentile world.

PERSECUTION AND DISPERSION

Between two descriptions of the persecution that scattered the church from Jerusalem (8:1,3–4) Luke mentions the burial of Stephen by godly men, who mourned deeply for him (verse 2). Thus the dispersion of Jesus' messengers is directly traced to Stephen's bold witness and martyrdom. The spread of the gospel to Antioch in Syria will likewise be linked to Stephen's death (11:19). Just as the disciples of John the Baptist claimed his body for burial (*Mark* 5:29) and as Joseph of Arimathea and Nicodemus requested the body of Jesus (*John* 19:38–42), so these men showed both piety and courage in arranging a respectful burial and offering public lament for Stephen. To identify with one such as Stephen, against whom both the people and the leaders had vented their rage, was risky.

In the Old Testament, scattering or dispersion was the judgement of God. The arrogant were scattered from Babel (*Gen.* 11:9). The Lord threatened to scatter his people from his land if they broke faith with him (*Deut.* 28:64). When they did, he kept his word, dispersing them among the nations (*Ezek.* 36:19).

This dispersion of the church, however, was a sign of God's judgment, not on those scattered but on the scatterers, on persecutors such as Saul whose zeal to destroy the church only served to spread the word about Jesus more broadly. Having given

Israel's capital city abundant opportunity to hear the message of the Messiah, God was taking his good news elsewhere. Moreover, the apostles themselves, who stayed in Jerusalem as others scattered, were unscathed by Saul's violent fervour as he went from house to house, seeking out those homes in which believers gathered for worship and fellowship.

THE POWER OF THE SCATTERED WORD

Philip, second to Stephen among the servants to the widows (6:5), is an example of how those who had been scattered preached the Word wherever they went. The word *preaching* is 'announcing good news' (from which our 'evangelize' comes), and Philip would later be called 'the evangelist' (21:8). The content of the good news he proclaimed is clear: he proclaimed the Christ (8:5), namely, the good news of the kingdom of God and the name of Jesus Christ (verse 12).

The Samaritans were a border people, perceived by Jews to be on the fringe between God's people and the Gentiles, the Lord's enemies. Samaritan religion revered the books of Moses but no other part of the Old Testament. They anticipated not a royal Messiah descended from David but a last-days 'Restorer,' a prophet like Moses (see *Deut.* 18:15). Despite their respect for Moses, Samaritans were viewed as foreigners to Israel (*Luke* 17:18) and grouped with the Gentiles as outside the community of God's covenant (*Matt.* 10:5). Yet, precisely because they were outsiders, Jesus reached out to a Samaritan leper, cleansing his uncleanness (*Luke* 17:16), and to a Samaritan woman, sharing her cup and offering to her his 'living water' (*John* 4:7–10). Which individuals or groups do you mentally categorize as just beyond the perimeter of God's love and saving power?

Samaritans were also open to a syncretistic absorption of pagan elements into their religion. In that particular city a magician named Simon had been practising his craft for some time, amazing the populace, so that they gave him their attention and acclaimed him as the Great Power of God – an incarnation of divine wonder-working might – agreeing with his own boasts that he was someone great. Key terms in the summary of Simon's previous influence (verses 9–11) also describe Philip's ministry, showing that Jesus' Word overpowered Simon's magic. Suddenly the crowds paid close attention to Philip's preaching, and Simon himself was amazed by the great miracles he saw (verse 13; Greek: 'great powers,' like Simon's title, the Great Power).

Although the signs that Philip did – exorcisms and healings – attracted the Samaritans' attention and produced great joy in that city, it was the message he preached that changed their hearts. As he announced the good news that God's reign had dawned in Jesus the Messiah (not only the Prophet promised by Moses but also the King descended from David), many believed and were baptized. In fact, Simon himself believed and was baptized, although later events would show how ephemeral his 'belief' was. Even when proclaimed by a servant of widows, Jesus' name and gospel overpower the rival forces of magic, bringing wholeness and freedom to a city long oppressed by Satan. The persecution was painful, and the scattering seemed to be a setback. Yet through these trials God broadcast his Word like fertile seed into new fields. Do you see your setbacks as opportunities to tell the good news of Christ in new venues?

22

The Free Gift of the Spirit

Now when the apostles at Jerusalem heard that Samaria had received the word of God, they sent to them Peter and John, ¹⁵ who came down and prayed for them that they might receive the Holy Spirit, ¹⁶ for he had not yet fallen on any of them, but they had only been baptized in the name of the Lord Jesus. ¹⁷ Then they laid their hands on them and they received the Holy Spirit. ¹⁸ Now when Simon saw that the Spirit was given through the laying on of the apostles' hands, he offered them money, ¹⁹ saying, "Give me this power also, so that anyone on whom I lay my hands may receive the Holy Spirit." ²⁰ But Peter said to him, "May your silver perish with you, because you thought you could obtain the gift of God with money! ²¹ You have neither part nor lot in this matter, for your heart is not right before God. ²² Repent, therefore, of this wickedness of yours, and pray to the Lord that, if possible, the intent of your heart may be forgiven you. ²³ For I see that you are in the gall of bitterness and in the bond of iniquity." ²⁴ And Simon answered, "Pray for me to the Lord, that nothing of what you have said may come upon me."
²⁵ Now when they had testified and spoken the word of the Lord, they returned to Jerusalem, preaching the gospel to many villages of the Samaritans (Acts 8:14–25).

Because the Samaritans constituted a covenantal 'no man's land' between Israel and the pagan world, their incorporation into the church was a milestone, marking a new phase in the expansion of God's kingdom. For this reason God waited to bestow his Spirit until apostles from the mother church in Jerusalem were present to welcome, and to witness God's welcome of, these new brothers and sisters in Christ. The Spirit also performed a winnowing function in Samaria, sifting true faith from its counterfeit (*Luke* 3:16–17). Simon's faith, which initially seemed as genuine as that of his fellow–citizens, proved to be both superficial and ephemeral.

THE SPIRIT GATHERS SAMARITANS INTO THE CHURCH

Luke's comment that the apostles in Jerusalem heard that Samaria had accepted the Word of God anticipates the arrival of a similar report concerning the Gentiles (11:1). In both cases Peter was present when the Spirit came on believers belonging to a new religious and ethnic category. At Cornelius' house Peter was accompanied by six Jewish-Christian brothers from Joppa, whose circumcised status enhanced their credibility as witnesses to God's gift of his Spirit to uncircumcised Gentiles (10:23, 45; 11:12). In Samaria Peter was joined by John, who once wanted to call down lightning on a Samaritan village (*Luke* 9:54). If John, of all people, joined Peter in testifying to God's embrace of Samaritans, who could dispute his testimony?

In the Samaritans' experience, faith in Jesus was not immediately accompanied by the gift of the Holy Spirit. Luke shows that this was not typical by noting that, although they had been baptized in Jesus' name, the Holy Spirit had not yet come upon any of them (8:16). Luke is not referring to the Spirit's role in regeneration, but to the Spirit's gifting of believers to serve others. No one enters God's kingdom by faith unless he has been born of the Spirit, for faith itself is the product of God's resurrection power (*John* 3:5, *Eph.* 2:4–10). In normal Christian experience, as the Spirit imparts spiritual life, he enfolds believers into Christ's Body and imparts gifts for service (*1 Cor.* 12:13). In the case of the Samaritans, however, the Spirit's incorporating grace was separated from his regenerating grace, postponed until apostles were present to mediate the Spirit's gifts through prayer and the laying on of hands.

GOD'S GIFT IS NOT FOR SALE

Luke does not tell us how Simon saw that the Spirit was given through the laying on of the apostles' hands. Although the Spirit works secretly and invisibly (*John* 3:8), in Samaria he showed his presence in some tangible sign, as he had at Pentecost and would in Cornelius' house (2:2–3; 10:45–46). Simon had been impressed by Philip's miracles, but the power to bestow the Spirit was what he wanted at all costs. Religious professionals in the Roman world happily paid extravagant amounts for their appointment to serve in pagan temples, confident that their investment would reap a profitable return. Simon no doubt saw the promise of profit in the apostles' power, and was eager to part with silver to learn their secret.

The secret, of course, was that the Spirit is not a commodity to be traded on the market, but the Sovereign who gives himself freely to those who surrender to his grace. When Peter referred to the gift of God, he used a term that in Acts always refers to the Holy Spirit (2:38; 10:45; 11:17). Peter's sharp rebuke shows how far Simon's mind-set is from the faith that receives the good gifts of God. Peter consigned Simon, with his silver, to destruction. Simon had no part or share with the apostles in their ministry, just as Judas had thrown away his 'share' in that ministry for love of money (1:17). With revelatory insight Peter saw Simon's heart as God does. It was not right with God, but was poisoned and bound in sin's chains. In describing Simon as full of bitterness, Peter used terms employed by Moses to describe the 'bitter poison' of worshipping the idols of the nations (*Deut.* 29:18). The books of Moses, which even Samaria received as God's Word, condemned Simon's attempt to reduce the Lord to an idol to be manipulated for his own profit or prestige. His only hope lay in wholehearted repentance and humble prayer for forgiveness of the intents of his heart.

Whether Simon pleaded for Peter's intercession because he was truly repentant or out of terror at Peter's destructive power, Luke does not say. Instead Luke leaves the apostle's words ringing in our ears, cautioning us against the illusion that we can coerce God as though he were a genie, rather than bowing to him as Lord. And Luke turns our attention back to the Word of the Lord, tracing the apostles' return route to Jerusalem, evangelizing Samaritan villages along the way.

Simon's attempt to control and manipulate sovereign grace was especially crass, but we too have ways by which we try to put God in our debt, or to force his hand. Even our devotion, self–discipline, and self–sacrifice can be turned into tools to 'leverage' our desires from God. Do you need to heed Peter's call to repent from efforts to control what can only be received as a gift of sheer grace?

23

Scripture and Grace
Opened to an Outcast

Now an angel of the Lord said to Philip, "Rise and go towards the south to the road that goes down from Jerusalem to Gaza." This is a desert place. [27] And he rose and went. And there was an Ethiopian, a eunuch, a court official of Candace, queen of the Ethiopians, who was in charge of all her treasure. He had come to Jerusalem to worship

[28] and was returning, seated in his chariot, and he was reading the prophet Isaiah. [29] And the Spirit said to Philip, "Go over and join this chariot." [30] So Philip ran to him and heard him reading Isaiah the prophet and asked, "Do you understand what you are reading?" [31] And he said, "How can I, unless someone guides me?" And he invited Philip to come up and sit with him. [32] Now the passage of the Scripture that he was reading was this:

"Like a sheep he was led to the slaughter
and like a lamb before its shearer is silent,
so he opens not his mouth.
[33] In his humiliation justice was denied him.
Who can describe his generation?
For his life is taken away from the earth."

[34] And the eunuch said to Philip, "About whom, I ask you, does the prophet say this, about himself or about someone else?" [35] Then Philip opened his mouth, and beginning with this Scripture he told him the good news about Jesus. [36] And as they were going along the road they came to some water, and the eunuch said, "See, here is water! What prevents me from being baptized?"

37-38 And he commanded the chariot to stop, and they both went down into the water, Philip and the eunuch, and he baptized him. 39 And when they came up out of the water, the Spirit of the Lord carried Philip away, and the eunuch saw him no more, and went on his way rejoicing. 40 But Philip found himself at Azotus, and as he passed through he preached the gospel to all the towns until he came to Caesarea (Acts 8:26–40).

Philip's boundary-bursting outreach made an even more radical breakthrough after Samaria. Directed by an angel of the Lord, he travelled into what was once Philistine territory to meet a powerful Gentile official, who, despite his longing for the God of Israel, was doubly excluded from the Lord's sanctuary in Jerusalem. The treasurer of Ethiopia was puzzling over Isaiah's prediction of a suffering Servant, and the Spirit had scheduled their appointment so that Philip could provide the key that unlocks Scripture – and God's kingdom. Here we see that God's grace breaks down the wall that separated Israel from the nations, and that the Old Testament finds its focus and fulfilment in Jesus, the Servant who suffered for the guilty, so that we might not be eternal outcasts.

TO A GENTILE IN GENTILE TERRITORY

Luke calls attention to the Gentile environment of Philip's encounter with the Ethiopian eunuch by mentioning Gaza at the beginning of the passage and Azotus (formerly called Ashdod) at the end. Gaza and Ashdod were two of the five cities of the Philistines, who harassed Israel during the period of the judges and received judgement from God's hand (*Josh.* 13:1–5, *1 Sam.* 6:17; 17:1–54, *Zeph.* 2:4–7).

Philip came upon a travelling carriage (or chariot) in which a dignitary from Ethiopia was returning home after coming to Jerusalem to worship at the temple. In the Greco-Roman world Ethiopian referred not to the modern nation but to dark-skinned people of the upper Nile, south of Egypt, particularly the kingdom of Nubia, which was governed by a succession of queens, each bearing the title 'the Candace'. In the Old Testament, this region was called Cush (*Psa.* 68:31, *Zeph.* 2:12). Well beyond the Roman Empire's far-flung borders, it epitomized the very ends of the earth.

From the standpoint of ethnicity and of geography, this supervisor of the Nubian queen's treasury had crossed great distances to draw near to the sanctuary of God. He could not, however, break through the final barrier: he was a eunuch. In the pagan world this condition qualified him for high office, for eunuchs were trusted to oversee aspects of the royal court that required high security, such as harems and treasuries. The Mosaic Law, however, excluded emasculated men from the assembly of the Lord (*Deut.* 23:1). Their physical defect, like that of the lame, symbolized the spiritual defilement that makes every one of us unfit to approach God, if left to ourselves (*Lev.* 21:17–21). Though he had made the pilgrimage to worship, his connection to the covenant people could have been no closer than that of an uncircumcised God–fearer, forbidden to enter the temple further than the Court of the Gentiles. Thus, despite his position of power, the Ethiopian was doubly excluded – by race and by physical defect – from the worshipping community of Israel.

Are you trapped by spiritual defects that keep you at arm's length from God? Philip's Bible study with the eunuch has good news for you.

THE KEY THAT UNLOCKS SCRIPTURE

Under orders of the Spirit, Philip approached the Ethiopian's carriage and heard him reading aloud (as the ancients usually did) from the prophecy of Isaiah. The eunuch admitted that he could not understand the Scripture – could not discern whether the prophet described his own sufferings or those of another – without someone to guide him into its meaning. The verb translated *guides* reflects this metaphor: he needs a guide, just as Jesus promised that the Spirit of truth would 'guide' his disciples into all truth (*John* 16:13). Jewish interpreters debated whether the servant in Isaiah 53 was Israel as a community or some holy Israelite of the past. Philip, however, held the key that unlocks the true meaning of the prophet's words: he began from that very passage of Scripture and told him the good news about Jesus. Scripture is not always transparent. We all need guides, pastors and teachers, to lead us into its truths. Trustworthy guides always lead us step by step, through the Bible's diverse times and themes, to Jesus.

At the end of Luke's gospel two crestfallen pilgrims, leaving Jerusalem, learned from Jesus himself that Moses and the prophets had predicted the Christ's sufferings and subsequent glory (*Luke* 24:26–27). Now Christ's witness, Philip, showed this pilgrim, also returning home from Jerusalem, that Jesus was the One to whom the prophet pointed, the servant who was led like a sheep to slaughter, enduring injustice without threats of retaliation (see *1 Pet.* 2:22–23). The servant's premature death seemed to dash hopes of descendants, a loss with which a eunuch could empathize. Yet Philip announced the good news that flows from the servant's sufferings. The song that describes the servant's sufferings also announces his glorification (*Isa.* 52:13, *Acts* 3:13) and the justification of the transgressors, whose punishment he bore (*Isa.* 53:5, 10–12, *Luke* 22:37).

In fact, Isaiah's prophecy gave special hope and encouragement to outcasts, assuring foreigners that the Lord would not exclude them from his people and promising eunuchs access to his temple, and a legacy better than sons and daughters (*Isa.* 56:3–8). In this Ethiopian, who was both a foreigner and a eunuch, these promises found fulfilment.

NOTHING PREVENTS THE GENTILES

When they came to water by the road, the eunuch, having grasped the welcome extended to him through Jesus, asked, 'What prevents me from being baptized?' Peter would ask the same question, using the same verb, regarding the baptism of the Gentile Cornelius and his friends (10:47; see also 11:17). Through his angel and his Spirit God was directing his gospel-bearing messengers to the Gentiles, first to an Ethiopian eunuch and then to a Roman centurion (8:26, 29; 10:3, 19). Jesus' death had broken down the wall of ceremonial regulations between Israel and the nations, so that now nothing but unbelief prevents the Gentiles from approaching the living God (*Eph.* 2:11–22).

Philip immediately baptized his newborn brother, who had travelled from the ends of the earth to be found by God's grace. (Verse 37, containing the eunuch's confession of faith, does not appear in the oldest Greek manuscripts.) Then, suddenly, the Spirit of the Lord snatched Philip away, as the Spirit had miraculously transported Israelite prophets (*1 Kings* 18:12, *2 Kings* 2:16, see also *Ezek.* 11:24). Although the eunuch saw Philip no more, he proceeded home in the joy of the Holy Spirit, fulfilling God's ancient promises to welcome worshippers from Cush as his own redeemed people (*Psa.* 87:3–4, *Zeph.* 3:10). As the eunuch went south, Philip went north, proceeding from Azotus to Caesarea, capital of the Roman province of Judea, preaching the gospel in all the towns between. Philip's coastal ministry would continue for many years (21:8). It set the stage for Peter's visit to such coastal towns as Lydda and Joppa (9:32–43), from which he would be summoned to Caesarea to speak the good news to Cornelius and his household (10:1–48).

Have you seen the wide–stretched arms of God's grace, ready to embrace individuals, classes, and races that you and I might exclude, if it were up to us? Thank God that 'there is a wideness in God's mercy' (F. W. Faber), for only the outstretched arms of Jesus, the suffering and glorified servant, could draw you to the Father.

24

From Persecutor to Apostle

But Saul, still breathing threats and murder against the disciples of the Lord, went to the high priest [2] *and asked him for letters to the synagogues at Damascus, so that if he found any belonging to the Way, men or women, he might bring them bound to Jerusalem.* [3] *Now as he went on his way, he approached Damascus, and suddenly a light from heaven flashed around him.* [4] *And falling to the ground he heard a voice saying to him, "Saul, Saul, why are you persecuting me?"* [5] *And he said, "Who are you, Lord?" And he said, "I am Jesus, whom you are persecuting.* [6] *But rise and enter the city, and you will be told what you are to do."* [7] *The men who were travelling with him stood speechless, hearing the voice but seeing no one.* [8] *Saul rose from the ground, and although his eyes were opened, he saw nothing. So they led him by the hand and brought him into Damascus.* [9] *And for three days he was without sight, and neither ate nor drank.*

[10] *Now there was a disciple at Damascus named Ananias. The Lord said to him in a vision, "Ananias." And he said, "Here I am, Lord."* [11] *And the Lord said to him, "Rise and go to the street called Straight, and at the house of Judas look for a man of Tarsus named Saul, for behold, he is praying,* [12] *and he has seen in a vision a man named Ananias come in and lay his hands on him so that he might regain his sight."* [13] *But Ananias answered, "Lord, I have heard from many about this man, how much evil he has done to your saints at Jerusalem.* [14] *And here he has authority from the chief priests to bind all who call on your name."* [15] *But the Lord said to him, "Go, for he is a chosen instrument of mine to carry my name before the Gentiles and*

kings and the children of Israel. [16] For I will show him how much he must suffer for the sake of my name." [17] So Ananias departed and entered the house. And laying his hands on him he said, "Brother Saul, the Lord Jesus who appeared to you on the road by which you came has sent me so that you may regain your sight and be filled with the Holy Spirit." [18] And immediately something like scales fell from his eyes, and he regained his sight. Then he rose and was baptized; [19] and taking food, he was strengthened (Acts 9:1–19a).

The conversion of Saul is one of three watershed events highlighted in Acts, along with the outpouring of the Spirit at Pentecost and the conversion of the Gentiles in Cornelius' home. Multiple references to each event underscore its importance, as we find in Old Testament historical narratives (for example, Creation, *Gen.* 1–2; Isaac's bride, *Gen.* 24; the Ten Commandments, *Exod.* 20 and *Deut.* 5). The Spirit's arrival is promised (*Acts* 1:5, 8); reported (2:1–11); interpreted (2:33, 38–39); and remembered (11:15–17; see also 10:44–46). The conversion of Cornelius and his friends is recounted by Luke (10:1–48), repeated by Peter (11:4–17), and recalled again by Peter at the crucial council of apostles and elders (15:7–11). Saul's transformation from violent persecutor into vigorous propagator is narrated by Luke (*Acts* 9), then reported by Paul to a mob in the temple (*Acts* 22) and to King Agrippa (*Acts* 26).

The conversion of Saul, who would become apostle to the Gentiles (*Rom.* 1:5; 11:13), occurs between the conversions of two Gentiles, the Ethiopian eunuch and the Roman centurion Cornelius. Saul's and Cornelius' conversions are linked by striking parallels, such as the visions granted both to Christ's servants (Ananias and Peter, 9:10–17; 10:9–17) and to their unlikely audiences (Saul and Cornelius, 9:3–8, 12; 10:3–6), confirming that God himself is orchestrating these watershed events.

Saul himself would later acknowledge that his zeal for his ancestral traditions and righteousness through law keeping drove him to persecute the church (*Gal.* 1:13–14, *Phil.* 3:5–6). He had agreed that Stephen deserved death for speaking of changes to the customs received from Moses, and he blindly saw his duty to lie in eradicating this dangerous sect devoted to Jesus. Yet the blinding glory of the risen Lord Jesus restored his spiritual sight, transformed him into a humbled recipient and an eager publicist of God's unmerited grace (*1 Tim.* 1:12–16), and sent him to the Gentiles, who were excluded from God's covenant with Israel.

AN ENEMY ARRESTED

As the word of Christ, carried by Philip and other dispersed Christians, was bringing salvation and life to Samaritans and an Ethiopian, Saul was still breathing out murderous threats against the Lord's disciples. As he had arrested both men and women in Jerusalem (8:3), now he expanded his campaign into the Dispersion. The high priest issued letters instructing the synagogues of Damascus in Syria to assist Saul's efforts to seize and extradite men or women associated with the Way. The Jewish monastic community that produced the Dead Sea Scrolls had referred to itself as 'the Way', but Christians probably derived this self–designation from Jesus himself, who told his disciples, 'I am the way, the truth, and the life,' stressing that the Father can be reached by no other road (*John* 14:6). In Acts the gospel itself is called 'the way of salvation' (16:17) and 'the way of the Lord' (18:25–26), and the Christian movement is designated simply 'the Way' (19:9, 23; 22:4; 24:14, 22). So Saul set off on the road (9:17; the same Greek word as that translated way) north, seeking to eradicate the Way associated with Jesus' Name.

Saul would be a different man before he reached Damascus. The light that suddenly flashed from heaven was the brilliant glory of God himself and signalled a momentous revelation from the Almighty (*Luke* 2:9). Old Testament prophets were called through a vision of God's glory in radiant, overpowering light (*Isa.* 6:1–4, *Ezek.* 1:27–28). Like some of these prophets before him, Saul was now called by the repetition of his name, 'Saul, Saul' (*Exod.* 3:4, *1 Sam.* 3:4, see also *Gen.* 46:2). His travelling companions heard the sound of the heavenly voice but did not perceive the form of the speaker. Paul would later comment that they saw the light but did not understand the speaker's words (22:11). Their perception of the light and thunderous sound showed that Saul's vision was not the subjective product of his own imagination, but the content of the revelation was intelligible only to Saul, as was the case with Daniel (*Dan.* 10:7).

Earlier prophets were terrified by the Lord's consuming presence and their own defilement (*Isa.* 6:5, *Dan.* 10:8), but Saul had more reason for fear, for the heavenly Speaker accused him: 'Why are you persecuting me?' Addressing the Speaker with reverent respect as Lord, Saul asked his identity. Saul's zeal for God's glory had been boundless, and for the honour of God's name he had carried his 'holy war' beyond Jerusalem. Who, then, could this awesome Personage be, who considered pious, zealous, righteous Saul his enemy?

The answer must have stunned Saul: '*I am Jesus, whom you are persecuting.*' Jesus had told his disciples that he would identify himself so closely with them in their mission and their suffering that the treatment they received from others, for good or ill, he would count as done to himself (*Luke* 10:16, *Matt.* 25:40). The union of believers with our Lord and Saviour, which is implied in Jesus' first words to Saul, would be central to the gospel that Saul would preach to the nations; those who are 'in Christ' by faith have died with Christ, have been raised with him, and have been seated with him in heaven itself (*Gal.* 2:20, *Rom.* 6:2–14, *Eph.* 2:4–6). In pursuing, arresting, and trying to destroy Jesus' people, Saul had opposed Jesus himself. Believing that he was serving the God of Israel, he had shown himself to be hostile to the Lord and his Christ (4:25–27, citing *Psa.* 2).

Instead of the condemnation that he deserved, however, Saul received the Lord's mercy in the form of a new assignment, diametrically opposed to his previous intentions. He must proceed to Damascus, there to await orders. Yet Saul did not walk away unscathed from his encounter with the Light of the World: blinded by Jesus' glory and humbled by his helplessness, he needed others to lead him by the hand. The Lord warned Israel that, if they turned their back on him and his covenant, they would be struck with blindness at midday (*Deut.* 28:28–29, see also *Isa.* 59:10). Saul's physical blindness portrayed the darkness that had engulfed his heart, the wilful ignorance that powered his persecution of the church and its Lord (*1 Tim.* 1:13, see also *2 Cor.* 4:3, 6).

Paul would later lament the blindness of so many of his kinsmen, whose zeal to achieve their own righteousness kept them from seeing and submitting to the righteousness of Christ, which is God's free gift. Even we who affirm intellectually that we are made right with God by grace alone through faith alone may succumb to blindness of heart, trying to make ourselves worthy of God's favour rather than surrendering to his humbling, amazing grace.

A WITNESS COMMISSIONED

Ananias of Damascus differed radically in character from the infamous Ananias who had died for lying to the Holy Spirit (5:1–11). The Ananias sent to pray for Saul and to welcome him into the circle of Jesus' disciples in Damascus was 'a devout man according to the law, well spoken of by all the Jews' (22:12). Moreover, he was ready to do what Jesus commanded, even when it entailed personal risk.

When the Lord Jesus called him to seek out Saul, Ananias humbly raised the obvious objection: Saul was notorious for his violence against the church in Jerusalem, and the report had preceded him that he was authorized to arrest Christian disciples in Damascus. But Jesus' answer revealed Saul's new identity and provided a preview of his role in the gospel's spread 'to the ends of the earth' (*Acts* 13 – 28). Saul was the Lord's chosen instrument, a vessel now to be filled with Jesus' name. Paul would use this word to describe himself as a 'jar of clay' carrying God's treasure, the gospel (*2 Cor.* 4:7). Saul would carry that name before Gentiles, kings, and the people of Israel. In subsequent chapters we will hear Paul addressing each of these audiences. Moreover, as Saul had afflicted others who call on Jesus' Name (9:14, see 2:21), so he would suffer for that Name. Luke will tell of assassination conspiracies, slander, stoning, beating, imprisonment, and shipwreck.

So Ananias went to Saul, addressing him as *Brother*, not so much because both could trace their lineage to the patriarchs but rather because both had become sons of God through faith in Jesus the Messiah. Saul's sight was restored and, more importantly, he was filled with the Holy Spirit, whose presence signifies inner cleansing and enfolds new members into the Body of Christ (*Acts* 15:8–9, *1 Cor.* 12:13).

In many ways Saul's conversion was unique. None of us have undergone his sudden, radical reversal from violent, self–righteous persecutor to Christ–centred apostle. Nevertheless, he is God's object lesson for us, the prime exhibit of the saving power of pride–shattering grace: 'But I received mercy for this reason, that in me, as the foremost [of sinners], Jesus Christ might display his perfect patience as an example to those who were to believe in him' (*1 Tim.* 1:16). In Saul of Tarsus we see 'works righteousness' at its best hitting a dead end, and we see Christ's grace in embracing his enemies, as they come to the end of themselves.

25

God's Tale of Two Cities

For some days he was with the disciples at Damascus. ²¹ And *immediately he proclaimed Jesus in the synagogues, saying, "He* *is the Son of God." ²¹ And all who heard him were amazed and* *said, "Is not this the man who made havoc in Jerusalem of those* *who called upon this name? And has he not come here for this* *purpose, to bring them bound before the chief priests?" ²² But Saul* *increased all the more in strength, and confounded the Jews who* *lived in Damascus by proving that Jesus was the Christ.*

²³ When many days had passed, the Jews plotted to kill him, *²⁴ but their plot became known to Saul. They were watching the* *gates day and night in order to kill him, ²⁵ but his disciples took* *him by night and let him down through an opening in the wall,* *lowering him in a basket.*

²⁶ And when he had come to Jerusalem, he attempted to join *the disciples. And they were all afraid of him, for they did not* *believe that he was a disciple. ²⁷ But Barnabas took him and* *brought him to the apostles and declared to them how on the road* *he had seen the Lord, who spoke to him, and how at Damascus* *he had preached boldly in the name of Jesus. ²⁸ So he went in* *and out among them at Jerusalem, preaching boldly in the name* *of the Lord. ²⁹ And he spoke and disputed against the Hellenists.* *But they were seeking to kill him. ³⁰ And when the brothers* *learned this, they brought him down to Caesarea and sent him* *off to Tarsus.*

³¹ So the church throughout all Judea and Galilee and Samaria *had peace and was being built up. And walking in the fear of the* *Lord and in the comfort of the Holy Spirit, it multiplied* (Acts 9:19b–31).

The 180–degree reversal in the direction of Saul's life was evident immediately. On the one hand he suddenly began to proclaim the Name of Jesus, whose adherents he had persecuted. On the other, because he preached that Jesus is God's Son and Messiah, he began to suffer the persecution that he had inflicted on others. Yet the Christian family rallied to the aid of their newborn brother, orchestrating Saul's escape from would-be assassins. This pattern – bold preaching, murderous plot, narrow escape – appeared in both Damascus and Jerusalem, the two cities in which Saul began his service as 'preacher, apostle, and teacher' of God's good news (*1 Tim.* 2:7, *2 Tim.* 1:11).

DAMASCUS: ASTONISHMENT, CONSPIRACY, AND ESCAPE

Ananias must have introduced Saul to the Christian community at Damascus. This introduction assuaged their fears, for Luke comments simply that Saul spent several days with the disciples in Damascus. The disciples in Jerusalem would be less ready to welcome their persecutor.

Saul launched immediately into his mission as the carrier of Jesus' Name (9:15), starting in the very synagogues that he had once hoped to enlist as allies in his crusade against Jesus' followers. Now Saul was preaching that Jesus is the Son of God (9:20), the Christ (9:22), and proving his claims from the Scriptures, as he would later do elsewhere (17:2–3). Although Luke's Gospel emphasizes that Jesus is God's Son (*Luke* 1:32, 35; 3:22; 4:41), this title is used only here in the book of Acts. Yet this summary of Saul's early preaching agrees with his epistles, in which Paul traces his conversion to the revelation of God's Son (*Gal.* 1:15–16) and describes his message as the gospel of God's Son, Jesus Christ our Lord (*Rom.* 1:1–4). Christian communication with the non-Christian culture today often focuses on points of ethical and political controversy: sexuality, abortion, and the like. Such topics, though important for a society's well being, cannot change hearts as the Son of God can.

Saul's synagogue audience, knowing his record and reputation, was astonished by his new message and by the vigour and persuasiveness with which he advocated it. He had raised havoc in Jerusalem among those who called on Jesus' name – a fact that would often grieve him (*Gal.* 1:13, 23, *1 Cor.* 15:9, *1 Tim.* 1:13). How, then, could he now advocate the very Name that he had sought to eradicate? Some of Saul's Jewish listeners were not only mystified by his reversal. They also were frustrated by their own inability to refute his biblical case for Jesus as the suffering and glorified Messiah. As Stephen's opponents had resorted to violence when they could not answer his arguments, so in Damascus some Jews conspired to kill Saul, watching the city gates day and night to prevent his escape. He would later recall that this Jewish conspiracy had the support of the city governor (*2 Cor.* 11:32–33).

The Lord Jesus, however, had other plans. Saul learned of the plot, and under the cloak of night disciples lowered him in a large hamper through a window in the city wall. God does not promise us comfortable or safe lives. Paul's lengthy list of his sufferings for the gospel, climaxing in the escape at Damascus, makes this clear (*2 Cor.* 11:23–33). Yet we can rest assured that no enemy can cut short the witness that God intends for us to bear.

JERUSALEM: SUSPICION, CONSPIRACY, AND ESCAPE

Saul's welcome by the church in Jerusalem was, understandably, less than warm. These believers had borne the brunt of his rage against the name of Jesus. They doubted his claim to believe and viewed his efforts to join them as infiltration by one still intent on ravaging the church, imprisoning and intimidating its members.

One man, however, took the risk of getting to know the new Saul. Barnabas, aptly renamed 'Son of Encouragement' by the apostles (4:36), heard Saul out and believed his story. Perhaps Barnabas, who belonged to the Dispersion (Cyprus), had Christian contacts in Damascus who confirmed Saul's words, but Luke makes no mention of this. Rather, we see in Barnabas a man 'full of the Holy Spirit and of faith' (11:24), who believed that God can transform his worst enemy and who placed not only his property but now his life at the disposal of his Lord. Barnabas brought Saul to the apostles and told them Saul's story, notably that he had seen the Lord and heard the Lord's word of commission and that Saul had responded by boldly proclaiming the name of Jesus in Damascus. Through Barnabas' intervention the apostles welcomed Saul as a brother. Seeing the risen

Lord Jesus was a key qualification for the apostolic calling that he shared with them (*1 Cor.* 9:1), for it meant that he too could bear witness to Christ's resurrection (1:21–22; 22:14–15). This he did in Jerusalem, preaching boldly in the name of the Lord. We might assume that Saul's boldness was a product of his personality as a man who threw himself wholeheartedly into whatever cause gripped him, whether killing Christians or preaching Christ. That assumption would be mistaken. Saul would later remind Christians that his preaching was hampered by 'weakness . . . fear and much trembling' (*1 Cor.* 2:3), and he would plead for prayer, that he might declare the gospel fearlessly (*Eph.* 6:19–20, *Col.* 4:3–4). Christian boldness is neither brash self–confidence nor unflinching fearlessness. It is God's gift, given to those who ask (4:29, 31). When was the last time you begged for the grace to declare Christ's Name more boldly?

Saul's adversaries in debate were Grecian Jews from the Dispersion, such as those North African and Asian Jews in the Synagogue of the Freedmen, who opposed Stephen (6:9–10). Saul, whose zeal to persecute Christians was once inflamed by Stephen's witness (22:20), now became, in effect, Stephen's replacement. In Jerusalem, as in Damascus, enemies incapable of answering Saul's 'case for Jesus' resorted to plotting his demise, hoping to silence his message. Yet again the brothers discovered the plot and moved Saul out of harm's way, sending him from the seaport Caesarea to Tarsus, his home town (Acts 9:11; 21:39; 22:3). There Saul would stay until retrieved by Barnabas to serve the fledgling church of Antioch in Syria (11:25–26, see also *Gal.* 1:21).

The result of Saul's conversion was a time of peace for the church in Judea, Galilee, and Samaria. (Note that Luke regards many congregations, spread throughout three districts, as one church.) Yet the church's progress depended not on tranquil outward circumstances but on its relationship to its Lord: the comfort of the Holy Spirit and the fear of the Lord. This blend of comfort and awe produced both spiritual and numerical growth. 'Was being built up' is a metaphor for spiritual maturing (*Eph.* 4:16).

Times of crisis often drive us to our knees and draw us to the Lord in desperate need, spurring spiritual growth. Do you also seek his grace, to grow deep and reach out, in times of peace?

26

Jesus Raises the Helpless

Now as Peter went here and there among them all, he came down also to the saints who lived at Lydda. ³³ *There he found a man named Aeneas, bedridden for eight years, who was paralysed.* ³⁴ *And Peter said to him, "Aeneas, Jesus Christ heals you; rise and make your bed." And immediately he rose.* ³⁵ *And all the residents of Lydda and Sharon saw him, and they turned to the Lord.*

³⁶ *Now there was in Joppa a disciple named Tabitha, which, translated, means Dorcas. She was full of good works and acts of charity.* ³⁷ *In those days she became ill and died, and when they had washed her, they laid her in an upper room.* ³⁸ *Since Lydda was near Joppa, the disciples, hearing that Peter was there, sent two men to him, urging him, "Please come to us without delay."*

³⁹ *So Peter rose and went with them. And when he arrived, they took him to the upper room. All the widows stood beside him weeping and showing tunics and other garments that Dorcas made while she was with them.* ⁴⁰ *But Peter put them all outside, and knelt down and prayed; and turning to the body he said, "Tabitha, arise." And she opened her eyes, and when she saw Peter she sat up.* ⁴¹ *And he gave her his hand and raised her up. Then calling the saints and widows, he presented her alive.* ⁴² *And it became known throughout all Joppa, and many believed in the Lord.* ⁴³ *And he stayed in Joppa for many days with one Simon, a tanner* (Acts 9:32–43).

The spotlight turns again to Peter in this narrative of two 'raising up' miracles that Jesus accomplished through him. To a paralysed man and to a dead woman Peter issued identical commands, 'Rise!' (9:34, 40). In both cases not only were the individuals raised up to active life but also many others turned to the Lord in faith (verses 35, 42). Peter was following in Philip's footsteps through towns in the coastal Plain of Sharon, arriving at the port city of Joppa. From Joppa Peter would be escorted by delegates of Cornelius to Caesarea, to preach the gospel to a gathering of Gentiles in the centurion's home. Thus Peter's coastal ministry would open the door for salvation to spread to the nations.

THE PARALYSED AENEAS RAISED

Peter travelled westward from Jerusalem toward the Mediterranean; he reached the ancient town of Lydda, where there was already a gathering of the *saints*. The title *saints*, meaning 'holy, consecrated people,' which appears often in Paul's letters, is applied to Christians in Acts only four times: twice here (again in verse 41) and twice in connection with Saul's persecution (9:13; 26:10). The raising of Aeneas and of Tabitha strengthened groups of saints, already gathered in these coastal towns, presumably through Philip's witness while travelling from Azotus to Caesarea (8:40).

Aeneas had been paralysed, unable to stir from his mat for eight years. The longevity of his disability underscores the miraculous power at work in his healing, as did the advanced age of the crippled man who was healed at the temple gate (3:2, 6; 4:22). On that earlier occasion Peter took pains to stress that Jesus' name, not Peter's power or piety, was the source of saving power (3:12, 16). Likewise in Lydda, Peter's pronouncement pointed away from himself to the risen Lord who raises the powerless: 'Jesus Christ heals you.' Like the paralysed man whom Jesus healed (*Luke* 5:24–25), Aeneas was instructed to attend to the mat on which he had been lying, showing that his healing was instantaneous and complete. No follow–up therapy was needed to strengthen atrophied muscles.

Such signs attested Peter's apostolic authority, but they did so by pointing away from the apostle and towards the Lord who had commissioned him. Though we are not apostles, we too are charged as Jesus' witnesses to point others away from ourselves (and their own resources) to Jesus, who alone saves (4:12). As we do, we will see people turned to the Lord, the direction of their lives reversed

180 degrees, from indifference and rebellion to faith, hope, and love toward Jesus the Messiah.

THE DECEASED TABITHA RAISED

The death of a disciple named Tabitha was a crushing blow to the church at Joppa, and especially to its poor widows, who had been clothed through Tabitha's generosity. Luke translates her Aramaic name, Tabitha, 'gazelle', for his Greek readers as Dorcas.

Although we are not told whether Aeneas believed before Peter found him, Luke tells us much about the fruit of Tabitha's faith. Because she was always doing good and helping the poor (literally, 'full of good deeds and compassionate donations'), the widows whom she had clothed mourned her death deeply. Leaders had been ordained in Jerusalem to co–ordinate mercy ministry to widows (6:1–7), but Tabitha rightly saw such service as the privilege of every Christian (20:35, *1 John* 3:17–18, *1 Tim.* 5:16).

The disciples sent two of their number to Lydda, ten miles away, to beg Peter to come at once to Joppa. Why their urgent request for Peter's presence? Mary and Martha had wanted Jesus to come quickly when their brother fell ill, and they reproached him when he arrived, they thought, too late (*John* 11:3, 21, 32). These Christians, however, did not send for Peter until after Tabitha's death. No doubt they needed the apostle's comfort in their grief. Yet, although the apostles had not yet raised any dead, the placement of Tabitha's body in an upper room to await Peter's arrival suggests that these saints may have hoped not merely for comfort in sorrow, but for life from the dead.

The raising of Tabitha shows that Peter stood in the tradition of the ancient prophets Elijah and Elisha and especially of his Lord Jesus, on whose power he depended. Like Jesus when he raised Jairus' daughter and like Elisha, Peter sent everyone out of the room, leaving him alone with the body of the deceased (*Mark* 5:40, *2 Kings* 4:33). Like Elisha also, Peter fell to his knees in prayer; for he knew that, unlike Jesus who is 'the resurrection and the life' (*John* 11:25; 5:21), in himself he had no power to raise the dead. Peter called the godly woman's Aramaic name, 'Tabitha, arise,' almost an echo of Jesus' Aramaic command to Jairus' daughter, 'Talitha cumi!' (*Mark* 5:41). Tabitha opened her eyes, awaking to life, as did the

Shunammite woman's son (*2 Kings* 4:35). She sat up, as did the widow's son at Nain, restored to life by Jesus (*Luke* 7:15). As Elijah and Jesus gave sons back to their widowed mothers, restoring protection to the bereft (*1 Kings* 17:23, *Luke* 7:15), so Peter presented Tabitha to the saints, and especially to the widows for whom she had provided. The prophets foreshadowed and the apostle echoes the life-giving power of the risen Lord, who stands at the centre of history.

As reports of the resurrection power of Jesus swept through the city, drawing many to faith in the Lord, God set the stage for the gospel's next advance by settling Peter in the home of a tanner named Simon, whose daily work with animal hides rendered him perpetually unclean, according to the rabbis. God was about to show Peter that no person was to be dismissed as being incurably defiled, beyond the reach of the Spirit's purifying grace. If Christ can raise up the paralyzed and reverse death itself, we must see that his mercy is strong and wide enough to transform people from every occupation, clan, and nation.

27

God Speaks to a Gentile

At Caesarea there was a man named Cornelius, a centurion of what was known as the Italian Cohort, ² a devout man who feared God with all his household, gave alms generously to the people, and prayed continually to God. ³ About the ninth hour of the day he saw clearly in a vision an angel of God come in and say to him, "Cornelius." ⁴ And he stared at him in terror and said, "What is it, Lord?" And he said to him, "Your prayers and your alms have ascended as a memorial before God. ⁵ And now send men to Joppa and bring one Simon who is called Peter. ⁶ He is lodging with one Simon, a tanner, whose house is by the seaside." ⁷ When the angel who spoke to him had departed, he called two of his servants and a devout soldier from among those who attended him, ⁸ and having related everything to them, he sent them to Joppa (Acts 10:1–8).

We now reach the third and final watershed event in the book of Acts. Each of these events is highlighted by repeated references to them throughout the book: (1) *Pentecost*: the Spirit speaks good news in the tongues of the Gentiles (2; 1:8; 11:15–17, *Luke* 3:16; 24:49); (2) *Paul*: God commissions the apostle to the Gentiles (9; 22:3–16; 26:12–18); and now (3) *Cornelius*: God gives the Gentiles his Spirit (10; 11:5–18; 15:7–11). In the conversion of Samaritans and the Ethiopian eunuch, God gave glimpses of his passion to embrace outsiders in his grace and enfold them into his people. Now God's heart for all the nations is fully displayed and is to be attested by Peter and the Jewish believers who accompanied him to Caesarea.

A 'GOOD' ALIEN

Cornelius is introduced first in his connection with the occupying forces of the powerful, pagan Roman Empire. He was a centurion, commander of one hundred soldiers, posted to Caesarea. Located on the Mediterranean coastline north of Joppa, Caesarea was a cosmopolitan city, built by Herod the Great and named for Caesar Augustus. It was the provincial capital of Judea under the Roman governors, so a military presence is not surprising. The troops under Cornelius' command were part of the Italian Cohort, or Regiment. Their affiliation with Italy reinforces Cornelius' link with the imperial capital that had subjugated Israel, to the outrage of devout Jews. Rome was in Peter's day what Nineveh had been in Jonah's. (Recall the prophet's reluctance to warn God's enemies of impending judgement, in case they repented and the LORD relented.) Cornelius was an alien in God's land and, worse yet, a representative of the pagan power that oppressed God's people.

Yet Cornelius was a most untypical alien. He was devout and God-fearing, and his family followed his lead. *God-fearing* was a term applied to Gentiles who adhered to Judaism's faith in one God and to the Ten Commandments, but who baulked at circumcision and the kosher dietary restrictions of Leviticus. Because God-fearers were uncircumcised and ate 'unclean' foods, observant Jews kept them at arm's length (see also 11:3), while respecting their monotheistic faith and moral uprightness.

Cornelius' piety showed itself in his prayers and his charitable gifts for 'the people'. His generosity to Israelites in particular explains why he was 'well spoken of by the whole Jewish nation' (10:22). Like the centurion at Capernaum, for whom Jewish elders had interceded (*Luke* 7:3–5), Cornelius' longing for Israel's God motivated his concrete generosity toward Israel's people.

A GRACIOUS COMMAND

God sent his angel to Cornelius at three in the afternoon: the 'hour of prayer' and evening sacrifice at the temple in Jerusalem (3:1, see also *Luke* 1:10). Cornelius' 'spiritual clock' was set to temple time, so the angel appeared in a vision as Cornelius' prayer coincided with those of Israel in the sanctuary.

Calming Cornelius' fear, the angel assured him, *Your prayers and your alms have ascended as a memorial before God.* The Old Testament background of this statement explains its significance. Cornelius' prayers were like Israel's pleas for relief from Egyptian bondage, which 'went up' from earth to God's heavenly court (*Exod.* 2:23). His gifts were a memorial offering, like the sacrifices presented by Israel to worship God and seek forgiveness (*Lev.* 2:2; 5:12). They were not the achievements of self–righteousness, but his heart–cries for rescue and atonement. Therefore the angel promised a messenger who would bring words of salvation (11:14).

Responding immediately to the angel's instruction, Cornelius summoned two servants and a *devout soldier* (note his influence on military subordinates!) and sent them south to Joppa, to retrieve Simon Peter from the house of Simon the tanner. Do you share Cornelius' hunger for God's Word of grace, his urgent quest to hear God's messengers?

28

God Cleanses the Defiled

*The next day, as they were on their journey and approaching
the city, Peter went up on the housetop about the sixth hour to
pray. ¹⁰ And he became hungry and wanted something to eat,
but while they were preparing it, he fell into a trance ¹¹ and saw
the heavens opened and something like a great sheet descending,
being let down by its four corners upon the earth. ¹² In it were
all kinds of animals and reptiles and birds of the air. ¹³ And there
came a voice to him: "Rise, Peter; kill and eat." ¹⁴ But Peter
said, "By no means, Lord; for I have never eaten anything that
is common or unclean." ¹⁵ And the voice came to him again a
second time, "What God has made clean, do not call common."
¹⁶ This happened three times, and the thing was taken up at once
to heaven.*

*¹⁷ Now while Peter was inwardly perplexed as to what the
vision that he had seen might mean, behold, the men who were
sent by Cornelius, having made inquiry for Simon's house,
stood at the gate ¹⁸ and called out to ask whether Simon who
was called Peter was lodging there. ¹⁹ And while Peter was
pondering the vision, the Spirit said to him, "Behold, three men
are looking for you. ²⁰ Rise and go down and accompany them
without hesitation, for I have sent them." ²¹ And Peter went
down to the men and said, "I am the one you are looking for.
What is the reason for your coming?" ²² And they said,
"Cornelius, a centurion, an upright and God-fearing man, who
is well spoken of by the whole Jewish nation, was directed by a
holy angel to send for you to come to his house and to hear what
you have to say." ²³ So he invited them in to be his guests* (Acts
10:9–23a).

Having set matters in motion from Cornelius' side, God prepared Peter to welcome Cornelius' delegation and to respond to their request. The vision granted to Peter confirmed the one received by Cornelius, showing that the apostle's evangelization of the Gentiles was merely a response to God's sovereign initiative. Just as complementary visions to Saul (9:12) and to Jesus' messenger Ananias (9:10) confirmed God's call to Saul as apostle to the Gentiles, so now complementary visions to Cornelius (10:3) and to Jesus' messenger Peter (10:19) confirm God's ingathering of the Gentiles in his grace through faith.

A SHOCKING COMMAND

As Cornelius' servants and soldier were nearing Joppa and asking the whereabouts of Simon's residence, Peter sought solitude for prayer on the house's flat roof. His hunger apparently disturbed his prayer and set servants to work preparing a noon meal, but God would use that hunger to teach Peter a world-shaking lesson. Peter *fell into a trance*, a deep sleep like that of Adam when God created Eve (*Gen.* 2:21) and of Abraham when God's fiery glory passed between animal carcasses, securing God's covenant promises (*Gen.* 15:12). The mode of revelation differed from the way that Cornelius, wide–awake, saw God's angel clearly, but the divine origin and authority were the same. Peter saw heaven opened, as often occurred when God disclosed unseen realities to his spokesmen (*Luke* 3:21, *Acts* 7:56, *Rev.* 4:1; 19:11), and something like a vast sheet or tablecloth being lowered by its four corners. Prophets often employed vague comparisons when trying to convey heavenly realities that transcend our ordinary experience (*Exod.* 24:10, *Ezek.* 1:22, 26, 28).

More important than the container were its contents: all kinds of animals, reptiles, and birds of the air – every variety of livestock and wildlife that God had created (*Gen.* 1:24, 30) and preserved in the ark built by Noah (*Gen.* 6:20). In Noah's ark, however, a distinction was made between 'clean' and 'unclean' animals (*Gen.* 7:2–3), foreshadowing the Levitical dietary laws (*Lev.* 11). God had set Noah and his family apart from their ungodly neighbours, just as he would set Israel apart from theirs. The distinction in diet between 'clean' or holy and 'unclean' or common symbolized that sovereign discrimination by which the Lord consecrated Israel to himself (*Lev.* 20:24–26).

Against this background God's command to Peter was shocking: Kill and eat any of the creatures he saw in the vision, even those on the forbidden list of Leviticus 11. Peter's sharp retort, *By no means, Lord!* is more emotional than logical. How dare he address the Speaker as Lord and refuse him in the same breath? In fact, his reaction reproduced that of the ancient priest and prophet Ezekiel, when God commanded him to eat food prepared in a non-kosher way (*Ezek.* 4:9–14). Both resisted God's command to violate the Law's purity regulations, protesting that they had never eaten ceremonially unclean meat. God had different lessons to teach his two servants: Ezekiel must eat in order to symbolize Israel's defilement, like the Gentiles. Peter must partake in order to picture the Gentiles' cleansing to become God's people, like Israel.

Jesus had taught that what defiles people is not the food that enters their mouths but the words that leave their mouths, which reveal the corrupt motives of sin-stained hearts. The Evangelist, with hindsight imparted by the Holy Spirit, noted that Jesus' teaching 'declared all foods clean' (*Mark* 7:19). Peter, however, had not yet seen Jesus' point and needed correction by the heavenly voice: 'What God has made clean, do not call common.' Amazingly, Peter dared to refuse God's command (and receive God's rebuke) not once but three times. Although he had not come to Joppa to hop on a ship as Jonah had done (*Jon.* 1:3), this 'son of Jonah' (see also *Matt.* 16:17) was no more willing to mingle with Gentiles than the prophet had been. On the other hand, the Lord used Peter's stubbornness to drive home his own message repeatedly: when God performs the cleansing, no mere human can contradict his verdict. The threefold repetition of the vision, like Pharaoh's twin dreams in Joseph's day, showed 'that the thing is fixed by God and God will shortly bring it about' (*Gen.* 41:32).

God was about to cleanse for himself what had been considered incorrigibly defiled. His focus of concern was not the menu, but men and women (10:28). On the other hand, kosher food laws were themselves an obvious barrier that isolated Israel, socially as well as religiously, from the Gentile peoples all around them – as Peter's critics would hasten to point out (11:3)! In cultures around the world and throughout time, and especially in Peter's Middle Eastern setting, to share a meal is to share fellowship, establishing a bond; to shun a meal is to shun friendship, repudiating a stranger. Is there a class or category of people that you have avoided or mentally dismissed as beyond the reach of Christ's cleansing grace? Is there anyone with whom you would not eat?

SURPRISING VISITORS

As Peter pondered the meaning of his threefold vision, its interpretive key stood knocking at the courtyard gate. The Spirit, who had instructed Philip to approach the Ethiopian official's carriage (8:29), now informed Peter about his surprising visitors downstairs. Peter must not hesitate to go with them for they had not only been sent by a Roman centurion but by the divine Spirit himself (*I have sent them*). The verb translated *hesitate* occurs four times in Acts. All refer to God's welcome of Cornelius and his fellow-Gentiles, emphasizing that believers must not obstruct (10:20; 11:12) or criticize (11:2) this extension of God's grace, for in the gospel the Lord himself refuses to discriminate between Jew and Gentile (15:9).

Cornelius' delegation informed Peter of their master's reputation for righteousness and of the angelic vision he had received, adding now the detail (not previously mentioned) that Cornelius was awaiting what Peter would have to say upon entering the centurion's home (see also verse 33). In the message carried by Peter lay salvation for Cornelius and his household (11:14). Through successive retellings of Cornelius' vision, the spotlight is focused ever more pointedly on the saving power of God's Word in the mouth of God's messenger.

Though himself a guest of Simon the tanner, Peter extended hospitality to the Gentile representatives of a Gentile military officer, bringing them under the roof on which he had puzzled over God's cleansing of the unclean, and seating them at table with himself and his host. Fissures were weakening the wall between Jew and Gentile, between insider and alien. Through those cracks Peter glimpsed what he would soon see clearly: the blazing glory of Christ's grace, purifying all sorts of human hearts by faith (15:9–11).

29

Peace to All Peoples
Through the Lord of All

The next day he rose and went away with them, and some of the brothers from Joppa accompanied him. ²⁴ And on the following day they entered Caesarea. Cornelius was expecting them and had called together his relatives and close friends. ²⁵ When Peter entered, Cornelius met him and fell down at his feet and worshipped him. ²⁶ But Peter lifted him up, saying, "Stand up; I too am a man." ²⁷ And as he talked with him, he went in and found many persons gathered. ²⁸ And he said to them, "You yourselves know how unlawful it is for a Jew to associate with or to visit anyone of another nation, but God has shown me that I should not call any person common or unclean. ²⁹ So when I was sent for, I came without objection. I ask then why you sent for me."

³⁰ And Cornelius said, "Four days ago, about this hour, I was praying in my house at the ninth hour, and behold, a man stood before me in bright clothing ³¹ and said, 'Cornelius, your prayer has been heard and your alms have been remembered before God. ³² Send therefore to Joppa and ask for Simon who is called Peter. He is lodging in the house of Simon, a tanner, by the sea.' ³³ So I sent for you at once, and you have been kind enough to come. Now therefore we are all here in the presence of God to hear all that you have been commanded by the Lord."

³⁴ So Peter opened his mouth and said: "Truly I understand that God shows no partiality, ³⁵ but in every nation anyone who fears him and does what is right is acceptable to him. ³⁶ As for the word that he sent to Israel, preaching good news of peace through Jesus Christ (he is Lord of all), ³⁷ you yourselves know

what happened throughout all Judea, beginning from Galilee after the baptism that John proclaimed: [38] how God anointed Jesus of Nazareth with the Holy Spirit and with power. He went about doing good and healing all who were oppressed by the devil, for God was with him. [39] And we are witnesses of all that he did both in the country of the Jews and in Jerusalem. They put him to death by hanging him on a tree, [40] but God raised him on the third day and made him to appear, [41] not to all the people but to us who had been chosen by God as witnesses, who ate and drank with him after he rose from the dead. [42] And he commanded us to preach to the people and to testify that he is the one appointed by God to be judge of the living and the dead. [43] To him all the prophets bear witness that everyone who believes in him receives forgiveness of sins through his name" (Acts 10:23b–43).

A two-day journey brought Cornelius' three messengers, Peter, and six of the brothers from the church in Antioch (10:23; 11:12) to Cornelius' home in Caesarea in the late afternoon, around the time that the angel had appeared to Cornelius four days earlier (10:30). Cornelius was not only eagerly expecting their arrival, but he had also gathered a large group of his relatives and close friends to hear the message from God that Peter brought. In the Roman world the language of 'friendship' was applied to social and economic obligations linking patrons and their dependents as well as to relationships of affection and camaraderie. The word rendered *close* in *close friends* carries overtones of obligation in other contexts (see the use of 'necessary' in *Phil.* 2:25), so probably the crowd gathered by Cornelius included not only his family members and social intimates but also inferiors who benefited from Cornelius' favour. He spared no effort to ensure that all within his sphere of influence would have the opportunity to hear the message of salvation that God was sending through Simon Peter (11:14).

When Cornelius fell at Peter's feet in reverence, it was a spontaneous gesture of profound honour well known in the ancient Near East, but rarely would an officer of the occupying Roman forces greet a Jewish fisherman with such deference. Peter, however, was no mere fisherman, but the messenger of God promised in the angelic vision; and Cornelius was no typical Gentile centurion, but a man already humbled by grace and hungry for the living God. He was a fulfilment of Isaiah 45:14, which promised that Gentiles would bow down before Israel, confessing, 'Surely God is with you!' (see also *1 Cor.* 14:25).

COMPLEMENTARY VISIONS

Upon entering Cornelius' home and finding a crowd assembled, Peter reminded the group that association with Gentiles, especially in a Gentile's house, was forbidden for Jews. It was one thing for Peter to welcome Cornelius' delegation into Simon's home to eat kosher Jewish food at the tanner's table, and quite another for Peter and his fellow Jews to enter a Gentile home, where Levitical scruples were not observed in preparing food! Yet Peter had grasped the implications of his rooftop vision. God himself had taught him not to call any man impure or unclean – ceremonially defiled and defiling others. At a later point in Antioch, under peer pressure, Peter would retreat in practice from this gospel-informed breakthrough (*Gal.* 2:11–16), but in Caesarea and in Jerusalem he stood true to the new insight that God had given him despite the criticism he received (11:2). He was ready not only to associate with Cornelius and company but also to serve them, when the centurion clarified the purpose for which he had summoned Peter.

Cornelius briefly described his vision four days earlier and the instruction to seek Peter out in Simon the tanner's home in Joppa. Luke as narrator identified Cornelius' visitant as an angel, a superhuman messenger sent from God's heavenly court. From Cornelius' vantage point as the recipient of the vision the angel appeared as a man in bright, shining clothes, the form typically ascribed to angels in their encounters with humans (1:10, *Luke* 24:4). Just as the angel assured him that his charitable gifts had been remembered before God (10:31), so now the group was assembled in the presence of God to hear the message that the Lord had commanded Peter to speak. God the Holy Spirit was about to show his presence by giving birth to the first Gentile church in a burst of joyful worship. We all do well to cultivate Cornelius' sensitivity to the reality that we live before the face of God, especially when gathered with others to hear God's Word.

GOOD NEWS TO PEOPLE OF EVERY NATION

Peter's brief (probably abbreviated) gospel presentation was interwoven with his 'new' insight, that God cares for and announces salvation to all the peoples of the world. First, Peter denied that God shows partiality along ethnic lines. In this he echoed Moses, who called Israel to love aliens because they had been oppressed aliens in Egypt and because the LORD their God 'is not partial and takes no bribe' (*Deut.* 10:17–19). Second, he affirmed that God welcomes people from every nation who fear him and do what is right. He was not claiming that God's welcome is based on their works, for he would go on to promise forgiveness of sins through faith in Jesus' name (10:43; see also 15:9). Rather, doing right – such as Cornelius' prayers and alms – displays a heart that fears the Lord, casting itself on divine mercy in humble trust. Third, Peter stressed that Jesus Christ, sent by God to tell the good news of peace to Israel (see also *Isa.* 52:7, *Eph.* 2:17), is Lord of all, not only the Messiah of Israel.

Peter prefaced his message with '*you yourselves know*', for he assumed that the circle gathered around a God-fearer who enjoyed the respect of the Jewish people would be well aware of the controversial ministry of Jesus of Nazareth. God had indeed prepared his salvation 'in the sight of all people', and Peter now realized that the Gentiles were not merely onlookers, but beneficiaries of the light of revelation (*Luke* 2:30–32, *Isa.* 52:10).

Peter's summary of the gospel highlights the fact that God anointed Jesus *with the Holy Spirit and with power* – a reference to the descent of the Spirit at Jesus' baptism, interpreted when Jesus read Isaiah 61 in the synagogue at Nazareth (*Luke* 3:22; 4:18). In the power of the Spirit Jesus established God's kingdom by assaulting Satan's domain, healing and liberating those who were oppressed by the devil. Blessing flowed from him because God was with him, as Nicodemus had recognized (*John* 3:2).

Nevertheless, Jesus was killed by the leaders of his own people in the most shameful way: by hanging him on a tree, as a sign of God's curse upon him (*Deut.* 21:23, see also *Acts* 5:30). Yet the divine repudiation that hanging on a tree symbolized is set alongside the vindication that God awarded Jesus in the resurrection. If Jesus arose as the Holy One on whom death could not keep its grip (2:24, 27;

3:14–15), whose curse was he bearing as he hung on the tree? Paul would answer: 'Christ redeemed us from the curse of the law by becoming a curse for us – for it is written: "Cursed is everyone who is hanged on a tree"' (*Gal.* 3:13).

Peter and his fellow apostles were witnesses selected in advance by God to testify not only to Jesus' pre–crucifixion deeds of power and mercy but also to his post–resurrection life and reign. Their testimony that Jesus is risen from the dead was not the fruit of wishful thinking or hallucination, for they ate and drank with him after he rose. These were among the many convincing proofs that Jesus presented to his apostles and, through them, to Theophilus and us and the church throughout the ages, whose faith is founded on the apostles' witness (1:3, *Luke* 24:36–43, *John* 20:24–29).

Jesus also charged his apostles to declare his future role as judge of the living and the dead. Paul would later tell Athenian philosophers that Jesus' resurrection had put everyone everywhere on notice that their Judge had been appointed by God, and their turning from idols to the only God who lives and saves must not be postponed (17:30–31, see also *Isa.* 45:22). We rightly rejoice in Jesus' resurrection as confirming his divine claims, vindicating his cause, and promising our victory over the last enemy, death. We must also heed the apostolic warning that the resurrection of Jesus designates him as the Judge to whom all will give account on the last day.

Peter was just beginning his remarks (see 11:15), and his mention of the prophets' testimony about Jesus would probably have introduced another section of his sermon, in which Scriptures would be cited to show their fulfilment in Jesus. On the Day of Pentecost Peter had cited Joel 2 and Psalms 16 and 110; in Solomon's Portico he had quoted Moses' promise of a great prophet (*Deut.* 18:15) and God's promise that Abraham's seed would bless the nations (*Gen.* 22:18). What prophetic Scriptures Peter now meant to cite we do not know, for suddenly the sovereign Spirit interrupted his preacher, flooding Gentile hearts with faith at the mention of forgiveness in Jesus' name and filling Gentile mouths with praises to God in the tongues of the nations.

In these few sentences Peter had presented the truths at the heart of God's good news: Jesus the Messiah, Lord of all, was empowered by the Spirit to liberate the devil's captives, died under a curse deserved by others, and was raised up by God to reign and to judge. This was according to the Scriptures, which promise forgiveness of sins to everyone – from every people – who believes in Jesus' Name. Reflect on the meaning of each element in this concise gospel summary until your heart is moved to wonder, to gratitude, and to a joyful desire to spread the news.

30

The Gentile Pentecost

While Peter was still saying these things, the Holy Spirit fell on all who heard the word. [45] *And the believers from among the circumcised who had come with Peter were amazed, because the gift of the Holy Spirit was poured out even on the Gentiles.* [46] *For they were hearing them speaking in tongues and extolling God. Then Peter declared,* [47] *"Can anyone withhold water for baptizing these people, who have received the Holy Spirit just as we have?"* [48] *And he commanded them to be baptized in the name of Jesus Christ. Then they asked him to remain for some days* (Acts 10:44–48).

At the mention of forgiveness in Jesus' name, the Holy Spirit, whose mission it is to glorify the Son (*John* 16:12–15), fell upon the Gentiles who were listening to Peter. The two words that Luke uses to describe his coming connect this event with the Spirit's prior descents in Acts. '*Fall on*' appears in Acts 8:16: the Spirit did not fall upon the believers of Samaria until the apostles, Peter and John, arrived. '*Pour out*' belongs to the anointing imagery of Joel 2:28–32, cited by Peter at Pentecost (2:17–18, 33). Just as at Pentecost the Spirit ushered the disciples into the age of Christ's reign and later brought Samaritans (on the boundary between Israel and the Gentiles) into the new people of God, so now the Spirit was opening a new chapter in the spread of salvation 'to the ends of the earth': Gentiles are welcomed as children of Abraham not through circumcision and commandment keeping, but through faith alone.

The descent of the Spirit in Cornelius' home parallels Pentecost in other details as well. The Spirit signified his presence in the

Gentile believers by enabling them to speak in tongues, as had occurred at Pentecost (2:4). Some scholars see the lack of the word '*other*' in 10:46, in contrast to 2:4, as implying that the Gentiles' tongue-speaking was ecstatic speech, unlike the supernatural ability to speak intelligible human dialects at Pentecost (2:8–11). But their conclusion rests too much on the absence of a single word, especially in view of the direct correspondence that Peter, a participant in both events, saw between the two: 'The Holy Spirit fell on them just as on us at the beginning' (11:15).

The Gentile believers' speech also corresponded to that of the disciples at Pentecost in its content. Then the *mighty works of God* were declared (2:11). Now Cornelius and his associates were *extolling God* (literally, 'making God great,' that is, extolling his greatness).

The Spirit's arrival evoked the same astonishment in the observers of both events. At Pentecost Dispersion Jews were 'amazed and astonished' to hear unlettered Galileans speaking the dialects of distant nations (2:7). At Caesarea the circumcised believers who had accompanied Peter from Joppa (see also 10:23) were amazed to observe that God had poured out his Spirit even on the Gentiles (verse 45). In both events the Holy Spirit came as God's free gift, showing his amazing grace (2:38; 10:45; 11:17; see also 8:20).

Finally, faith is accompanied by baptism in the name of Jesus Christ, in which new disciples were publicly numbered with Jesus' people, and named and claimed as Jesus' property (2:38; 10:48). Peter's rhetorical question, *Can anyone withhold water for baptizing these people?* (in Greek: 'Can anyone prevent water, that these should not be baptized?'), links Cornelius with that earlier Gentile convert from Ethiopia, who asked Philip, 'See, here is water! What prevents me from being baptized?' (8:36). Some would soon try to prevent the church's welcome of Gentile outsiders by faith alone, without their submission to Israel's ceremonial distinctives (11:2; 15:1). Peter's logic, however, was flawless: when God himself insists on welcoming outsiders, it is both impudent and dangerous to try to stand in his way (11:17)! Again we confront the question: Is there anyone at all whom we have dismissed as beyond the reach of God's amazing grace?

31

Peter Answers Objections

Now the apostles and the brothers who were throughout Judea heard that the Gentiles also had received the word of God. ² So when Peter went up to Jerusalem, the circumcision party criticized him, saying, ³ "You went to uncircumcised men and ate with them." ⁴ But Peter began and explained it to them in order: ⁵ "I was in the city of Joppa praying, and in a trance I saw a vision, something like a great sheet descending, being let down from heaven by its four corners, and it came down to me. ⁶ Looking at it closely, I observed animals and beasts of prey and reptiles and birds of the air. ⁷ And I heard a voice saying to me, 'Rise, Peter; kill and eat.' ⁸ But I said, 'By no means, Lord; for nothing common or unclean has ever entered my mouth.' ⁹ But the voice answered a second time from heaven, 'What God has made clean, do not call common.' ¹⁰ This happened three times, and all was drawn up again into heaven. ¹¹ And behold, at that very moment three men arrived at the house in which we were, sent to me from Caesarea. ¹² And the Spirit told me to go with them, making no distinction. These six brothers also accompanied me, and we entered the man's house. ¹³ And he told us how he had seen the angel stand in his house and say, 'Send to Joppa and bring Simon who is called Peter; ¹⁴ he will declare to you a message by which you will be saved, you and all your household.' ¹⁵ As I began to speak, the Holy Spirit fell on them just as on us at the beginning. ¹⁶ And I remembered the word of the Lord, how he said, 'John baptized with water, but you will be baptized with the Holy Spirit.' ¹⁷ If then God gave the same gift to them as he gave to us when we believed in the Lord Jesus Christ, who was I that I could stand in God's way?" ¹⁸ When they heard these

*things they fell silent. And they glorified God, saying, "Then to
the Gentiles also God has granted repentance that leads to life"*
(Acts 11:1–18).

When Peter returned to Jerusalem, he met a firestorm of
criticism over his by-now notorious friendliness with
uncircumcised Gentiles. We now see why Luke took such pains to
record God's initiative in breaking down the wall of ceremonial
regulations that had excluded Gentiles from the people of his
covenant: the angelic visitor to Cornelius, Peter's vision about
cleansing (of both foods and persons), the Spirit's directive to
accompany Cornelius' messengers, and the Spirit's descent on the
Gentiles as Peter preached about Jesus.

We also understand why, in response to the Spirit's coming, Peter
phrased the question as he did: 'Can anyone withhold water for
baptizing these people, who have received the Holy Spirit just as we
have?' (10:47) There were, in fact, some in the church at Jerusalem
who would, if they could, forbid the baptism of Gentiles unless the
latter were circumcised to show their commitment to keep all the
regulations of the Law of Moses, ceremonial as well as moral.

Moreover, we see God's wisdom in providing corroborating
witnesses who could stand with Peter and confirm his testimony
regarding the astonishing event that they had observed together.
Those brothers from Joppa who were mentioned incidentally as
accompanying Peter to Caesarea (10:23) and whose adherence to the
circumcision deepened their astonishment when the Gentiles
received the Holy Spirit (10:45) proved to be the ideal circle of
witnesses (fulfilling the requirement of multiple witnesses, *Deut.*
19:15, *Matt.* 18:16) to testify that God had indeed bypassed
circumcision and welcomed the Gentiles simply by faith.

PETER ACCUSED

In words closely parallel to his account of the earlier report to
Jerusalem concerning Samaria (8:14), Luke now records that *the
apostles and the brothers who were throughout Judea heard that the
Gentiles also had received the word of God.* The parallel wording
identifies these two events as major transitions in the ethnic

expansion of the gospel and the church founded on it. First the Samaritans, who mingled fidelity to the Law of Moses with pagan practices, and now the Gentiles, were being included into the new people of God. These summaries highlight not the Spirit's miraculous demonstrations but his Word-confirming and Word-spreading role. What matters is not that the Gentiles have spoken in tongues, but that the word of Jesus, which elicits faith and brings reconciliation with God, has taken root in their hearts.

When Peter returned to Jerusalem, the report of events in Cornelius' home had preceded him. Sadly, some in the church were preoccupied with the suspicion, which was probably correct, that Peter's staying several days in a Gentile household would have exposed him to non-kosher food. This mattered more to them than the news that Gentiles had believed the message of Christ. These Jewish believers were not only circumcised themselves (as all Jews and Gentile proselytes were) but were also adamant that Gentiles coming to faith in Jesus must also undergo circumcision if they were to join the church. The expression, *the circumcision party*, literally 'those of the circumcision' (as in 10:45), focuses not on their personal condition but on their conviction of what should be required of others. Since one's table company and one's menu were so intimately connected, God had appropriately given Peter a menu-related vision to show the expanding circle of companions with whom Jesus' followers could (and must!) break bread.

PETER ANSWERS

Peter answered the charge of defilement through table fellowship with *uncircumcised men* (literally 'men who have uncircumcision', as his accusers labelled the Gentiles, categorizing uncircumcision as a disease) by retelling the narrative that Luke's readers have already read.

Narrative repetition, in detail and in close proximity to the original account, while it may frustrate impatient modern readers, was a recognized device by which biblical historians emphasized the monumental importance of watershed events. In addition to the twin narrations of the search for Isaac's bride mentioned earlier (*Gen.* 24), note the recapitulation of the instructions for the tabernacle and its furnishings (*Exod.* 25–30) in their actual construction (*Exod.* 36–39) and the repetition of the Ten Commandments at the beginning and conclusion of Israel's wilderness wanderings (*Exod.* 20, *Deut.* 5).

Peter's retelling therefore varies little from Luke's account, which immediately precedes it: Peter's vision in Joppa and the Lord's threefold rebuke of the apostle; the delegation from Caesarea and their return to their master, accompanied by Peter and 'these six brothers' from Joppa; the coming of the Spirit upon the Gentiles as Peter was in the opening portion of his sermon; and Peter's conclusion that he could not prevent and dared not hinder God from incorporating the Gentiles into his church without circumcision, as God so evidently intended to do.

Several added details in Peter's report are worth noting:

(1) Along with four-footed (domesticated) animals, reptiles, and birds, Peter said that he also saw wild beasts in the sheet. The inclusion of predators means that the menu presented to Peter encompassed not only the diversity in Noah's ark but also the wide range of animal life created by God in the beginning (*Gen.* 1:24, 30).

(2) Peter omitted mention of Cornelius' prayers and alms (see also 10:4, 22, 31), but he made explicit that what Cornelius awaited was a message that would bring salvation to him and his household (11:14). Thus the emphasis shifts from the positive fruit of Cornelius' anticipatory faith to his deep spiritual longing, which his own prayers and gifts could not satisfy. He and those near him needed a rescue that they could not achieve by their own best efforts. They needed the forgiveness of sins that comes only through the name of Jesus (see also 10:43).

(3) The mention of Cornelius' household recalls Peter's Pentecost promise to his hearers and their children (2:39). Although tracing one's descent from faithful parents provides no protection to the presumptuous rebel, still the ancient promise to Abraham holds: covenant grace flows along the limbs of family trees and flourishes in homes where God is revered (*Gen.* 17:7; 18:19, *Josh.* 24:15).

(4) Peter's interpretation of the descent of the Spirit on Cornelius and his circle now explicitly linked that event with Pentecost. Listening to the Gentiles speak in other tongues, Peter remembered the Lord Jesus' words, which had contrasted John's water baptism to the Holy Spirit baptism that occurred at Pentecost (1:5). God gave the Gentiles the same gift, the Spirit, as he had given his assembled

disciples in the upper room fifty days after his suffering. God had united them to his supremely Anointed One, Jesus, in the same way: through their believing in the Lord Jesus Christ. Clearly God saw the Gentiles' uncircumcised condition as no obstacle to their immediate inclusion into the community of his grace, and those who do not dare to pit themselves against God's purposes must also welcome such outsiders with corresponding warmth.

AN AWESTRUCK CONCLUSION

Peter's report silenced the objections of his accusers. '*They fell silent*' means they had no further objections – although of course their silence was not absolute, for they praised God in wonder, 'Then to the Gentiles also God has granted repentance that leads to life.' Nor did the silencing of objections necessarily imply universal assent. Elsewhere this verb shows people silenced not because they are persuaded but because they cannot muster credible counter arguments (*Luke* 14:4, *Acts* 21:14). Opposition to God's welcome of believing Gentiles would resurface in Antioch (15:1) and elsewhere (*Gal.* 5:1–6, *Phil.* 3:2–10).

Although there may have been silent detractors, the church joined Peter in praising God for his gift to the Gentiles. Repentance itself – the change of heart from self to God, from sinful pride to humble trust – only comes as a gift from God. Peter had said as much to Jewish audiences on previous occasions (3:26; 5:31). Since it is a gift undeserved by its recipients, not dependent on their worthiness but expressive of God's mercy, repentance is always an amazing grace, producing a life that overflows in thanksgiving.

32

God's Gift Exchange
Unites Jews and Greeks

Now those who were scattered because of the persecution that arose over Stephen travelled as far as Phoenicia and Cyprus and Antioch, speaking the word to no one except Jews. ²⁰ But there were some of them, men of Cyprus and Cyrene, who on coming to Antioch spoke to the Hellenists also, preaching the Lord Jesus. ²¹ And the hand of the Lord was with them, and a great number who believed turned to the Lord. ²² The report of this came to the ears of the church in Jerusalem, and they sent Barnabas to Antioch. ²³ When he came and saw the grace of God, he was glad, and he exhorted them all to remain faithful to the Lord with steadfast purpose, ²⁴ for he was a good man, full of the Holy Spirit and of faith. And a great many people were added to the Lord. ²⁵ So Barnabas went to Tarsus to look for Saul, ²⁶ and when he had found him, he brought him to Antioch. For a whole year they met with the church and taught a great many people. And in Antioch the disciples were first called Christians.

²⁷ Now in these days prophets came down from Jerusalem to Antioch. ²⁸ And one of them named Agabus stood up and foretold by the Spirit that there would be a great famine over all the world (this took place in the days of Claudius). ²⁹ So the disciples determined, everyone according to his ability, to send relief to the brothers living in Judea. ³⁰ And they did so, sending it to the elders by the hand of Barnabas and Saul (Acts 11:19–30).

The scene has shifted and the actors have changed, but the theme remains the same: God is bringing Gentiles into the church as his redeemed people. As believers scattered from Jerusalem, some travelled along the coast through Phoenicia, some went west across the sea to Cyprus, and some north to Antioch, the third city of the Empire (after Rome and Alexandria) and the chief metropolis of Syria. At Antioch Jewish Christians from the Dispersion broke through the ethnic barrier, as Peter had done at Caesarea, to bring the gospel to Greeks. The fruit of their witness was a flourishing multi-ethnic congregation, active in evangelism, noted in the community, generous in helping brothers, and eventually pivotal in the gospel's expansion to points west.

SCATTERED SEED GERMINATES AMONG THE GREEKS

The sowers of the Lord's Word in Phoenicia, Cyprus, and Antioch had been scattered by the persecution instigated by Stephen's martyrdom, just as Philip had been scattered to Samaria (8:1, 4–5). Though exiled from home by the hostility of Judaism's leaders, these believers still spoke the Word to their fellow-Jews. Nor did the cosmopolitan mix of Antioch, crossroads between East and West, intimidate them into a ghettoized withdrawal. Some from Cyprus and the North African city of Cyrene, accustomed to contact with Gentiles, started telling the good news of the Lord Jesus to Greeks as well.

Luke uses a Hebrew metaphor, *The hand of the Lord was with them*, to indicate that the Holy Spirit's presence, power, and approval rested on their efforts, causing the Word to bear a rich harvest, turning many to the Lord in faith (see *Exod.* 9:3, *Isa.* 66:14, *Luke* 1:66, *Acts* 4:28, 30). The principle, 'Out of the abundance of the heart the mouth speaks', holds true positively as well as negatively (*Matt.* 12:34); and the joy of these believers in Jesus broke forth into speech, to fellow–Jew and Gentile stranger alike. What speech spills from your mouth, revealing the reality that fills your heart?

GIFTS FROM DISTANT BROTHERS

News of large–scale conversions of Gentiles in Antioch called for confirmation by a representative of the mother church in Jerusalem, just as Peter and John had been sent to Samaria to verify the gospel's impact there (8:14). This time, instead of sending apostles, the church found the ideal delegate in Barnabas. A Cypriot from the Dispersion himself, Barnabas was so highly regarded in Jerusalem that the apostles themselves had nicknamed him, 'Mr Encouragement' (4:36). Like Stephen, Barnabas was full of the Holy Spirit and faith (see also 6:5). His faith had proved its mettle when he had dared to get close enough to Saul, the former persecutor, and had discovered the genuineness of Saul's faith (9:27). Barnabas risked believing that God's grace could work in unlikely places, so he rejoiced when he 'saw the grace of God' (as Luke literally expresses it) at work in new believers. The heart filled with the Spirit of the Father is overjoyed when the lost are found (*Luke* 15:7, 10, 32). True to his name, he encouraged their perseverance in devotion to the Lord.

To grow strong, new Christians need instruction as well as encouragement. Barnabas saw that the fledgling Antioch church needed another teacher who had already shown boldness and skill in demonstrating from the Scriptures that Jesus is the Christ: namely, Saul, who had returned to his home city (9:22, 27–30). Retrieving Saul from Tarsus, Barnabas taught with him for an entire year, grounding great numbers of people deeply in the faith. Three times in this brief passage Luke calls attention to the large numbers of converts (11:21, 24, 26). God is not indifferent to how many people experience his grace (see also also 2:41, 47; 4:4; 5:14). He spreads a large and lavish feast of salvation, and refuses to have a single place at his table empty (*Luke* 14:23)!

The distinction between the church, with its bold announcement that Jesus is Lord and its welcome of Gentiles, and the non-messianic Jewish community became so obvious that the pagan neighbours of believers coined a new term, *Christians*, to identify this dynamic movement. The title appears twice elsewhere in the New Testament, being used on both occasions by those outside the faith (*Acts* 26:28, *1 Pet.* 4:16). It identifies believers as people loyal to Christ, just as Herodians were partisans of Herod (*Mark* 3:6).

The church at Jerusalem gave further gifts to Antioch in the persons of prophets, who were gifted to reveal God's mysteries (*1 Cor.* 13:2; 14:5, 24–25, 29–31). Among the risen Lord's gifts to his church, prophets are second only to apostles in importance (*1 Cor.* 12:28). With the apostles they constitute the foundation of the church as God's new temple, for through them the mystery of Christ has been revealed (*Eph.* 2:20; 3:5). We have access to that once–for–all foundation through the completed New Testament.

GIFTS TO DISTANT BROTHERS

Agabus prophesied a severe famine that would impact the entire Empire, and Luke comments that this prophecy was fulfilled when Claudius was emperor. A major flooding of the Nile in 45 AD damaged and reduced the Egyptian harvest, sending grain prices sky-rocketing throughout the Roman world for several years. A severe famine struck Judea also from 46 to 48 AD.

This word from the Lord gave the Christians of Antioch opportunity to express their gratitude for spiritual gifts received from the church of Jerusalem (Barnabas, Saul, the prophets) and their solidarity with their suffering brothers in Judea. Paul would later write about an offering that Gentile churches were eagerly collecting for impoverished believers in Judea: 'For, if the Gentiles have come to share their [the Jews'] spiritual blessings, they ought also to be of service to them in material blessings' (*Rom.* 15:27).

The exchange of gifts, spiritual and material, between congregations separated by distance signifies our unity in Christ, despite our diversity of race and culture. Such tangible expressions of unity should distinguish the church today in a world ripped apart by ethnic and nationalistic loyalties.

33

Death and Deliverance

About that time Herod the king laid violent hands on some who belonged to the church. ² He killed James the brother of John with the sword, ³ and when he saw that it pleased the Jews, he proceeded to arrest Peter also. This was during the days of Unleavened Bread. ⁴ And when he had seized him, he put him in prison, delivering him over to four squads of soldiers to guard him, intending after the Passover to bring him out to the people. ⁵ So Peter was kept in prison, but earnest prayer for him was made to God by the church.

⁶ Now when Herod was about to bring him out, on that very night, Peter was sleeping between two soldiers, bound with two chains, and sentries before the door were guarding the prison. ⁷ And behold, an angel of the Lord stood next to him, and a light shone in the cell. He struck Peter on the side and woke him, saying, "Get up quickly." And the chains fell off his hands. ⁸ And the angel said to him, "Dress yourself and put on your sandals." And he did so. And he said to him, "Wrap your cloak around you and follow me." ⁹ And he went out and followed him. He did not know that what was being done by the angel was real, but thought he was seeing a vision. ¹⁰ When they had passed the first and the second guard, they came to the iron gate leading into the city. It opened for them of its own accord, and they went out and went along one street, and immediately the angel left him. ¹¹ When Peter came to himself, he said, "Now I am sure that the Lord has sent his angel and rescued me from the hand of Herod and from all that the Jewish people were expecting."

¹² When he realized this, he went to the house of Mary, the mother of John whose other name was Mark, where many were gathered together and were praying. [13] And when he knocked at the door of the gateway, a servant girl named Rhoda came to answer. [14] Recognizing Peter's voice, in her joy she did not open the gate but ran in and reported that Peter was standing at the gate. [15] They said to her, "You are out of your mind." But she kept insisting that it was so, and they kept saying, "It is his angel!" [16] But Peter continued knocking, and when they opened, they saw him and were amazed. [17] But motioning to them with his hand to be silent, he described to them how the Lord had brought him out of the prison. And he said, "Tell these things to James and to the brothers." Then he departed and went to another place.

[18] Now when day came, there was no little disturbance among the soldiers over what had become of Peter. [19] And after Herod searched for him and did not find him, he examined the sentries and ordered that they should be put to death (Acts 12:1–19a).

Luke is drawing to a close his description of the second phase of the gospel's expansion, 'in all Judea and Samaria' (1:8, see also 8:1; 9:31). As the first phase (Jerusalem) closed with Stephen's martyrdom and the third phase (the end of the earth) will end with Paul imprisoned at Rome, so this second phase closes with a sobering reminder that the explosive outreach of the church to the Gentiles was accompanied by persecution from people in power. Yet persecution served the spread of the gospel rather than silencing it. Stephen's death scattered the message of Jesus out from Jerusalem. Although Paul's custody in Rome would inhibit his physical mobility, he could still proclaim God's kingdom and the Lord Jesus Christ 'without hindrance' (28:31). So also at the close of this second phase, King Herod, the persecutor, finds his plot against the church thwarted and his own life forfeit for blasphemous arrogance, while the Word of God goes on growing (12:24).

KING HEROD MOVES AGAINST THE APOSTLES

Herod the king was Herod Agrippa I, grandson of Herod the Great and nephew of Herod Antipas, to whom Pilate had sent Jesus for trial. Through his friendship with the Emperors Caligula and Claudius, Agrippa had acquired the title 'king' (denied to his uncles) and amassed a realm (under Rome, of course) comparable in extent to that of his grandfather. Yet his hold on the Transjordan, Decapolis, Galilee, Perea, Judea and Samaria was tenuous, so he looked for ways to ingratiate himself with his restive Jewish subjects. One such way was to strike at the leaders of the movement that persisted in proclaiming Jesus to be the Messiah, despite the Sanhedrin's condemnation of Jesus and harsh treatment of his apostles.

In a terse sentence, seven words in Greek, Luke records the death of James, the first apostle to be martyred. James belonged to Jesus' inner circle along with his brother John and Simon Peter. These three witnessed Jesus' transfiguration, and Jesus asked them to accompany him during his anguished prayer in Gethsemane. Jesus had warned his disciples that men would 'lay hands on' them (see also *Acts* 12:1) and persecute them (*Luke* 21:12). Between Stephen and James other believers, not named by Luke, had laid down their lives for the faith (9:1; 26:10).

Herod's execution of James with the sword (Roman style, not Jewish) had its desired result: the Jews were pleased. So he took the further step of seizing Peter, intending to try and execute him publicly after the Passover and Feast of Unleavened Bread. The apostles were following the footsteps of their Master, who had appeared before another Herod at Passover time (*Luke* 22:7; 23: 8–12).

Until the end of the eight-day feast Herod placed Peter under extremely heavy security, probably in the Fortress Antonia that overlooked the Temple grounds. Every night four squads of four soldiers each – two chained to the prisoner, the other two standing guard outside the cell door – stood three-hour watches to ensure that the escape that had embarrassed the Sanhedrin would not be repeated (5:17–26). Such short watches provided no excuse for drowsiness on duty.

Meanwhile, an even more powerful force was at work to effect Peter's escape: the church was earnestly praying to God for him.

PETER'S SLEEPWALK TO FREEDOM

Peter slept so soundly, secure in God's purpose whether it meant life or death (see also *Phil.* 1:20–24), that the angel struck his side to awaken him. As he stood in response to the angel's command, both chains dropped from his wrists. Neither the chains' clatter nor the heavenly light that flooded the cell roused the guards (see also *Luke* 2:9). The prisoner himself was so groggy that the angel gave him step-by-step dressing instructions: 'Dress yourself and put on your sandals' (as at the first Passover, *Exod.* 12:11), then, 'Wrap your cloak around you and follow me.' Peter drifted as in a dream by the angel's side past the first and second guards to the forbidding iron gate that barred his way to the city beyond and freedom. But the gate swung open of its own accord!

Suddenly Peter found himself alone in the street, the angel having vanished. He realized that what he had assumed was a vision or dream was sober reality: 'The Lord has sent his angel and rescued me from the hand of Herod', just as he had sent his angel to rescue Moses from Pharaoh's hand at the first Passover (*Exod.* 18:4, where the Greek translation reads, 'God . . . rescued me from the hand of Pharaoh,' as in Acts 12:11).

Peter headed immediately for the spacious home of Mary, a regular meeting place for the believers. Mary's son, *John, whose other name was Mark*, would play a future role in Acts, accompanying his cousin Barnabas and Saul at the start of their first mission into Cyprus and Asia (12:25; 13:5, 13) and becoming the occasion of their later disagreement (15:37–40). Later still, however, Paul would express appreciation for Mark (*Col.* 4:10, *2 Tim.* 4:11, see also *1 Pet.* 5:13). Mark's life would illustrate how God perseveres until his grace overcomes our instabilities.

EARNEST BUT UNBELIEVING PRAYERS

The church was at prayer for Peter when he arrived and knocked at the gate leading into Mary's courtyard. The servant Rhoda, assigned door-keeping duties, was apparently a believer, for the sound of Peter's voice shouting for entrance so filled her with joy that she forgot to open the gate, leaving him in the street as she reported the good news to the praying saints inside. They dismissed her as delusional, but she remained adamant. They speculated that Peter had already been slain and his guardian angel was roaming Jerusalem's streets (*Psa.* 91:11, *Matt.* 18:10, *Heb.* 1:14). Meanwhile, the astonishing truth stood knocking at the gate.

The humbling, even humorous, humanity of these early Christians shows that the welfare of the church rests on God's faithfulness, not our feeble faith. First, Peter passed through the prison's open doors like a sleepwalker, only realizing that his deliverance was no dream in the cool night air of the street outside. Then Rhoda was so thrilled to hear Peter's voice that she forgot to let him into her mistress's home. When Rhoda reported to the praying Christians that Peter was standing outside, they were prepared to entertain any theory except the truth that God had answered their prayers. That the Lord would flex his arm to save such frail and foolish folk is a tribute to his grace alone.

As Peter had been singled out by name to receive the news of Jesus' resurrection (*Mark* 16:7), so now James and the brothers must be told of Peter's miraculous release from prison and death. This James, the brother of Jesus (*Gal.* 1:19, *Matt.* 13:55), would emerge as a 'pillar' of the Jerusalem church and take a leading role in the Apostolic Council that secured the Gentiles' place in the church, apart from circumcision (15:13; 21:18, *Gal.* 2:9, 12).

In this passage God shows how radically his good purposes for his children vary from one person to the next. For James the son of Zebedee, Herod's persecution brought swift death. In Peter's case, the persecutor's plans were thwarted as the apostle walked to freedom (and his hapless guards paid for his escape with their lives). But the differences lay only in the short run. In the long run, Peter knew that death as a prisoner awaited him, for Jesus had told him so (*John* 21:18–19). In the even longer run, a glorious resurrection awaits James and Peter and all who hold faith fast to the end, to whom Jesus says, 'Be faithful unto death, and I will give you the crown of life' (*Rev.* 2:10).

34

God Defends His Glory and Grows His Word

Then he went down from Judea to Caesarea and spent time there.
²⁰ Now Herod was angry with the people of Tyre and Sidon,
and they came to him with one accord, and having persuaded
Blastus, the king's chamberlain, they asked for peace, because
their country depended on the king's country for food. ²¹ On an
appointed day Herod put on his royal robes, took his seat upon
the throne, and delivered an oration to them. ²² And the people
were shouting, "The voice of a god, and not of a man!"
²³ Immediately an angel of the Lord struck him down, because
he did not give God the glory, and he was eaten by worms and
breathed his last.
²⁴ But the word of God increased and multiplied.
²⁵ And Barnabas and Saul returned from Jerusalem when they
had completed their service, bringing with them John, whose other
name was Mark (Acts 12:19b–25).

Each phase of the gospel's expansion (Jerusalem, Judea and Samaria, the end of the earth) was accompanied not only by healing miracles but also by signs of judgement on God's enemies. In Jerusalem judgement struck within the church as Ananias and Sapphira died for their lie to the Holy Spirit (5:1–11). In the third phase, blindness will strike Elymas the sorcerer, who tries to dissuade the proconsul of Cyprus from listening to the gospel (13:6–11). In the present section we have seen Saul the persecutor struck blind and then restored to sight in the name of Jesus (9:8–9, 17–19). Now this section closes with an extreme judgement: the angel of the Lord strikes down Herod Agrippa, the persecutor of God's people and usurper of God's praises.

GOD'S ANGEL STRIKES AGAIN

Herod had returned to Caesarea Maritima, the seaside city built by his grandfather in honour of Caesar Augustus. His growing political and economic influence explains the eagerness with which the Phoenician cities of Tyre and Sidon tried to placate his anger through the mediation of Blastus, Herod's personal attendant. As Luke notes, coastal cities were dependent for food on farmlands in the interior, which lay within Agrippa's domain. (In ancient times Hiram of Tyre and Solomon of Israel had signed a lumber-for-food exchange treaty, *1 Kings* 5:10–12).

The Jewish historian Josephus, who also records the sudden death of Agrippa, indicates that the appointed day was a festival in honour of Caesar – probably the celebration of the city's founding in March or of Caesar's birthday in August (*Antiquities of the Jews*, 19.343–351). Josephus describes the royal robes worn by Herod as 'woven completely of silver', which glittered with the rays of the sun, causing the crowds to marvel.

Josephus' account agrees with Luke's affirmation that it was while the crowd extolled Herod as no mere man but a god and he accepted their accolades that he was struck down with an intense terminal illness. In commenting, the angel of the Lord struck him down, Luke engages in word play, reusing the verb that described the Lord's angel striking Peter's side to awaken him. For Peter the blow of God's angel meant life and freedom; for Herod that blow meant death.

Josephus mentions the symptom of excruciating abdominal pain, while Luke says that Herod was *eaten by worms*. The deaths of Antiochus IV Epiphanes, the Syrian king who defiled the Temple and provoked the Maccabean resistance (*2 Maccabees* 9:9), and Herod the Great (Josephus, *Antiquities*, 17.168–170) were attributed to their being consumed by worms. The decomposition that usually occurs in the grave preceded and precipitated the death of these tyrants. Isaiah punctured the pretensions to divinity of Babylon's king:

'All your pomp has been brought down to the grave, along with the noise of your harps; maggots are spread out beneath you, and worms cover you. How you have fallen from heaven, O morning star, son of the dawn! You have been cast down to the earth, you who once laid low the nations! You said in your heart, " . . . I will make myself like the Most High"' (*Isa.* 14:11–14).

So end all who refuse to give God glory, seizing the praise that is his alone. How often do we, in more subtle ways, usurp the honour that belongs by rights to God himself (*Rom.* 2:21, *John* 12:43)? Rejoice that Jesus, who always glorified the Father and over whom death's decay had no hold, endured the wrath that we glory-thieves deserve (*John* 12:28, *Acts* 2:31).

THE WORD GOES ON GROWING

Luke concludes this second section by contrasting Herod's miserable end with the continuing growth of Jesus' Word. The organic metaphor of growth (see also *Mark* 4:14) appeared earlier in Acts 6:7 and will reappear in 19:20. Because faith comes by hearing, Luke highlights apostolic preaching and portrays the growth of the church as the fruitful growth of the Word (see also *Col.* 1:6).

Finally, Luke prepares us for the next phase of gospel expansion by noting the return of Barnabas and Saul from Jerusalem to Antioch. The famine predicted by Agabus finally occurred in 46 AD, after Herod's demise, so the completion of Barnabas' and Saul's mission in Jerusalem chronologically fits here. As they returned, accompanied by John Mark, to the multi-ethnic church in cosmopolitan Antioch, God was positioning them to receive his call to bring salvation to the ends of the earth.

35

Darkness and Daybreak

Now there were in the church at Antioch prophets and teachers, Barnabas, Simeon who was called Niger, Lucius of Cyrene, Manaen a member of the court of Herod the tetrarch, and Saul. ² While they were worshipping the Lord and fasting, the Holy Spirit said, "Set apart for me Barnabas and Saul for the work to which I have called them." ³ Then after fasting and praying they laid their hands on them and sent them off.

⁴ So, being sent out by the Holy Spirit, they went down to Seleucia, and from there they sailed to Cyprus. ⁵ When they arrived at Salamis, they proclaimed the word of God in the synagogues of the Jews. And they had John to assist them. ⁶ When they had gone through the whole island as far as Paphos, they came upon a certain magician, a Jewish false prophet named Bar-Jesus. ⁷ He was with the proconsul, Sergius Paulus, a man of intelligence, who summoned Barnabas and Saul and sought to hear the word of God. ⁸ But Elymas the magician (for that is the meaning of his name) opposed them, seeking to turn the proconsul away from the faith. ⁹ But Saul, who was also called Paul, filled with the Holy Spirit, looked intently at him ¹⁰ and said, "You son of the devil, you enemy of all righteousness, full of all deceit and villainy, will you not stop making crooked the straight paths of the Lord? ¹¹ And now, behold, the hand of the Lord is upon you, and you will be blind and unable to see the sun for a time." Immediately mist and darkness fell upon him, and he went about seeking people to lead him by the hand. ¹² Then the proconsul believed, when he saw what had occurred, for he was astonished at the teaching of the Lord (Acts 13:1–12).

World missions begin in worship. We have seen the gospel break through the ethnic barrier between Judaism and the Gentiles in the case of the Ethiopian, Cornelius, and the church in Antioch. Geographically as well the gospel has moved beyond Israel's borders. Yet the Mediterranean Sea was the barrier between Israel and the distant islands at 'the end of the earth': 'Sing to the Lord a new song, his praise from the end of the earth, you who go down to the sea, and all that fills it, the coastlands and their inhabitants' (*Isa.* 42:10; see also 11:10–11; 41:5; 49:1, 6; 66:19). Therefore it was when Barnabas and Saul sailed across the sea to Cyprus that the third phase of witness announced in Acts 1:8 was launched. The Spirit's commission came as the church's prophets and teachers were worshipping the Lord.

WORSHIP EXPANDS WITNESS

The prophets and teachers of the church in Antioch reflected the city's cosmopolitan composition. Barnabas (first in the list), though sent from Jerusalem, had been born in Cyprus. Saul (last in the list), though educated in Jerusalem, was born in Tarsus of Cilicia (22:3). Simeon's Latin nickname *Niger* means 'black', so he probably belonged to one of the dark-complexioned peoples of north Africa. Lucius likewise hailed from North Africa, from Cyrene in Libya. Manaen had belonged to élite society in Roman-occupied Palestine as a childhood friend of Herod the tetrarch, the Herod who ordered John the Baptist's execution and eagerly interrogated Jesus.

The leaders' fasting expressed earnestness and expectancy: the blessing that they sought from the Lord was more urgent than food itself. Although Jesus' disciples did not fast while he was present with them, he prepared them to fast in the future in a way that only their Father would see (*Matt.* 6:17–18; 9:14–15). To these earnest worshippers the Holy Spirit spoke through one of the prophets: 'Set apart for me Barnabas and Saul for the work to which I have called them.' Saul was a vessel chosen to carry Jesus' name before Gentiles, kings, and the people of Israel (*Acts* 9:15). He had borne witness to Israelites in Jerusalem and taught Gentile Christians in Antioch (11:26), but this call of the Spirit launched a new phase in Saul's ministry. Paul would later use the Spirit's language to affirm that he had been 'set apart' from his mother's womb, and then called by grace to proclaim God's Son (*Gal.* 1:15, *Rom.* 1:1). Now the apostle to the Gentiles was about to enter into the work for which God had prepared him. The word *work*, so common but here so meaningful, will mark a milestone when Paul and Barnabas return to Antioch 'where they had been commended to the grace of God for the *work* that they had fulfilled' (14:26). The leaders' prayer with fasting and laying on of hands here is not ordination to office, as in the case of the seven servants (6:6) and the elders of new churches (14:23). Barnabas and Saul were already teachers of the church, so their co-workers placed hands on them to identify with them in their mission and to entrust them to God's grace for their labours. Thus through the church they were sent on their way by the Holy Spirit himself.

JEWISH DARKNESS AND GENTILE DAYBREAK

From Seleucia, the port of Antioch, Barnabas and Saul (accompanied by John Mark) sailed westward to Salamis, the eastern port of Cyprus. They employed the strategy that would characterize Paul's work elsewhere, proclaiming God's Word first in Jewish synagogues. This priority had a pragmatic advantage in that the synagogue audience was familiar with the Scriptures, but it was motivated primarily by principle: God's promises to Israel's patriarchs demanded that the gospel be announced 'to the Jew first, and also to the Greek' (*Rom.* 1:16; 2:9–10; 15:8–9, *Acts* 3:26; 13:46–47).

The first Gentile whose meeting with the missionaries Luke records was the proconsul, Sergius Paulus, who governed the island from Paphos, on the southwestern coast. Luke describes him as an intelligent man, whose insight is seen in his summoning Barnabas and Saul to hear the message they carried from God.

A member of his own court, however, stood as an obstacle to his hearing God's Word: a Jewish sorcerer and false prophet by the name of Bar-Jesus ('son of *Jehovah-saves*'). Even educated Romans placed weight on omens and divination, and the Jews had a reputation throughout the Empire for 'inside knowledge' of divine operations. It is not so surprising therefore that Sergius Paulus had employed a Jewish 'prophet' as a consultant. Bar-Jesus' other name, Elymas, is interpreted to mean 'sorcerer' (Greek, *magos*). It is probably derived either from an Aramaic word meaning 'sage' or a Hebrew term, 'dream-interpreter', explaining his role as advisor to the procurator.

Bar-Jesus proved himself to be a false prophet by opposing the Word of God spoken by Barnabas and Saul, and by trying to turn Sergius Paulus away from the faith. From this point on Saul – whose Roman name, Paul, is here introduced as he moves on to Gentile territory – took the lead in proclaiming the gospel and answering its enemies, and hereafter he will be listed first or alone as the team leader (13:13, 42, 46, 50, 14:1,3; etc.). Paul asserted that Bar–Jesus' character contradicted his name: instead of being 'son of *Jehovah–saves*', he was a son of the devil (see also *John* 8:44). The sorcerer, full of all kinds of deceit and villainy, stood in sharp contrast to the apostle, who was filled with the Holy Spirit to deliver God's indictment against this false prophet. Bar–Jesus presumed to speak in the Lord's name while perverting the right ways of the Lord (see also *Hos.* 14:9). His message was the opposite of John the Baptist's call to repentant readiness: 'Prepare the way of the Lord, make his paths straight' (*Luke* 3:4, *Isa.* 40:3). Bar-Jesus wanted to preserve the status quo at all costs!

Paul declared that the hand of the Lord – God's powerful presence – was against Bar-Jesus, as it had been against unfaithful Israel (*Judg.* 2:15, *1 Sam.* 12:15). The sorcerer would experience the covenant curse of blindness, as Saul himself had been struck blind at midday, needing someone to guide him (*Deut.* 28:28–29, *Acts* 9:8). Both men illustrated in microcosm the blindness of Israel, the Lord's servant, as the following account of Jewish opposition and Gentile welcome towards God's Word at Pisidian Antioch will demonstrate (*Isa.* 42:19–20, *Acts* 13:40–48). Yet, as Paul's blindness had been temporary, so would Elymas' be – a promise of grace is extended, even as the Lord had promised a cure of Israel's blindness through his Servant (*Isa.* 42:6–7, 16).

Darkness descended immediately on the Jewish false prophet, even as light burst on the Gentile ruler, who believed for he was astonished at the teaching of the Lord. As often occurs in the Gospels, what astonished the procurator was not the miraculous works of Jesus, but the authoritative words of Jesus (*Luke* 4:32, *Mark* 1:22; 6:2; 11:18). Only when you are amazed by the grace revealed in the Gospel will you grasp the meaning of the miracles performed by Jesus' messengers in Jesus' Name.

36

Paul's 'Inaugural' Sermon

Now Paul and his companions set sail from Paphos and came to Perga in Pamphylia. And John left them and returned to Jerusalem, ¹⁴ *but they went on from Perga and came to Antioch in Pisidia. And on the Sabbath day they went into the synagogue and sat down.* ¹⁵ *After the reading from the Law and the Prophets, the rulers of the synagogue sent a message to them, saying, "Brothers, if you have any word of exhortation for the people, say it."* ¹⁶ *So Paul stood up, and motioning with his hand said:*

"Men of Israel and you who fear God, listen. ¹⁷ *The God of this people Israel chose our fathers and made the people great during their stay in the land of Egypt, and with uplifted arm he led them out of it.* ¹⁸ *And for about forty years he put up with them in the wilderness.* ¹⁹ *And after destroying seven nations in the land of Canaan, he gave them their land as an inheritance.* ²⁰ *All this took about 450 years. And after that he gave them judges until Samuel the prophet.* ²¹ *Then they asked for a king, and God gave them Saul the son of Kish, a man of the tribe of Benjamin, for forty years.* ²² *And when he had removed him, he raised up David to be their king, of whom he testified and said, 'I have found in David the son of Jesse a man after my heart, who will do all my will.'* ²³ *Of this man's offspring God has brought to Israel a Saviour, Jesus, as he promised.* ²⁴ *Before his coming, John had proclaimed a baptism of repentance to all the people of Israel.* ²⁵ *And as John was finishing his course, he said, 'What do you suppose that I am? I am not he. No, but behold, after me one is coming, the sandals of whose feet I am not worthy to untie.'*

²⁶ *"Brothers, sons of the family of Abraham, and those among you who fear God, to us has been sent the message of this salvation.* ²⁷ *For those who live in Jerusalem and their rulers, because they did not recognize him nor understand the utterances of the prophets, which are read every Sabbath, fulfilled them by condemning him.* ²⁸ *And though they found in him no guilt worthy of death, they asked Pilate to have him executed.* ²⁹ *And when they had carried out all that was written of him, they took him down from the tree and laid him in a tomb.* ³⁰ *But God raised him from the dead,* ³¹ *and for many days he appeared to those who had come up with him from Galilee to Jerusalem, who are now his witnesses to the people.* ³² *And we bring you the good news that what God promised to the fathers,* ³³ *this he has fulfilled to us their children by raising Jesus, as also it is written in the second Psalm,*

" 'You are my Son,
  today I have begotten you.'

³⁴ *And as for the fact that he raised him from the dead, no more to return to corruption, he has spoken in this way,*

" 'I will give you the holy and sure blessings of David.'

³⁵ *Therefore he says also in another psalm,*

" 'You will not let your Holy One see corruption.'

³⁶ *For David, after he had served the purpose of God in his own generation, fell asleep and was laid with his fathers and saw corruption,* ³⁷ *but he whom God raised up did not see corruption.* ³⁸ *Let it be known to you therefore, brothers, that through this man forgiveness of sins is proclaimed to you, and by him everyone who believes is freed from everything* ³⁹ *from which you could not be freed by the law of Moses.* ⁴⁰ *Beware, therefore, lest what is said in the Prophets should come about:*

⁴¹ *" 'Look, you scoffers,*
  be astounded and perish;
  for I am doing a work in your days,
    a work that you will not believe, even if one tells it to you.'"

⁴² *As they went out, the people begged that these things might be told them the next Sabbath.* ⁴³ *And after the meeting of the synagogue broke up, many Jews and devout converts to Judaism*

followed Paul and Barnabas, who, as they spoke with them, urged
them to continue in the grace of God (Acts 13:13–43).

Paul's team sailed north from Cyprus to the coast of Asia Minor, with Perga in the region of Pamphylia as their first destination. (Paul's emerging leadership is implied in the reference to the missionary team as *Paul and his companions*.) Here John Mark abandoned the mission to return home. Luke records no rationale for his departure, but Paul's negative reaction when Barnabas later proposed taking Mark on another trip shows that Paul saw Mark's departure as unjustified (15:37–40). Perhaps Mark was intimidated by the leaders' plan to make the dangerous trip over the Taurus Mountains to Pisidian Antioch in the interior.

Why did Paul and Barnabas target Antioch rather than more accessible coastal cities? The extended family of Sergius Paulus was prominent in Pisidian Antioch, so possibly his offer of introduction influenced their decision. This Antioch (one of sixteen named after Antiochus by his son Seleucus Nikator three centuries earlier) had become a Roman colony and therefore wielded significant political and economic influence in its area, the Phrygian region of the Roman province of Galatia, near the border with Pisidia. A sizeable Jewish community resided in Antioch as well. Antioch was strategic for reaching the interior of Asia Minor, consistent with Paul's priority of bringing the Gospel first to the Jewish Dispersion, and then to Gentiles.

Rabbinic sources show that the reading of the Law of Moses and a related text from the Prophets, together with the recitation of the 'Hear, O Israel' (*Deut.* 6:4–5) and prescribed prayers, typically opened the synagogue liturgy. Then, at the invitation of the presiding elder – only one served at a time, but the synagogue rulers who had previously held the office served as advisors – an exposition of the Scripture was given by a man in the congregation or a visiting rabbi. (Paul may have been recognized as such because of his earlier association with the Sanhedrin in Jerusalem.) The 'word of exhortation' (see also *Heb.* 13:22) was a sermon that explained the biblical text and its relevance to the congregation. Here we have our first sample of Paul's preaching, although Paul had already preached extensively (9:20–22, 28–29; 11:26; 13:1, 5, 7). It is addressed to an audience of Dispersion Jews, Gentile proselytes (converts to Judaism), and Gentile God-fearers who were on the outskirts of the Jewish community (13:16, 26, 43). Paul's sermon has affinities with Peter's Pentecost sermon, especially in the way it shows from Scripture (*Psa.* 16:10 cited in both) and eyewitness testimony that Jesus is the Messiah who fulfils God's promises to David. Like Stephen's speech (*Acts* 7) it begins with a thematic survey of Israel's history in covenant with God, although the theme emphasized by Paul (God's grace to Israel) differs from that stressed by Stephen (Israel's resistance to deliverers sent by God). Israel's history illustrated both themes, as Psalms 105 (God's grace) and 106 (Israel's rebellion) show.

The sermon is in three sections, each introduced by words of address to the listeners: *Men of Israel and you who fear God* (13:16); *Brothers, sons of the family of Abraham, and those among you who fear God* (verse 26); and *Let it be known to you therefore, brothers* (verse 38). *Section One* (verses 16–25) surveys God's generosity to Israel from the Exodus to John the Baptist, with a focus on David. *Section Two* (verse. 26–37) narrates the sufferings and resurrection of Jesus, showing from Scripture that they fulfilled the holy and sure blessings promised to David. *Section Three* (verses 38–41) draws the application, promising forgiveness and justification to all who believe, and warning against unbelief.

GOD'S GRACE IN THE HISTORY OF ISRAEL

God's grace to his people began with his choosing them – a choice, Moses emphasized, based not on their worthiness or prominence, but on his own love and faithfulness (*Deut.* 4:37; 7:6–8; 10:15; see also 9:5–6). His mercy was shown in the way he made the people great (literally, 'exalted') in Egypt; for, despite the cruel slavery to which they were subjected, their numbers multiplied (*Exod.* 1:9). Even more clearly he showed kindness by bringing Israel out of Egypt 'with uplifted arm', as Moses had reminded them (*Deut.* 4:34; 5:15; 9:26, 29).

The spelling of the key verb in verse 18 varies in the Greek manuscripts. The change of a single letter makes the difference between *'he put up with them'* (ESV) and 'he carried them gently'.

Both are true, but Paul's emphasis on God's grace and his other echoes of Deuteronomy probably tips the scales in favour of 'carried gently', drawn from Moses' reminder of God's paternal care in the desert (*Deut.* 1:31).

Dispossessing the seven nations in Canaan (see also *Deut.* 7:1), God caused Israel to inherit their land. This process – from the people's growth in Egypt, through the forty years in the wilderness, and climaxing with the conquest under Joshua – occurred over a period of approximately 450 years.

God's gifts to Israel included the judges and then, in Samuel's time, the king they requested, the Benjamite Saul, son of Kish. Paul passes over in silence Israel's repeated apostasies, which necessitated God's gift of judges, and the Lord's displeasure with Israel's request for a king (*1 Sam.* 8:7–9). His theme is God's generosity. Therefore also Saul's disobedience is left implicit in the comment that God removed him and the contrast to David, 'a man after my heart, who will do all my will'. God's testimony on behalf of David blends words from Psalm 89:20 ('I have found David my servant'), 1 Samuel 13:14 (Samuel's rebuke to Saul: 'The LORD has sought out a man after his own heart and appointed him leader'), and, surprisingly, Isaiah 44:28 (where the Lord describes King Cyrus of Persia, 'He is my shepherd and will accomplish all that I please'). In supporting the rebuilding of Israel's temple Cyrus, though a Gentile, was behaving as kings should, doing the will of the great King. The sequel to Paul's sermon will show Gentiles more eager to heed God's call than the natural children of Abraham. (Of course, neither David nor Cyrus did *all* God's will. Their description looks ahead to Jesus, whose complete obedience to God shows what human rulers should be.)

Paul's mention of David provides opportunity to introduce God's greatest gift to Israel, *the Saviour, Jesus,* descended from David, as promised in 2 Samuel 7:12. Jesus' descent from the seed of David, an essential qualification of his Messiahship, is affirmed throughout the New Testament (*Matt.* 1:1, 6, 17, *Luke* 1:32, 69, *Rom.* 1:3, *Rev.* 5:5). Paul will revisit this theme in his interlocking exposition of Psalms 2 and 16 and Isaiah 55:3 in the sermon's second section (13:32–37).

Before he sent the Saviour, God sent John to prepare the people by preaching a baptism expressive of repentance (*Luke* 3:3–14). John made clear that he himself was not the long-awaited Messiah but was preparing the way for One so exalted that John was unworthy to perform the slave's task of removing his sandals (*John* 1:19–27).

SALVATION IN THE SUFFERING AND RISEN SON

The message of salvation, which was now sent both to Abraham's biological children and to Gentile God-fearers as Abraham's spiritual children, centres on the suffering and resurrection of Jesus the Saviour, the theme of the second section. Paul made three points about Jesus' death at the hands of the people and rulers of Jerusalem:

Jesus' condemnation was motivated by culpable ignorance. The compact Greek syntax of verse 27 indicates that Jesus' persecutors were ignorant not only of his identity but also of the 'voices' (literally) of the prophets that are read each Sabbath. If they had understood the Scriptures that they heard so often, they would have recognized Jesus and 'would not have crucified the Lord of glory' (*1 Cor.* 2:8, see also *John* 5:45–47). Their ignorance was inexcusable, yet forgivable (3:17, 19, see also *1 Tim.* 1:13).

Jesus' condemnation was undeserved. Paul refers to Pilate's verdict that Jesus had committed no crime worthy of death (*Luke* 23:4), as Peter had earlier stressed (3:13). In fact, this miscarriage of justice had been perpetrated not just against one innocent of capital crime, but against the Lord's Holy One (13:35, citing *Psa.* 16:10).

Nevertheless Jesus' condemnation fulfilled the Scriptures. Although those who demanded Jesus' death did so in ignorance and injustice, their actions fulfilled God's promises spoken through the prophets. Only when all that was written about his suffering had been fulfilled was he taken down from the tree and buried. Paul's reference to the cross as the tree implies the divine curse under which Jesus died, despite his innocence (*Deut.* 21:23). That curse was rightfully ours but Jesus endured it, setting us free from it (*Gal.* 3:13, see also *Acts* 5:30; 10:39).

God would not allow the verdict of ignorant humans against Jesus to stand: he raised him from the dead, as those who had accompanied him from Galilee to Jerusalem were testifying, for he had appeared to them after his resurrection over a period of many days (see also 1:3, 21–22; 10:41). Paul bypassed mention of Jesus' appearance to himself on the road to Damascus to focus on the testimony of those who knew Jesus intimately. Just as they were bearing witness to 'the people' in Jerusalem, Judea, Samaria, and Galilee, so Paul and Barnabas were bringing to the Dispersion (and the Gentiles) this good news of God's promises fulfilled.

The resurrection marks the fulfilment of the second Psalm, in which the Christ was declared to be God's Son, enthroned on God's holy hill. At his birth, baptism, and transfiguration Jesus had been identified as God's Son (*Luke* 1:35; 3:22; 9:35). But the New Testament typically finds the fulfilment of Psalm 2:7 in Jesus' resurrection, when he had endured the rage of rebellious peoples (*Psa.* 2:1–2, cited in *Acts* 4:25–26) and was constituted the Son of God in power by his resurrection from the dead (*Rom.* 1:4). The resurrection fulfils God's promise to place David's son – who was God's Son – on David's throne forever (*2 Sam.* 7:12–14, *Heb.* 1:5, *Acts* 2:30).

Isaiah 55:3 and Psalm 16:10 share two key words, so Paul skilfully uses these verses to interpret each other: (1) '*Will give*': God, who gave so generously to Israel in the past, will give to Israel's children the blessings he had faithfully promised to David. He does so because he kept the promise of Psalm 16:10: 'You will not give (ESV: will not let) your Holy One see corruption.' Although David died and was gathered to his fathers in the grave (*1 Kings* 2:10), where his body underwent decay, his Messianic Descendant was raised the third day and did not see decay. Christ's resurrection benefited not only himself but also his people: '*you*' in verse 34 is plural, not singular. Not to Jesus alone, but to all who trust him God gives the sure and pure promises of David, as Paul has stressed (*to us* and *to you* in verses 26, 32–33, 38). (2) '*Holy*': The blessings promised to David are holy because they are bound up with God's Holy One, Jesus the Saviour, whom death could not hold, as Peter had affirmed in citing Psalm 16 at Pentecost (2:24–28). By bringing Christ up from the grave, God secured salvation for us. In Christ, the Holy One, God granted David's highest hopes to us. Do you marvel over the grace that we confess in the Nicene Creed, that the unique, eternal Son of God, very God of very God, 'for us and for our salvation' became man, suffered and died, was raised and seated at God's right hand, and will come again with glory?

THE IMPERATIVE OF FAITH

In concluding Paul again addressed his audience as 'brothers', including in this familial title not only ethnic Israelites and Gentile proselytes (13:43), but also God-fearing Gentiles who had not been circumcised. Both God's promise (verses 38–39) and his warning (verses 40–41) should move them to trust in Jesus.

Through Jesus God promises to every believer forgiveness of sins, justification from all the offences that the Law of Moses cannot clear from our record. Thus in Paul's 'inaugural' sermon (in Acts) we hear the good news of divine grace, bringing justification through faith alone – the gospel so richly revealed in Paul's epistles to the Galatians and the Romans:

'A person is not justified by works of the law, but through faith in Jesus Christ, so we also have believed in Christ Jesus, in order to be justified by faith in Christ and not by works of the law, because by works of the law no one will be justified' (*Gal.* 2:16; see also 3:8–14, *Rom.* 3:28).

'There is therefore now no condemnation for those who are in Christ Jesus. For the law of the Spirit of life has set you free in Christ Jesus from the law of sin and death. For God has done what the law, weakened by the flesh, could not do. By sending his own Son in the likeness of sinful man and for sin, he condemned sin in the flesh, in order that the righteous requirement of the law might be fulfilled in us, who walk not according to the flesh but according to the Spirit' (*Rom.* 8:1–3).

The law's holy demands were a wall that excluded Gentiles (*Eph.* 2:14–15) and a yoke that overpowered Jews (*Acts* 15:10–11), for the law was not designed to enable sinful people to rectify their relationship with God (*Gal.* 3:21). To humble faith God gives the perfect righteousness of Jesus, his Holy One.

To the gospel promise Paul added a prophetic warning from Habakkuk 1:5. The marvel that scoffers would not believe in Habakkuk's day was the desolation of Judah by Nebuchadnezzar's Babylonian army. In Paul's day the marvel was Jesus' resurrection and its implication: that Christ's death throws open heaven's gate to all who believe, Jew and Gentile alike.

THE LISTENERS' OPENNESS TO THE WORD

The general response was an eagerness to hear more on the following Sabbath. For many, both Jews and devout proselytes, the Word pierced more deeply. They *followed* Paul and Barnabas, not just physically, but in the pilgrimage of faith in Jesus. Consequently the missionaries urged these new disciples to continue in the grace of God (see also 11:23; 14:22). Our endurance in faith is not fuelled by our own will-power any more than our justification results from our own law-keeping. We continue, as we began, in the grace of God. The apostles' exhortation to perseverance would prove to be a timely precaution, as opposition from unbelieving Jews hardened in the coming week.

37

Jewish Rejection and Gentile Joy

The next Sabbath almost the whole city gathered to hear the word of the Lord. [45] But when the Jews saw the crowds, they were filled with jealousy and began to contradict what was spoken by Paul, reviling him. [46] And Paul and Barnabas spoke out boldly, saying, "It was necessary that the word of God be spoken first to you. Since you thrust it aside and judge yourselves unworthy of eternal life, behold, we are turning to the Gentiles. [47] For so the Lord has commanded us, saying,

" 'I have made you a light for the Gentiles,
that you may bring salvation to the ends of the earth.' "

[48] And when the Gentiles heard this, they began rejoicing and glorifying the word of the Lord, and as many as were appointed to eternal life believed. [49] And the word of the Lord was spreading throughout the whole region. [50] But the Jews incited the devout women of high standing and the leading men of the city, stirred up persecution against Paul and Barnabas, and drove them out of their district. [51] But they shook off the dust from their feet against them and went to Iconium.[52] And the disciples were filled with joy and with the Holy Spirit (Acts 13:44–52).

T he scene at the Antioch synagogue the following Sabbath was a replay of the gospel's encounter with Sergius Paulus and Bar-Jesus on Cyprus, but now at the community level. God-fearing Gentiles had reported to all those within their sphere of influence that Paul and Barnabas had good news of forgiveness and God's approval, to be received simply by trusting in Jesus the Saviour. As a result (Luke generalizes) almost the whole city, not only Gentiles previously attracted to Jewish monotheism but even those immersed in paganism, overran the synagogue to hear the missionaries' message. As the Jewish sorcerer Bar-Jesus tried to prevent his Gentile patron from believing the Gospel, so at Antioch unbelieving Jews sought to dissuade the curious Gentiles from embracing Paul's message. But the gospel overcame its opponents' slanders to bring salvation to all whom God had appointed for eternal life.

JEALOUSY AND JOY

The sight of the Gentile crowds gathered to hear the Lord's Word filled the majority of the Jewish community with jealousy. Luke typically identifies jealousy as the motive behind Jewish opposition to the Gospel (5:17; 17:5), while greed and civic pride prompted Gentiles to resist the faith and persecute its preachers (16:19–21; 19:24–28). Faithful Jews hoped that God–fearing Gentiles who attended synagogue services would eventually convert to Judaism, submitting to circumcision and shouldering 'the yoke of the Torah'. Now Paul and Barnabas were proclaiming that the God of Israel had sent his Messiah to bring salvation to Jew and Gentile alike, granting, by faith, a right relationship to God that could not be achieved through the Law of Moses. Of course the Jews were jealous over the Gentiles' interest in this new message!

Paul and Barnabas answered boldly that a divine necessity compelled their announcing God's saving Word to the Jews first. In other cities, they would continue to do so, mindful of God's faithful promises to the patriarchs (14:1; 17:2, *Rom.* 1:16; 15:8). Since the Jewish community at Antioch had, by and large, rejected the invitation to God's salvation feast, unconsciously judging themselves unworthy of eternal life (see also *Matt.* 22:8), God had appointed Gentiles to receive this blessed life of the age to come. As Jewish leaders were slandering God's good news, Paul and Barnabas were fulfilling the calling given to Israel through Isaiah, being *a light for the Gentiles* and bringing salvation to the ends of the earth (*Isa.* 49:6). The aged Simeon had seen in the infant Jesus 'a light for revelation to the Gentiles' as well as the glory of Israel (*Luke* 2:32). In Acts 1:8 the risen Lord alluded to Isaiah 49:6, showing his apostles that God's kingdom was bigger than their dreams for Israel. Jesus the faithful

Servant is the Lord who commissions his servants to proclaim his saving light to all peoples to the ends of the earth.

To this announcement the Gentiles responded with joy, *glorifying the word of the Lord*. Three times in this text the gospel is called *the word of the Lord* to emphasize that this saving message comes from the Lord Jesus (13:44, 48, 49; see also 4:29; 8:25; 16:32; 11:20–24). The general joy in the Gentile community bore lasting fruit only in those whom God had appointed for eternal life. The unusual word *appointed* used to express God's sovereign election (see also the more usual word in 13:17) probably evokes the metaphor of God's book of life, in which he has 'inscribed' the names of his own (*Exod.* 32:32–33, *Psa.* 69:28; 87:6, *Dan.* 12:1, *Luke* 10:20, *Rev.* 3:5; 13:8; 17:8; 20:12, 15; 21:27). When Israel rejects its Messiah, God still has his chosen ones, who will feast at his banquet table (*Luke* 14:21–24).

BANISHMENT AND JOY

As *the word of the Lord* filled Antioch and overflowed throughout the region, opposition from Jewish quarters mounted. Women belonging to the Gentile aristocracy had attached themselves to the synagogue as God-fearers and were influenced by the synagogue leadership to oppose Paul and Barnabas. Perhaps the leading men of the city who joined the opposition were their husbands. Elsewhere wealthy and God-fearing women would welcome the gospel (16:14; 17:4, 12) and the persecutors would be drawn from lower classes (17:5). Both the prominent (such as Theophilus) and the poor confront the invitation to faith and the danger of unbelief. Paul and Barnabas were banished from the environs of Antioch and moved east to Iconium, but not before shaking the city's dust from their feet as a sign of God's indictment (*Luke* 9:5, *Acts* 18:6). Jews shook dust from their feet and clothing when returning home from 'unclean' Gentile areas. Now Christ's messengers signify that unbelieving Judaism has become 'unclean' by rejecting its Messiah and his gift of forgiveness. Yet they left behind disciples filled with the joy of salvation through the presence of the Holy Spirit.

Is your joy in God's amazing grace fresh and vibrant? Does it overflow when the gospel and the Spirit draw outsiders into the family of God?

38

A City Divided

Now at Iconium they entered together into the Jewish synagogue and spoke in such a way that a great number of both Jews and Greeks believed. ² But the unbelieving Jews stirred up the Gentiles and poisoned their minds against the brothers. ³ So they remained for a long time, speaking boldly for the Lord, who bore witness to the word of his grace, granting signs and wonders to be done by their hands. ⁴ But the people of the city were divided; some sided with the Jews and some with the apostles. ⁵ When an attempt was made by both Gentiles and Jews, with their rulers, to mistreat them and to stone them, ⁶ they learned of it and fled to Lystra and Derbe, cities of Lycaonia, and to the surrounding country, ⁷ and there they continued to preach the gospel (Acts 14:1–7).

I conium lay ninety miles east of Antioch along the Roman thoroughfare that linked Ephesus in the West with Tarsus and Antioch of Syria in the East. In addition to its native Phrygians, the city had been home to Jews and Greeks since the reign of the Seleucids and attracted Roman settlers when Claudius became Emperor. Thus the gospel reached another ethnically diverse city in Galatia. Following their normal practice, Paul and Barnabas began their evangelistic ministry in the synagogue, bringing the good news to the Jews first, as well as to the Gentile God-fearers who already stood on the fringes of the covenant people.

JEWS AND GENTILES BELIEVE – AND DISBELIEVE

The brevity of Luke's summary concerning Iconium sets in sharp focus the divisive effects of the gospel, which had also surfaced at

Antioch. As many Jews and Gentile proselytes responded positively to Paul's preaching the first Sabbath in Antioch (13:43), so in Iconium a great number of Jews and Gentiles believed. As unbelieving Jews in Antioch not only opposed Paul and Barnabas themselves but also stirred up opposition from Gentile quarters (13:45, 50), so in Iconium Jews who disobeyed God's summons to repentance and faith agitated among the Gentile population and turned them not only against the apostles, but also against all the brothers who constituted this new church.

BOLD WITNESS DIVIDES THE CITY

Because of this opposition Paul and Barnabas stayed long in Iconium, grounding these persecuted believers in *the word of his grace*. Paul would later commit the Ephesian elders to the same *word of his grace*, stressing the gospel's power to protect Christians under attack, whether from without or from within (20:32). Unpopularity and persecution in themselves did not intimidate the apostles into silence or flight. On the contrary, Paul would later cite the combination of an open door for ministry with the presence of opposition as his reason for remaining in Ephesus (*1 Cor.* 16:8–9). Too often, I suspect, we use opposition as an excuse for flight rather than an encouragement to persevere where God has placed us.

Through signs and wonders the Lord added his confirming testimony to that of his servants, as he had done earlier in response to prayer (4:29–30). The result was a sharp division in the populace, with some identifying with the Jews who opposed the gospel, while others sided with the apostles. The good news always acts like a sword, dividing families and friends (*Matt.* 10:34–39). The same message of the cross that emits the fragrance of life to believers also repels unbelievers as the stench of death (*2 Cor.* 2:14–16).

CONSPIRACY AND ESCAPE

Finally the generalized hostility congealed into a conspiracy to humiliate and kill the apostles. Among the conspirators were Jews and Gentiles, as well as community leaders. Stoning was the prescribed punishment for blasphemers (*Lev.* 24:14) and would make the execution look like 'mob justice', if Roman authorities launched an inquiry.

Learning of the plot, the apostles fled south-east into Lycaonia, preaching the good news in Lystra and Derbe. They were prepared to endure opposition, arrest, mistreatment, and (if need be) death for the sake of Jesus' name, but they were not misguided masochists, trying to achieve virtue through martyrdom. As long as avoiding death furthered his mission to the nations, Paul would take steps – whether flight by night or legal appeal – to prolong his 'fruitful labour' (*Phil.* 1:22). What mattered was that Christ be glorified, whether in Paul's living or in his dying. Is that what matters above all to you?

39

The Living God Calls
Pagans to Turn Around

*Now at Lystra there was a man sitting who could not use his feet.
He was crippled from birth and had never walked. ⁹ He listened
to Paul speaking. And Paul, looking intently at him and seeing
that he had faith to be made well, ¹⁰ said in a loud voice, "Stand
upright on your feet." And he sprang up and began walking.
¹¹ And when the crowds saw what Paul had done, they lifted up
their voices, saying in Lycaonian, "The gods have come down
to us in the likeness of men!" ¹² Barnabas they called Zeus, and
Paul, Hermes, because he was the chief speaker. ¹⁴ And the priest
of Zeus, whose temple was at the entrance to the city, brought
oxen and garlands to the gates and wanted to offer sacrifice with
the crowds. ¹⁴ But when the apostles Barnabas and Paul heard
of it, they tore their garments and rushed out into the crowd,
crying out, ¹⁵ "Men, why are you doing these things? We also
are men, of like nature with you, and we bring you good news,
that you should turn from these vain things to a living God, who
made the heaven and the earth and the sea and all that is in them.
¹⁶ In past generations he allowed all the nations to walk in their
own ways. ¹⁷ Yet he did not leave himself without witness, for he
did good by giving you rains from heaven and fruitful seasons,
satisfying your hearts with food and gladness." ¹⁸ Even with these
words they scarcely restrained the people from offering sacrifice
to them.*

*¹⁹ But Jews came from Antioch and Iconium, and having
persuaded the crowds, they stoned Paul and dragged him out of
the city, supposing that he was dead. ²⁰ But when the disciples
gathered about him, he rose up and entered the city, and on the
next day he went on with Barnabas to Derbe (Acts 14:8–20).*

L ystra marked a new departure in the witness of Paul and Barnabas. Apparently there was no local synagogue, their customary starting point, in Lystra; so the apostles preached directly to pagan Gentiles who had no exposure to Judaism and the Scriptures. For those not acquainted with God's special revelation to Israel the apostles laid a foundation in the general revelation that confronts all races, showing that the Creator of all things has shown kindness through rain and harvest, food and joy. Their 'sermon' to the Lystrans was not a full gospel presentation, but an emergency address hastily spoken to forestall blasphemous idolatry. Nevertheless it anticipates the way that Paul would present the gospel in other pagan venues, moving from God's display of his power and kindness in creation and providence to the announcement of salvation and coming judgement in Christ (17:22–31, see also *Rom.* 1:18–3:26).

THE LAME LEAPS AGAIN

Luke invites us to notice the similarities between Paul's healing of the Gentile lame man at Lystra and Peter's earlier healing of a Jewish lame man outside the Temple in Jerusalem. Each had been lame from his mother's womb (ESV: *from birth*, 3:2; 14:8). On both the apostles fixed their gaze (ESV translates the same verb with *directed his gaze at* in 3:4, and *looking intently at* in 14:9). When healed through the apostles' commands, both jumped to their feet (3:8; 14:10). The observers of both miracles mistakenly attributed them to the apostles' own power, an inference that the apostles immediately repudiated.

These parallels show that Paul's outreach to Gentiles exhibited as much divinely-given authority and blessing as did Peter's ministry to the Jewish people (*Gal.* 2:7–9). The similarities also reinforce the unity of the one gospel of Jesus Christ, though preached to diverse audiences. Whether in Jerusalem or Lystra, the leaping of the lame signals the fulfilment of God's promise to open blind eyes, unstop deaf ears, cause the lame to leap like a deer, and make the mute tongue to shout for joy (*Isa.* 35:5–6, *Luke* 7:22). God's kingdom has invaded this wounded world through Jesus' Word and Spirit!

MISTAKEN FOR GODS

In astonishment the Lystrans leaped to the conclusion that two of the gods had come to them in human form. They identified Barnabas with Zeus, king of the gods, perhaps because of his age and sedate bearing. Paul, who did the talking, they took to be Hermes, the messenger of the Greek deities.

In their local Lycaonian dialect, which the apostles did not understand, the pagans discussed how best to welcome their divine visitors. They had good reason to show lavish hospitality and reverence. The Roman poet Ovid (*Metamorphoses* 8.611–724) records a legend from this region about Zeus and Hermes travelling incognito, seeking shelter, only to be refused by everyone in a particular town except an elderly couple. Philemon and his wife Baucis, despite their own poverty, hastened to meet their guests' needs. The gods, revealing their true identities, transformed the couple's humble hovel into a temple, making Philemon and Baucis its priests and caretakers. They and their house-temple were transported to a hilltop, to observe the flood that destroyed their inhospitable neighbours.

Those familiar with this local myth would believe that when Zeus and Hermes walked the earth in human form, they were to be welcomed warmly and sacrificially. No wonder the priest in charge of the temple of Zeus outside the city gates brought sacrificial bulls decked with floral garlands to slay for the gods who had made a lifelong lame man leap!

THE KINDNESS OF THE CREATOR

The appearance of the priest with the bulls revealed to the apostles what the townspeople intended to do. Tearing their clothes to express dismay over the blasphemy of worshipping mere men as gods (see also *Mark* 14:63), they rushed into the crowd, shouting their protest. They insisted that they were merely human, sharing the same emotions as their hearers. Their implication that the true God is different from his human creatures was a criticism of the Greek myths, in which the gods were portrayed as experiencing all-too-human passions, including sexual lust (Zeus supposedly fathered children by eight goddesses and fifteen human women!).

Paul and Barnabas were bringing good news from the living God. Though formerly he had let the nations go their own way, worshipping products of their own imaginations (see also *Rom.* 1:28), now he commanded them to turn from worthless idols to himself and find salvation (*Isa.* 45:22, see also *Acts* 3:19, *1 Thess.* 1:9). The apostles echoed the ancient prophets in calling pagan idols *vain things*, since such 'gods' cannot benefit their worshippers (*1 Sam.* 12:21, *Jer.* 2:5; 8:19). By contrast, the living God made heaven and earth and sea and everything in them (alluding to *Psa.* 146:6, *Exod.* 20:11, *Neh.* 9:6).

Even before sending the good news of Jesus the Saviour through Paul and Barnabas, the Creator had not left himself without a testimony addressed to all the nations. His kindness was shown in the rain that he sent, producing crops that filled human hearts with food and gladness (*Jer.* 5:24, *Psa.* 145:16, *Lev.* 26:4). Rain, sunshine, and countless other benefits which come to 'the righteous and the unrighteous' exhibit the Creator's kindness, his common grace that extends even to his enemies (*Matt.* 5:45). They therefore strip every excuse from those who foolishly persist in trusting and serving any created thing – not only graven images, but also our own academic, economic, political, or athletic resources or achievements (*Rom.* 1:20).

The immediate objective of the apostles' impromptu speech was to stop the sacrificial ritual, and this they accomplished only with difficulty. They did not introduce the specifics of Jesus' ministry, in the way that Paul when preaching in Athens would later speak of Jesus' resurrection and role as judge (17:30–31; see also verse 18). But they did announce God's call to turn from idols to himself as good news, a new phase in God's gracious dealings with the Gentiles.

THE FICKLE CROWD

The Jewish communities of Antioch and Iconium, fuelled by the same misguided zeal that had once driven Saul's own wide-ranging war on the church, reached Lystra for the purpose of turning these fickle pagans against Paul and Barnabas, whom they had hailed as gods. The plot that had been frustrated at Iconium succeeded at Lystra. Having stoned Paul, they dragged his dead (as they thought) body outside the city to be exposed to the elements and scavengers (see also *Mark* 12:8).

A group of Christian disciples had been gathered by the gospel, however. As they encircled Paul's body (in grief? in prayer?), Paul revived. The apostle would list this stoning among his apostolic credentials (*2 Cor.* 11:25), and would remind Timothy, a native of Lystra, that he had witnessed Paul's sufferings in this region (*2 Tim.* 3:11, see also *Acts* 16:1). Perhaps the experience of standing over the apostle's bruised and bloodied body as a young Christian helped to forge Timothy (despite his timidity) into Paul's trusted 'son' and co–worker in the gospel (*Phil.* 2:19–23, *1 Tim.* 1:18, *2 Tim.* 1:6–8, 12). For many of us the cost of faithfulness to the gospel is far less than this. Are we ready to pay it?

40

Mission Accomplished!

*When they had preached the gospel to that city [Derbe] and had
made many disciples, they returned to Lystra and to Iconium
and to Antioch, ²² strengthening the souls of the disciples,
encouraging them to continue in the faith, and saying that
through many tribulations we must enter the kingdom of God.
²³ And when they had appointed elders for them in every church,
with prayer and fasting they committed them to the Lord in whom
they had believed.
²⁴ Then they passed through Pisidia and came to Pamphylia.
²⁵ And when they had spoken the word in Perga, they went down
to Attalia, ²⁶ and from there they sailed to Antioch, where they
had been commended to the grace of God for the work that they
had fulfilled. ²⁷ And when they arrived and gathered the church
together, they declared all that God had done with them, and
how he had opened a door of faith to the Gentiles. ²⁸ And they
remained no little time with the disciples* (Acts 14:21–28).

S till aching from his stoning the day before, Paul left with
Barnabas for Derbe, sixty miles south-east of Lystra. There they
made many disciples – using the verb in Jesus' Great Commission:
'make disciples of all nations' (*Matt.* 28:19; see also 13:52; 27:57).
Becoming a Christian entails a radical shift of allegiance to learn from
and follow Jesus, whatever the cost (*Luke* 14:27).

STRENGTHENING THE SAINTS
From Derbe the shortest, easiest, and safest route back to Antioch
in Syria would have been the well-paved Roman road east through

Tarsus, Paul's home town in Cilicia. To travel westward instead, retracing their steps through Lystra and Iconium to Pisidian Antioch, meant revisiting sites where Paul and Barnabas had been threatened or attacked. Then they would again face the arduous trek over the Taurus Mountains to Perga in Pamphylia and its seaport, Attalia, to catch a ship to Syria.

Yet a consideration more pressing than travel convenience drove the apostles' decision to revisit these cities: each was now an outpost of the coming kingdom of God, for in each a group of Jesus' disciples, newborn in the faith, were gathering. Instead of counting converts, the apostles sought to establish churches, so they returned to *'strengthen the souls of the disciples'*. As Barnabas had encouraged the new church in Syrian Antioch to persevere in faith (11:23), so the apostles did now for the churches of Galatia. Return visits to strengthen new believers would be a recurring pattern in Paul's ministry (15:41; 18:23; see also 16:5).

It might seem strange that the apostles' encouragement addressed the harsh reality of persecution: '*Through many tribulations we must enter the kingdom of God.*' Yet Christian hope does not deny the sufferings of this present age, which are often increased by the world's hostility to Christ and his followers. Paul would later urge the Christians of Thessalonica not to be unsettled by trials: 'You yourselves know that we are destined for this. For when we were with you, we kept telling you beforehand that we were to suffer affliction' (*1 Thess.* 3:3–4). Yet the hope of the gospel puts present troubles into perspective as insignificant when compared to the glory to be revealed to us when God's kingdom arrives in its fullness (*Rom.* 8:18).

In addition to offering personal encouragement, the apostles provided for ongoing stability and growth by appointing several elders in each church. In established congregations leaders were identified through the discernment of all the members (6:3), but for these young churches the apostles themselves designated men of spiritual maturity and wisdom as leaders (20:28). Since the Exodus, elders had provided wise leadership, first in Israel's wilderness encampment and later in its settled cities (*Exod.* 3:16; 18:13–26, *Num.* 11:24–30, *Deut.* 1:9–18; see also 19:12; 21:3–9). The church in Jerusalem was led by elders from very early on (*Acts* 11:30). Paul would later instruct his associates regarding the qualities to be sought in elders (also called overseers or bishops) (*1 Tim.* 3:1–7, *Titus* 1:5–9). The mutual accountability of a plurality of elders safeguards both the flock and its shepherds (20:28–31), but ultimately the apostles placed their converts into stronger, surer hands, entrusting them to the Lord, in whom they had put their trust.

REPORTING GOD'S GREAT WORK

Paul and Barnabas knew how meaningful it was to commit these churches to the Lord, for when they began their journey the church of Syrian Antioch had committed them to the grace of God for the work they had now fulfilled. The repetition of *work*, from the Holy Spirit's original call to them (13:2), closes this section as it began, with Paul and Barnabas in Antioch, reporting all that God had accomplished as he had opened the door of faith so that Gentiles could enter his kingdom. (On the 'opened door' metaphor, see *1 Cor.* 16:9, *2 Cor.* 2:12, *Col.* 4:3.) When Peter had reported what God did in Cornelius' house, the church marvelled that God had given repentance even to Gentiles (*Acts* 11:18). Here the same sovereign initiative is described in terms of faith.

We who believe from among the world's nations should give constant thanks to the gracious God who opened the door of faith to us, and strengthens our souls through the shepherds he provides.

41

Not Circumcision, But Faith

But some men came down from Judea and were teaching the brothers, "Unless you are circumcised according to the custom of Moses, you cannot be saved." ² *And after Paul and Barnabas had no small dissension and debate with them, Paul and Barnabas and some of the others were appointed to go up to Jerusalem to the apostles and the elders about this question.* ³ *So, being sent on their way by the church, they passed through both Phoenicia and Samaria, describing in detail the conversion of the Gentiles, and brought great joy to all the brothers.* ⁴ *When they came to Jerusalem, they were welcomed by the church and the apostles and the elders, and they declared all that God had done with them.* ⁵ *But some believers who belonged to the party of the Pharisees rose up and said, "It is necessary to circumcise them and to order them to keep the law of Moses."*

⁶ *The apostles and the elders were gathered together to consider this matter.* ⁷ *And after there had been much debate, Peter stood up and said to them, "Brothers, you know that in the early days God made a choice among you, that by my mouth the Gentiles should hear the word of the gospel and believe.* ⁸ *And God, who knows the heart, bore witness to them, by giving them the Holy Spirit just as he did to us,* ⁹ *and he made no distinction between us and them, having cleansed their hearts by faith.* ¹⁰ *Now, therefore, why are you putting God to the test by placing a yoke on the neck of the disciples that neither our fathers nor we have been able to bear?* ¹¹ *But we believe that we will be saved through the grace of the Lord Jesus, just as they will"* (Acts 15:1–11).

God's abundant blessing on the mission to the Gentiles and the controversy it provoked stand at the central point of Acts, the theological watershed in the gospel's advance 'to the end of the earth.' The resolution of the conflict by the apostles and elders of the church in Jerusalem would recognize indisputably that God had opened wide the door to salvation, welcoming all people to enter by faith in 'the grace of the Lord Jesus'.

In 'ancient days' (ESV: *in the early days*, 15:7), when Cornelius and his friends believed and received the Spirit, Peter's report to the Jerusalem church had silenced opposition to his fellowship with Gentiles. Since then the aggressive cross-cultural witness of the church in Syrian Antioch and of its emissaries among the Gentiles of Phrygia and Lycaonia made it clear that the reception of Gentiles apart from circumcision was no longer the exception but the rule. This trend alarmed those who, believing that Jesus was Messiah, still treasured Israel's covenantal distinctives. They pressed their objection to Paul's grace- and faith-based, circumcision-free gospel, first at Antioch and then at Jerusalem.

THE CONFLICT OVER THE GENTILES

Long before Moses received the Law at Sinai, God had set apart his people by circumcision, an 'everlasting covenant' in the flesh of Abraham and his sons (*Gen.* 17:7). Although Jesus had extended grace to individual Gentiles, he never spoke of abolishing circumcision as the sign that sets the heirs of God's promises apart from others. It is not surprising, then, that despite the Cornelius incident some Jewish Christians continued to insist that the Gentiles who were pouring into the church had to be circumcised as proselytes to Judaism would be, in order to share in the salvation promised to Abraham and fulfilled in the Messiah.

When some holding this view arrived at Antioch from Judea and began to teach that Gentile believers must be circumcised, Paul and Barnabas strongly disputed their claim. The issue was so significant and the opposing views so irreconcilable that appeal was made outside the Antioch congregation to the authority and wisdom residing in the apostles and elders of the mother church in Jerusalem. This appeal shows the close relationship of congregations in the early church, functioning not as autonomous units but as parts of an interconnected whole, though separated by distance and ethnicity. This interconnection is further seen in the fact that the decision reached at Jerusalem would be binding not only at Antioch but also in the churches of Galatia (16:4).

Paul and Barnabas, with other delegates, were *sent on their way* (that is, their travel expenses were funded) by the church. As they travelled south through Phoenicia and Samaria, the apostles reported how God had converted the Gentiles to himself (see also 3:19; 14:15; 15:19; 26:18; *Isa.* 45:22). Their report occasioned great joy, as the Gentiles themselves had rejoiced upon hearing that God had sent his light to them (13:48). Jesus himself, when criticized for consorting with the unworthy, taught that those attuned to the Father's gracious heart always rejoice when the lost are found – and the more lost, the better, for in retrieving them his grace shines most brightly (*Luke* 15:7, 10, 32).

When they reached Jerusalem, Paul and Barnabas received a warm welcome from the church and its leaders, to whom they reported all that God had done through them to draw in the Gentiles. Both here and in Acts 14:27 the text reads '*All that God had done with them*', implying their privilege as God's co–workers (*1 Cor.* 3:9). Nevertheless the controversy over the Gentiles' status immediately flared up in Jerusalem, stirred up by believers belonging to the party of the Pharisees, who showed their separateness from Gentiles and non–observant Jews by rigorously adhering to rabbinical tradition.

THE COUNCIL OF APOSTLES AND ELDERS

The question before the council was how the Gentiles could receive salvation, entering the community that inherits God's promises. The Holy Spirit's answer (15:28) came not through a new word of revelation delivered by prophet or apostle, but through much discussion, brought to a conclusion by three speeches.

(1) Peter retold his experience as the apostle through whom God first evangelized uncircumcised Gentiles.

(2) Paul and Barnabas reported God's work among the Gentiles through them.

(3) James interpreted these events in the light of the Scriptures.

Although apostles participated, they did so not as announcers of new revelation but as fellow elders who shared responsibility for God's flock (see also *1 Pet.* 5:1). In other words, the deliberative process followed by this council – interpreting the church's experience in the light of Scripture – was the same as that employed by 'ordinary' pastors and elders in later generations.

Peter's speech reminded the group that God's sovereign choice, not Peter's own initiative, led to his preaching the gospel to the Gentiles gathered by Cornelius (10:1–11:18). Three times he mentions the *faith* that constitutes the real boundary between alienation and salvation: (1) When Peter preached, the Gentiles believed (15:7); (2) God purified their hearts by faith (verse 9); and (3) through the grace of the Lord Jesus Jewish Christians are saved by believing, just as the Gentiles are (verse 11).

Jesus had warned money-loving Pharisees that external compliance without inward devotion does not impress God, who knows hearts (*Luke* 16:15; see also 18:9–14). Now Peter drew the corollary: a person's external defilement does not prevent the heart–knowing God from imparting inward purity through humble faith. God testified to his acceptance of the Gentiles by the gift of his Holy Spirit – just as he had done for Peter and other Jewish believers on the day of Pentecost! In words that Paul would later echo, Peter affirmed that God makes no distinction between Jew and Gentile in his way of salvation through faith alone, by grace alone (see also *Rom.* 3:22–24; 10:12).

Peter turned the tables on the opponents of grace, charging them with the classic sin that brought Israel's wilderness generation to their desert graves: 'Why are putting God to the test?' (*Exod.* 17:2, 7, *Num.* 14:22, *Deut.* 6:16, *Psa.* 78:18, 41, 56, see also *Acts* 5:9). Now that God's better way of simple faith is fully revealed in Jesus, to lay the yoke of the Law, which the rabbis lauded as Israel's glory, on Gentile necks is like longing for the 'security' of Egyptian slavery. In fact, submission to the Law for acceptance with God was an unbearable yoke of slavery for Jew and Gentile alike (*Gal.* 5:1). For all their external compliance, no Israelite could bear the weight of the Law's heart-searching demand for absolute loyalty to the Lord of the covenant. The only yoke that fallen folk of any race can bear is the yoke of Jesus, made light because he bore the Law's demand for holy righteousness, inside and out, in our place (*Matt.* 11:30, *Rom.* 10:3–4, *Phil.* 3:6–9).

Peter's gospel is identical to Paul's: the righteousness that no one can achieve through law–keeping, Jesus gives through faith (*Acts* 13:38–39, *Gal.* 2:15–16). Have you abandoned your futile attempt to earn God's approval, bowing to his humbling mercy?

42

James Cites Prophecies of the Gentiles' Inclusion

And all the assembly fell silent, and they listened to Barnabas and Paul as they related what signs and wonders God had done through them among the Gentiles. ¹³ After they finished speaking, James replied, "Brothers, listen to me. ¹⁴ Simeon has related how God first visited the Gentiles, to take from them a people for his name. ¹⁵ And with this the words of the prophets agree, just as it is written,

¹⁶ " 'After this I will return,
and I will rebuild the tent of David that has fallen;
I will rebuild its ruins,
and I will restore it,
¹⁷ that the remnant of mankind may seek the Lord,
and all the Gentiles who are called by my name,
says the Lord, who makes these things
¹⁸ known from of old.'

¹⁹ Therefore my judgement is that we should not trouble those of the Gentiles who turn to God, ²⁰ but should write to them to abstain from the things polluted by idols, and from sexual immorality, and from what has been strangled, and from blood. ²¹ For from ancient generations Moses has had in every city those who proclaim him, for he is read every Sabbath in the synagogues" (Acts 15:12–21).

P eter's reminder of what God had done through him to evangelize the Gentiles, together with his conclusion that Jew and Gentile alike depend wholly on the grace of God, silenced the critics, as his original report had done (see also 11:18). The calm in the council provided Barnabas and Saul an opportunity to enter as evidence the miracles by which God had signified his purpose to welcome Gentiles without imposing circumcision on them. Barnabas is named first again, for the first time since they ministered on Cyprus. Perhaps because of the honour accorded him by the apostles (4:36–37; 11:22–24), it was prudent for him to take the lead in presenting the evidence of God's grace to the Gentiles. Luke briefly summarizes the missionaries' report to show that what turned the tide of debate was not merely an appeal to experience, but the interpretation of that experience in the light of God's Word. James would offer that interpretation.

A PEOPLE FOR GOD'S NAME

This James was first mentioned as a church leader in Acts 12:17, after the martyrdom of the Apostle James (12:2). He is James 'the Lord's brother', with whom Paul met when he returned to Jerusalem as a Christian (*Gal.* 1:19) and who was recognized as a 'pillar' of the mother church along with Peter and John (*Gal.* 2:9). Although Jesus' brothers did not believe in him during his earthly ministry (*John* 6:5), after his resurrection Jesus appeared to James (*1 Cor.* 15:7). The linguistic similarities between the Epistle of James and this speech of James and the council's letter, which is derived from it, confirm that he is that epistle's author (compare *Acts* 15:13 with *James* 2:5, 15:14 with *James* 1:27, 15:17 with *James* 2:7, 15:23 with *James* 1:1).

James tied God's present welcome of the Gentiles to Old Testament hope and promise. Simeon (the Hebrew form of Simon) had narrated how God *visited the Gentiles* to gather from them a people for his name. In biblical history, when God '*visits*', he intervenes to save his people and judge their enemies (*Exod.* 3:16; 4:31, *Luke* 1:68; 7:16). In the past the Gentiles were the enemies to be judged, but now God was fulfilling Zechariah 2:11, to which James alluded: 'Many nations (Gentiles) will be joined with the LORD in that day and will become my people.'

James quoted 'the words of the prophets' from Amos 9:11–12, weaving in words from Jeremiah 12:15 (*I will return*) at the beginning, and Isaiah 45:11 (*known from of old*) at the end. In Amos' prophecy the dynasty of David is portrayed as a collapsed tent. The exile to Babylon and subsequent subjugation of Judah made the everlasting 'house' that God had built for David look like a heap of ruins (*2 Sam.* 7:11–16, see also *Psa.* 89). But the resurrection of Jesus, the son of David, meant the restoration of Davidic dominion over the Gentiles.

The Hebrew text, reflected in our English versions of Amos, speaks of David's descendants possessing the remnant of Edom, representative of Gentile nations that previously harassed Israel. The Greek Septuagint, quoted in Acts, speaks of *the remnant of men* (*Adam*, 'mankind', differs from *Edom* only in vowel points) seeking the Lord (the Hebrew verbs *possess* and *seek* are spelled almost identically). Perhaps the Septuagint translators worked from a different Hebrew text.

Despite these variations, James' purpose for citing Amos 9:11–12 is found in both versions: the restoration of David's dynasty in the Messiah marks the point when the Gentiles bear the Lord's name – literally, his name is 'called over them', claiming them as 'a people for his name', as James had said in his opening. The closing words from Isaiah 45:21 stress that God planned long ago to include the Gentiles (see *Gen.* 12:3). Now he issues a worldwide invitation: 'Turn to me and be saved, all the ends of the earth; for I am God, and there is no other' (*Isa.* 45:22).

NO BURDEN FOR THE GENTILES

Since God was fulfilling his promise to place his name on the Gentiles, James fully concurred with Peter's refusal to impose the yoke of the Law on them. The council, in turn, would agree with James.

James did recommend that the Gentiles be advised to abstain from four defiling practices: food polluted by idols, sexual immorality, the meat of strangled animals, and blood (repeated in Acts 15:29; 21:25). Neither James nor Paul nor the Gentile Christians viewed these guidelines as demanding law observance in order to join the church that Jesus saves. Rather, these stipulations were greeted with joy by the Gentiles (15:31) and carried by Paul well beyond Antioch (16:4).

Scholars disagree regarding the meaning and rationale of these prohibitions. Some believe that the practices to be avoided are drawn from holiness regulations in Leviticus 17–18, which applied to Israelite and resident alien alike (*Lev.* 17:8). Thus the rationale would be to advise Gentiles to exercise their Christian liberty prudently, in ways that would not hinder their fellowship with Jewish believers. The Leviticus laws forbade sacrifices elsewhere than at the Lord's sanctuary (= idolatry) (17:8–9), eating blood (17:10–12), eating meat from which the blood had not been drained (= strangled animals) (17:13–14), and incest and other forms of sexual impurity (18:6–20). Yet nowhere in the New Testament is sexual practice treated as morally and spiritually 'indifferent', falling within the sphere of one's liberty in Christ. More likely is the view that these four practices together constituted a complex of pagan, idolatrous worship in which Gentiles who trust in Jesus must no longer participate. Paul would tell the Corinthians that, while eating meat once offered to an idol in one's home does not defile, participating in feasts at idols' temples was a different matter (*1 Cor.* 8–10). Idolatry and sexual immorality were often intertwined (*1 Cor.* 10:7–8). Pagan sacrificial ritual included strangling victims (to 'capture' their life-breath) and drinking their blood (to absorb their vital power).

James urged the council to clarify for the Gentiles precisely what Paul was eager to stress to his converts: To become Christians, Gentiles need not become Jews, but they cannot remain pagans! We must flee sexual immorality and idolatry, for we are not our own, but belong to a new Master (*1 Cor.* 6:18–20; 10:14, see also *1 Thess.* 1:9; 4:1–9). The purity of our Saviour reflected in our lives should be a winsome witness to those who hear Moses read in synagogues each Sabbath (*Acts* 15:21), as well as to others who long for integrity in our increasingly-paganizing culture.

43

Encouragement for the Gentiles

Then it seemed good to the apostles and the elders, with the whole church, to choose men from among them and send them to Antioch with Paul and Barnabas. They sent Judas called Barsabbas, and Silas, leading men among the brothers, [23] *with the following letter: "The brothers, both the apostles and the elders, to the brothers who are of the Gentiles in Antioch and Syria and Cilicia, greetings.* [24] *Since we have heard that some persons have gone out from us and troubled you with words, unsettling your minds, although we gave them no instructions,* [25] *it has seemed good to us, having come to one accord, to choose men and send them to you with our beloved Barnabas and Paul,* [26] *men who have risked their lives for the sake of our Lord Jesus Christ.* [27] *We have therefore sent Judas and Silas, who themselves will tell you the same things by word of mouth.* [28] *For it has seemed good to the Holy Spirit and to us to lay on you no greater burden than these requirements:* [29] *that you abstain from what has been sacrificed to idols, and from blood, and from what has been strangled, and from sexual immorality. If you keep yourselves from these, you will do well. Farewell."*

[30] *So when they were sent off, they went down to Antioch, and having gathered the congregation together, they delivered the letter.* [31] *And when they had read it, they rejoiced because of its encouragement.* [32] *And Judas and Silas, who were themselves prophets, encouraged and strengthened the brothers with many words.* [33] *And after they had spent some time, they were sent off in peace by the brothers to those who had sent them.*

[34-35] *But Paul and Barnabas remained in Antioch, teaching and preaching the word of the Lord, with many others also* (Acts 15:22–35).

James's conclusion clinched the argument that the Holy Spirit had been building through Peter's remarks and the report brought by Barnabas and Saul: circumcision must not be imposed on the Gentiles as a condition of salvation, but the Gentiles must refrain from the defiling practices of pagan worship to signal their allegiance to Jesus and to quell slander of his Name by Jews, who were steeped in the Law. The council would communicate this decision not only by letter but also in the person of two of its respected leaders, Judas (called Barsabbas) and Silas. The latter was to become Paul's colleague in future ministry (15:40, *1 Thess.* 1:1, *2 Thess.* 1:1, *2 Cor.* 1:19, see also *1 Pet.* 5:12).

THE ENCOURAGING LETTER

The letter exhibits the great pastoral wisdom of the apostles and elders not only in the decision they reached but also in the way they communicated it. Its greeting reassures the Gentile Christians of their secure status in the family of God. Then the council repudiates those Judean teachers whose insistence on circumcision had distressed and confused Gentile believers. In contrast to those troublemakers, the council expresses its solidarity with Barnabas and Paul. Finally, the letter summarizes the council's decision itself.

The Gentile believers' place in the family of God is indicated in the twofold use of *brothers*, one for the letter's authors, the other for its recipients. As Jews addressed fellow-Jews as 'brothers' because of their shared ancestor Abraham (see also *Acts* 2:29, 37; 3:17; 7:2), so the leaders of the Jerusalem church embraced believing Gentiles as brothers united in Christ, through whom they had become Abraham's seed and heirs by faith (*Gal.* 3:29; *Rom.* 4:11). The letter addresses Christians not only in Antioch but also in Syria, the Roman province of which Antioch was capital, and Cilicia, the north-west region of the same province. Its contents applied to Gentile churches elsewhere as well (16:4).

In explaining the rationale for the letter the council addressed the issue of leadership, legitimate and illegitimate. The Judean teachers who had disrupted the church at Antioch with their demand that Gentiles be circumcised (15:1) had no authorization from the apostles or elders in Jerusalem. The council strongly disavowed their teaching, describing its effects with two pejorative verbs, disturbed and troubling, one of which Paul applied to Judaizers among the Galatian churches (*Gal.* 1:7; 5:10). On the other hand, the letter commended Barnabas and Saul, well known to believers in Antioch, whom the apostles and elders called affectionately 'our beloved' and commended for their costly devotion to the Name of Jesus.

Because Paul recognized that the credibility of his gospel was intertwined with his credibility as its messenger, he took pains to defend his apostolic calling and conduct (*Gal.* 1:11–2:16, *2 Cor.* 1:12–6:12). Similarly, the council affirmed Barnabas and Paul as respected co-workers, in preparation for announcing its agreement with their understanding of the gospel and its implications for Gentiles. Moreover, along with these missionaries the council had sent Judas and Silas, who would confirm orally the letter's encouraging message.

Finally, the letter announced the decision that the council reached through deliberation. This deliberation is implied by *it has seemed good . . . to us* (15:28), repeating a Greek verb used earlier in verses 22 and 25. Their unanimity is expressed in verse 25 with a Greek adverb meaning *'with one accord'* (see also 1:14; 2:46; 4:24; 18:12). In this unanimity they recognized God's direction of his church: this is no mere human verdict, but rather *it seemed good to the Holy Spirit.* The decision was not to burden the Gentiles with the requirement of circumcision and the Law's other ceremonial regulations, but only to insist on their dissociation from pagan worship, represented by the four elements previously listed by James, with a slight variation of terminology and order. James spoke first of two general categories, the 'pollutions' of idols and sexual immorality, then of two particular practices entailed in pagan sacrificial rituals, ingesting strangled animals and blood. The letter groups the three sacrificial terms together – what has been sacrificed to idols, blood, strangled animals – and concludes with the sexual perversions practised in pagan worship. Gentiles need not become Jews, but they must cease being pagans when they come under Christ's lordship.

THE ENCOURAGING LEADERS

When the delegation reached Antioch and delivered the letter, its reading evoked joy in the Gentiles, whose standing by faith in the grace of God was clearly affirmed. The letter brought encouragement in two senses:

(1) It comforted Gentile hearts with the assurance that the Father had welcomed them by faith alone; and
(2) it exhorted (the Greek verb often includes this sense) them to demonstrate the reality of their faith by shunning the idol temples (as Paul would exhort the Corinthians, *1 Cor.* 10:14–22).

Judas and Silas, who were not only elders but also prophets, personally reinforced the letter's encouragement through their own preaching and teaching, strengthening their Gentile brothers in Christ. Faithful pastors know our constant need as believers to have our hearts strengthened through the gospel of grace (see also 14:22; 15:41; 18:23, *Heb.* 13:9). Even after Judas and Silas returned to Jerusalem, Paul and Barnabas remained in Antioch, where they spoke the good news contained in the Lord's Word (the word *preached* represents the Greek 'evangelized, spoke good news'). The power for the growth of the church is the Word of the Lord, applied by the heart-changing Spirit of God.

[Verse 34, which appears in the KJV, states that Silas remained in Antioch. It is absent from the oldest manuscripts and has been thought by some to be a later copyist's attempt to explain how Silas became Paul's partner (verse 40).]

44

A Traumatic Argument

And after some days Paul said to Barnabas, "Let us return and visit the brothers in every city where we proclaimed the word of the Lord, and see how they are." ³⁷ Now Barnabas wanted to take with them John called Mark. ³⁸ But Paul thought best not to take with them one who had withdrawn from them in Pamphylia and had not gone with them to the work. ³⁹ And there arose a sharp disagreement, so that they separated from each other. Barnabas took Mark with him and sailed away to Cyprus, ⁴⁰ but Paul chose Silas and departed, having been commended by the brothers to the grace of the Lord. ⁴¹ And he went through Syria and Cilicia, strengthening the churches (Acts 15:36–41).

God is a realist, and calls his people to be realistic about their own flaws. In the aftermath of fruitful ministry, we sometimes stumble over our own shortcomings, as Elijah wallowed in self-pity after the great triumph over Baal at Mount Carmel (*1 Kings* 18 – 19). Thus we rediscover that the gospel advances and the church grows not through our power or piety, but through the name of Jesus (3:12, 16). So it was that Paul and Barnabas having stood together to face persecution from without and opposition from within the church, having seen the joyful resolution of the controversy over their Gentile converts, and having carried on further fruitful evangelism at Antioch, so bitterly disagreed that their collaboration in ministry was shattered. Paul will occupy centre stage throughout the rest of the book of Acts, but he is not the hero of the story. The risen Lord Jesus is.

The argument began with a pastoral proposal from Paul, with which Barnabas readily concurred: they would retrace their steps through Cyprus and Galatia, visiting the churches planted on the earlier trip to observe their progress and deepen the disciples' faith. Barnabas proposed reuniting their original team by inviting his cousin John Mark, who had been their assistant in Cyprus but abandoned the project in Pamphylia, before the inland trek over the Taurus Mountains (13:5, 13).

Paul's negative reaction was immediate and adamant. Both the Greek word order and the vocabulary of Acts 15:38 reflect his strong refusal to take Mark again. The description of Mark as *'one who had withdrawn from them . . . and had not gone with them to the work'* appears early in the sentence for emphasis. The verb *withdrawn from* is more negative than the verb describing his departure in 13:13; in fact, the verb used here sometimes refers to apostasy (*Luke* 8:13, *Heb.* 3:12). Finally, the mention of the *work* recalls the start and conclusion of that great enterprise of evangelizing Gentiles in Cyprus and Galatia (13:2; 14:26). Such instability, Paul believed, disqualified Mark from participating in a second mission.

Barnabas was equally convinced that his cousin should have another opportunity to prove himself faithful. This was characteristic of this 'son of encouragement' who risked acquaintance with Saul, once a violent persecutor, and later invited him into a shared ministry (9:26–27; 11:25–26). Yet their *sharp disagreement* generated heated emotions (see the related verb in *Acts* 17:16 and *1 Cor.* 13:5) and divided the former co-workers.

Luke's sparse account invites commentators to speculate about other sources of irritation (*Gal.* 2:13), to try to apportion blame, or even to excuse the rift as resulting from inevitable, legitimate differences in priorities. Luke, however, has shown how believers and their leaders can resolve conflicts, maintaining the unity of the Spirit (6:1–7; 15:1–29). Wherever the responsibility for the breakdown lay, this breach between brothers was inexcusable. Barnabas' mentoring of Mark eventually restored Paul's confidence (*Col.* 4:10, *2 Tim.* 4:11, *Philem.* 24); but that is not to say that Paul was wrong to consider Mark unprepared for the rigours of mission so soon after his failure.

Without justifying either disputant, Luke shows how the sovereign God advances his kingdom through his flawed servants. God doubled his work force as Barnabas and Mark set sail for Cyprus, while Paul enlisted the Judean prophet Silas and took the overland route to the north-west, visiting the churches of Syria and Cilicia. That God uses sinful servants never excuses our sin, but it always glorifies his grace

45

The Gospel Crosses the Aegean

Paul came also to Derbe and to Lystra. A disciple was there, named Timothy, the son of a Jewish woman who was a believer, but his father was a Greek. ² He was well spoken of by the brothers at Lystra and Iconium. ³ Paul wanted Timothy to accompany him, and he took him and circumcised him because of the Jews who were in those places, for they all knew that his father was a Greek. ⁴ As they went on their way through the cities, they delivered to them for observance the decisions that had been reached by the apostles and elders who were in Jerusalem. ⁵ So the churches were strengthened in the faith, and they increased in numbers daily.

⁶ And they went through the region of Phrygia and Galatia, having been forbidden by the Holy Spirit to speak the word in Asia. ⁷ And when they had come up to Mysia, they attempted to go into Bithynia, but the Spirit of Jesus did not allow them. ⁸ So, passing by Mysia, they went down to Troas. ⁹ And a vision appeared to Paul in the night: a man of Macedonia was standing there, urging him and saying, "Come over to Macedonia and help us." ¹⁰ And when Paul had seen the vision, immediately we sought to go on into Macedonia, concluding that God had called us to preach the gospel to them.

¹¹ So, setting sail from Troas, we made a direct voyage to Samothrace, and the following day to Neapolis, ¹² and from there to Philippi, which is a leading city of the district of Macedonia and a Roman colony. We remained in this city some days. ¹³ And on the Sabbath day we went outside the gate to the riverside, where we supposed there was a place of prayer, and we sat down and spoke to the women who had come together. ¹⁴ One who heard *us was a woman named Lydia, from the city of Thyatira, a seller of purple goods, who was a worshipper of God. The Lord opened her heart to pay attention to what was said by Paul. ¹⁵ And after she was baptized, and her household as well, she urged us, saying, "If you have judged me to be faithful to the Lord, come to my house and stay." And she prevailed upon us* (Acts 16:1–15).

Paul's intention for this second trip into Asia Minor was to strengthen churches established on his first journey, but God had a more extensive mission planned. Paul and Silas revisited the churches of Galatia, picking up en route a helper to replace John Mark. Having accomplished their original objective, they wanted to move into the province of Asia or into Bithynia, but the Spirit of God vetoed both initiatives. Instead the Lord directed their steps to Troas, a northern port on the Aegean Sea. There God sent Paul a night vision that explained the closed doors to Asia and Bithynia: Macedonia, across the Aegean Sea, needed the good news about Jesus.

A NEW HELPER AT LYSTRA

Paul and Silas walked north-west through the Cilician Gates, a pass through the Taurus Mountains, eventually reaching Derbe and Lystra. Luke's Greek highlights the new co-worker they discovered there: 'And behold! A certain disciple was there, by name Timothy.' Timothy would become the helper that John Mark had failed to be. In fact, Timothy would become much more: Paul's 'true child in the faith' (*1 Tim.* 1:2, see also *2 Tim.* 1:2). Despite recurring illness and his natural timidity, Timothy consistently put others' needs above his own (*1 Tim.* 5:23, *2 Tim.* 1:7–8, *Phil.* 2:19–23). Paul would even identify Timothy with himself in the authorship of his epistles (*2 Cor.* 1:1, *Phil.* 1:1, *Col.* 1:1, *1 Thess.* 1:1 [with Silas], *2 Thess.* 1:1 [with Silas], *Philem.* 1). The fact that believers both in Lystra and in nearby Iconium vouched for Timothy's maturity convinced Paul that Timothy must be added to his team.

Timothy's status with respect to Judaism was irregular, however. His mother was a Jewish Christian, but his father had been Greek. Rabbis discouraged such mixed marriages, but when they occurred, the children of a Jewish mother were considered Jewish, belonging to God's covenant (see also *1 Cor.* 7:14 regarding children of Christian/pagan marriages). Although his mother Eunice taught him the Scriptures from infancy, Timothy's Gentile father had forbidden his circumcision (*2 Tim.* 1:5; 3:15). Knowing Timothy's Gentile paternity and uncircumcised status, local Jews would regard him as an uncircumcised Jew, in violation of the Abrahamic covenant (*Gen.* 17:14). His presence on Paul's and Silas' team would hinder outreach to the synagogues, among whom Paul was always willing to live as a Jew, observing the Law, in order to win the Jews (*1 Cor.* 9:20). So Paul, although adamantly against any attempt to impose circumcision on Gentile believers, circumcised Timothy to clarify the latter's status as a Jewish Christian. Just as Gentiles need not become Jews, so Jews do not have to act like Gentiles to belong to Jesus the Messiah. The rumour that Paul discouraged Jews from circumcising their sons was false (*Acts* 21:21). More importantly, for Paul the advance of the gospel outweighed personal comfort. Does it for you?

The decisions reached by the apostles and elders in Jerusalem impacted the advance of the Gospel, safeguarding Gentile freedom from circumcision but also summoning Gentiles to single–minded allegiance to Christ. Therefore Paul and Silas (one of the council's delegates) communicated these decisions to the Galatian churches, as they had in Syria and Cilicia. Thus Paul strengthened his Gentile brothers' faith as he had planned (see also 14:22; 15:41), and the churches' spiritual vitality bore fruit in numerical expansion. The Galatian churches' daily growth reproduced the earlier pattern in Jerusalem and Syrian Antioch (2:47; 4:4; 5:14; 6:7; 11:21).

A CRY FOR HELP AT TROAS

Paul had taken the initiative to strengthen the churches of south Galatia, fulfilling his responsibility as a servant of the gospel. The next phase of his journey would show God's sovereignty in directing his messengers. Paul, Silas, and Timothy had planned, after revisiting the churches in Iconium and Antioch, to work their way west through the province of Asia to the Aegean coast, probably targeting its world-famous metropolis, Ephesus. The Holy Spirit, however, forbade or prevented this route. How he did so, Luke does not tell us. Probably he revealed his intention to Paul directly or through Silas' prophetic gift, as he had spoken to Philip and to Peter (8:29; 10:19). Deflected northward, they reached the border of the Mysian region of Asia, from which they tried to travel north-east into Bithynia, near the Black Sea. Again the Spirit blocked their way. Now he is called the Spirit of Jesus to remind us that, whenever the Spirit acts, he is the agent through whom Jesus continues his ministry of deed and word (1:1). God would not always bypass these regions: Paul would later have a long ministry in Ephesus (19:1–41; 20:17–38), and the gospel would reach Bithynia as well (*1 Pet.* 1:1).

At this point, however, God's plan overrode Paul's agenda. The apostle's trusting submission to his Master's sovereign wisdom never kept him from initiating and implementing plans, but Paul had learned flexibility, following as the Lord took the lead to build his church. Later Paul would write to the Romans that he had often planned to visit them but had been prevented from doing so, especially by the evangelistic openings in the eastern Mediterranean (*Rom.* 1:13; 15:19–22). When he finally reached Rome through the Empire's legal system, it was in answer to his prayer 'that now at last by God's will the way may be opened for me to come to you' (*Rom.* 1:10; see also 15:32, *Acts* 18:21). We could avoid much worry and frustration by trusting our Father's wisdom and love, when his providence thwarts our dreams.

God's itinerary became clear when the team reached Troas. They may have thought that Troas itself, a port city and Roman colony, was the venue for evangelism to which the Holy Spirit had been pushing them, but a vision sent to Paul at night made clear God's objective in bringing them to the coast. In the vision Paul saw a man from Macedonia, to the west across the sea, appealing for help. Of course, the help that Paul's team could provide was the gospel of Jesus Christ, so they concluded that this vision was God's direction to sail west, bringing the message of salvation to the nation from which Alexander the Great, centuries earlier, had launched his world empire. Now Macedonia would meet a Lord who, though crucified in weakness, had risen to rule a kingdom of worldwide dimensions and eternal duration. A fourth member joined the team at this point, as the change of pronouns in verse 10 implies: 'We sought to go . . .

God had called us . . . ' Here begins the first of four sections in which Luke signals his own participation in the events he narrates.

GOD OPENS A BUSINESSWOMAN'S HEART AT PHILIPPI

The winds were with the ship for their voyage past the island of Samothrace to Neapolis, the port serving Philippi, took only two days (see 20:6). Alexander the Great's father, Philip, had renamed Philippi after himself when he captured it from the Thracians. Caesar Augustus had honoured the city by naming it a colony, so that its citizens (including many retired military personnel) enjoyed the privileges of Roman citizenship. It is no surprise, then, that when the Name of Jesus liberated a fortune–teller from demons, her owners masked their greed behind a façade of civic pride in being Romans (16:21).

Apparently Philippi lacked the minimum quorum (*minyan*) of ten Jewish men needed to form a synagogue. In Paul's typical strategy the next best thing would be a place of prayer where worshippers of Israel's God would gather informally to call on his Name, and Paul's team expected to find such a place outside the city gates along the river bank. There they met a group of women, the most prominent of whom was Lydia, a businesswoman who imported the costly purple cloth for which her native Thyatira, in Asia, was famous. Apparently God had prospered her trade, for she headed a household capable of extending hospitality to Paul and his colleagues. She was a worshipper of God, a Gentile God-fearer like Cornelius and so many others who believed in Jesus through Paul's preaching in synagogues (10:2; 13:16; 17:4).

As Paul spoke, the Lord empowered his word as only he can: he opened Lydia's heart to welcome and trust his message of grace. Luke here presents another picture to illustrate the Holy Spirit's sovereign life-giving work. Earlier he spoke of God and Christ 'granting repentance' (11:18; see also 3:26); of God 'opening a door of faith' (14:27); and of those 'appointed to eternal life' believing (13:48). Paul would use other images: resurrection of the dead (*Eph.* 2:1–10); God's light illuminating darkened hearts (*2 Cor.* 4:4–6); new creation (*2 Cor.* 5:16–17); and rebirth (*Titus* 3:5, see also *John* 3:3–8). However it is expressed, the truth is always the same: when anyone comes to Jesus in faith, it is because the Father draws him or her by his Word and Spirit (*John* 6:44). All glory goes to God. The faith in Lydia's heart immediately showed itself in her actions. She was baptized, as were the members of her household, both servants and other dependents. Moreover, she insisted on opening her home to Paul and his co-workers. By accepting her hospitality they showed their acceptance of Lydia herself as a believing sister, just as Jesus' dining with outcasts signified the Father's welcome (*Luke* 15). When we hear God's gracious 'Welcome home', we respond by opening our homes to others (*Rom.* 12:13, *Gal.* 6:6, *Heb.* 13:2, *3 John* 5–8).

46

Christ's Prisoners Set Others Free

*As we were going to the place of prayer, we were met by a slave
girl who had a spirit of divination and brought her owners much
gain by fortune-telling.* [17] *She followed Paul and us, crying out,
"These men are servants of the Most High God, who proclaim
to you the way of salvation."* [18] *And this she kept doing for many
days. Paul, having become greatly annoyed, turned and said to
the spirit, "I command you in the name of Jesus Christ to come
out of her." And it came out that very hour.*

[19] *But when her owners saw that their hope of gain was gone,
they seized Paul and Silas and dragged them into the
marketplace before the rulers.* [20] *And when they had brought them
to the magistrates, they said, "These men are Jews, and they are
disturbing our city.* [21] *They advocate customs that are not lawful
for us as Romans to accept or practice."* [22] *The crowd joined in
attacking them, and the magistrates tore the garments off them
and gave orders to beat them with rods.* [23] *And when they had
inflicted many blows upon them, they threw them into prison,
ordering the jailer to keep them safely.* [24] *Having received this
order, he put them into the inner prison and fastened their feet in
the stocks.*

[25] *About midnight Paul and Silas were praying and singing
hymns to God, and the prisoners were listening to them,* [26] *and
suddenly there was a great earthquake, so that the foundations
of the prison were shaken. And immediately all the doors were
opened, and everyone's bonds were unfastened.* [27] *When the jailer
woke and saw that the prison doors were open, he drew his sword
and was about to kill himself, supposing that the prisoners had
escaped.* [28] *But Paul cried with a loud voice, "Do not harm*

yourself, for we are all here." ²⁹ *And the jailer called for lights and rushed in, and trembling with fear he fell down before Paul and Silas.* ³⁰ *Then he brought them out and said, "Sirs, what must I do to be saved?"* ³¹ *And they said, "Believe in the Lord Jesus, and you will be saved, you and your household."* ³² *And they spoke the word of the Lord to him and to all who were in his house.* ³³ *And he took them the same hour of the night and washed their wounds; and he was baptized at once, he and all his family.* ³⁴ *Then he brought them up into his house and set food before them. And he rejoiced along with his entire household that he had believed in God.*

³⁵ *But when it was day, the magistrates sent the police, saying, "Let those men go."* ³⁶ *And the jailer reported these words to Paul, saying, "The magistrates have sent to let you go. Therefore come out now and go in peace."* ³⁷ *But Paul said to them, "They have beaten us publicly, uncondemned, men who are Roman citizens, and have thrown us into prison; and do they now throw us out secretly? No! Let them come themselves and take us out."* ³⁸ *The police reported these words to the magistrates, and they were afraid when they heard that they were Roman citizens.* ³⁹ *So they came and apologized to them. And they took them out and asked them to leave the city.* ⁴⁰ *So they went out of the prison and visited Lydia. And when they had seen the brothers, they encouraged them and departed* (Acts 16:16–40).

In addition to Lydia, a God-fearer familiar with God's promises in Scripture, Luke profiles two others in Philippi who were transformed by the power of Jesus' Name. The fortune–telling slave and the keeper of the city jail were obviously entangled in the miseries that Satan and sin have introduced into the world, the former as a victim and the latter as a victimizer. Yet the power of Jesus' Name set both free.

LIBERATION AND FALSE ARREST

Paul, Silas, Timothy, and Luke continued to meet with Lydia and others each Sabbath at the place of prayer near the river, and the mention of 'the brothers' gathered at Lydia's house indicates that Paul's preaching ministry in Philippi bore fruit (16:40). On one occasion the apostolic band was met by a slave girl who had 'a Python spirit', a demon that was believed to make her an oracle and able to foretell the future. According to Greek myth, the god Apollo had slain the serpent oracle Python to establish his own oracle at Delphi, in Achaia. The pagans of the Graeco-Roman world, from the naïve illiterate to the educated nobility, consulted omens and oracles to try to pierce the veil of the unknown future, especially when embarking on new ventures. The Lord had taught Israel that no god but he could foretell the future because none but he controls history (*Isa.* 43:8–13; 46:5–10). Yet even Israel had to be warned against consulting those who practised divination (*Deut.* 18:9–15).

The girl's 'gift' turned a tidy profit for her owners, and it was her economic profitability, not her insight into future or spiritual realities, that they valued. During Jesus' ministry unclean spirits recoiled from his holiness, confessing him to be 'the Holy One of God' and 'Son of the Most High God' (*Mark* 1:24, *Luke* 8:28). So now the Python spirit, speaking through the girl's shouts, identified Paul's company as 'servants of the Most High God' who brought news of 'a way of salvation.' (The ESV's '*the* way' makes her announcement sound more definite than it is in Greek.) Although formally her statement was true, in the pagan context of Philippi, 'the Most High God' could refer to Zeus or a deity served by one of the Eastern cults, and virtually every god offered 'salvation' from some problem or other – physical illness, danger at sea, frustration in romance, economic hardship, or some other trouble. Paul was upset by her incessant 'testimony' not only because it came from an untrustworthy source (see also *Mark* 1:34) but also because its wording was so vague that it subsumed Jesus to pagan polytheism. In the authority of Jesus' Name he expelled the demon, setting its victim free. Jesus' Name functioned not as a magic incantation but as divine revelation, expressing Paul's dependence on his Lord's power to save and calling the girl and the bystanders to faith (see also *Acts* 3:16).

When the spirit left the girl, so did her owners' hope of profit (the same Greek verb appears in verses 18 and 19). Their reaction revealed how little stock they had put in her prophecies. Whereas she identified Paul and Silas as bearers of a divine message of salvation, they accused Jesus' messengers of fomenting civil disruption. They dragged the two missionaries (apparently Timothy and Luke escaped their notice) into the marketplace to face Philippi's two colonial magistrates. Hiding the greed that was their real motive, they appealed to civic pride and anti-Semitic prejudice to win over the magistrates and the gathering mob: 'These men are Jews, and . . . advocate customs that are not lawful for us as Romans to accept or practice.' Since Philippi had been made a colony by Augustus, every Philippian citizen could boast of Roman citizenship.

In their haste to quell the disturbance, the magistrates bypassed investigation and proceeded directly to the humiliating punishment of the strangers, which the crowd so vociferously desired. They ordered the two police officers, who carried bundles of rods with an axe symbolizing their authority to inflict corporal and capital punishment, to wield their rods on Paul and Silas' bared backs. (These 'rod–bearers' are the officers sent by the magistrates in verses 35–38.) In addition to five floggings at Jewish hands, Paul had been beaten with rods three times by Romans by the time he wrote 2 Corinthians (*2 Cor.* 11:24–25). He was still stinging from the humiliation received at Philippi when he reached Thessalonica (*1 Thess.* 2:2). Then the troublemakers were hustled to the custody of the city jailer, probably a hardened retired army officer, who took seriously his orders to guard them securely. Indifferent to their pain, he neither washed their open wounds nor fed them, but immediately fastened their feet in stocks in the jail's inmost cell.

OPEN DOORS AND OPEN HEARTS

Bruised and bleeding from the beating and immobilized by the stocks, Paul and Silas nevertheless found in God's grace reason to pray and sing well into the night, with an audience of fellow–inmates eavesdropping on their praises to God. When Paul wrote from another prison, urging the Philippians to join his rejoicing in his sufferings for their faith, those who remembered that strange hymn singing at midnight could attest to his joy in adverse circumstances (*Phil.* 1:12, 18, 29–30; 2:17–18). When adversity dampens our mood, we need to sink the roots of our joy more deeply into the Lord himself, rather than relying on surface circumstances (*Phil.* 4:4).

Suddenly the Lord signalled his sovereign, saving presence by a strong earthquake, as at Sinai, at Calvary, and at the Jerusalem church's prayer meeting (*Exod.* 19:18, *Matt.* 27:51, *Acts* 4:31). The prison's foundations were shaken, locked cell doors thrown open, and chains dislodged from the walls. The jailer, shaken from his sleep and seeing cell doors standing open, assumed that his prisoners had escaped and drew his sword to commit suicide, rather than face public dishonour and execution (as Peter's guards had suffered, 12:19). Paul's shout stopped him. Such was the influence of the missionaries over their fellow-inmates that none had seized the opportunity to escape.

With lanterns the jailer jumped from street level down into the basement where the prison cells were, and found its whole inmate population accounted for. Trembling, he fell before Paul and Silas, terrified at the divine power that attended them. Bringing them up and out into the courtyard, he asked, 'What must I do to be saved?' Had he heard their preaching, or the slave girl's bizarre advertisement, or their songs in the night? What he meant by 'saved' in his question is hard to know, but Paul and Silas answered in terms of the comprehensive salvation – from sin, guilt, condemnation, alienation, and ultimately from death, physical and eternal – that the Lord Jesus gives to those who believe in him. As in the cases of Cornelius and Lydia, the promise embraces not only the jailer but also those belonging to his house, who heard the gospel as Paul and Silas preached and who together received baptism (11:14; 16:15, see also *John* 4:53, *1 Cor.* 1:16).

Just as Lydia's faith moved her to offer immediate hospitality, so the jailer's faith alerted him to the cruel indifference that he had earlier shown towards these prisoners. Now he washed their wounds and set food before them at his table, his terror of disgrace and death transformed into exultant joy by his new-found faith in God through Jesus Christ. When serving hurting brothers and sisters feels more like a burdensome chore than a joyful privilege, we need to refresh our wonder at the grace that shook the jailer's world and melted his hardened heart.

THE GOSPEL VINDICATED

In the morning the magistrates sent their bailiffs, the 'rod–bearers', to the jail with orders to release Paul and Silas. No doubt they reasoned that the crowd had dispersed, the beating and night in jail had taught those two Jews not to spread their strange customs in their noble Roman colony, public order had been maintained, and so the case could be closed quietly. Receiving this news, the jailer rejoices to release his fathers in the faith in peace.

Paul, however, would not let the incident end so easily. He sprang a shocking surprise for the officers to convey to their superiors: the despised objects of the mob's ire, whom the magistrates summarily condemned to a beating without inquiry or trial yesterday, were in fact Roman citizens themselves! (This information is just as much a surprise to us, Luke's readers, but we will see Paul invoke his rights of citizenship again in 22:25–28 and 25:10–12.) Whether the tumult had prevented Paul and Silas from revealing their citizenship, or whether they had chosen to forego an exemption from suffering that other believers could not claim, the magistrates were still to blame for their failure to ascertain the identity of the accused and the facts of the case before rushing to an expedient but unjust judgement.

Paul's Greek imitates that of his accusers. They had said, 'These men . . . *who are Jews* . . . announce customs not lawful for us . . . *who are Romans.*' Now Paul said, 'They publicly beat us, though we were not judged guilty . . . men *who are Romans* . . . and now privately they throw us out?' Such unjustified humiliation of a Roman citizen could be grounds for stripping a city of its status and privileges as a colony and have even worse consequences for the magistrates themselves. It is no wonder that the magistrates were gripped with fear when they learned of their hasty miscarriage of justice, and that they hurried to the jail to appease Paul and Silas.

Paul's demand for a public, face-to-face apology from the magistrates was not motivated by a vengeful eye-for-eye lust, or an embarrassment-for-embarrassment retaliation. His concern was to set the record straight regarding the slander broadcast by the slave girl's owners and apparently legitimized by the magistrates. Although Christians confessed 'Jesus is Lord', affirming allegiance to a king higher than Caesar (*Acts* 17:7), their faith was neither disruptive of Roman social order nor treasonous toward its government. In fact, Luke's narrative repeatedly shows the opponents of the gospel as the disturbers of the peace and of the community's well being (for example, 18:12–17; 19:23–41). This point would reassure Theophilus, whose 'most excellent' title implies influential status within the imperial power structure. More importantly, it shows that Paul practised the respect for civil authority that he enjoined upon other Christians (*Rom.* 13:1–7, see also *1 Pet.* 2:13–17). Without idolizing state or society, we must adorn the reputation of the gospel through peaceable neighbourliness and honour toward the leaders and institutions established by God to maintain order.

Upon their release Paul and Silas went to Lydia's house, which had become the church's gathering place. They encouraged the brothers who had gathered there, perhaps with the same perspective that Paul would later write to them, that both faith in Christ and suffering for him are gifts granted by God (*Phil.* 1:29–30, see also *Acts* 14:22). Having strengthened the church, Paul, Silas, and Timothy (leaving Luke in Philippi, as the switch to third-person pronouns implies) granted the magistrates' nervous request that they leave the city.

47

Disturbers of the Peace

*Now when they had passed through Amphipolis and Apollonia,
they came to Thessalonica, where there was a synagogue of the
Jews. ² And Paul went in, as was his custom, and on three
Sabbath days he reasoned with them from the Scriptures,
³ explaining and proving that it was necessary for the Christ to
suffer and to rise from the dead, and saying, "This Jesus, whom
I proclaim to you, is the Christ." ⁴ And some of them were
persuaded and joined Paul and Silas, as did a great many of
the devout Greeks and not a few of the leading women. ⁵ But the
Jews were jealous, and taking some wicked men of the rabble,
they formed a mob, set the city in an uproar, and attacked the
house of Jason, seeking to bring them out to the crowd. ⁶ And
when they could not find them, they dragged Jason and some of
the brothers before the city authorities, shouting, "These men who
have turned the world upside down have come here also, ⁷ and
Jason has received them, and they are all acting against the
decrees of Caesar, saying that there is another king, Jesus." ⁸ And
the people and the city authorities were disturbed when they heard
these things. ⁹ And when they had taken money as security from
Jason and the rest, they let them go.*

*¹⁰ The brothers immediately sent Paul and Silas away by night
to Berea, and when they arrived they went into the Jewish
synagogue. ¹¹ Now these Jews were more noble than those in
Thessalonica; they received the word with all eagerness,
examining the Scriptures daily to see if these things were so.
¹² Many of them therefore believed, with not a few Greek women
of high standing as well as men. ¹³ But when the Jews from
Thessalonica learned that the word of God was proclaimed by*

Paul at Berea also, they came there too, agitating and stirring up the crowds. [14] Then the brothers immediately sent Paul off on his way to the sea, but Silas and Timothy remained there. [15] Those who conducted Paul brought him as far as Athens, and after receiving a command for Silas and Timothy to come to him as soon as possible, they departed (Acts 17:1–15).

The experience of Paul, Silas, and Timothy at Thessalonica and Berea illustrates the diverse responses that the gospel elicited in the Jewish synagogues of the Dispersion, and still evokes today. At Thessalonica conversion of many God-fearing Gentiles and prominent women provoked unbelieving Jews to jealousy, and they recruited a mob of unsavoury Gentiles to stir up a riot against Paul and company. At Berea, on the other hand, the Jewish community gave Paul a fair hearing, testing his message by the Scriptures. As a result many Jews, as well as Greek noblewomen and men, came to faith. The Thessalonian Jews' relentless pursuit of the missionaries to Berea revealed the hypocrisy of their charge that Christianity threatened the peace and order of society. In fact, it was the enemies of the gospel who provoked the civil unrest that so alarmed Roman authorities.

PERSUASION AND PERSECUTION AT THESSALONICA

Thessalonica was a strategic objective as Paul's team travelled west along the well-maintained Roman highway, the Via Egnatia, from Philippi. The distance was 100 miles, divided roughly into thirds by Amphipolis and Apollonia, in which, no doubt, they stayed overnight. (Even on horseback the whole journey would have taken three days.) Although Amphipolis was a prominent city, Paul was eager to reach Thessalonica because it had a Jewish community large enough to sustain a synagogue. Thessalonica was also the capital of the province of Macedonia, and for this reason too it was a strategic site for fulfilling the call issued through Paul's vision at Troas, to 'help' the Macedonians by bringing the good news of Jesus (16:9).

Luke calls attention to Paul's custom of targeting first the synagogue congregation, composed of Jews and God-fearing

Gentiles, in Thessalonica as in other cities (13:5, 14; 14:1; 17:10; 18:4; 19:8). At the synagogue Paul would find people familiar with the Scriptures given to Israel. In Thessalonica Paul had opportunity over three Sabbaths to open up these Scriptures (ESV: *explaining* represents the same verb as in *Luke* 24:32: 'He . . . opened to us the Scriptures') and set before his hearers the surprising message that it was necessary for the Christ to suffer and then rise from the dead – the same truth that Jesus' disciples could not see until he opened their minds to it (*Luke* 24:26, 45–47). Perhaps Paul cited such Scriptures as Psalm 16 and Isaiah 53, which we have heard expounded elsewhere in Acts. Having shown the suffering-to-glory agenda set out for the Messiah in Scripture, Paul affirmed that Jesus is this Messiah. Jesus fits the profile and fulfils these divine promises.

The seed of the Word bore different proportions of fruit from different categories of 'soils'. Some of the Jews were persuaded (the negative reaction of the majority will soon be seen), whereas a large number of God-fearing Greeks believed, and of the prominent women not a few. *Not a few*, which reappears in Greek at the end of verse 12, is Luke's understatement for a sizeable number (see also the singular '*no small*' translated in various ways in 12:18; 14:28; 15:2; 19:23–24; 27:20).

The conversion to Christ of so many God-fearers, whom the Jews had hoped to draw into proselyte status, inflamed the jealousy of most Jews, as had happened at Pisidian Antioch (13:45; see also 5:17). The same Greek word expresses both jealousy and zeal (*Gal.* 1:14, *Phil.* 3:6, *Rom.* 10:2) and in our own attitudes the line between them is often very fine. We can easily believe that we are defending God's glory when we are actually avenging our own bruised egos, as the Jews did here (see *Mark* 9:38–41).

Instead of trying to refute Paul's biblical arguments, the Jews resorted to violence, recruiting Gentile thugs who were loitering in the marketplace to create a disturbance and simulate a ground swell of public outrage against Paul and Silas. They stormed the house of Jason, who had extended hospitality to Paul's team and had also opened his home as a gathering place for the church. When the mob failed to find the missionaries, they seized Jason and other brothers who had gathered there and dragged them before the city officials. This mob violence and false accusation marked just the beginning of persecutions suffered by the Thessalonian church (1 Thess. 2:14, 2 Thess. 1:4–7).

The mixed mob of Jews and Gentiles made no mention of the original motives for the Jews' anger: their rejection of Paul's Christ-centred reading of Scripture and their envy at the gospel's impact upon God-fearing Gentiles. Instead they accused Jason of harbouring troublemakers who travelled from town to town fomenting civil unrest, disobedience to Caesar's decrees, and treasonous allegiance to another king, Jesus. Perhaps the rumours of the missionaries' arrest at Philippi on charges of spreading customs unlawful for Roman citizens had reached Thessalonica, but these opponents did not know or chose to suppress the end of the story, the magistrates' public apology. In proving that Jesus is the Christ, Paul did affirm that Jesus is king, but Jesus' rule dictated not revolution against Rome, but respectful submission to human rulers. Nevertheless such charges were calculated to get the officials' attention, for authorities throughout the Empire feared few things more than mob violence, riot, or any allegation that they would condone disloyalty to the Emperor.

The city officials, though alarmed by the accusations, responded with prudent caution. Perhaps they had heard of the Philippian magistrates' embarrassment and did not want to imitate their error. The officials required Jason and the other brothers to post bond, financially guaranteeing that their guests would not provoke disorder or promote rebellion, and then they released them. By night, to forestall a secret assault, the brothers sent Paul and Silas (with Timothy, verse 14) away from Thessalonica, and they made their way west fifty miles to Berea, where another sizeable Jewish community with its own synagogue resided.

SEARCHERS OF THE SCRIPTURES AT BEREA

The Berean Jews exhibited more noble character than the Thessalonians in the open and discerning hearing they gave to Paul as he spoke in their synagogue. Because he argued from the Scriptures that God had purposed for the Messiah to suffer and to rise from the dead, they turned to the Scriptures to test Paul's claims on behalf of Jesus. In fact, they interacted with Paul not only on the Sabbath but every day, diligently pursuing the truth in God's Word.

It was no coincidence, then, when many of the Jews of Berea believed, for in testifying about Jesus the Scriptures create and strengthen faith in him (*John* 5:39–40). Many of the city's socialites and Greek men also believed. As in Thessalonica, the conversion of prominent women is noted. Although God calls men to exercise sacrificial leadership in family and church, throughout Acts he highlights his welcome of women as well as men into his family (*Acts* 2:18; 5:14; 9:2, 36–42; 12:12–17; 16:13–15; 17:34; 18:18–26).

The Jews of Thessalonica were so hostile to God's Word that they travelled the two days' journey to Berea to stir up another mob to attack Paul there. Luke uses two verbs, agitating and stirring up, to emphasize the irony that the gospel's enemies are guilty of the very civil disruption with which they accused Paul and Silas (16:20–21; 17:6–7; see also 19:40). Long ago King Ahab of Israel labelled Elijah the 'troubler of Israel' because the prophet had announced that the Lord would humble his idolatrous people through a severe drought. Elijah rightly responded that Ahab was the real trouble maker for Israel because the king had abandoned the Lord's commands and imposed Baal–worship upon God's people (*1 Kings* 18:17–18). Likewise in Paul's day the disturbers of the peace were not the servants of King Jesus, but those who resisted his truth and reign.

We too must adorn the gospel that we announce through lives of integrity, peaceful harmony, and respectful submission: 'Give thought to do what is honourable in the sight of all. If possible, so far as it depends on you, live peaceably with all . . . Pay to all what is owed to them: taxes to whom taxes are owed, revenue to whom revenue is owed, respect to whom respect is owed, honour to whom honour is owed (*Rom.* 12:17–18; 13:7).

48

Making Known the Unknown God

Now while Paul was waiting for them at Athens, his spirit was provoked within him as he saw that the city was full of idols. ¹⁷ *So he reasoned in the synagogue with the Jews and the devout persons, and in the marketplace every day with those who happened to be there.* ¹⁸ *Some of the Epicurean and Stoic philosophers also conversed with him. And some said, "What does this babbler wish to say?" Others said, "He seems to be a preacher of foreign divinities" – because he was preaching Jesus and the resurrection.* ¹⁹ *And they took hold of him and brought him to the Areopagus, saying, "May we know what this new teaching is that you are presenting?* ²⁰ *For you bring some strange things to our ears. We wish to know therefore what these things mean."* ²¹ *Now all the Athenians and the foreigners who lived there would spend their time in nothing except telling or hearing something new.*

²² *So Paul, standing in the midst of the Areopagus, said: "Men of Athens, I perceive that in every way you are very religious.* ²³ *For as I passed along and observed the objects of your worship, I found also an altar with this inscription, 'To the unknown god.' What therefore you worship as unknown, this I proclaim to you.* ²⁴ *The God who made the world and everything in it, being Lord of heaven and earth, does not live in temples made by man,* ²⁵ *nor is he served by human hands, as though he needed anything, since he himself gives to all mankind life and breath and everything.* ²⁶ *And he made from one man every nation of mankind to live on all the face of the earth, having determined allotted periods and the boundaries of their dwelling place,* ²⁷ *that they should seek God, in the hope that they might feel their way*

*towards him and find him. Yet he is actually not far from each one of us, * [28] *for*

" '*In him we live and move and have our being*';
as even some of your own poets have said,
" '*For we are indeed his offspring.*'

[29] *Being then God's offspring, we ought not to think that the divine being is like gold or silver or stone, an image formed by the art and imagination of man.* [30] *The times of ignorance God overlooked, but now he commands all people everywhere to repent,* [31] *because he has fixed a day on which he will judge the world in righteousness by a man whom he has appointed; and of this he has given assurance to all by raising him from the dead.*"

[32] *Now when they heard of the resurrection of the dead, some mocked. But others said, "We will hear you again about this."* [33] *So Paul went out from their midst.* [34] *But some men joined him and believed, among them Dionysius the Areopagite and a woman named Damaris and others with them* (Acts 17:16–34).

Paul's speech before the Greek intelligentsia in the Areopagus is the longer of only two samples of his evangelistic presentation to Gentiles who lacked previous exposure to the Scriptures. The other, his address at Lystra, had the limited objective of stopping the blasphemy that the Lystrans were unwittingly about to commit (*Acts* 14:15–17). It therefore did not mention Jesus' death and resurrection, the heart of Paul's gospel. At Athens, most of Paul's speech laid the foundation that pagan Greeks needed in order to grasp the significance of Christ's work: one God created and rules all, man's identity as God's image shows the folly of idolatry, etc. In conclusion, Paul referred to the great shift between the past, when God 'overlooked' but did not condone pagan ignorance, and the present, in which God summons all people everywhere to turn to himself for refuge from his coming judgement. The certainty and nearness of that judgement have been demonstrated in the resurrection of the Man designated by God to be Judge of all.

This speech is an invaluable and unparalleled model for our communication of the unchanging gospel in our increasingly pagan and biblically ignorant culture. With wisdom imparted by the Holy

Spirit, Paul conveyed God's truth without distortion in a conceptual idiom intelligible to the ancient world's intellectual élite.

STRANGE IDEAS PIQUE THE ATHENIANS' CURIOSITY

Since Paul himself had become the target of the rabble–rousers' assaults, the brothers at Berea sent him off to the coast, while Silas and Timothy remained to solidify the young church. Some accompanied Paul as he travelled south to Athens. On their return they delivered his command that Silas and Timothy should join him soon.

As he awaited them, he was outraged to observe the abundance of idols that dominated the city's art, architecture, and public life. Not only did images of the deities of the Greek pantheon fill the magnificent temples on the Acropolis that rose above the city, but also shrines and monuments to Hermes and other gods lined the marketplace, the centre of economic and academic life. Athens had declined in political influence since its heyday in the fifth and fourth centuries before Christ, but when Paul arrived it was still legendary throughout the Roman Empire for its artwork, its intellectual sophistication, and its devotion to the gods.

To his weekly dialogues with Jews and Gentile God-fearers in the synagogue, Paul added daily conversation with whomever he could engage in the Athenian marketplace, where both commerce and the clash of world-views took place. Epicurean and Stoic philosophers in particular took an interest in Paul's strange ideas, though dismissing him with an attitude of smug superiority: 'What does this babbler wish to say?' They understood him to be advocating gods foreign to Athens. This was among the crimes for which Socrates was put to death 450 years before, but the Athens of Paul's day was more tolerant. In fact, the Athenians were intellectual dilettantes, famous for their restless, insatiable appetite for any new idea. They thought they heard Paul patching together a match between a Jewish god, 'Jesus', and his female consort with a Greek name, 'Resurrection' (*Anastasis*). Several Greek deities bore the names of abstract qualities – Fate, Mercy, Effort, Shame, – so their confusion is understandable.

The philosophers brought Paul to a meeting of the Areopagus, the governing council of Athens that had authority to regulate the many visiting lecturers who were drawn by the city's academic reputation. Though his audience expressed scepticism toward Paul's foreign ideas, he saw their inquiry as an opportunity to call them to turn 'to God from idols to serve the living and true God, and to wait for his Son from heaven, whom he raised from the dead, Jesus who delivers us from the wrath to come' (*1 Thess.* 1:9–10).

THE GOD WHOM THEY KNEW THEY DID NOT KNOW

Paul's speech skilfully blends bridge-building and confrontation. On certain points he agreed with his cultured despisers, especially in their common critique of the naïve idolatry of the masses, who virtually equated images of gold, silver or stone with the deities they represented. At other points, particularly as he moved to the themes of coming judgement, repentance, and resurrection, his message challenged core tenets of both Epicureanism and Stoicism.

Epicurus and Zeno (founder of Stoicism – named after the covered porch or *stoa* in which Stoics gathered to debate) were contemporaries who lived three centuries before Christ's birth. Epicurus was a consistent materialist: not only the human body but even the soul is made of very fine matter, which dissolves into the atmosphere at death. The gods, if they exist, are serenely indifferent to human actions, neither needing worship nor meddling in people's lives. The wise person neither fears divine retribution nor hopes for reward beyond the grave. Rather, he imitates the gods in aloof enjoyment of pleasure. Epicureans would agree with Paul on the folly of gross idolatry but recoil at the thought that God would raise the dead or judge humanity.

While Epicureans exaggerated divine transcendence to the elimination of immanence, Stoicism did the opposite, moving almost to pantheism. The divine was the Logos, a rational principle permeating and integrating all things into an interconnected order, a cosmos. Stoic poets such as Aratus of Soli said of the Logos, 'We are all his offspring', meaning that each contains the divine spark of life and rationality. The wise person recognizes his connection with everything else in the universe through the Logos, cultivating an attitude of self-sufficient contentment, impervious to changing circumstance. History is an unending cycle of order followed by chaos followed by order. Stoics would applaud Paul's insistence on God's nearness (and his quotation of their own poet), but they would reject his announcement that history has a direction, moving from times of ignorance to the time of repentance, and finally to the day of judgement.

In this speech Paul never quoted the Old Testament Scriptures, as he did in synagogues. Instead of citing Scripture, he began with God's self-revelation in creation, providence, and especially in the character of man, affirming that even on the basis of these indirect disclosures from the Creator his hearers should have known him better than they did. Although Paul's explicit appeal is to general rather than special revelation, the content of his message is thoroughly biblical, even alluding to scriptural wording at points.

Paul opened with an ambiguous compliment. From the shrines that filled the city, Paul saw that 'in every way you are very religious'. This seems to be a compliment ('You are serious about pleasing your deities'); but Paul's word is double-edged, sometimes carrying a disparaging connotation as in Festus' dismissive reference to Judaism as 'their own religion' (*Acts* 25:19). In view of Paul's distress over idol-ridden Athens, he apparently felt both pity and revulsion over the Athenians' ardent but misguided religiosity.

His point of contact was an altar dedicated 'To the unknown god'. The deities of the Greek pantheon were believed to supervise every area of life: love and war, science and art, land and sea, labour and leisure, health and finances. Yet a lingering unease, lest some unnamed god had been overlooked and remained unappeased, had prompted the erection of several altars to 'unknown gods', as other ancient authors attest. Paul seized on this admission of ignorance by the 'knowledge capital' of the ancient world to announce the true God whom they never knew.

In contrast to the Epicureans' view of the gods as aloof and the Stoic view of the divine as a principle immersed in the universe, Paul announced the Creator who is distinct from the world but also engages with his creatures, who rules as Lord and supplies 'life and breath and everything'. Paul paraphrased God's self-description in

Isaiah 42:5: 'This is what God the Lord says – he who created the heavens and stretched them out, who spread out the earth and all that comes out of it, who gives breath to its people, and life to those who walk on it' (see also *Gen.* 2:7). That the living God cannot be contained in man-made temples is another Old Testament theme (*1 Kings* 8:27, *Isa.* 66:1–2), as is Paul's assertion that God is not dependent on his creatures' service (*Psa.* 50:10–12). Yet God's independence is not disengagement. Not only does he give life to his creatures generally, but he also shows special interest in humanity, creating the diverse ethnic groups from one man (*Gen.* 5; 10) and controlling the time and space dimensions in which they live. The *allotted periods and the boundaries of their dwelling place* (17:26) refer either to natural phenomena, the change of seasons and the borders between habitable regions and wilderness (*Psa.* 74:17), or to God's sovereignty over the history of the rise and fall of nations and over the boundaries between them (*Deut.* 32:8). God's purpose was to draw human beings into a quest to discover their Creator. Twice Paul used the Greek optative mood (*That they might feel their way towards him and find him*), rare in the New Testament, to imply how unlikely it would be for fallen man's blind groping to achieve true knowledge of God, despite the Creator's nearness as the sustainer of all his creatures (see also *Job* 12:10).

Yet, God's common grace enabled pagan poets to glimpse the kinship between God and man that exposes the folly of representing deity through images crafted of gold, silver, or stone. Paul quoted the Stoic Aratus, 'We are his offspring', finding in the poet's words a reflection of man's creation in the image of God. (In this sense Adam is God's son, just as Adam's son bore his likeness, *Luke* 3:38, *Gen.* 5:1–3.) Israelite psalmists and prophets satirized the folly of worshipping the products of one's own craft (*Psa.* 115:4–8, *Isa.* 44:9–20, *Jer.* 10:3–5). Sophisticated Epicureans and Stoics realized this, but they failed to see that their own mental conceptions of deity, whether as distant pleasure-seekers or as an impersonal rational principle, were equally human inventions.

Finally, Paul announced that the time of the Gentiles' ignorance of the true God had ended. No longer would he let the nations 'walk in their own ways', as Paul had said in Lystra (14:16). With the resurrection of the Man appointed to judge the world, the God who created all the nations to inhabit the whole earth summons all people everywhere to repent, turning to him for rescue from his righteous judgement (see also *Isa*. 45:22).

FOOLISHNESS TO GREEKS, BUT WISDOM FOR THOSE GOD SAVES

With the mention of Jesus' resurrection Paul was 'turning the corner' in his argument from the necessary foundation – the distinction between the Creator and his creatures, his self–sufficiency and personality, his revelation in providence and in man – to the answer to his interrogators' question, What did he mean when he spoke of Jesus and Resurrection? He introduced the central theme of his preaching, Jesus' death and resurrection as the hinge on which all history turns. He also moved the discussion from the realm of philosophical debate into that of personal responsibility. Finally, he made explicit that the resurrection he announced entailed a return to embodied life from the dead, a prospect repugnant to Greek philosophies generally, not only Epicureanism and Stoicism but also the Platonic tradition.

Consequently he was interrupted by the derision of the majority in the council, while others, though unconvinced, expressed interest in further discussion at a later time. Only Dionysius, a member of the council, a woman named Damaris, and some others became believers. These apparently meagre results were not attributable to a flawed strategy, as some have misunderstood 1 Corinthians 2:2 to imply. Paul's address before the Areopagus is presented as a laudable apostolic pattern for introducing sophisticated pagans to God's revealed truth. In a single encounter God's Spirit transformed sophisticated pagans into sincere disciples, using Paul's argument from God's general revelation in creation and his display of divine justice, power, and mercy in raising the Lord Jesus.

In our post-Christian and pagan culture, Paul shows how comprehensive our witness must be, introducing people ignorant of biblical basics (however intellectual they may be) to such truths as God's supremacy and self-disclosure in creation, providence, and human nature, laying the foundation that they need if they are to grasp the gospel of his grace.

49

Christianity at the Crossroads

*After this Paul left Athens and went to Corinth. ² And he found
a Jew named Aquila, a native of Pontus, recently come from
Italy with his wife Priscilla, because Claudius had commanded
all the Jews to leave Rome. And he went to see them, ³ and because
he was of the same trade he stayed with them and worked, for
they were tentmakers by trade. ⁴ And he reasoned in the
synagogue every Sabbath, and tried to persuade Jews and
Greeks.*

*⁵ When Silas and Timothy arrived from Macedonia, Paul
was occupied with the word, testifying to the Jews that the Christ
was Jesus. ⁶ And when they opposed and reviled him, he shook
out his garments and said to them, "Your blood be on your own
heads! I am innocent. From now on I will go to the Gentiles."
⁷ And he left there and went to the house of a man named Titius
Justus, a worshipper of God. His house was next door to the
synagogue. ⁸ Crispus, the ruler of the synagogue, believed in the
Lord, together with his entire household. And many of the
Corinthians hearing Paul believed and were baptized. ⁹ And the
Lord said to Paul one night in a vision, "Do not be afraid, but
go on speaking and do not be silent, ¹⁰ for I am with you, and no
one will attack you to harm you, for I have many in this city
who are my people." ¹¹ And he stayed a year and six months,
teaching the word of God among them.*

*¹² But when Gallio was proconsul of Achaia, the Jews made
a united attack on Paul and brought him before the tribunal,
¹³ saying, "This man is persuading people to worship God
contrary to the law." ¹⁴ But when Paul was about to open his
mouth, Gallio said to the Jews, "If it were a matter of*

wrongdoing or vicious crime, O Jews, I would have reason to accept your complaint. ¹⁵ But since it is a matter of questions about words and names and your own law, see to it yourselves. I refuse to be a judge of these things." ¹⁶ And he drove them from the tribunal. ¹⁷ And they all seized Sosthenes, the ruler of the synagogue, and beat him in front of the tribunal. But Gallio paid no attention to any of this (Acts 18:1–17).

Corinth was the crossroads of Achaia, both geographically and culturally. Julius Caesar rebuilt a new Corinth a century after the old city had been razed by Roman troops, and by Paul's day Corinth was a flourishing centre of political power, commerce – and sexual licence. Corinth was a Roman colony and the capital of the province of Achaia, from which the procurator governed. North-south land routes intersected east-west sea routes at Corinth. Occupying the isthmus that joined southern Achaia to the rest of Greece and Macedonia to the north, Corinth boasted twin ports, Cenchrea on the Aegean Sea and Corinth itself on the Adriatic. Much distance and time could be saved by sailing goods from Asia Minor into Cenchrea, transporting them by land over the narrow isthmus, and loading them on to ships bound for Italy.

Port cities populated by sailors often exhibit moral laxness. Even in the decadent Roman Empire, however, Corinth had become a byword for sexual depravity. Yet the city also had a well-established Jewish community, with a synagogue. This metropolis would pose a challenge to Christ-centred living (as 1 and 2 Corinthians show), but it would also become a springboard for the gospel. Paul settled in Corinth for one and a half years, patiently planting seed for others to water and laying a foundation on which others would build (*1 Cor.* 3:6, 10).

AQUILA AND PRISCILLA, HOSPITABLE CO–WORKERS

Upon his arrival Paul met a Jew named Aquila and his wife Priscilla. Paul had much in common with this couple: they were Jews from the Dispersion (Pontus was in northern Asia Minor, on the Black Sea), they practised his trade, and had been forced to move because of their faith in Jesus the Messiah. According to the second-century historian Suetonius, the Emperor Claudius' edict expelling the Jews from his capital was prompted by civil unrest among the Jewish population of Rome 'instigated by Chrestus'. Many scholars believe that 'Chrestus' is an alternate Latin transliteration for the Greek 'Christos' (Christ), and that the turmoil among Roman Jews was over whether Jesus is Messiah. To restore tranquillity to the city, Claudius ordered all Jews out of Rome. Although this edict was never repealed, eventually its enforcement was neglected and Jews, including Priscilla and Aquila, resettled in Rome (*Rom.* 16:3–4).

Wherever this couple appears in the New Testament, we see other believers enjoying their hospitality, as Paul did at Corinth. In their home the gifted preacher Apollos was instructed more accurately in God's way (18:26). While they lived at Ephesus and then at Rome the churches of those cities met in their home (*1 Cor.* 16:19, Rom. 16:3–5, 2 Tim. 4:19). In our day, isolated as we are by individualism and stressed by over-commitment, believers need to rediscover the joys of this ministry, exemplified in the practice of Priscilla and Aquila, of opening our homes to others.

Paul not only lodged with them but also laboured beside them at their shared trade, tent making. Unlike the Sophists and other professional orators, Paul refused to make his audience pay for his announcement of God's free gift. Instead, he supported himself and his team by hard work, providing an example of responsibility and generosity to younger believers (*Acts* 20:34, *1 Cor.* 4:12, *1 Thess.* 2:9, *2 Thess.* 3:7–9). Paul insisted that the church should meet the material needs of its teachers (*1 Cor.* 9:7–14, *Gal.* 6:6), but he was willing to forego that right in order to offer God's grace free of charge (*1 Cor.* 9:15–18).

TO JEWS FIRST, THEN TO GENTILES (AGAIN)

Before Silas and Timothy came from Macedonia, Paul's work-days were filled with tent making, and his Sabbaths with attempts to persuade Jews and Greeks in the synagogue. The arrival of his colleagues enabled him to devote all his time to testifying that Jesus is the promised Christ. Thus Luke refers to the generous gifts from such Macedonian churches as Philippi, who showed gratitude for God's grace by supporting Paul's outreach to others (*Phil.* 4:15–16,

2 Cor. 11:8–9). Their donations freed Paul to devote more time to his calling as God's ambassador.

Eventually the opposition of unbelieving Jews hardened, and their abuse of the gospel made the synagogue an inhospitable venue for further witness. As he had at Pisidian Antioch, Paul saw Jewish intransigence as freeing him to focus on the Gentiles (13:45–48). With reference to the imagery of Ezekiel's prophecy, Paul announced that he had discharged his responsibility as a watchman, sounding the alarm, so that those who refused to heed would be bringing their impending bloodshed upon their own heads (*Ezek.* 3:16–19; 33:1–9). Paul would later remind elders of the Ephesian church that he was innocent of the blood of all, for he had proclaimed the whole purpose of God to Jews and Greeks with the tears of urgent compassion (20:18–31, especially verses 26–27). In a gesture of judgement the apostle shook from his robes even the motes of the synagogue, as he had shaken Antioch's dust from his sandals, renouncing contact with the stubborn unbelievers among his own people (13:51, see also *Neh.* 5:13, *Luke* 10:10–11).

Paul did not have to travel far to find a base for his ongoing proclamation: next door to the synagogue was the house of Titius Justus, a Gentile God-fearer who had believed and who opened his home to the church. Many Corinthians believed and submitted to baptism, including one of special note: the synagogue ruler himself, Crispus, came to faith with his whole household. He became one of the few in Corinth to be baptized by Paul himself (*1 Cor.* 1:14–16). Unlike the entrenched Jewish leaders elsewhere, Crispus did not react defensively to Paul's message but listened with the openness of the Bereans, putting it to the test of Scripture and finding it true. Thus in Corinth the gospel was indeed the power of God for salvation, to the Jew first and also to the Greek.

DIVINE ENCOURAGEMENT FOR THE FEARFUL PREACHER

We might have expected such a fruitful ministry, including the strategic conversion of a Jewish 'pillar' such as Crispus, to boost Paul's confidence. In fact, however, Paul honestly acknowledged the apprehension and abject helplessness he felt at Corinth: 'I was with you in weakness and in fear and much trembling' (*1 Cor.* 2:3).

To bolster his trembling spokesman's courage the Lord Jesus spoke to Paul at night in a vision. His words combined gentle rebuke, a stirring mandate, and strong promises. The tense of the verb in the rebuke, '*Do not be afraid*', called Paul to abandon the terror to which he had surrendered: 'Stop fearing.' The mandate called Paul to continue speaking in Jesus' name, allowing no intimidation to silence him. The Lord reinforced his summons to resist fear with the promise of his presence, as he often did when calling his servants to daunting tasks: '*I am with you*' (see also *Exod.* 3:12, *Josh.* 1:5, 9, *Jer.* 1:8). Jesus also promised his preacher protection from harm, not for Paul's personal comfort but because many people in Corinth were Jesus' property, given to him by the Father (*John* 6:37, 39). No one could stop them hearing Christ's life-giving voice, as he laid claim to their hearts through Paul's gospel. So Paul stayed for a further eighteen months, grounding this church, which stood at the crossroads of trade and power, in the Word of God.

OPPOSITION THWARTED (AGAIN)

The vision prepared Paul for a new legal assault by the Jews who opposed the gospel. Gallio, brother of the philosopher Seneca in Claudius' court, became proconsul of Achaia in AD 51 or 52. The complaint that the Jews lodged with Gallio alleged that Paul persuaded people to worship God in ways contrary to the law of Moses. They claimed that Paul was advocating a new religion, not the ancient Judaism that Rome had tolerated. New religious movements often had political by-products disruptive of the *Pax Romana*, thus propagating a new faith was considered a serious crime. If the proconsul of an entire province judged Christianity a dangerous novelty, his decision could be cited as a legal precedent throughout the Empire.

Paul was prepared to demonstrate from the Scriptures that he was preaching nothing but what Moses had foretold. He had opened his mouth to do so when the proconsul dismissed the whole proceeding, refusing to adjudicate an internal controversy within the Jewish community. When the plaintiffs and the accused had been ejected from Gallio's courtroom, Sosthenes, who had succeeded Crispus as synagogue ruler, was the one who suffered harm rather than Paul. We are not told the identity or motive of those who beat Sosthenes.

Possibly Gentiles took advantage of the Jewish leaders' humiliation to express anti-Semitic hostility; or perhaps the Jews themselves were venting frustration at this setback to their public image. In any case, Jesus proved true to his word: none could harm Paul because through him Jesus was gathering his many people. Like the witnesses in John's mysterious vision, who symbolize the suffering and testifying church, Paul was invincible, as are we ourselves, until our mission on earth is complete (*Rev.* 11:5–7).

50

Travels and Teachers

After this, Paul stayed many days longer and then took leave of the brothers and set sail for Syria, and with him Priscilla and Aquila. At Cenchreae he had cut his hair, for he was under a vow. [19] *And they came to Ephesus, and he left them there, but he himself went into the synagogue and reasoned with the Jews.* [20] *When they asked him to stay for a longer period, he declined.* [21] *But on taking leave of them he said, "I will return to you if God wills," and he set sail from Ephesus.*

[22] *When he had landed at Caesarea, he went up and greeted the church, and then went down to Antioch.* [23] *After spending some time there, he departed and went from one place to the next through the region of Galatia and Phrygia, strengthening all the disciples.*

[24] *Now a Jew named Apollos, a native of Alexandria, came to Ephesus. He was an eloquent man, competent in the Scriptures.* [25] *He had been instructed in the way of the Lord. And being fervent in spirit, he spoke and taught accurately the things concerning Jesus, though he knew only the baptism of John.* [26] *He began to speak boldly in the synagogue, but when Priscilla and Aquila heard him, they took him and explained to him the way of God more accurately.* [27] *And when he wished to cross to Achaia, the brothers encouraged him and wrote to the disciples to welcome him. When he arrived, he greatly helped those who through grace had believed,* [28] *for he powerfully refuted the Jews in public, showing by the Scriptures that the Christ was Jesus* (Acts 18:18–28).

Ephesus, the political, cultural, and commercial centre of the Roman province of Asia, now becomes the stage on which the drama of the gospel's growth unfolds. Ephesus was the site of the world famous Temple of Artemis, which attracted pilgrims from the whole Empire to its annual festival. The city was also a financial and commercial centre, where overland trade routes from the east joined the sea lanes of the Aegean and Mediterranean Seas.

The Holy Spirit had blocked Paul's plan to evangelize Ephesus earlier in this journey (16:6), but on his return to Palestine the apostle visited the city briefly, promising to return if God permitted. Meanwhile the Lord raised up another powerful preacher in Ephesus, Apollos, who received instruction from Paul's co-workers, Priscilla and Aquila.

TRAVELS TO ASIA AND SYRIA

In the respite from persecution produced by Gallio's refusal to adjudicate the Jews' charges, Paul continued his ministry at Corinth for some time. Finally he prepared to depart for Syria (referring not just to the region around Antioch but to the whole Roman province, which included Judea). Jerusalem must have been an intended destination, for before embarking at Cenchrea Paul shaved his hair to conclude a Nazirite vow he had taken (*Num.* 6:2, 5, 9, 18). The rest of the ritual would be to offer a sacrifice at the temple and burn the hair 'devoted' to God on the altar. This vow may have been Paul's expression of thanks for Christ's promised protection in Corinth. Paul's vow belies the charge that he disregarded the law's relevance to Jews (18:13; 21:21–26, see also *1 Cor.* 9:20).

Paul, Priscilla, and Aquila sailed east to Ephesus. As usual, Paul reasoned from the Scriptures in the Jewish synagogue. His listeners apparently shared the fair-minded openness of the Bereans, asking Paul to prolong his stay. On his heart, however, was the completion of his vow in Jerusalem. He declined their invitation but promised to return 'if God wills'. His ready submission of his plan to God's will, mentioned repeatedly in his epistles (*Rom.* 1:10; 15:32, *1 Cor.* 4:19; 16:7, see also *James* 4:15), shows us how heartfelt trust in God's sovereignty works out in practice.

Leaving Priscilla and Aquila in Ephesus to work at tent making and church building, Paul sailed to Caesarea. From there he went up to greet the church in Jerusalem before he went down to Antioch, from which he and Silas had been sent. Although Jerusalem is not mentioned by name, it is implied. The verbs *go up* and *go down* typically designate travel to and from Jerusalem and the temple there (21:15, *Luke* 2:42, 51; 10:30–31; 18:10, 31, *Acts* 3:1; 11:2; 15:2). In addition to reporting to the church, Paul no doubt visited the temple to complete his vow.

After a sojourn in Antioch, he retraced his steps on the second journey, travelling again to the churches of Galatia and Phrygia, again with the purpose of strengthening the disciples (see also 15:36, 41). As restless as Paul was to reach regions where Jesus' name had not been heard (*Rom.* 15:20, *2 Cor.* 10:15–16), he had equal concern to fortify his spiritual children in the faith. Their immaturity was his deepest parental (maternal!) anguish (*Gal.* 4:19), and their progress was among his highest joys (*Phil.* 1:3–8; 4:1). May God give us like passion to help our brothers and sisters grow strong in his grace!

A GIFTED TEACHER WHO NEEDED TEACHERS

As Paul travelled westward through central Asia Minor, a new and powerful evangelist arrived at Ephesus by sea. Apollos had belonged to the prosperous community of Dispersion Jews in Alexandria, Egypt, the second largest city in the Empire. Years earlier this community had translated the Scriptures into Greek (the Septuagint), and in Apollos' day the philosopher Philo led its intellectual life. Apollos himself was an eloquent speaker and 'powerful [ESV: *competent*] in the Scriptures'. His description recalls those of Jesus, a prophet 'mighty in deed and word' (*Luke* 24:19), and of Moses, 'mighty in his words and deeds' (*Acts* 7:22). His proclamation about Jesus and the way of the Lord was accurate, and his zeal was energized by the Holy Spirit. Luke describes him as 'boiling in the Spirit' – with a fervour stimulated by God's Spirit – in words similar to Paul's exhortation: 'Be fervent in spirit' (*Rom.* 12:11). In both passages the reference is to the Holy Spirit, not our human spirit.

There was, however, a piece missing from Apollos' message: he knew only John's baptism, never having been taught about the new covenant initiation rite established by the risen Lord Jesus. In

Christian baptism the triune God places his name on his people (*Matt.* 28:19, see also *Acts* 2:38) and our union with Christ in his death and resurrection is portrayed (*Rom.* 6:3–4, *Gal.* 3:27). Apollos understood, believed, and preached the gospel of Christ, but he knew nothing of this new sacrament in which the use of water preaches the same gospel. As they heard Apollos, Priscilla and Aquila recognized the gap in his previous training. With the humble wisdom of Christ's true servants they neither ignored Apollos' error nor embarrassed him in public. Rather, they took him aside into their home, and there supplied his lack. Not intellectual aggression but gentle persuasion characterizes mature teachers who reflect Jesus, the Servant of the Lord (see also *2 Tim.* 2:24–26, *Matt.* 12:17–21).

Apollos' desire to preach in Achaia received the hearty endorsement of his Ephesian brothers. They wrote a letter of commendation, like those mentioned elsewhere in the New Testament, endorsing his teaching and urging the churches to support him (*Col.* 4:10, *Rom.* 16:1–2, *3 John* 8–12, see also *2 Cor.* 3:1–3). Such communications express the churches' unity, despite the distances that separate them. In Corinth Apollos' gifts bore fruit both inside and outside the church. Outside, Apollos' biblical insight, deep conviction, and oratorical skills made him a formidable debater, demonstrating to other Jews that the suffering and risen Jesus is the promised Messiah. Within the church, he built up those who by grace had believed. By grace reminds us that faith, which unites us to Christ, is itself God's gift: 'For by grace you have been saved through faith. And this is not your own doing; it is the gift of God' (*Eph.* 2:8).

.

51

Christ's Power Pierces
Pagan Darkness

And it happened that while Apollos was at Corinth, Paul passed through the inland country and came to Ephesus. There he found some disciples. ² And he said to them, "Did you receive the Holy Spirit when you believed?" And they said, "No, we have not even heard that there is a Holy Spirit." ³ And he said, "Into what then were you baptized?" They said, "Into John's baptism." ⁴ And Paul said, "John baptized with the baptism of repentance, telling the people to believe in the one who was to come after him, that is, Jesus." ⁵ On hearing this, they were baptized in the name of the Lord Jesus. ⁶ And when Paul had laid his hands on them, the Holy Spirit came on them, and they began speaking in tongues and prophesying. ⁷ There were about twelve men in all.

⁸ And he entered the synagogue and for three months spoke boldly, reasoning and persuading them about the kingdom of God. ⁹ But when some became stubborn and continued in unbelief, speaking evil of the Way before the congregation, he withdrew from them and took the disciples with him, reasoning daily in the hall of Tyrannus. ¹⁰ This continued for two years, so that all the residents of Asia heard the word of the Lord, both Jews and Greeks.

¹¹ And God was doing extraordinary miracles by the hands of Paul, ¹² so that even handkerchiefs or aprons that had touched his skin were carried away to the sick, and their diseases left them and the evil spirits came out of them. ¹³ Then some of the itinerant Jewish exorcists undertook to invoke the name of the Lord Jesus over those who had evil spirits, saying, "I adjure you by the Jesus, whom Paul proclaims." [14] Seven sons of a Jewish high priest named Sceva were doing this. [15] But the evil spirit answered them, "Jesus I know, and Paul I recognize, but who are you?" [16] And the man in whom was the evil spirit leaped on them, mastered all of them and overpowered them, so that they fled out of that house naked and wounded. [17] And this became known to all the residents of Ephesus, both Jews and Greeks. And fear fell upon them all, and the name of the Lord Jesus was extolled. [18] Also many of those who were now believers came, confessing and divulging their practices. [19] And a number of those who had practised magic arts brought their books together and burned them in the sight of all. And they counted the value of them and found it came to fifty thousand pieces of silver. [20] So the word of the Lord continued to increase and prevail mightily.

[21] *Now after these events Paul resolved in the Spirit to pass through Macedonia and Achaia and go to Jerusalem, saying, "After I have been there, I must also see Rome." [22] And having sent into Macedonia two of his helpers, Timothy and Erastus, he himself stayed in Asia for a while* (Acts 19:1–22).

Paul had a prolonged ministry at Ephesus, the most influential city on the Aegean's eastern shore, just as he had preached at length in Corinth on the western shore. He debated with Jews, proselytes, and God-fearers in the synagogue for three months. Then for two years he taught in the lecture hall of Tyrannus. After resolving to leave Ephesus, he remained in Asia while his assistants prepared the churches of Macedonia and Achaia for his visit en route to Jerusalem and, eventually, Rome. Thus, as Paul would remind the church's elders, he proclaimed the gospel in Ephesus over a three-year period (20:31). Through Paul's ministry of word and deed, to Jew and Gentile alike, God's kingdom broke into this major pagan stronghold with life-changing power.

DRAWING JOHN'S DISCIPLES INTO THE AGE OF THE SPIRIT

The opening reminder that Paul reached Ephesus during the period that Apollos was preaching in Corinth not only orients readers to the timing of their respective ministries (Apollos was watering the seed that Paul had planted in Achaia, *1 Cor.* 3:6). It also invites us to compare and contrast Apollos with the twelve disciples whom Paul met at Ephesus. Although *disciples* in Acts normally refers to Christian believers, something about this group must have struck Paul as unusual because he asked them if they had received the Holy Spirit upon coming to faith.

Their answers to Paul's questions identified them as belonging to a residual pocket of Old-Testament, anticipatory faith that had somehow been bypassed by the news of Jesus' redemptive work. They responded: 'We have not even heard that there is a Holy Spirit.' Like Apollos, they had received John's baptism of repentance but had not been baptized into the name of the Lord Jesus. Paul even needed to inform them that Jesus was the Name of the Coming One for whom John prepared the way.

If they had been exposed to John's teaching at all, they must have been aware of the existence of the Spirit of God (*Luke* 3:16). Probably their confession of ignorance means, 'We have not heard that the Holy Spirit has come into people's experience, as God promised he would in the last days.' Similar wording in John 7:39 carries this significance: 'The Spirit had not been given [literally, *was not yet*], because Jesus was not yet glorified.' They needed to be brought up to date with God's saving agenda. When they heard Paul's call to believe, they immediately submitted to baptism *in the name of the Lord Jesus* (see also *Acts* 2:38; 8:16; 10:48), and, with the laying on of Paul's hands, they received the Spirit, who showed his presence through prophecy and tongues. Like the Samaritan believers who received the Spirit (8:15–17) and the Gentiles in Cornelius' house (10:44–46), this group made up of John's disciples were joined to the one body of Christ, which had been baptized by the Spirit on the Day of Pentecost (*1 Cor.* 12:13).

Like Apollos they had known only John's baptism, but their differences to Apollos outweigh this similarity. Before Priscilla and Aquila set him straight on baptism, Apollos had received instruction in the Lord's way and taught accurately about Jesus. He was fervent in the Spirit, whereas they did not know that God had bestowed this Gift to his church. Luke preserved both accounts to show Theophilus the range of understanding and misunderstandings current even among those associated with the Jesus movement, and to emphasize that the full and accurate gospel was told by apostles like Peter and Paul (and now preserved in Luke's two volumes, *Luke* 1:1–4).

THE PERSUASIVE WORD OF CHRIST'S KINGDOM

On Paul's brief stop at Ephesus en route to Jerusalem, the Jews had asked him to stay and teach longer. Now, upon his return, they opened their synagogue for a full three months to his presentations about the coming of God's kingdom in the suffering and resurrection of Jesus the Messiah. Although many were persuaded, others eventually became stubborn or hardened, like the ancient Pharaoh in the face of God's power (*Exod.* 8:15; 9:35). They publicly maligned the Way – the only way to God (*John* 14:6) – as Paul preached this Way that he once persecuted (*Acts* 22:4).

Paul protected impressionable young believers from the opponents' verbal poison by moving to the lecture hall of Tyrannus, there continuing his public ministry for two more years. The result of this prolonged ministry was that the Word of the Lord reached both Jews and Gentiles not only in Ephesus but throughout the province of which it was capital (see also 20:21). The church at nearby Colosse was probably planted by Epaphras during this time (*Col.* 1:7), and the origins of many of the churches addressed in the Book of Revelation probably date from this period as well (*Rev.* 1:4, 11).

THE POWERFUL SIGNS OF CHRIST'S KINGDOM

Ephesus was a pagan centre dominated not only by the idolatry of the Temple of Artemis but also by flourishing magical and spiritualist trades that claimed to be able to control unseen powers. To gain the Ephesians' attention, the Lord kindly condescended to show his power at work in Paul in very tangible ways, pushing back the oppressive dominion of Satan. Power is the theme of this section. In Greek 'powers' (ESV: *miracles*) opens verse 11, which literally reads, 'Powers beyond the usual God was doing through Paul's hands.' Likewise 'grew in power' is the final word of the summary that closes the section in verse 20.

God made even the sweaty headbands and work aprons that Paul used as he worked again in Priscilla's and Aquila's leather shop the means by which his healing power flowed to people afflicted by illness and demonic possession. As Israel's sufferers had reached out for the tassels on Jesus' robe (*Mark* 5:27; 6:56) and sought healing in Peter's shadow (*Acts* 5:15–16), so now people grabbed any cloth that had touched Paul's skin and rushed it to their suffering loved ones. AIDS and other epidemics make it natural for us to view disease as the contagious aggressor, and good health as a fragile oasis in a wasteland of suffering. In Jesus and his apostles, however, health and wholeness proved contagious and the miseries that plague human life were forced to retreat.

Although God accommodates his self-disclosure to our limited and confused capacities, he will not let us mistake his sovereign power for a force subject to our manipulation. A notorious failed attempt to use Jesus' name as a magic talisman convinced everyone who heard of it that the Jesus whom Paul preached was no mere wonder-worker, but the Lord to be revered.

Greeks and Romans respected Jews as experts on things spiritual and especially as exorcists. If the Jews' God had forbidden them to speak his name, the pagans reasoned, that name must be very strong, and those allied to so strong a God should be able to enlist his power against lesser spirits that oppressed people. Some Jewish exorcists tried to employ the name of Jesus to expel evil spirits. After all, Jesus was known to have released many from demonic enslavement, and now his messenger Paul was doing the same in Ephesus. When the seven sons of Sceva, a Jewish chief priest (or so he claimed), tried to manipulate Jesus' name in this way, their attempt backfired. They addressed the evil spirit that controlled a man, 'I adjure you by the Jesus, whom Paul proclaims.' The spirit retorted: 'Jesus I know, and Paul I recognize, but who are you?' Evil spirits knew Jesus only too well, and trembled (*Luke* 4:38, 41; 8:28, see also *James* 2:19), and they recognized Paul as a servant of the Most High God (*Acts* 16:17). But the attempt by the sons of Sceva to tap into the power of Jesus at a safe distance, without submission to Jesus, made a mockery of their appeal to his name. Only to true servants, submissive to his authority, does the Lord Jesus delegate authority to advance his kingdom of grace, liberating Satan's slaves.

The evil spirit prompted his tormented host to leap on these seven would-be exorcists, beating and stripping them until they fled the house in pain and shame, naked and bleeding. Before he met Jesus, the Gerasene demoniac had lived among the dead, naked and bleeding from self-inflicted wounds (*Mark* 5:5, *Luke* 8:27). Now the sons of Sceva resembled him. Those who try to combat the powers of evil through techniques and stratagems of power rather than through humble trust in the Jesus preached by Paul will find themselves beaten by an Enemy far stronger and more cunning than they.

Ironically, the fact that Jesus' name did not 'work' when used as a magic word causes the Ephesian populace to magnify Jesus' name all the more. Here, clearly, was a Lord too majestic to be used, and too jealous for his own honour merely to be added to the pantheon of Hellenistic deities. Apparently even some Christian believers suddenly realized for the first time that faith in Jesus and participation in Ephesus' magic and occult industries were incompatible. Those who practised sorcery – casting spells, reading omens, and trying to pierce the veil of the unknown in other forbidden ways (*Deut.* 18:10–13) – confessed their evil practices, showing the genuineness of their repentance by assembling the scrolls prescribing occult rituals to be burned publicly. They calculated that this bonfire of the vanities had consumed scrolls worth 50,000 silver drachmas – a costly response to Christ's exclusive claim on their loyalty. Is your heart clinging to any rival of Jesus, afraid that it will cost too much to follow Jesus only?

Luke summarized the growth of the church in Jerusalem (6:7), Judea and Samaria (12:24; see also 9:31) as the growth of the Word of the Lord. Now he does so a third time, as the Word moves out toward the ends of the earth, adding that the Word was not only growing but also flexing its strength by turning many from darkness to light.

FUTURE PLANS

Before the last and most dangerous confrontation between the gospel and the entrenched paganism of Ephesus, Paul had already resolved to return to Jerusalem via Macedonia and Achaia, after which he hoped at last to satisfy his deferred desire to preach in the imperial capital, Rome (see also *Rom.* 1:13). Luke's Greek suggests that Paul's decision was reached 'in the Spirit', although the Spirit also made clear along the way that sufferings awaited Paul in Jerusalem (see also 20:22–23; 21:10–11). Paul's letters show that his main purpose was to present an offering from the Gentile churches to aid needy Jewish believers, and that he saw this gift as the Gentiles' expression of thanks for the gospel and as a token of the whole church's unity (*1 Cor.* 16:1–4, *2 Cor.* 8 – 9, *Rom.* 15:25–28). Having sent Timothy and Erastus ahead to help the churches gather together their offerings, Paul continued working in Asia to allow time for these preparations.

Even in his travel plans Paul did not succumb to the dichotomy between reaching the lost and serving the saints that often pulls Christians and churches to one or the other extreme. Both priorities were precious to his Lord, so Paul pursued both with all his energy.

52

The Camp of the Goddess Confounded

About that time there arose no little disturbance concerning the Way. [24] *For a man named Demetrius, a silversmith, who made silver shrines of Artemis, brought no little business to the craftsmen.* [25] *These he gathered together, with the workmen in similar trades, and said, "Men, you know that from this business we have our wealth.* [26] *And you see and hear that not only in Ephesus but in almost all of Asia this Paul has persuaded and turned away a great many people, saying that gods made with hands are not gods.* [27] *And there is danger not only that this trade of ours may come into disrepute but also that the temple of the great goddess Artemis may be counted as nothing, and that she may even be deposed from her magnificence, she whom all Asia and the world worship."*

[28] *When they heard this they were enraged and were crying out, "Great is Artemis of the Ephesians!"* [29] *So the city was filled with the confusion, and they rushed together into the theatre, dragging with them Gaius and Aristarchus, Macedonians who were Paul's companions in travel.* [30] *But when Paul wished to go in among the crowd, the disciples would not let him.* [31] *And even some of the Asiarchs, who were friends of his, sent to him and were urging him not to venture into the theatre.* [32] *Now some cried out one thing, some another, for the assembly was in confusion, and most of them did not know why they had come together.* [33] *Some of the crowd prompted Alexander, whom the Jews had put forward. And Alexander, motioning with his hand, wanted to make a defence to the crowd.* [34] *But when they recognized that he was a Jew, for about two hours they all cried out with one voice, "Great is Artemis of the Ephesians!"*

³⁵ And when the town clerk had quieted the crowd, he said, "Men of Ephesus, who is there who does not know that the city of the Ephesians is temple keeper of the great Artemis, and of the sacred stone that fell from the sky? ³⁶ Seeing then that these things cannot be denied, you ought to be quiet and do nothing rash. ³⁷ For you have brought these men here who are neither sacrilegious nor blasphemers of our goddess. ³⁸ If therefore Demetrius and the craftsmen with him have a complaint against anyone, the courts are open, and there are proconsuls. Let them bring charges against one another. ³⁹ But if you seek anything further, it shall be settled in the regular assembly. ⁴⁰ For we really are in danger of being charged with rioting today, since there is no cause that we can give to justify this commotion." ⁴¹ And when he had said these things, he dismissed the assembly (Acts 19: 23–41).

In the last recorded event of Paul's extended ministry at Ephesus, Paul does not speak a word, despite his desire to defend his co-workers from a mob that had been whipped into a frenzy of religious zeal and civic pride. Luke records the riot stirred up by the Ephesian silversmiths not to introduce another Pauline sermon, but to illustrate that the enemies of the Way, not its advocates, are responsible for the social unrest that attends the spread of Christ's Word. This riot completes the pattern of responses to Paul's gospel proclamation from the Jewish community and from the Gentiles, which we have seen elsewhere (Antioch, Iconium, Philippi, Thessalonica, Corinth): first Paul preaches in the synagogue, persuading many Jews and God-fearing Gentiles but evoking the opposition of others (19:8–9); then he preaches to pagans in public venues, converting so many that those who profit from the pagan establishment, threatened by the Word's growing power, retaliate through mob violence (19:10–41).

THE PROFITABILITY OF GODDESS-WORSHIP THREATENED

Toward the end of Paul's time in Ephesus a major disturbance concerning the Way was provoked by a certain Demetrius, leader of the silversmiths' guild associated with the world famous Temple of Artemis. One of the seven wonders of the ancient world, this temple attracted worshippers from throughout the Empire, especially for the annual festival of drama, feasting, processions and other pageantry held in honour of the goddess around the time of the spring equinox. Small terracotta replicas of the temple and its idol have been found throughout the Mediterranean world, but Demetrius and his co-workers made more expensive silver souvenirs to be purchased by pilgrims for their shrines at home. The Temple of Artemis was a dominant economic power in Ephesus, a banking institution with large reserves and a landlord holding title to vast farmlands outside the city.

Demetrius argued that Paul's preaching threatened both the profitability and the reputation of the silversmiths' craft by misleading multitudes in Ephesus and throughout the province, convincing them that handmade items are not gods. Paul had said precisely this to the philosophers at Athens, and no doubt he made the same case whenever introducing pagans to their Creator (17:24, 29). Demetrius was right: the truth that Paul preached threatened both of the idols whom the silversmiths served, not only the great goddess Artemis but also the money they made from her devotees. In fact, their strongest motive was 'covetousness, which is idolatry' (*Col.* 3:5). Many today think themselves too sophisticated to worship deities fashioned from stone or silver; yet they serve and trust the idol of finance, oblivious to the hollow ring of its promises.

So crass a motive as monetary profit had to be hidden behind one that would arouse the ardour of the whole Ephesian populace. Therefore Demetrius closed by raising the spectre that Paul's insults could rob their world-renowned deity of her rightful majesty. This shocking prospect filled the craftsmen with rage. They set out into the streets chanting at the top of their voices, 'Great is Artemis of the Ephesians', and soon a raucous mob joined in the shout.

THE DEVOTEES OF GODDESS–WORSHIP CONFUSED

Luke's record of the riot reflects the chaos of the crowd. The rioters could not get their hands on the culprit they sought, Paul. Instead, they grabbed two of Paul's Macedonian co-workers, Gaius and

Aristarchus, and dragged them into the city's great amphitheatre (seating 24,000, and still standing today) for an 'emergency' assembly of the Ephesian citizenry. According to Acts 20:4, not long after this crisis Paul would be accompanied by Aristarchus, by Gaius of Derbe (in Galatia), and by others as he travelled through Achaia and Macedonia. Apparently Paul had two companions called Gaius from different regions (Macedonia and Galatia). The name was common: another Gaius was Paul's host in Corinth (*Rom.* 16:23, *1 Cor.* 1:14), and yet another hosted itinerant preachers sent by the Apostle John (*3 John*). Faithful Aristarchus, not intimidated by hardships, would endure shipwreck and imprisonment with Paul (27:2, *Col.* 4:10).

Since the rage of the crowd swirled around these brothers, Paul wanted to enter the theatre to speak on their behalf. He was dissuaded, however, by a surprising coalition of counsellors. Not only the disciples, his Christian brothers, but also Paul's friends among the Asiarchs urged Paul not to place himself at risk in the unruly mob. Asiarchs had political and religious pre-eminence as priests of the sanctuaries dedicated to the goddess Roma and the Emperor. Those who counted themselves Paul's friends were perhaps his patrons. In view of their link with Rome they felt special responsibility to shield this Roman citizen from the harm that could come from the clash of his own boldness with the unpredictable violence of an angry mob. Paul endured intense persecution at Ephesus, but on this occasion he was spared (20:19, *1 Cor.* 15:32, *2 Cor.* 1:8–9).

Those gathered in the theatre knew from the silversmiths' chant that the glory of their goddess had been challenged, but in the confusion many had no idea from where the challenge had come. In the turmoil the Jews put forward one of their own, Alexander, to offer some sort of defence. He was shouted down before the direction of his remarks could be heard. Possibly he would have tried to distance the Jewish community from Paul's criticism of man–made gods, deflecting the ire of the idolaters exclusively on the Christians. If that was his purpose, it was a sad symptom of tolerant compromise with the surrounding pagan atmosphere, at odds with the ancient prophets' exposé of the emptiness of an idol (*Isa.* 44:9–20; 46:1–7, *Jer.* 10:3–5, *Psa.* 115:4–8). Then again, possibly Alexander's defence would have affirmed Israel's faith that the Lord alone is God, as Paul did, and then defended the Jews' freedom to practise their convictions. We will never know because the crowd drowned out his comments with two hours of mind-numbing adulation of their divine patroness.

THE ADVOCATES OF GODDESS-WORSHIP REBUKED

Only the authority of the city clerk could quell the tumultuous mantra, 'Great is Artemis of the Ephesians!' As the highest civic official, he was the city's liaison to the Roman provincial government of Asia, which had its seat in Ephesus. Ephesus was a 'free city', enjoying some autonomy to establish and enforce its own laws under the Empire's overarching authority. Such privileges could be quickly revoked, however, if the proconsul of Asia decided that the city could not control its unruly elements. Thus, when the clerk had silenced the roars of the crowd, he delivered a speech to defuse the situation. His remarks reinforce Luke's reassurance to Theophilus that the Christian faith is not a revolutionary movement intent on sowing discord or undercutting social order.

The clerk's argument is twofold. *First*, the reputation of Artemis and Ephesus stands secure, undiminished by the words or activities of the Christians. *Second*, Demetrius and the silversmiths are the ones who have put the welfare of the city at risk by precipitating this illegal and disorderly assembly.

The first argument seems to rest either on a legal technicality or on a misunderstanding of the implications of the gospel. It was undeniable that Ephesus was known throughout the world as the guardian of the largest and grandest temple to Artemis (four times the size of the Athenian Parthenon). What is unrecorded elsewhere is the presence there of an image of the goddess that had fallen from heaven, although such meteors were associated with other temples (e.g., the shrine to Artemis at Taurus). The city clerk affirmed the innocence of Aristarchus and Gaius, asserting that 'they have neither robbed temples or blasphemed our goddess.' It is easy to agree that they were innocent of the former charge, but harder to see how a pagan whose loyalty to Artemis seems unquestionable could understand Paul's critique of idolatry as anything but 'blasphemy' against the goddess. Perhaps the clerk's point was that no one could testify to hearing from Aristarchus and Gaius the disparaging comments about the goddess that Paul would have made. Perhaps he felt that the image that fell from heaven was exempt from Paul's critique of hand-made gods. But it is equally possible that Demetrius grasped more accurately than did the city clerk the real implications of Paul's message: the Christian faith did indeed place the goddess's reputation at risk, not through slanders but through the sober truth of the living God!

The clerk's second argument repeats a common motif in Acts: those who oppose the gospel, not those who promote it, break the laws of the state and disrupt the tranquillity of social order. Philippi's magistrates reacted precipitously to a crowd whipped to a frenzy by those who had lost profit when Jesus freed their clairvoyant slave from demonic oppression. In so doing, they violated the rights of Roman citizens. The Jewish community of Corinth asked the proconsul for an adverse ruling against Paul, only to have Gallio rebuff their petition as an exclusively Jewish quarrel. Now in Ephesus it was Demetrius and the other craftsmen, not Paul and his colleagues, who placed the city in *danger* (this Greek word is used by Demetrius in verse 27 and the clerk in verse 40, and nowhere else in Acts). Legal, orderly avenues were open for Demetrius to pursue his complaint against Paul, either in the proconsul's provincial court or when the municipal citizenry gathered in its regular assembly. (An Ephesian inscription mentions one *legal assembly* per month.) The present gathering, however, had no legal warrant that could be offered in defence if the proconsul called the city to account for rioting. With this reasonable warning the clerk managed to disperse the mob.

Like our Lord, Christians need not and must not advance the cause of his kingdom by means of the violence employed by our enemies. Our weapons are far stronger, having divine power to dismantle every 'lofty opinion raised against the knowledge of God' and to 'take every thought captive', subduing it to Christ's authority (*2 Cor.* 10:4–5). With such an arsenal we can repay evil with calm kindness and forthright witness, watching God win his victory in his way.

53

Reunions and Farewells

After the uproar ceased, Paul sent for the disciples, and after encouraging them, he said farewell and departed for Macedonia. ² When he had gone through those regions and had given them much encouragement, he came to Greece. ³ There he spent three months, and when a plot was made against him by the Jews as he was about to set sail for Syria, he decided to return through Macedonia. ⁴ Sopater of Berea, the son of Pyrrhus from Berea, accompanied him; and of the Thessalonians, Aristarchus and Secundus; and Gaius of Derbe, and Timothy; and the Asians, Tychicus and Trophimus. ⁵ These went on ahead and were waiting for us at Troas, ⁶ but we sailed away from Philippi after the days of Unleavened Bread, and in five days we came to them at Troas, where we stayed for seven days.

⁷ On the first day of the week, when we were gathered together to break bread, Paul talked with them, intending to depart on the next day, and he prolonged his speech until midnight. ⁸ There were many lamps in the upper room where we were gathered. ⁹ And a young man named Eutychus, sitting at the window, sank into a deep sleep as Paul talked still longer. And being overcome by sleep, he fell down from the third story and was taken up dead. ¹⁰ But Paul went down and bent over him, and taking him in his arms, said, "Do not be alarmed, for his life is in him." ¹¹ And when Paul had gone up and had broken bread and eaten, he conversed with them a long while, until daybreak, and so departed. ¹² And they took the youth away alive, and were not a little comforted (Acts 20:1–12).

In the aftermath of the near riot, Paul acted on his earlier resolve to return to Jerusalem via Macedonia and Achaia. His epistles to the Corinthians and the Romans reveal one purpose for this trip, which is mentioned only briefly in Acts 24:17: 'I came to bring to bring alms to my nation.' These offerings, collected from the Gentile congregations of Macedonia, Achaia, and presumably Galatia and Asia, were a concrete expression of the church's unity, spanning geographic and demographic distances (*1 Cor.* 16:1–4, *2 Cor.* 8–9, *Rom.* 15:25–29). A second purpose for this swing from west (Macedonia and Greece) to east (Syria and Jerusalem) was to encourage the churches previously planted, as was Paul's custom (see also *Acts* 14:21–22; 15:36, 41). Although another Jewish plot grimly foreshadowed greater suffering ahead, the life-giving power of the gospel was illustrated in the resurrection of a dead youth at Troas.

REUNION AND FAREWELL IN MACEDONIA AND GREECE

The Corinthian correspondence exposes Paul's strained and sometimes stormy relations with the Corinthian church during his ministry at Ephesus. Pastoral concerns for the Corinthians prompted Paul to change his travel itinerary – whether to visit Macedonian churches (Philippi, Thessalonica, Berea) first and then go south to Corinth, or vice versa, we do not know (*1 Cor.* 16:5, *2 Cor.* 1:12 – 2:4, 12–13; 7:5–7). But the Corinthian church interpreted these changes as mere vacillation. Luke spares his readers these disturbing details, recording simply Paul's travels: northwards firstly to Macedonia (from which he wrote 2 Corinthians), and then into Greece. Luke does not mention that the northern phase included outreach as far west as Illyricum on the Adriatic Sea (*Rom.* 15:19). These omissions focus our attention on Paul's encouragement of his fellow Christians (20:1–2, 12). The encouragement of Christian brothers and sisters is a privilege and responsibility for all believers (*Heb.* 3:13).

Paul's three months in Greece were probably spent primarily in Corinth, enjoying his reconciled relationship with the Corinthians, about whom Titus' report had given him hope (*2 Cor.* 7:6–7). The letter (lost to us) that Paul had written with tears had borne sweet spiritual fruit (*2 Cor.* 2:4; 7:8–13). During these months he wrote his majestic epistle to the Romans, presenting his gospel to the church in the capital of the Empire in anticipation of his first visit there. He asked the Roman Christians to pray for his deliverance from the unbelievers in Judea (*Rom.* 15:31). God would orchestrate that deliverance and Paul's trip to Rome, as only he, in his wise sovereignty, could.

After those winter months, when sea travel was risky, Paul was ready to set sail from Cenchrea. Learning of another plot of the Jews, perhaps to attack him once the ship was at sea, he went north by land instead. For this return route via the churches of Macedonia, Galatia and Asia, he had amongst his company representatives from Macedonia (Sopater of Berea, Aristarchus and Secundus of Thessalonica), from Galatia (Gaius of Derbe, Timothy of Lystra [*Acts* 16:1]) and from Asia (Tychicus and Trophimus). These were probably the delegates selected by the Gentile congregations to safeguard their offerings for needy Christians in Judea and to express in person the Gentiles' gratitude to their Jewish brothers and sisters (*1 Cor.* 16:3, *2 Cor.* 8:18–24). From prison Paul would later commend Timothy (*Phil.* 2:19–24, *2 Tim.* 1:2, 8), Aristarchus (*Col.* 4:10, see also *Acts* 27:2), and Tychicus (*Col.* 4:7–9, *Eph.* 6:21–22) as co-workers who shared his sufferings.

WORSHIP AND RESURRECTION AT TROAS

Paul observed the seven-day Feast of Unleavened Bread with the Philippian church, no doubt showing them its fulfilment in Christ, the final Passover Lamb, and the inner purity it evokes in us for whom he died (*1 Cor.* 5:7–8). Then, Luke writes, '*we* sailed away from Philippi' (in Macedonia) to Troas in Asia, indicating that he had now rejoined Paul's group, having remained at Philippi on Paul's second journey (the '*we*' pronouns ceased at 16:40).

Paul and company spent a full seven days in Troas, gathering with the church to break bread on the eve of their departure, *on the first day of the week.* This was not merely a social event but an assembly for worship, in which Paul preached and the Lord's Supper was observed, as the reference to breaking bread, literally *the* bread, after midnight, in verse 11 shows. (The definite article is omitted in most translations but is present in Greek. See also *Luke* 22:19; 24:30, 35, *Acts* 2:42, *1 Cor.* 10:16.) The church worshipped on the first day of the week, which had been set apart by the Lord's resurrection as the Lord's Day (*Luke* 24:1, *Rev.* 1:10).

Since Paul intended to leave the following day, he made the most of this last opportunity to encourage the Christians at Troas, where his earlier stays had been abbreviated (16:8–10, *2 Cor.* 2:12–13). To set the scene for a fatal accident, Luke emphasizes that Paul 'prolonged his speech' until midnight, talking on and on. With his physician's acumen Luke notes also that many oil lamps were in the upstairs room where the church met, raising the temperature and reducing the oxygen level. A young man, Eutychus, found himself gradually overcome by drowsiness as he sat in an open window, and when he dropped off to sleep he dropped backward to the street, three storeys below. Rushing downstairs, those who first reached him found him *dead*. Paul, however, threw himself on the lad and embraced him, as the prophets Elijah and Elisha had thrown themselves on the deceased sons of bereaved mothers (*1 Kings* 17:17–24, *2 Kings* 4:33–36). Jesus' resurrection power flowed through his servant, and Paul restored the boy alive to those who loved him, just as Jesus himself had raised and returned a young man to his mourning mother (*Luke* 7:11–15, see also *Acts* 9:36–41).

Paul led the church in celebrating the Supper, and continued his encouraging words until dawn. The promises of God's Word, confirmed by the miraculous sign of God's life–giving power, brought the believers great encouragement. The ESV's *not a little comforted* conveys one meaning of the Greek verb, but obscures the connection with Paul's earlier *encouragement* of Christians in Ephesus and Macedonia (20:1–2). Encouragement is the theme that opens and closes this passage. Although threats loomed on the horizon for the apostle, his concern was that fellow Christians stand fast in their hope, resting on Christ's sufficiency. Do you share his selfless focus on others' growth in Christ?

54

Charge to Watchmen and Shepherds

But going ahead to the ship, we set sail for Assos, intending to take Paul aboard there, for so he had arranged, intending himself to go by land. ^{14} And when he met us at Assos, we took him on board and went to Mitylene. ^{15} And sailing from there we came the following day opposite Chios; the next day we touched at Samos; and the day after that we went to Miletus. ^{16} For Paul had decided to sail past Ephesus, so that he might not have to spend time in Asia, for he was hastening to be at Jerusalem, if possible, on the day of Pentecost.

^{17} Now from Miletus he sent to Ephesus and called the elders of the church to come to him. ^{18} And when they came to him, he said to them:

"You yourselves know how I lived among you the whole time from the first day that I set foot in Asia, ^{19} serving the Lord with all humility and with tears and with trials that happened to me through the plots of the Jews; ^{20} how I did not shrink from declaring to you anything that was profitable, and teaching you in public and from house to house, ^{21} testifying both to Jews and to Greeks of repentance toward God and of faith in our Lord Jesus Christ. ^{22} And now, behold, I am going to Jerusalem, constrained by the Spirit, not knowing what will happen to me there, ^{23} except that the Holy Spirit testifies to me in every city that imprisonment and afflictions await me. ^{24} But I do not account my life of any value nor as precious to myself, if only I may finish my course and the ministry that I received from the Lord Jesus, to testify to the gospel of the grace of God. ^{25} And now, behold, I know that none of you among whom I have gone

about proclaiming the kingdom will see my face again.
²⁶ Therefore I testify to you this day that I am innocent of the
blood of all of you, ²⁷ for I did not shrink from declaring to you
the whole counsel of God. ²⁸ Pay careful attention to yourselves
and to all the flock, in which the Holy Spirit has made you
overseers, to care for the church of God, which he obtained with
his own blood. ²⁹ I know that after my departure fierce wolves
will come in among you, not sparing the flock; ³⁰ and from among
your own selves will arise men speaking twisted things, to draw
away the disciples after them. ³¹ Therefore be alert, remembering
that for three years I did not cease night or day to admonish
everyone with tears. ³² And now I commend you to God and to
the word of his grace, which is able to build you up and to give
you the inheritance among all those who are sanctified. ³³ I
coveted no one's silver or gold or apparel. ³⁴ You yourselves know
that these hands ministered to my necessities and to those who
were with me. ³⁵ In all things I have shown you that by working
hard in this way we must help the weak and remember the words
of the Lord Jesus, how he himself said, 'It is more blessed to give
than to receive.'"
³⁶ And when he had said these things, he knelt down and prayed
with them all. ³⁷ And there was much weeping on the part of all;
they embraced Paul and kissed him, ³⁸ being sorrowful most of
all because of the word he had spoken, that they would not see
his face again. And they accompanied him to the ship (Acts
20:13–38).

P aul was hurrying to reach Jerusalem by Pentecost. Seven weeks
separated Pentecost from Passover, which he had celebrated in
Philippi, and Luke's detailed itinerary indicates that over three of
those had elapsed: seven days for the Feast of Unleavened Bread,
five crossing the Aegean, seven at Troas, and four or five sailing down
the Asian coast (20:5, 13–15). Perhaps Paul wanted to present the
offerings from the Gentiles at the harvest-related Feast of Weeks,
which Jewish tradition also associated with Gentiles hearing God's
Word at Sinai, along with Israel (*Exod.* 19:1; 34:22, *Deut.* 16:9–12,
see also *Acts* 2:1). He could not risk delay at Ephesus, whether

through prolonged ministry or opposition, so he bypassed its port, landing further south instead at Miletus. Yet concern for the Christians in Ephesus moved him to invest several days to summon and await the church's elders, so that he might charge and encourage them for their shepherding responsibilities in his absence.

In the context of the book of Acts, Paul's address to the Ephesian elders is his last message preached in a predominantly Gentile venue, and the only one addressed to Christians. These are Paul's 'closing words' to the Gentiles, his unique sphere of evangelistic witness and pastoral ministry. Paul's words also derive poignancy from his announcement that these believers, among whom Paul had ministered daily for several years, would not see his face again. This statement, more than any other, pierced the elders' hearts with pain.

Paul's speech is a farewell discourse, similar to the parting words of other leaders in redemptive history: Jacob's farewell to his sons (*Gen.* 49–50); Moses' sermons on the plains of Moab (the whole of Deuteronomy); Joshua's charge to Israel (*Josh.* 23:1–24:27); Samuel's speech after confirming Saul as king (*1 Sam.* 12:1–25); and Jesus' upper room discourse (*John* 13–17) in which he prepared his disciples for his death but also for his presence in a new way, through the Spirit of Truth. Second Timothy and 2 Peter are apostolic farewell discourses in written form, preparing the church for life after the apostles' deaths. At transition points in covenantal leadership, the departing leader directed God's people to look back to God's past faithfulness and ahead to future challenges and to their own faithfulness.

LOOKING BACK AND LOOKING FORWARD

The structure of Paul's speech shows how the past and the future are interrelated. Paul began with the past, reciting his faithfulness in teaching everything beneficial to everyone everywhere (20:17–21). Then he looked to the future, announcing his departure for Jerusalem and his expectation that they would not see him again (verses 22–25). Then he drew conclusions from his past faithfulness and his future absence. Regarding the past, Paul repeated the words *I did not shrink from declaring* (verses 20, 27) to support the claim that his faithful preaching of God's whole will exonerated him from responsibility for the blood of his hearers (verses 26–27). Mentioning his departure again (verse 29), he predicted future dangers for the church and charged the elders to protect God's sheep (verses 28–32). Finally, Paul committed them to God's care for the future, recalling his own past pattern of generosity as an example of Christ-like servant-hood (verses 33–35). Paul rehearsed his integrity in office not to defend his reputation from criticism but to teach the elders through his own example, to engrave indelibly on their memories the picture of his tireless, tearful, truth-telling service as a pattern for their own ministry as shepherds of God's flock.

PAUL, THE FAITHFUL WATCHMAN

When Paul declared, 'I am innocent of the blood of all of you', he was referring to God's sobering metaphor when he charged Ezekiel with his prophetic responsibility. God compared his spokesman to a watchman posted on the city wall to be on the lookout for impending attacks (*Ezek.* 3:18–19; 33:1–9). If the watchman, seeing danger on the horizon, sounds his trumpet in alarm, citizens who fail to take warning have only themselves to blame when they are destroyed. The watchman has done his job and is innocent of their blood. But if he fails to sound the trumpet – if the prophet fails to deliver God's warning of judgement and call to repentance – then as the wicked die God will hold the watchman, his spokesman, accountable for their blood.

Our message is not our own, but God's. It has urgent, life-or-death consequences. Although the watchman himself cannot bring either the judgement or the rescue, what he does or fails to do has eternal consequences. So Paul's affirmation is his way of saying, 'I have been a faithful watchman, I have fully discharged my duty to deliver God's message.' Notice the reasons for Paul's confidence:

He brought a complete message. He held back nothing that would benefit his listeners. He proclaimed the whole will of God. He did not trim his message to appeal to their tastes or avoid their prejudices. Paul spoke the language of his audience and bridged the gap between their present understanding and God's full revelation, but Paul dared not sift through God's revelation, discarding some truths as less profitable. Everything *profitable* was simply *the whole counsel of God*, his redemptive plan, promised in the Old Testament and fulfilled in the gospel. According to his hearers' capacities, feeding milk to babies and meat to the mature, Paul preached the whole truth that God had revealed, with Christ as the integrating centre point (see also *Col.* 1:27, *1 Cor.* 2:2). At other points Paul summarized his message in other ways: *repentance toward God and faith in our Lord Jesus Christ* (20:21); *the gospel of the grace of God* (verse 24); *the kingdom* (verse 25); and *the word of God's grace* (verse 32).

He addressed a comprehensive audience, which included both Jews and Greeks (verse 21). He did not prefer people like himself before others who were different; nor people with historic covenantal connections before raw pagans (or vice versa). Paul knew that absolutely everybody he met, upstanding or down and out, self-respecting or scorned by others, needed the grace offered in the gospel of Christ.

He was compelled by a compassionate motive. He spoke with self-forgetting urgency because he was utterly focused on the eternal, spiritual well-being of those he served, not on his own comfort or convenience. He ministered with all humility, not to boost his ego or enhance his reputation, but to draw others to Jesus. Twice Paul mentioned the tears with which he persuaded others as revealing his longing that they turn from dead idols to find life in the Lord Jesus. Paul knew that God had sovereignly chosen a people for himself, whom he would surely regenerate, preserve, and glorify. Yet that assurance never bred in Paul a cold indifference to his hearers. Rather, with tears he urged people to repent and believe: 'We implore you on behalf of Christ, be reconciled to God' (*2 Cor.* 5:20). The purity of Paul's motives was also seen in the troubles he endured through the plots of the Jews (*Acts* 20:19; see also 19:9). Rejection by his own people – the ancient covenant people – wounded Paul deeply, but he endured it for the sake of bringing good news to the Gentiles. The same Spirit who compelled his travel to Jerusalem foretold sufferings waiting him there, yet Paul's single-minded purpose was to complete the mission entrusted to him by his Lord.

He preached with committed consistency, everywhere and all the time. He taught both *in public and house to house.* Publicly, Paul preached in open venues such as the synagogue (19:8) and the lecture hall of Tyrannus (19:9). *House to house* refers primarily to gatherings of believers in the larger homes of affluent Christians (see also *Rom.* 16:5, *1 Cor.* 16:19, *Col.* 4:15, *Philem.* 2), but it would also include private ministry to individuals and families. Paul's passion to bring the gospel to people was not limited to settings in which he could gain fame or be the centre of attention. He was also eager to share God's truth in settings that were out of the public eye. While supporting his team from his tent-making trade (20:34), Paul preached and persuaded night and day for three years (verse 31). He did not approach the ministry as an 8-to-5, forty-hour-per-week job. Nor did he fly into a city, rack up statistics, and leave. Whenever possible, Paul stayed long enough to help new Christians put their roots down deeply into the truth of Christ.

In his comprehensive ministry – constantly preaching God's whole truth with urgent compassion to all sorts of people in various venues – Paul set the pace for the elders who would build on the foundation he laid.

ELDERS, THE FAITHFUL SHEPHERDS

When Paul began to address the elders' responsibilities in the future, he turned to another Old Testament metaphor: 'Care for [or shepherd] the church of God.' Through Jeremiah and Ezekiel, God had rebuked Israel's leaders as unfaithful shepherds, and he had promised to replace them (*Jer.* 23:1–6, *Ezek.* 34:2–23). Israel's leaders had scattered the sheep rather than gathering them, and had exploited rather than feeding and protecting them. In their selfish indifference they did not retrieve the stray, bandage the wounded, nor discipline the strong rams that bullied the weak. Therefore the Lord himself would come to seek, bind up, and discipline. He would appoint over them a single Shepherd, the righteous Branch descended from David. Jesus, the good Shepherd, fulfils these promises (*John* 10).

Jeremiah 23:4 also predicts a *plurality* of faithful shepherds, replacing Israel's unfaithful kings and priests. The fulfilment of this promise is the body of elders or overseers now given to the church, charged by Paul here and by Peter in 1 Peter 5:2 to shepherd the flock of God – to feed, protect, and discipline God's people for their growth in grace. Through such shepherds Jesus, the chief Shepherd, now cares for his sheep. Paul mentions several factors to motivate elders to care conscientiously for God's flock.

Elders are appointed by the Holy Spirit (20:28a). They hold office not out of their own initiative, but because God the Spirit, working through the discernment of the church, recruited and installed them in the task.

God paid an infinite price to acquire his flock (verse 28b). God purchased his church 'with his own blood', or 'the blood of his Own'. The Greek adjective 'his own' may refer directly to the blood (applying the title 'God' to Jesus, as in *Rom.* 9:5); or it could express God's relationship to the One who shed his blood. Because he is 'God's own' Son, beloved by the Father, the costliness of his death demonstrates the magnitude of God's love toward his church (see also *Rom.* 8:32; 5:10). On either interpretation, Paul's purpose was to emphasize the infinite investment God has made in his church. He procured this treasure at the highest price imaginable and expects his shepherds to guard it with care.

God's flock will face dangers from without and within (*Acts* 20:29–30). In the apostle's absence savage wolves, itinerant false prophets and teachers, would attack the flock from outside, spreading infectious heresy like gangrene (*2 Tim.* 2:17; see also 3:1–9; 4:3, *1 John* 2:18–23, *2 John*, *2 Pet.* 2, *Jude* 3–16). Even more alarming was Paul's prediction that predators would arise '*from among your own selves*', as some elders become intoxicated by their influence over others and twist the gospel to attract disciples to themselves rather than to Jesus. In view of this danger Paul's exhortation 'Pay careful attention to yourselves' (20:28) is not merely reflexive, calling each elder to individual self-examination, though that is included (*1 Tim.* 4:16). It is primarily corporate and reciprocal: 'Pay careful attention to each other.' (The reflexive and reciprocal pronouns are sometimes interchangeable in New Testament Greek, for example *1 Pet.* 4:8–10.) Therefore a renewed call to vigilance, 'Therefore be alert', comes on the heels of the warning about deceptive shepherds (20:31). This mutual accountability is the principle underlying the apostles' practice of appointing a plurality of elders in each church (14:23), to guard each other from error and arrogance, and the flock from abuse.

GOD, THE FAITHFUL PROTECTOR

With these heavy responsibilities and sombre warnings ringing in the elders' ears, how inexpressibly sweet the apostle's next words must have sounded: 'I commend you to God and to the word of his grace, which is able to build you up and to give you the inheritance among all those who are sanctified' (20:32). This statement is climactic in two respects.

(1) It climaxes the various ways within this speech that Paul has characterized the Word of God. It is God's Word of unmerited favour, which grants believers a share in the saints' heavenly inheritance (see also 26:18; *Col.* 1:12).

(2) It climaxes a series of texts in which believers are entrusted to the Lord for safekeeping. As Paul and Barnabas retraced their steps through Lystra, Iconium, and Pisidian Antioch, they appointed elders in each church, commending them to the Lord 'in whom they had believed' (14:23). Paul and Barnabas themselves had been entrusted to God's grace, through prayer with fasting, when they first set out from Antioch in Syria (14:26; see also 13:3). Likewise, when Paul and Silas set out on the second journey, the church entrusted them to the Lord's grace (15:40).

As watchmen and shepherds, elders must protect the sheep from outside predators and sometimes, sadly, even from each other. With this weighty duty, however, comes the heartening promise of Jesus, 'I will never leave you nor forsake you' (*Heb.* 13:5), and his assurance, 'I will build my church' (*Matt.* 16:18). We are not orphans, left to our own devices, for Jesus comes to us and accompanies us, in his Spirit of truth (*John* 14:18).

55

Paul's Face Fixed
Toward Jerusalem

And when we had parted from them and set sail, we came by a straight course to Cos, and the next day to Rhodes, and from there to Patara. *² And having found a ship crossing to Phoenicia, we went aboard and set sail. ³ When we had come in sight of Cyprus, leaving it on the left we sailed to Syria and landed at Tyre, for there the ship was to unload its cargo. ⁴ And having sought out the disciples, we stayed there for seven days. And through the Spirit they were telling Paul not to go on to Jerusalem. ⁵ When our days there were ended, we departed and went on our journey, and they all, with wives and children, accompanied us until we were outside the city. And kneeling down on the beach, we prayed ⁶ and said farewell to one another. Then we went on board the ship, and they returned home.*

⁷ When we had finished the voyage from Tyre, we arrived at Ptolemais, and we greeted the brothers and stayed with them for one day. ⁸ On the next day we departed and came to Caesarea, and we entered the house of Philip the evangelist, who was one of the seven, and stayed with him. ⁹ He had four unmarried daughters, who prophesied. ¹⁰ While we were staying for many days, a prophet named Agabus came down from Judea. ¹¹ And coming to us, he took Paul's belt and bound his own feet and hands and said, "Thus says the Holy Spirit, 'This is how the Jews at Jerusalem will bind the man who owns this belt and deliver him into the hands of the Gentiles.'" ¹² When we heard this, we and the people there urged him not to go up to Jerusalem. ¹³ Then Paul answered, "What are you doing, weeping and breaking my heart? For I am ready not only to be imprisoned

but even to die in Jerusalem for the name of the Lord Jesus."
14 And since he would not be persuaded, we ceased and said, "Let
the will of the Lord be done."
15 After these days we got ready and went up to Jerusalem.
16 And some of the disciples from Caesarea went with us, bringing
us to the house of Mnason of Cyprus, an early disciple, with
whom we should lodge (Acts 21:1–16).

A t first glance this section seems to be little more than a travel
itinerary, listing ports of call and lengths of stay. Some scholars
plausibly speculate that behind such passages lies a diary that Luke
kept daily as they journeyed. In the midst of the times and places,
however, Luke is developing a more profound and ominous theme.
Everywhere Paul stopped, it seems, he heard foreboding warnings
of suffering awaiting him in Jerusalem. His brothers and sisters, even
those on his own team, drew the obvious conclusion that Paul should
change course to avoid the afflictions ahead. Paul, however, though
equally convinced by the Holy Spirit's predictions, drew the opposite
conclusion. Since the same Spirit who foretold suffering had
constrained his heart to make this visit – especially, as his epistles
show, to deliver the offering from the Gentile churches – Paul was
determined to face with courage whatever hardship lay before him
for the sake of Jesus' Name. Moving resolutely toward suffering in
Jerusalem, Paul was walking in the footsteps of his Saviour.

PROGRESSING TO JERUSALEM

The heart-wrenching farewell from the Ephesian elders, following
prayer offered on their knees (20:36–37), would be repeated at other
stops along Paul's route to Jerusalem. Paul's announcement that
prison and hardships awaited him in Jerusalem (verse 23) hung like
a dark cloud over his every gathering with believers along the way.
Three times in these verses Jerusalem is mentioned by name as the
site of the apostle's impending suffering (21:4, 11, 13). A distinctive
feature of Luke's Gospel is the travel narrative that begins with the
words, '[Jesus] set his face to go to Jerusalem' (*Luke* 9:51), and
mentions that dire destination frequently thereafter (9:53; 13:33;
18:31; 19:11; see also 9:31). Luke's Greek wording is literally, 'he

fixed his face firmly', an allusion to the Suffering Servant's flinty resolve to endure shame and pain for God's sake (*Isa.* 50:7). Now it was Paul, servant of Jesus the Servant, whose resolve to reach Jerusalem and the hardships it held could not be deflected.

Paul and his company, including our author Luke and the delegates of the Gentile churches entrusted with their offerings (see also 20:4), took a small coastal vessel around the south-west tip of Asia Minor. They harboured overnight on the islands of Cos and Rhodes before reaching the port of Patara on the mainland. There they booked passage on a larger cargo ship that could navigate the open sea and was departing for Tyre in Phoenicia, a major port some distance south of Syrian Antioch (and therefore much closer to Judea). Passing the island of Cyprus, visible off to their left, the ship landed at Tyre, probably within a week of setting out from Patara.

While the ship was being unloaded, Paul's group sought out the Christians of Tyre, with whom they stayed a week. Those scattered in the aftermath of Stephen's martyrdom evangelized throughout Phoenicia (11:19), and Paul and Barnabas had visited Phoenician churches when travelling from Antioch to the council in Jerusalem (15:3); so Paul apparently knew disciples at Tyre. Their deep affection for Paul was evident in their efforts to dissuade him from going to Jerusalem. Luke's comment that it was '*through the Spirit*' that they urged Paul not to proceed seems puzzling, since Paul had decided '*in the Spirit*' to make this trip (19:21) and felt himself '*compelled by the Spirit*' to follow through, even though the Holy Spirit also warned of troubles to come (20:22–23). Here Luke is summarizing the sort of exchange that he will narrate in more detail in connection with Agabus' prophecy at Caesarea: the Spirit revealed to a prophet the troubles awaiting Paul in Jerusalem, whereupon believers, who loved him, tried to persuade him to avoid these pains, as Peter had when Jesus foretold his own sufferings (*Matt.*16: 21–23). Their efforts, however, proved fruitless. When the ship had received new cargo and was ready to sail south, whole families – husbands, wives, and children – accompanied Paul and his colleagues to the wharf, kneeling with him in prayer on the beach before bidding them a sad farewell.

SUFFERINGS TO COME IN JERUSALEM

Disembarking at Ptolemais, the group enjoyed the fellowship and hospitality of brothers in Christ there before proceeding to Caesarea, the seaside capital of the province of Judea and the locale for Peter's groundbreaking evangelization of Cornelius and his friends. Even before that event Philip, one of the Seven appointed to distribute food to the church's widows, had reached Caesarea after evangelizing Samaria, the Ethiopian eunuch, and the coastal towns of old Philistia (8:40). Though ordained to mercy ministry, Philip's eagerness to tell the good news of Jesus (8:4–5, 12) warranted his being called the evangelist, a title that appears rarely in the New Testament (*Eph.* 4:11, *2 Tim.* 4:5). His four virgin daughters, who had the gift of prophecy, were living proof of the Spirit's coming at Pentecost, fulfilling God's promise, 'Your sons and daughters will prophesy' (2:17).

Luke calls attention, however, not to the prophecies of Philip's daughters, but to one brought by Agabus of Judea, who had earlier announced a coming famine, moving the church at Antioch to send relief to Jerusalem (11:28–30). This time Agabus performed a 'prophecy in action', in the tradition of the Old Testament prophets (*1 Kings* 11:29–32 [torn cloak]; *Isa.* 20:2–6 [nakedness]; *Jer.* 13:1–11 [linen belt]; 19:1–13 [clay jar]; *Ezek.* 4:1–17 [clay tablet, defiled bread]). Agabus took Paul's long cloth belt, normally wrapped several times around the waist, and tied himself up hand and foot. Then he invoked the Holy Spirit in the manner of the ancient prophets (see also 'Thus says the Lord', *Amos* 1:6, 9, 11, etc.) predicting, 'This is how the Jews at Jerusalem will bind the man who owns this belt and deliver him into the hands of the Gentiles.'

Agabus' prophecy underscores how Paul's treatment, though not identical to that of Jesus, nevertheless reflects the suffering of his Lord, whom Jewish leaders 'delivered over to the Gentiles' (*Luke* 18:32). Its fulfilment would occur in a surprising way, with Roman troops taking Paul into custody to protect him from mob violence – a protection turned into imprisonment by Jewish accusations and assassination plots. Yet Paul himself would later summarize this convoluted legal situation in terms that echoed Agabus' prediction:

'I was delivered as a prisoner from Jerusalem into the hands of the Romans' (28:17).

Again Paul's brothers and sisters, including Luke and others from Paul's entourage, reacted to the prediction with efforts to dissuade Paul from continuing his march toward trouble. Their tears hammered his heart, assaulting his resistance by appeal to his affection for them all. Still, he remained convinced that the Holy Spirit wanted him in Jerusalem. He had told the Ephesian elders that completing the mission given him by the Lord Jesus was worth more than his physical life (20:24), and now he asserted that he was ready to face not only prison but even death for the sake of Jesus' name. Suffering for the sake of this Name is the highest of privileges (5:41). From detention in Rome Paul would write, 'It is my eager expectation and hope that I will not be at all ashamed, but that with full courage now as always Christ will be honoured in my body, whether by life or by death' (*Phil.* 1:20). When our hearts echo Paul's self-forgetting commitment to Christ's cause, it means that we are learning Paul's secret: 'For to me to live is Christ, and to die is gain' (verse 21).

Unable to persuade the apostle to pursue safety rather than obedience, the Christians surrendered to God's sovereign authority, echoing Jesus' prayer of submission in Gethsemane: 'Let the will of the Lord be done' (see also *Luke* 22:42, *Matt.* 6:10). It will be done in any case, and ultimately, despite our fears, it will be good for his children, who trust in Jesus (*Rom.* 8:28–30).

Some believers accompanied Paul and his retinue to Jerusalem. Either en route or when they reached the city, the group lodged with Mnason, a Cypriot who had become a disciple early on (see also 11:19–20). The hospitality of men such as Mnason and Philip provided Luke ample opportunity to interview eyewitnesses, filling out the research into Christian origins on which his two–volume history is based (*Luke* 1:1–4). Luke's connection with Christian roots reassures not only Theophilus but also his twenty-first century readers that we can rely on his record of Jesus' words and deeds.

56

Chains in Jerusalem

When we had come to Jerusalem, the brothers received us gladly.
¹⁸ On the following day Paul went in with us to James, and all
the elders were present. ¹⁹ After greeting them, he related one by
one the things that God had done among the Gentiles through
his ministry. ²⁰ And when they heard it, they glorified God. And
they said to him, "You see, brother, how many thousands there
are among the Jews of those who have believed. They are all
zealous for the law, ²¹ and they have been told about you that
you teach all the Jews who are among the Gentiles to forsake
Moses, telling them not to circumcise their children or walk
according to our customs. ²² What then is to be done? They will
certainly hear that you have come. ²³ Do therefore what we tell
you. We have four men who are under a vow; ²⁴ take these men
and purify yourself along with them and pay their expenses, so
that they may shave their heads. Thus all will know that there
is nothing in what they have been told about you, but that you
yourself also live in observance of the law. ²⁵ But as for the
Gentiles who have believed, we have sent a letter with our
judgement that they should abstain from what has been sacrificed
to idols, and from blood, and from what has been strangled, and
from sexual immorality." ²⁶ Then Paul took the men, and the
next day he purified himself along with them and went into the
temple, giving notice when the days of purification would be
fulfilled and the offering presented for each one of them.

²⁷ When the seven days were almost completed, the Jews from
Asia, seeing him in the temple, stirred up the whole crowd and
laid hands on him, ²⁸ crying out, "Men of Israel, help! This is
the man who is teaching everyone everywhere against the people

and the law and this place. Moreover, he even brought Greeks into the temple and has defiled this holy place." ²⁹ For they had previously seen Trophimus the Ephesian with him in the city, and they supposed that Paul had brought him into the temple. ³⁰ Then all the city was stirred up, and the people ran together. They seized Paul and dragged him out of the temple, and at once the gates were shut. ³¹ And as they were seeking to kill him, word came to the tribune of the cohort that all Jerusalem was in confusion. ³² He at once took soldiers and centurions and ran down to them. And when they saw the tribune and the soldiers, they stopped beating Paul. ³³ Then the tribune came up and arrested him and ordered him to be bound with two chains. He inquired who he was and what he had done. ³⁴ Some in the crowd were shouting one thing, some another. And as he could not learn the facts because of the uproar, he ordered him to be brought into the barracks. ³⁵ And when he came to the steps, he was actually carried by the soldiers because of the violence of the crowd, ³⁶ for the mob of the people followed, crying out, "Away with him!" (Acts 21:17–36).

L uke recalibrates his camera into slow motion to record the conflict that Paul encountered in Jerusalem when he sought to demonstrate his loyalty to his Jewish heritage. The next two and a half chapters of Acts (21:17 – 23:35) record the events of a period of less than two weeks' duration (see also 24:11). As the Evangelists gave extended treatment to the week leading to Jesus' death (for example *Luke* 19:28–23:56), so here Luke slows his narrative pace to emphasize the importance of Paul's suffering at the hands of the Jewish leadership, which was foretold repeatedly as Paul travelled to Jerusalem. The outcome for Paul, at least at this time, would differ from that endured by his Lord. Nevertheless the apostle was following in the footsteps of the Suffering Servant, seeking opportunity to bear witness to the name of Jesus in every assault, conversation, or inquest.

WELCOME AND COUNSEL FROM BROTHERS IN CHRIST

Upon arriving in Jerusalem, Paul and his companions immediately received a warm welcome from their brothers in Christ. The following day they had a more official meeting with James and the elders of the Jerusalem church, in which they reported God's achievement in gathering Gentiles to faith in Jesus through Paul's ministry, as Paul had reported on earlier occasions (14:27; 15:4). The turning of the nations to faith is always God's work, however he may use his human servants to proclaim his Word (see also *Isa.* 45:22). Therefore the elders appropriately gave God alone all the glory for his conquest of the peoples by his sovereign grace (see also 11:18).

Since the delegates of the Gentile churches were present, their offering presumably was presented to James and the elders, but Luke does not mention it, although he will later indicate that this was Paul's purpose for coming to Jerusalem (24:17). Paul had requested prayer that the Gentiles' offering would be accepted by the church in Judea in the spirit of unity in which it was offered (*Rom.* 15:31). Perhaps he feared that slanders circulating among unbelieving Jews could dampen the mother church's enthusiasm for the mission to the Gentiles. Although James and the elders remained supportive of that outreach, they frankly acknowledged that Paul's reputation was suffering among many Jewish Christians. Perhaps Luke's silence about the offering at this point implies that suspicion prevented it from accomplishing the unifying purpose that Paul desired.

The report that thousands of Jews had believed shows that, despite the frustration that often met Paul's witness in the Dispersion, the gospel was still bearing abundant fruit in Judea. The problem posed by this growth was that these believers, who remained zealous in keeping the Law of Moses, had received misinformation about Paul's teaching and conduct among the Jewish Dispersion. Enemies of the gospel reported that Paul was urging Jews who trusted Jesus to abandon the Mosaic distinctives that had set Israel apart from the nations, particularly the circumcision of their children and customs such as the kosher dietary restrictions. Paul's epistles show that, while he insisted that circumcision not be imposed on Gentiles, he never demanded that Jewish believers abandon it. Its presence or absence was irrelevant to a person's relationship to God (*Gal.* 6:15, *1 Cor.* 7:19). In fact, for the sake of winning more Gentiles and Jews to Christ, in the liberty he enjoyed under Christ's law Paul himself was prepared either to live outside the Mosaic ceremonial regulations or to abide by them (*1 Cor.* 9:19–23). In Corinth Paul had fulfilled a Nazirite vow (18:18), and his hurry to reach Jerusalem for Pentecost showed that he still valued Israel's calendar of festivals (20:16; see also 20:6).

The scurrilous rumours alleging Paul's 'turning away' from Moses apparently caused zealous Jewish Christians to question the inclusion of the Gentiles, despite the Jerusalem council's earlier decision, which James and the elders now reaffirmed. The rumours may also have jeopardized their outreach to their unbelieving Jewish kinsmen, for whom Paul's heart ached (*Rom.* 9:1–3). Paul urged others to restrain their own freedom to avoid giving offence to Jews, Greeks, or God's church, pointing to his own example (*1 Cor.* 10:32 – 11:1). Therefore he readily heeded James's advice to demonstrate his respect for Israel's heritage by participating, in person and in payment for sacrificial animals, with four brothers who were soon to complete their own Nazirite vows. He promptly gave notice that in seven days' time he and the four brothers would appear at the temple to conclude their vow with the prescribed sacrificial offerings (*Num.* 6:13–21).

ACCUSED, BEATEN, AND ARRESTED

James's plan to pacify Jewish sensibilities and refute Jewish slanders against Paul seemed to backfire. In the temple Asian Jews recognized Paul from his effective ministry in Ephesus, and they reacted immediately and violently. They seized Paul and shouted wild accusations to gather a mob to join in their attack on this man, whom they considered highly dangerous to their Jewish way of life. Inadvertently echoing Stephen's accusers (see also 6:13–14), they charged that Paul taught against the Jewish people, the law, and this place, that is, the temple.

Specifically, they jumped to the conclusion that Paul had defiled the temple by bringing an uncircumcised Gentile – Trophimus of Ephesus (20:4), whom they had seen with Paul elsewhere – past the wall that separated the Court of the Gentiles from the temple precincts proper. That wall bore a sign, mentioned by ancient writers and recovered by modern archaeologists, warning Gentiles that they would face immediate, violent death for trespassing that boundary. We who know Paul's true motive for being in the temple find their accusation ludicrous, but their perception of Paul as an apostate from Judaism and their zeal for temple, Torah, and tradition made the accusation plausible to the crowds milling in the temple courts. The mob dragged Paul out to the Court of the Gentiles and closed the gates to protect the inner courts from defilement from his blood, as they began to beat him to death for his blasphemy.

A Roman cohort (one thousand soldiers) was garrisoned in the Fortress Antonia, which overshadowed the temple and provided quick access to its precincts when troops were needed to quell civil disturbances among the restive Jewish worshippers. News of the riot flew upstairs to the tribune, Claudius Lysius (23:26), who immediately raced downstairs with centurions and soldiers under their command. Since each centurion commanded one hundred troops, at least two hundred Roman infantrymen emerged from the fortress stairway. Not surprisingly, at their appearance, Paul's attackers withdrew.

Since Paul was obviously the occasion of the turmoil, Claudius Lysius had him arrested and chained by both hands. (In this surprising way Agabus' prediction was fulfilled: Jewish hostility placed Paul, bound, into Roman custody.) Unable to discern Paul's crime because of the conflicting shouts of the mob, the tribune commanded that Paul be brought up to his headquarters in the fortress. The zealous mob emerged from its momentary paralysis of intimidation, rushing the soldiers and their captive, who had to be carried to safety on the stairway leading up to the barracks. The mob continued to chant, 'Away with him!' just as an earlier crowd had demanded of the Procurator Pontius Pilate, 'Away with this man' (*Luke* 23:18) and 'Crucify him' (*Mark* 15:13).

Had James's plan backfired? Paul was in the temple to show his loyalty to the faith of Israel, and that worthy motive led to his being beaten as an apostate and defiler of the temple. Nor was this the first time that he had felt the pain of having his best intentions misconstrued in the worst light (*2 Cor.* 6:8–9, *Gal.* 1:10). Did Paul err in following James's advice? We might think so, if we look only at the short-term outcome. Careful reflection, however, leads to a different conclusion.

Paul's motive, after all, was not to avoid mistreatment at the hands of unbelievers, but to reassure Jewish Christians that he supported their continued adherence to the customs commanded by Moses. In the week before Paul's arrest, his participation with the four brothers who were completing their vow would have become known throughout the Jerusalem church, setting many believers' suspicions to rest. More importantly, as Paul had travelled to Jerusalem the Holy Spirit repeatedly announced the sufferings and imprisonment awaiting him there, most graphically only days before in the 'action prophecy' of Agabus (20:23; 21:4, 10–11). Paul did not expect to evade the suffering that God's purpose had in store for him, nor did he wish to. For the sake of Christ's cause and church Paul was willing to endure not only inconvenience but also hardship and even death. The riot at the temple would prove to be one of a series of interlocking events in God's plan to bring Paul to Rome, the capital of the Empire.

Often we gauge whether a decision has been right or wrong by the results that we see in the short run. Many of the factors that produce those results, however, lie beyond our control. God does not expect us to foresee the future, so he weighs our decisions according to the standards of his Word and the motives of our hearts. Choices made for the right reasons please our Father, whatever the immediate outcome may be.

57

Paul's Defence to the People of Israel

As Paul was about to be brought into the barracks, he said to the tribune, "May I say something to you?" And he said, "Do you know Greek? ³⁸ Are you not the Egyptian, then, who recently stirred up a revolt and led the four thousand men of the Assassins out into the wilderness?" ³⁹ Paul replied, "I am a Jew, from Tarsus in Cilicia, a citizen of no obscure city. I beg you, permit me to speak to the people." ⁴⁰ And when he had given him permission, Paul, standing on the steps, motioned with his hand to the people. And when there was a great hush, he addressed them in the Hebrew language, saying:

¹ "Brothers and fathers, hear the defence that I now make before you."

² And when they heard that he was addressing them in the Hebrew language, they became even more quiet. And he said:

³ "I am a Jew, born in Tarsus in Cilicia, but brought up in this city, educated at the feet of Gamaliel according to the strict manner of the law of our fathers, being zealous for God as all of you are this day. ⁴ I persecuted this Way to the death, binding and delivering to prison both men and women, ⁵ as the high priest and the whole council of elders can bear me witness. From them I received letters to the brothers, and I journeyed towards Damascus to take those also who were there and bring them in bonds to Jerusalem to be punished.

⁶ "As I was on my way and drew near to Damascus, about noon a great light from heaven suddenly shone around me. ⁷ And I fell to the ground and heard a voice saying to me, 'Saul, Saul, why are you persecuting me?' ⁸ And I answered, 'Who are you,

Lord?' And he said to me, 'I am Jesus of Nazareth, whom you are persecuting.' [9] Now those who were with me saw the light but did not understand the voice of the one who was speaking to me. [10] And I said, 'What shall I do, Lord?' And the Lord said to me, 'Rise, and go into Damascus, and there you will be told all that is appointed for you to do.' [11] And since I could not see because of the brightness of that light, I was led by the hand by those who were with me, and came into Damascus.

[12] "And one Ananias, a devout man according to the law, well spoken of by all the Jews who lived there, [13] came to me, and standing by me said to me, 'Brother Saul, receive your sight.' And at that very hour I received my sight and saw him. [14] And he said, 'The God of our fathers appointed you to know his will, to see the Righteous One and to hear a voice from his mouth; [15] for you will be a witness for him to everyone of what you have seen and heard. [16] And now why do you wait? Rise and be baptized and wash away your sins, calling on his name.'

[17] "When I had returned to Jerusalem and was praying in the temple, I fell into a trance [18] and saw him saying to me, 'Make haste and get out of Jerusalem quickly, because they will not accept your testimony about me.' [19] And I said, 'Lord, they themselves know that in one synagogue after another I imprisoned and beat those who believed in you. [20] And when the blood of Stephen your witness was being shed, I myself was standing by and approving and watching over the garments of those who killed him.' [21] And he said to me, 'Go, for I will send you far away to the Gentiles'" (Acts 21:37–22:21).

Despite the life-threatening beating from which he had just been rescued, Paul was unwilling to give up his attempt to vindicate the gospel in the eyes of his Jewish kinsmen. As he and the soldiers reached the top of the stairway and were about to enter the fortress, he respectfully requested permission to address the tribune, who expressed surprise at Paul's polished Greek.

Claudius Lysias had assumed that Paul might be the Egyptian prophetic pretender whose revolutionary movement had recently been put down by the Roman procurator, Felix. The Egyptian presented himself as a new Moses and Joshua. He had gathered to himself four thousand assassins (literally, 'dagger men'), and they had lived in the desert like Israel in Moses' day. According to the Jewish historian Josephus, the Egyptian predicted that Jerusalem's walls would fall like Jericho's when surrounded by his guerrillas, leaving Rome's occupation forces exposed. Instead, four hundred rebels were killed and another two hundred captured, while their leader escaped.

Paul insisted that he was a Jew, not an Egyptian, and that he was a citizen of Tarsus, a highly respected city, and not a terrorist from the wilderness. His command of Greek, his courtesy in addressing the tribune, and his claim to a status worthy of honour combined to persuade the commander to grant Paul permission to address the Jewish crowds milling in the temple precincts below. The apostle to the Gentiles would try again to convince his countrymen that faith in Jesus the Messiah is the fulfilment, not the repudiation, of God's covenant with Israel.

Paul's defence is an autobiographical account of his early training in Judaism and violent opposition to the Christian Way, of his life-changing meeting with the risen Lord near Damascus, and of a subsequent vision granted him in the very temple that he was accused of defiling. For the next several chapters Paul would offer his defence in various venues, adapting his presentations to the varying backgrounds of his Jewish and Gentile audiences (24:10; 25:8; 26:1–2). This speech at the temple is the second of the three narratives of Paul's conversion on the road to Damascus. (See *Acts* 9 and 26, discussed in Chapters 24 and 64). Through such repeated narration, as we have seen, Luke emphasizes the event's importance, adding details appropriate to each setting. This first report by Paul himself of how Jesus transformed him, is a direct response to the slander that he, Paul, advocated Jewish apostasy from the Law of Moses and the temple.

GOD'S ZEALOT

Paul began building bridges immediately by addressing the crowd in Aramaic. The original says 'the Hebrew dialect' and could refer to Hebrew, which was still a living, spoken language, especially in the context of temple worship. But the expression also included

Aramaic, the Semitic language most widely used by Jews in Palestine. Hearing Paul address them in their own language, the crowd settled into silence to catch his every word. He showed both respect and Jewish solidarity by addressing them as brothers and fathers, just as Stephen had in opening his defence (7:2).

Paul's early life showed his affinity for everything that his hearers held dear. He was a Jew. Although born in the Dispersion, in Tarsus of Cilicia, he had been brought up in this city, Jerusalem, from his early childhood. His rabbinical education was at the feet of Gamaliel, leader of the respected School of Hillel, whose wise moderation in response to the Christian movement Luke had recorded earlier (5:34–40). His training in their ancestral law had been thorough, even rigorous. A similar word to that rendered *strict* in the ESV appears in Paul's later description of the Pharisees, to whom he belonged, as 'the strictest party of our religion' (26:5); so Paul's education in the law entailed not only exhaustive detail but also scrupulous precision in application. His zeal for the Torah and for tradition was unsurpassed among his hearers, exhibiting itself especially in his violent persecution of Jesus' followers. These claims parallel Paul's retrospective on his pre-Christian life in his epistles (*Gal.* 1:13–14, *Phil.* 3:4–6). He had not spared women but arrested them along with male believers, handing them over to prison, punishment, and even death (*Acts* 8:3; 26:10). In seizing Christians he was 'persecuting this Way' (as the Greek reads literally), trying to eradicate what he then considered a false and dangerous path of life (9:2; 16:17; 18:25–26; 19:9, 23; 24:14, 22). Paul even summoned the high priest and the Sanhedrin's body of elders as witnesses to confirm his former zeal for the defence of Judaism by eradicating the threat posed by faith in Jesus. They could testify that his zeal led him to expand his campaign into the Dispersion, carrying letters authorizing the extradition of Christian Jews to Jerusalem for trial.

GOD'S CHOSEN WITNESS

It was about noon, as they approached Damascus, that a bright light from heaven suddenly surrounded Paul and his companions. The timing at midday implies that the heavenly light outshone the sun at its strongest. It also connects Paul's subsequent blindness with the ancient covenant curse that threatened Israel with the consequences of unfaithfulness: 'At midday you will grope about like a blind man in the dark' (*Deut.* 28:29). As we noticed in Acts 9:7, Paul's companions observed the objective reality of the vision, although its specific content was revealed only to him. They saw the light but not the glorious One who appeared to Saul in the light. They heard the sound but did not understand the voice of the divine Speaker who addressed him (9:7; 22:9, see also *Dan.* 10:7). This was no dehydration–induced hallucination!

Here Paul's narrative most closely parallels Luke's earlier account: the twofold address, 'Saul, Saul' (see also *Exod.* 3:4, *1 Sam.* 3:10); the challenging question, 'Why are you persecuting me?'; the mystified response, 'Who are you, Lord?'; and the stunning answer, 'I am Jesus, whom you are persecuting.' (Here Paul added the identification *of Nazareth*.) In persecuting Christian believers, Paul had persecuted the Way, but in fact his aggression was more personal, and more grave: he was persecuting the One whose radiant glory was so overpowering that he could only be called 'Lord'. Jesus the Lord so identifies with his people that he counts our sufferings as his own (*Luke* 10:16, *Matt.* 25:41–45).

Yet through Christ's amazing grace, Paul was not consumed by God's wrath but commissioned to God's work. A task had been assigned him, and instructions awaited him in Damascus. Paul's account of his meeting with the pious Ananias omits mention of the vision in which Jesus reassured the latter and sent him to pray for the church's former persecutor (9:10–17). Instead Paul focused on Ananias' devotion to the law and respected reputation in the whole Jewish community of Damascus. Here, then, is another witness on behalf of Paul's fidelity to Israel and her traditions: the man who ushered him into the Christian faith was himself well known for carefully keeping the commandments.

Through Ananias' word (by the authority of the Lord Jesus, 9:17) Paul received his physical sight again. More importantly, he received insight into his new mission. Ananias brought a word from the God of our fathers. This last phrase comes from the message of impending liberation that God gave Moses at the burning bush (*Exod.* 3:15–16), and it stresses that Paul still serves the God who redeemed his ancestors and claimed them by his covenant. God had chosen Paul to see and to hear, and to bear witness to what he had seen and heard.

In the Greek version of the account of the burning bush, Moses begged God to choose some other, more competent person to free Israel (*Exod.* 4:13). But God had made his selection. Likewise, Paul's years as an arrogant persecutor could not reverse the fact that Paul had been set apart from his mother's womb (*Gal.* 1:15–16). The call of sovereign grace was sure to come, and when it did it seized its quarry.

Paul saw the Righteous One, the obedient Servant who was wounded for others' sins and so justified many, constituting them right in God's sight (*Isa.* 53:5–6, 11). Jesus' identity as the Righteous One showed the injustice of Israel's mistreatment of him (*Acts* 3:14; 7:52), but Jesus' righteousness is also the only hope for Israel, or for any of us. Once Paul discovered that his pursuit of self–achieved righteousness had made him God's enemy, he gladly confessed his dependence on the righteousness of God, which comes not from law–keeping but through faith in Christ (*Phil.* 3:9). Like the Eleven, Paul could boast of the privilege lavished on him by divine mercy: 'Am I not an apostle? Have I not seen Jesus our Lord?' (*1 Cor.* 9:1).

Paul also heard words from the mouth of Jesus, and was responsible for delivering the message of God's saving purpose to all races and classes of people. He was under compulsion and had no alternative but to preach: 'Woe to me if I do not preach the gospel!' (*1 Cor.* 9:16). Jesus had called him, like the original apostles, to be his witness, testifying to what he had seen and heard (*Acts* 1:8, 22; 2:32; 3:15; 5:32; 13:31). Our faith is grounded in the apostles' eyewitness testimony (*Eph.* 2:20, see also *1 John* 1:1–3, *2 Pet.* 1:16–18, *Heb.* 2:3–4).

Ananias had instructed Paul to submit to baptism, signifying the washing away of his sins through faith in Jesus, on whose name Paul must call for salvation (*1 Cor.* 6:11). *Calling on his name* echoes God's promise through the prophet Joel, quoted by Peter at Pentecost (*Acts* 2:21, *Joel* 2:32, see also *Rom.* 10:13). Throughout Scripture to 'call on the name of the Lord' is to appeal for his rescue, admitting our helplessness and worshipping him in humble trust (*Gen.* 4:26; 13:4). In his blind pride Paul had hunted down those who called on Jesus' name (*Acts* 9:14). Now he was numbered among them.

GOD'S AMBASSADOR TO THE GENTILES

Paul's defence continued with his description of a vision, not previously mentioned in Acts, that he had received after his return from Damascus to Jerusalem. It occurred while he was praying in the temple – another piece of evidence refuting the charge that Paul had abandoned the law and scorned or defiled the holy place (21:28–29). The vision resembled Isaiah's call to be a prophet not only because both men saw the Lord but also because each was warned that Israel would reject his message (*Isa.* 6:9–13). Isaiah was sent to sow persistently in that resistant field, nourishing the hope of a remnant. The Lord Jesus called Paul, on the other hand, to leave Jerusalem right away. This must have been one factor in the brothers' decision to send Paul to Tarsus when his Hellenistic Jewish opponents conspired to kill him (*Acts* 9:29–30).

Paul at first protested against his Lord's marching orders, pointing out his well-known record as a persecutor of Christians, beginning with Christ's faithful martyr Stephen (7:58; 8:1). The word translated *witness* in verse 20 is the same word used to describe Paul's calling as a witness in verse 15. In Hellenistic Greek generally it refers to one who gives legal testimony. Because Jesus' witnesses were often called to seal their testimony with their lives, the term acquired the connotation we associate with martyr: a witness who is faithful even to the death (*Rev.* 2:14; see also verse 10; 12:11). Jesus himself is the faithful witness who sealed his testimony with his blood, confirming God's promise (*Rev.* 1:5, *1 Tim.* 6:13).

Paul believed that his 'track record' should reasonably evoke not hostility but curiosity over his radical change of heart. The Lord, however, overruled his servant's common sense: 'I will send you far away to the Gentiles.' Jesus had told his disciples that their dreams for Israel's restoration were too small, for God's kingdom would embrace the end of the earth (*Acts* 1:8). Peter had alluded to the global dimensions of the kingdom, though not yet aware of all its implications: 'For the promise is for you and for your children and for all who are far off, everyone whom the Lord our God calls to himself' (2:39). God had promised to proclaim peace to those far away and those near (*Isa.* 57:19). Now he revealed to Paul that the far away people to whom Christ's reconciling peace must be proclaimed are not just dispersed Jews, but also the Gentiles from all the peoples of the earth (*Eph.* 2:17–18).

Who but the Father of our Lord Jesus could turn his ancient people's hardness into blessing for the nations, grafting us wild branches into the root of his covenant mercy (*Rom.* 11:17–24)? He can also graft natural branches broken off in unbelief – Israelites such as Saul of Tarsus – back into Jesus, the life-giving root of David (*Rev.* 22:16). For that harvest of the gospel among both Gentiles and Jews we should pray and bear witness.

58

The Rights of a Roman Citizen

Up to this word they listened to him. Then they raised their voices and said, "Away with such a fellow from the earth! For he should not be allowed to live." ²³ And as they were shouting and throwing off their cloaks and flinging dust into the air, ²⁴ the tribune ordered him to be brought into the barracks, saying that he should be examined by flogging, to find out why they were shouting against him like this. ²⁵ But when they had stretched him out for the whips, Paul said to the centurion who was standing by, "Is it lawful for you to flog a man who is a Roman citizen and uncondemned?" ²⁶ When the centurion heard this, he went to the tribune and said to him, "What are you about to do? For this man is a Roman citizen." ²⁷ So the tribune came and said to him, "Tell me, are you a Roman citizen?" And he said, "Yes." ²⁸ The tribune answered, "I bought this citizenship for a large sum." Paul said, "But I am a citizen by birth." ²⁹ So those who were about to examine him withdrew from him immediately, and the tribune also was afraid, for he realized that Paul was a Roman citizen and that he had bound him (Acts 22:22–29).

Other historical sources indicate that anti-Gentile sentiment was increasing in Judea when Paul reached Jerusalem in the late 50s AD, and this may explain why the temple crowd flew into a rage when Paul mentioned that Jesus had sent him to the Gentiles. Whatever good will he had gained by recounting his credentials of Jewish loyalty was lost when he clarified that the far-away ones to whom Jesus had sent him were Gentiles.

AN IRATE MOB

The crowd resumed its chant, demanding, 'Away with such a fellow from the earth [or, perhaps, the promised land]!' (see *Deut.* 13:5;17:12). In their indignation they were throwing off their cloaks to free their arms to hurl whatever they could find at the blasphemer. Ironically, their target had once kept the cloaks of those who stoned Stephen (7:58). They tossed dust into the air to vent their rage at Paul, who stood on the stairs above them (see also *2 Sam.* 16:13).

Since Paul had spoken in Aramaic, the tribune did not understand his address. The mob's sudden shift from attentive silence to vociferous agitation, however, made it obvious that Paul had not pacified his opponents and needed to be removed from the temple precincts to bring the situation under control. Out of respect for Tarsus, Lysius had allowed this Jew to address the crowd. The result was more disturbance and the tribune was still no closer to understanding its cause. He commanded a centurion to interrogate Paul, using an instrument that Rome found effective in extracting the truth from stubborn witnesses. The scourge or *flagellum* had leather thongs in which bits of knucklebone and metal were embedded, so that each lash not only inflicted pain but also bruised and tore flesh. Roman scourging could break bones, and victims sometimes died from their wounds.

AN ASSERTIVE CITIZEN

As soldiers stretched and tied him to receive the lash, Paul played the trump card of his Roman citizenship, as he and Silas had done when beaten and imprisoned at Philippi (16:37). He quietly asked the supervising centurion, 'Is it lawful for you to flog a man who is a Roman citizen and uncondemned?' Imperial law from the time of Augustus banned the flogging of Roman citizens prior to a formal trial and sentencing. The centurion recognized the claim implied in the prisoner's question and immediately reported it to the tribune, who rushed back to question Paul personally.

Paul reaffirmed that he was indeed a Roman citizen. Whether or not he was carrying any proof of his citizenship, his claim could have been verified from the public records of Tarsus. Falsely claiming Roman citizenship was a capital crime, so a person already in Roman custody had nothing to gain from such a lie. Claudius Lysias' remark that he himself had acquired his citizenship at great cost implied that the privilege had been cheapened since then, so that even a Jew who was obviously *persona non grata* with his own people could afford it. Technically, Roman citizenship could not be bought. It was a privilege inherited by birth or conferred in recognition for faithful service to Rome or to a Roman citizen. During the reign of Claudius, however, citizenship was virtually for sale by the Empress and her circle, as well as others. A strategic bribe had brought citizen status to Lysias, opening the way for his promotion from centurion to tribune. If Lysias intended to devalue Paul's citizenship, he was in for one more surprise: Paul was a citizen by birth, having inherited the privilege from his father or grandfather. 'Old', second-generation citizenship was more highly regarded than that recently acquired, whatever the latter's price tag.

Understandably, the soldiers who had been ready to flog answers out of their prisoner suddenly drew back, as their commander himself was gripped with alarm. As armed temple police sent to arrest Jesus fell back in fear when they actually met him (*John* 18:6), so now a thousand Roman soldiers quailed in fear of their prisoner, Paul the servant of Jesus. If a Roman citizen had received the brutal treatment that Lysias had ordered it would have had dire consequences for the tribune's career and person. In his report to the governor he would put a positive spin on his role in the events (23:27).

Paul urged Christians to submit to human governments as God's ministers of justice, to punish criminals and defend the innocent (*Rom.* 13:1–7, see also *1 Pet.* 2:13–14). He also expected government officials to live up to their high calling. Although willing to suffer submissively for Jesus' sake when necessary, Paul did not hesitate to challenge those in power to wield that power justly. In this fallen world Christians are tempted to relate to flawed governments either with intimidated compliance or with defiant rebellion. Calm in his confidence that Christ is Lord of all, Paul shows us a God-glorifying response superior to either of these extremes.

59

Paul's Defence to the
Leaders of Israel

*But on the next day, desiring to know the real reason why he
was being accused by the Jews, he unbound him and commanded
the chief priests and all the council to meet, and he brought Paul
down and set him before them.*

¹ *And looking intently at the council, Paul said, "Brothers, I
have lived my life before God in all good conscience up to this
day."* ² *And the high priest Ananias commanded those who stood
by him to strike him on the mouth.* ³ *Then Paul said to him, "God
is going to strike you, you whitewashed wall! Are you sitting to
judge me according to the law, and yet contrary to the law you
order me to be struck?"* ⁴ *Those who stood by said, "Would you
revile God's high priest?"* ⁵ *And Paul said, "I did not know,
brothers, that he was the high priest, for it is written, 'You shall
not speak evil of a ruler of your people.' "*

⁶ *Now when Paul perceived that one part were Sadducees and
the other Pharisees, he cried out in the council, "Brothers, I am
a Pharisee, a son of Pharisees. It is with respect to the hope and
the resurrection of the dead that I am on trial."* ⁷ *And when he
had said this, a dissension arose between the Pharisees and the
Sadducees, and the assembly was divided.* ⁸ *For the Sadducees
say that there is no resurrection, nor angel, nor spirit, but the
Pharisees acknowledge them all.* ⁹ *Then a great clamour arose,
and some of the scribes of the Pharisees' party stood up and
contended sharply, "We find nothing wrong in this man. What
if a spirit or an angel spoke to him?"* ¹⁰ *And when the dissension
became violent, the tribune, afraid that Paul would be torn to*

pieces by them, commanded the soldiers to go down and take him away from among them by force and bring him into the barracks. ¹¹ The following night the Lord stood by him and said, "Take courage, for as you have testified to the facts about me in Jerusalem, so you must testify also in Rome." (Acts 22:30– 23:11).

Claudius Lysias and his troops had rescued Paul from a fatal beating at the hands of the Jewish mob and spared him the indignity and wounds of a flogging, but they also kept Paul chained in custody overnight (see also 21:33; 22:30; 26:29). Were they Paul's protectors, or was he their prisoner?

To figure out how to handle the case of this Jew who was a Roman citizen from Tarsus, the tribune still needed to discover why Paul's presence had provoked a riot in the temple. The chaotic and conflicting shouts of the mob had revealed nothing (21:33–34). Letting the prisoner address the crowd had made matters worse. Paul's Roman citizenship ruled out the possibility of whipping the truth out of him. Perhaps the Jewish leadership, the Sanhedrin composed of chief priests, biblical and legal scholars, and elders, could identify Paul's offences. In the governor's name Lysias ordered this council to assemble. The High Priest Ananias, always eager to curry favour with the Roman authorities, readily complied.

REBUKE AND RESPECT FOR A LAWLESS JUDGE

Paul looked intently at the Sanhedrin, gauging the spiritual openness of the priests, teachers, and elders, as he had that of the lame man at Lystra (14:9; see also 3:4). Then he launched into his defence, asserting that he had 'conducted himself as a citizen (ESV: *lived my life*) under God with all good conscience'. The verb '*conduct oneself as a citizen*' appears in the New Testament only here and in Paul's letter to Philippi, a colony whose citizens were privileged with Roman citizenship (*Phil.* 1:27; see also 3:20). Paul was a citizen of Tarsus, of Rome, and of Israel (*Acts* 21:39; 22:28, *Eph.* 2:12). What mattered most, however, was how he conducted himself before the Sovereign who examines the conscience. Paul was not claiming to have achieved sinless perfection. In fact, he had given up trusting in his own righteousness (*Phil.* 3:9) and now saw himself as the worst of sinners, who had persecuted Christ's church (*1 Tim.* 1:13–16). But in the matter before the court Paul knew, as God was his witness, that he had done nothing to provoke the riot (*Acts* 24:12). He had not violated the Torah or the temple, nor had he broken Caesar's laws (25:8).

Ananias the high priest reacted immediately with a command that Paul be punched in the mouth. Such an order was completely in character for Ananias, whom Josephus criticizes as dishonouring his office through greed and violence. Did he hear in Paul's profession of innocence an implied accusation against the Sadducean establishment, who had previously persecuted the church (4:1–3; 5:17–18; 9:1–2)? Paul shot back a rebuke, 'God is going to strike you', echoing the law's covenant curse (*Deut.* 28:22) and the prophetic picture of a wall about to fall, even though a coat of whitewash masks its inner decay (*Ezek.* 13:10–15). Paul not only called Roman authorities to follow due Roman process, he also expected Israel's leaders to observe the demand of God's law for impartial justice, in which punishment awaits conviction on the basis of evidence (*Lev.* 19:15, *Deut.* 25:1). He was outraged that one who presumed to judge according to the law would so flagrantly violate the law.

Paul's rebuke evoked its own rebuke from bystanders: 'Would you revile God's high priest?' The apostle's instantaneous response shows us God's grace at work on his heart. Paul's cause was just and his words about Ananias were true, but when the apostle learned that his retort had dishonoured the office of God's high priest, he humbly repented for the way he had spoken those words. God's law forbade speaking *evil of a ruler of your people* (see *Exod.* 22:28), and Paul was always under the law of Christ. Christ calls his followers to respect rulers for their office's sake, however unworthy their personal conduct (*Matt.* 23:2–3, see also *1 Pet.* 2:18). When leaders fail us, Christians in Western democracies too often mimic our culture's cynical contempt for authority. Paul's sudden reversal from prophetic wrath to repentant respect calls us to be counter-cultural, reflecting instead our Lord Jesus' calm endurance when he himself was struck for speaking truth (*John* 18:19–23).

DIVIDE AND CONQUER

Through his rabbinical education under Gamaliel and his association with the Jerusalem authorities, Paul knew well the theological differences between the Sadducees, who made up the temple establishment, and the legal experts, most of whom were Pharisees. Both parties were represented in the Sanhedrin. The high priest's arrogant abuse of power persuaded Paul that he needed to spotlight the Sadducee-Pharisee disagreement over the doctrine of resurrection in order to show his fellow-Pharisees that his Christian convictions were a faithful extension of their understanding of Judaism.

As Luke helpfully explains to his Gentile readers, Sadducees say that there is no resurrection, nor angels nor spirits. They denied both the bodily resurrection at the end of history and the intermediate state of the righteous in angelic or spirit form between death and the last day. (Belief that the dead could appear as a spirit or angel is reflected in *Luke* 24:37–39 and *Acts* 12:15.) They could not find these doctrines in the books of Moses, the only portion of the Old Testament that they recognized as authoritative. Therefore Jesus had turned to Moses' second book, Exodus, to show that the Sadducees' denial of the resurrection contradicted God's covenant faithfulness to the patriarchs (*Luke* 20:27–39).

The Pharisees, on the other hand, believed in a final resurrection as Israel's ultimate hope, and therefore in the personal survival of the righteous after death. In this respect Paul remained a loyal Pharisee when he discovered that Jesus had already been raised as the first–fruits of the final resurrection harvest (*1 Cor.* 15:20). The Creator who made man a psychosomatic unity would not allow death to have the last word. This hope, which had always been Paul's as a Pharisee, found fulfilment in Jesus the risen Lord. Although Paul had been slandered as despising the Law and defiling the temple, in his own mind the resurrection was the central issue separating him from the power bloc who controlled the temple. It was that conviction that he now proclaimed.

The effect was immediate division. Chaos and noisy confusion prevailed in the Jewish Sanhedrin, just as it had in the Gentiles' assembly at Ephesus (19:23). Legal scholars rose to the defence of

Paul, their fellow Pharisee, pronouncing him innocent of wrongdoing. They even held open the possibility that Jesus had appeared in spirit or angelic form to speak to Paul. Theirs would be the first of several opinions exonerating Paul before he reached Rome (23:29; 25:25–27; 26:32).

The conflict deteriorated from the verbal to the physical, to the point that Lysias again feared for Paul's safety and sent soldiers to retrieve Paul again into the safety of the Fortress Antonia. The question whether Paul had committed a crime warranting further custody still had not been answered.

SAFE PASSAGE TO ROME

Paul's snappish retort in reaction to the high priest's abuse may have been symptomatic of the strain he was experiencing. His every effort to vindicate the gospel in the eyes of his countrymen ended in controversy and even violence. In the night following the Sanhedrin debacle the Lord Jesus came, as he had at Corinth (18:9–10), to comfort his downcast and weary witness: 'Take courage, for as you have testified to the facts about me in Jerusalem, so you must testify also in Rome.'

For a long time Paul had been hoping and praying to reach Rome (19:21, *Rom.* 1:10), but the Spirit's predictions of suffering awaiting him in Jerusalem placed his plan in doubt (*Rom.* 15:31–32). Now Jesus spoke his sovereign *MUST*, which made Paul's arrival in Rome absolutely certain. 'Many dangers, toils, and snares' lay between Paul and his destination, as they do between ourselves and our heavenly home. But the Lord's invincible purpose guarantees every believer's arrival, just as certainly as Paul would reach Rome via the surprising route of legal appeal, storm, and shipwreck.

60

Assassins Thwarted

When it was day, the Jews made a plot and bound themselves by an oath neither to eat nor drink till they had killed Paul. ^{13} *There were more than forty who made this conspiracy.* ^{14} *They went to the chief priests and elders and said, "We have strictly bound ourselves by an oath to taste no food till we have killed Paul.* ^{15} *Now therefore you, along with the council, give notice to the tribune to bring him down to you, as though you were going to determine his case more exactly. And we are ready to kill him before he comes near."*

^{16} *Now the son of Paul's sister heard of their ambush, so he went and entered the barracks and told Paul.* ^{17} *Paul called one of the centurions and said, "Take this young man to the tribune, for he has something to tell him."* ^{18} *So he took him and brought him to the tribune and said, "Paul the prisoner called me and asked me to bring this young man to you, as he has something to say to you."* ^{19} *The tribune took him by the hand, and going aside asked him privately, "What is it that you have to tell me?"* ^{20} *And he said, "The Jews have agreed to ask you to bring Paul down to the council tomorrow, as though they were going to inquire somewhat more closely about him.* ^{21} *But do not be persuaded by them, for more than forty of their men are lying in ambush for him, who have bound themselves by an oath neither to eat nor drink till they have killed him. And now they are ready, waiting for your consent."* ^{22} *So the tribune dismissed the young man, charging him, "Tell no one that you have informed me of these things."*

^{23} *Then he called two of the centurions and said, "Get ready two hundred soldiers, with seventy horsemen and two hundred*

spearmen to go as far as Caesarea at the third hour of the night.
²⁴ Also provide mounts for Paul to ride and bring him safely to
Felix the governor." ²⁵ And he wrote a letter to this effect:

²⁶ "Claudius Lysias, to his Excellency the governor Felix,
greetings. ²⁷ This man was seized by the Jews and was about to
be killed by them when I came upon them with the soldiers and
rescued him, having learned that he was a Roman citizen. ²⁸ And
desiring to know the charge for which they were accusing him, I
brought him down to their council. ²⁹ I found that he was being
accused about questions of their law, but charged with nothing
deserving death or imprisonment. ³⁰ And when it was disclosed
to me that there would be a plot against the man, I sent him to
you at once, ordering his accusers also to state before you what
they have against him."

³¹ So the soldiers, according to their instructions, took Paul
and brought him by night to Antipatris. ³² And on the next day
they returned to the barracks, letting the horsemen go on with
him. ³³ When they had come to Caesarea and delivered the letter
to the governor, they presented Paul also before him. ³⁴ On
reading the letter, he asked what province he was from. And when
he learned that he was from Cilicia, ³⁵ he said, "I will give you
a hearing when your accusers arrive." And he commanded him
to be guarded in Herod's praetorium (Acts 23:12–35).

Jesus' midnight assurance that Paul would certainly be his witness
in Rome, as he had been in Jerusalem, came not a moment too
soon. The very next morning over forty zealous Jews swore
themselves to a pact to take Paul's life before they tasted another
meal. Their conspiracy would be thwarted through the sharp ears
of Paul's nephew and the decisive action of the Roman tribune.

This sequence of the Lord's encouragement by night followed by
a concerted attack from unbelieving Jews reproduces in Jerusalem
the pattern established previously in Paul's ministry among the
Dispersion. In Corinth the Lord Jesus came by night in a vision to
encourage Paul to preach fearlessly, promising to preserve him for
the sake of the 'many people' to whom Christ had laid claim in that
city (*Acts* 18:9–10). Luke then records the Jews' legal action against

Paul before the Proconsul Gallio, who dismissed their complaint as a quibble over disagreements internal to Judaism (18:12–17). In Jerusalem the Lord's encouragement again focused on his future ministry, to which his personal safety is subservient: 'You must testify also in Rome.' The next morning the Jewish assassins' plot would prompt Lysias to send Paul to the governor in Caesarea. In so doing the tribune echoed Gallio's opinion that the accusations against Paul concerned disputes over Jewish law that were of no concern to Rome (23:29). Thus Roman officials both outside and inside Judea treated Christianity as a variant of the faith of Israel, which posed no threat to the peace and order of the Empire.

MURDEROUS, TREACHEROUS ZEAL

The group of over forty Jews who bound themselves by an oath literally called down upon themselves God's *anathema*, God's curse, if they tasted food or drink before they had done away with Paul. Such an oath obviously demanded relatively quick action, and their plan was formulated to complete the 'hit' the next day.

They approached the chief priests and elders (that is, the Sadducees), not the Pharisees who had expressed sympathy for Paul's resurrection theology in the hearing the previous day. These leaders of the Sanhedrin would offer to reconvene the council to question Paul further and clarify for the tribune the character of Paul's crimes. The assassins, however, would waylay Paul and his bodyguards en route from the fortress to the council chamber, killing him on the spot. Whether they lost their lives in the process or in the predictable aftermath, when Roman forces would avenge the death of a Roman citizen, probably mattered no more to them than violent death did to the terrorists of September 11, 2001, or to suicide bombers in the Middle East.

Such a violent plan would appeal to the High Priest Ananias, who had actually been summoned to Rome to answer for his role in planning the ambush of Samaritan pilgrims. His breach of God's law in having Paul struck in the mouth seems mild when compared to these conspirators' utter disregard for the law's safeguards of the sanctity of truth, justice and life. Like Paul before his Damascus Road experience, seeing themselves as the law's most loyal defenders, they were its most flagrant violators. It is only when we surrender to Christ's grace, abandoning our quest for vindication through the law, that we begin to fulfil the law (*Rom.* 8:4; 3:31).

THE PLOT EXPOSED

Paul's sister's son, a young man in his late teens or twenties, lived in Jerusalem, presumably with his mother. This detail fits with Paul's statement that, though born in Tarsus, he had been raised by his parents in Jerusalem (22:3). How Paul's nephew learned of the assassination plot we are not told. The fact that he immediately warned Paul suggests that at least some in Paul's own family had not shunned him for his faith. Though in custody, Paul, as a Roman citizen, would enjoy the privilege of visits from family and friends, and the nephew immediately gained access to inform Paul that his life was in danger.

Paul summoned the centurion supervising his guards, asking him to conduct the young man to the tribune, for whom he had urgent information. Again Paul's citizenship came into play, for it gave him a higher social status than the centurion. The centurion immediately followed his prisoner's direction, taking the youth to his commander. Lysias somehow sensed that the nephew's information was highly sensitive, so he took him aside to a private venue where he could speak without concern for eavesdropping ears. The young man's report revealed his detailed and accurate knowledge of the assassination plot: the oath taken by the conspirators and their number, the ruse of a further hearing by the Sanhedrin, and even the fact that the chief priests were at that moment awaiting Lysias' promise that he would send Paul down to their chamber the following day. The tribune swore the youth to secrecy – the element of surprise was now on the side of Paul and his protectors – and dismissed him.

Here we see the seamless integration of God's sovereign purpose and the decisions of his responsible creatures. The assassination plot was bound to fail, for the Lord had guaranteed that Paul would testify in Rome. Yet God would accomplish his plan to preserve Paul not apart from but through the actions of his nephew and the Roman commander. When the biblical truth of God's sovereignty grips our hearts, it frees us from fear without producing fatalism or indifference.

DECISIVE ACTION

The tribune lost no time making preparations to transfer his prisoner to a safer venue. Summoning two centurions, he ordered them to prepare the two hundred infantrymen under their command to march that night, along with seventy mounted soldiers and an additional two hundred spearmen – or 'archers' or 'local police' (the Greek word is so rare that its meaning is uncertain). This force of four hundred and seventy represented almost half the cohort of one thousand that was stationed in Jerusalem. Lysias was taking no chances. He would not risk having his guard overcome and his important prisoner lost, even if word of the troops' movements got out and they were ambushed in northern Judea.

To introduce the prisoner and orient the governor to his 'case', the tribune summarized events in a brief but formal letter. It opens as Hellenistic letters typically do, identifying first the author (Claudius Lysias), then the recipient (His Excellency, Governor Felix), and then extending Greetings (see also 15:23, *James* 1:1). The Roman name Claudius preceding his personal name indicates that he acquired his citizenship during the reign of Claudius (AD 41–54). The honorific address of the governor as His Excellency (identical to *most excellent Theophilus*, Luke 1:3) was technically inappropriate in Felix's case. It belonged properly to members of the equestrian class, into which Felix, a freedman who was once a slave, could not gain entrance. Nevertheless, Felix was Lysias' superior, and a slightly excessive expression of respect could do no harm.

Lysias condensed and rearranged the events surrounding the riot in the temple to highlight his service to the Empire and its citizens. His letter implies that his first 'rescue' of Paul was motivated by his commitment to defend a Roman citizen, rather than to arrest an Egyptian revolutionary (21:28). The tribune also conveniently omitted the significant detail that, ignorant of Paul's citizenship, he had ordered that Paul be scourged in a preliminary interrogation. The rest of his summary, however, is accurate enough. Once he learned that Paul was a citizen, Lysias had genuinely become Paul's protector both in the tumult at the Sanhedrin and in acting quickly to transport Paul out of the reach of the conspirators.

From Luke's perspective the most important sentence in the letter is the statement that the Jewish leaders' complaint concerned questions about their law, and that no charge against Paul warranted death or imprisonment. Just as some of the Pharisees found no fault in Paul's theology (23:9), so a Gentile official could not find in the accusations against Paul's conduct any legal ground for the serious penalties (execution, incarceration, exile) that Rome reserved to itself to impose. Finally a Jewish king would render the verdict that Paul's actions deserved neither death nor prison, and that he could have been released from custody had he not appealed to Caesar (26:31–32).

Of course as he wrote the letter the tribune had not yet notified Paul's accusers that he had been sent to Caesarea and that they must present their case to the governor himself. Ancient letters, however, use verb tenses from the standpoint of the reader, not the writer. For example, in the original Galatians 6:11 reads: 'See with what large letters I wrote in my own hand.' Although the act of writing was present to Paul, it would be past by the time the Galatians read the letter. Likewise, by the time Felix received Lysias' letter, Paul's accusers would have been notified that he was in the governor's custody in Caesarea.

The soldiers and mounted cavalry set out, as commanded, under cover of darkness, in the third hour of the night (9:00–10:00 p.m.). Paul rode a horse or donkey, so their speed did not depend on his strength. They pressed hard to reach Antipatris on the Judea–Samaria border, thirty-seven miles to the north-west, the next morning. This haste put Paul virtually beyond reach of Jerusalem's murderous zealots, and over half way to the governor's palace in Caesarea. The four hundred foot soldiers, having escorted their prisoner to Judea's border, returned to reinforce their cohort in Jerusalem, while the seventy horsemen – still a sizeable security force – rode on with Paul to Caesarea. There they delivered the letter and the prisoner into the custody of the governor.

Felix's corruption and incompetence, well documented in other sources, would show themselves in his handling of Paul's case, but at least the governor began the process 'according to the book'. He learned that Paul's home province was Cilicia, which was then included in a large administrative unit that also included Syria and

Judea, supervised by the imperial legate of Syria. Lysias' letter indicated that the charges against Paul were so insubstantial as to be unworthy of the legate's attention, so the case properly fell within Felix's authority as governor of Judea. He promised to hear the case as soon as Paul's accusers arrived from Jerusalem.

Thus Paul's testimony about Christ would advance to a new level in the imperial hierarchy. Although the charges against Paul were untrue and his captivity undeserved, instead of wallowing in self-pity he exploited them as opportunities to speak for King Jesus. How do you view and use the injustices you suffer?

61

Paul's Defence to Governor Felix

And after five days the high priest Ananias came down with some elders and a spokesman, one Tertullus. They laid before the governor their case against Paul. [2] And when he had been summoned, Tertullus began to accuse him, saying:

"Since through you we enjoy much peace, and since by your foresight, most excellent Felix, reforms are being made for this nation, [3] in every way and everywhere we accept this with all gratitude. [4] But, to detain you no further, I beg you in your kindness to hear us briefly. [5] For we have found this man a plague, one who stirs up riots among all the Jews throughout the world and is a ringleader of the sect of the Nazarenes. [6] He even tried to profane the temple, but we seized him.

[7–8] By examining him yourself you will be able to find out from him about everything of which we accuse him."

[9] The Jews also joined in the charge, affirming that all these things were so.

[10] And when the governor had nodded to him to speak, Paul replied:

"Knowing that for many years you have been a judge over this nation, I cheerfully make my defence. [11] You can verify that it is not more than twelve days since I went up to worship in Jerusalem, [12] and they did not find me disputing with anyone or stirring up a crowd, either in the temple or in the synagogues or in the city. [13] Neither can they prove to you what they now bring up against me. [14] But this I confess to you, that according to the Way, which they call a sect, I worship the God of our fathers, believing everything laid down by the Law and written in the Prophets, [15] having a hope in God, which these men themselves accept, that there will be a resurrection of both the just and the unjust. *16* So I always take pains to have a clear conscience towards both God and man. *17* Now after several years I came to bring alms to my nation and to present offerings. *18* While I was doing this, they found me purified in the temple, without any crowd or tumult. But some Jews from Asia —*19* they ought to be here before you and to make an accusation, should they have anything against me. *20* Or else let these men themselves say what wrongdoing they found when I stood before the council, *21* other than this one thing that I cried out while standing among them: 'It is with respect to the resurrection of the dead that I am on trial before you this day.' "

22 But Felix, having a rather accurate knowledge of the Way, put them off, saying, "When Lysias the tribune comes down, I will decide your case." *23* Then he gave orders to the centurion that he should be kept in custody but have some liberty, and that none of his friends should be prevented from attending to his needs.

24 After some days Felix came with his wife Drusilla, who was Jewish, and he sent for Paul and heard him speak about faith in Christ Jesus. *25* And as he reasoned about righteousness and self-control and the coming judgement, Felix was alarmed and said, "Go away for the present. When I get an opportunity I will summon you." *26* At the same time he hoped that money would be given him by Paul. So he sent for him often and conversed with him. *27* When two years had elapsed, Felix was succeeded by Porcius Festus. And desiring to do the Jews a favour, Felix left Paul in prison (Acts 24:1–27).

P aul's trial before Governor Felix followed typical court procedures, with the filing of charges, the prosecution by the plaintiffs' spokesman, and an answer from the defendant. After hearing both sides of the case, the judge normally rendered a verdict. Felix, however, found himself in a difficult position, persuaded of Paul's innocence and unwilling to condemn a Roman citizen without cause, yet not daring to offend the Jewish leadership and risk another outbreak of resistance to his rule. He grasped at an excuse to postpone his decision and then prolonged this strategy for two years, until removed from office.

More important to Paul than his freedom was his opportunity to tell others about Jesus. His trial before Felix gave him a platform for proclaiming the resurrection as the point of contention between himself and his accusers, while emphasizing that his hope was taught in the Law and the Prophets and shared by his fellow Jews. Even more encouraging to Paul would have been the subsequent private interviews initiated by the governor, in which they discussed faith in Christ Jesus and God's call to repentance in view of coming judgement.

AN ELOQUENT PROSECUTOR

True to his word, the tribune Lysias notified Paul's accusers that his case had been remanded to the governor, and Paul himself moved to Caesarea. Accordingly, five days later a delegation of the Sanhedrin headed by the high priest himself appeared before Felix to submit their charges. Their seriousness in prosecuting Paul was shown not only by Ananias' presence but also by the fact that they had hired a professional orator to argue their case. The Greek term, from which our 'rhetoric' comes, includes public speakers in general, and in this case the ESV has translated it *spokesman*. Tertullus' speech, even in the brief summary preserved by Luke, shows his shrewd use of flattery, subtle threat, and evasion to win a verdict condemning the defendant.

Like the tribune in his letter, Tertullus opened by addressing Felix with a title technically above his station in society: 'Most excellent'. The first objective of a courtroom address was to curry favour with the judge. Tertullus accomplished this with consummate skill, expressing the Jewish community's gratitude for the extended peace they had enjoyed under Felix's rule. Actually Felix's tenure was marred by constant unrest and violent clashes between imperial forces and the oppressed Jewish and Samaritan populace. His hostility to his Jewish subjects exacerbated the problems. Yet peace was a Roman ideal, and Tertullus was about to accuse Paul of disturbing the peace throughout the Empire. Surely Felix, a champion of peace, could not condone one who disrupted social order! The prosecutor also praised the foresight behind the governor's reforms (which seem to have been as fictional as the peace). A leader who anticipated where dangerous trends could lead would have the visionary flexibility to silence a troublemaker, whether or not mundane details (such as Roman law and the evidence) actually established Paul's guilt.

Abbreviating his compliments out of regard for the governor's valuable time (another convention of legal rhetoric), Tertullus next presented his clients' two charges against Paul. First, the defendant spreads riots like the plague everywhere he goes. Tertullus called Paul a 'plague', a carrier of seditious infection that posed as great a danger to social tranquillity as the bubonic plague did to life itself in the Mediterranean's teeming ports. Luke's account has shown us the grain of truth at the core of the libel: everywhere that Paul went, turmoil followed. But the instigators of unrest and riot were the gospel's enemies, not its preacher (13:50; 14:2, 5, 19; 16:22; 17:5, 13; see also 19:23–29, 37–40).

Tertullus' second charge was that Paul had tried to desecrate the temple. This reflected the confused assumption of the Asian Jews, who presumed that Paul had brought his Gentile colleague, Trophimus of Ephesus, inside the balustrade separating the Court of the Gentiles from the Courts of the Women and of Israel (21:28–29). This offence, although not a breach of Roman law, was one that Rome allowed the Jewish Sanhedrin to adjudicate, as the posted warning sign implied (see Chapter 56). Paul, then, should be remanded to the Sanhedrin for judgement. Tertullus, speaking only for the Sadducean component of the Sanhedrin, gave the impression that the council itself had passed judgement on Paul, whereas Luke's readers remember that Paul fell into Roman hands through a mob in the temple and that the Sanhedrin itself was divided over his guilt or innocence. (Some manuscripts include a longer version of verses 6–8, in which Tertullus implies that Lysias' protection of Paul was illegitimate meddling in the Jews' internal religious concerns. These words are absent from the manuscripts used in our translation.)

Tertullus closed his argument by inviting the governor to interrogate the prisoner to verify his crimes. As the prosecutor rested his case, his distinguished Jewish clients added their verbal affirmation, not to amplify his argument but to apply their political pressure to the governor.

A CONFIDENT DEFENCE

Without a word, dramatizing his authority by god-like silence, Felix gave Paul the nod to present his defence. Paul too began with a compliment to win the judge's favour, although Paul's is restrained to the point of ambiguity. Paul would cheerfully present his defence before Felix because he knew that the latter had been judge over the Jewish people for many years. The comment implied that the governor's extended experience in Judea had given him an understanding of things Jewish. Paul did not, however, flatter Felix for fictional justice or wisdom, as Tertullus had celebrated Felix's fictional peace.

Paul knew that the Sanhedrin's accusations rested on second-hand 'testimony' from Asian Jews who were absent from the court and who seem, in fact, to have disappeared altogether after the riot in the temple. In response to the first charge, therefore, Paul argued that his peaceful conduct in Jerusalem during his recent visit refuted the charge that he was an itinerant rabble–rouser. He had gone up to Jerusalem to worship, and had spent no more than twelve days there. (The ESV's translation dates Paul's arrival in Jerusalem only twelve days before his trial, but he must be referring only to his time in Jerusalem itself. At least eighteen days, twelve of them in Jerusalem, had transpired between Paul's arrival at Jerusalem and the present trial. See 21:17–18, 26–27; 22:30; 23:12, 31–32; 24:1). None of his accusers could truthfully testify that they found him discussing controversial issues in the temple, the synagogues, or elsewhere in Jerusalem.

Paul was prepared to make one confession, however. By confessing an 'offence' that was no crime under Roman law, Paul showed his transparency without risking legal liability. He also turned the discussion to the real issue between Paul and his accusers – which was also the message that he wanted to announce to the governor. According to the Way (which Paul once persecuted, 9:2; 22:4) Paul worshipped the God who had made his covenant with Paul's forefathers. The temple establishment dismissed the Way as a *sect*. Tertullus had used this Greek term, from which we get 'heresy', in that pejorative sense (*sect of the Nazarenes*, 24:5), although the term itself simply referred to any sub-group within a larger religious community (5:17; 15:5; 26:5).

Paul's faith in Jesus was controlled, contoured, indeed compelled by what was written in the Law of Moses and the Prophets, Judaism's ultimate standard. To believe Moses' writings was to believe in Jesus' words and to embrace the atoning suffering and the resurrection glory of the Messiah (*John* 5:46–47, *Luke* 24:26–27, 44–49). Paul clung to the same hope as other Jews, that at the last day God would raise the bodies of both the righteous and the unrighteous, to face final judgment. Jesus taught this explicitly, as did the later Old Testament books (*John* 5:28–29, *Dan.* 12:2–3, *Isa.* 25:8; 26:19, *Job* 19:25–27; see also *2 Cor.* 5:10, *Rev.* 20:12–15). Although the Sadducees who were Paul's accusers, rejecting those later Scriptures, did not embrace this hope, Felix should know his subjects well enough to realize that the Jewish populace, influenced more by the Pharisees, expected a general resurrection to come. If Israel's leaders claimed to speak for Israel, they must admit that Israel hoped for resurrection, just as Paul did. In fact, it was resurrection hope that motivated Paul to keep his conscience clear, offending neither God nor men. This affirmation was not just a legal strategy, for Paul urged such blamelessness on his Gentile converts as well (*1 Cor.* 10:32–11:1).

Regarding the second charge of defiling the temple, Paul showed its absurdity by pointing out the purpose of his visit to Jerusalem. He had come to bring contributions for the relief of the poor among his people – the only mention in Acts of the Gentiles' offering, which mattered so much to Paul (*1 Cor.* 16, *2 Cor.* 8–9, *Rom.* 15) – and to present sacrificial offerings at the temple. Moreover, he was ceremonially clean (the same Greek word is rendered *purified* in Acts 21:26). How, then, could a ritually-purified Jew, peacefully presenting his offerings in God's house, be accused of compromising the temple's sanctity?

The instigators of the whole controversy were certain Jews from Asia . . . At this point in Paul's speech, an unexpected break in his grammar calls attention to their absence. The Sanhedrin had neglected (or been unable) to bring the only witnesses who might have substantiated their charges! Roman law punished witnesses who lodged accusations and then failed to confront the accused in court.

As far as the Sanhedrin members who were present, the only 'offence' to which they could testify was Paul's shout confessing a Pharisee's faith in the resurrection of the dead – an issue, as we have seen, on which the council itself was sharply divided. Again Paul brought his defence back to the resurrection, although without mentioning the Risen Lord by name. In synagogue or marketplace, in private conversation or public courtroom, whatever the occasion and wherever his starting point, Paul found a way to bring the subject around to the resurrection, the central reality that showed Christ's cross to be vicarious, his present lordship to be supreme, and his future return as Judge to be inevitable.

JUSTICE DELAYED

Paul did not need to mention Jesus by name, for Felix was well acquainted with the Way and would certainly have known so central a theme as the crucified Messiah's resurrection on the third day. Luke's comment is interesting. Did the governor's knowledge of Christian teaching precipitate a sudden decision to adjourn the trial, lest Paul's defence invade issues that Felix's guilty conscience wanted to have left unexplored? Or had the defence rested, so that prosecution and defendant were awaiting the judge's verdict? In that case Luke means that Felix knew the Christian community well enough to conclude that the charges against Paul were baseless. Yet, instead of vindicating Paul and offending Jewish dignitaries with whom Felix's relations were already rocky, the governor postponed his decision with the lame excuse that he needed to consult the tribune Lysias before announcing a verdict. The tribune's letter had made clear that his investigation turned up no evidence that Paul had committed a serious crime (23:29), so Felix was obviously buying time. His sympathy for Paul's cause and respect for Paul's Roman citizenship found expression in his orders that Paul be granted a measure of freedom while imprisoned and that none of his friends be prevented from caring for him.

Perhaps Luke and other friends had shared Paul's midnight ride (note the plural *mounts*, 23:24) or made their way to Caesarea in the days after his escape. A week before Paul had been pummelled in the temple courtyard and slapped in the face. Then he had endured a hard, sixty-mile ride. Perhaps now, at last, his wounds received medical attention from 'Luke, the beloved physician' (*Col.* 4:14). We know that Luke was with Paul in Caesarea two years later (note *we should sail*, 27:1).

Something in Paul's defence piqued the governor's curiosity about the hope that gave the apostle such calm confidence. With his wife Drusilla he summoned Paul to a private audience, at which the apostle presented his message about faith in the Messiah Jesus. That faith pointed to Christ's cross as revealing God's righteous wrath against human sin, a preview of coming judgment as well as the gracious way of escape for those who turn from their self-absorbed lives and submit to the risen Lord. Drusilla was Felix's third wife, a daughter of the nominally Jewish King Herod Agrippa I. She was the teenage bride of a minor eastern king when Felix had become infatuated with her beauty and wooed her away from her royal husband. Paul's discussion of *self-control*, which had sexual connotations then as now, and *the coming judgment*, terrified the governor. He brought the interview to a sudden close, promising to recall Paul when convenient. His ambivalence brings to mind Herod Antipas' mixed reaction to John the Baptist, on the one hand eager to hear the prophet (whom he imprisoned), on the other troubled because John rebuked his theft of his brother's wife (*Mark* 6:17–20).

Felix did send for Paul repeatedly over the next two years, but not to hear more about the Messiah and the justice, self-control, and hope that his Spirit imparts. Felix hoped that Paul, a citizen whose offering for the poor revealed his financial connections outside Palestine, would offer a bribe to buy his release. Such bribes were strictly forbidden and harshly punished, but Felix was not above cutting corners if he could get away with it. On the other hand, keeping Paul in custody ingratiated him with the Jewish leadership in Jerusalem. When recalled to Rome to be reprimanded and narrowly escape punishment, Felix left Paul in custody, his legal case undecided. Felix's preferred response to life-challenging truth and costly decisions was procrastination. It did not serve him well in the end. Upon reaching Rome he dropped from history's pages, while his prisoner's words still change the lives of millions.

62

Paul Appeals to Caesar

Now three days after Festus had arrived in the province, he went up to Jerusalem from Caesarea. ² And the chief priests and the principal men of the Jews laid out their case against Paul, and they urged him, ³ asking as a favour against Paul that he summon him to Jerusalem – because they were planning an ambush to kill him on the way. ⁴ Festus replied that Paul was being kept at Caesarea and that he himself intended to go there shortly. ⁵ "So," said he, "let the men of authority among you go down with me, and if there is anything wrong about the man, let them bring charges against him."

⁶ After he stayed among them not more than eight or ten days, he went down to Caesarea. And the next day he took his seat on the tribunal and ordered Paul to be brought. ⁷ When he had arrived, the Jews who had come down from Jerusalem stood around him, bringing many and serious charges against him that they could not prove. ⁸ Paul argued in his defence, "Neither against the law of the Jews, nor against the temple, nor against Caesar have I committed any offence." ⁹ But Festus, wishing to do the Jews a favour, said to Paul, "Do you wish to go up to Jerusalem and there be tried on these charges before me?" ¹⁰ But Paul said, "I am standing before Caesar's tribunal, where I ought to be tried. To the Jews I have done no wrong, as you yourselves know very well. ¹¹ If then I am a wrongdoer and have committed anything for which I deserve to die, I do not seek to escape death. But if there is nothing to their charges against me, no one can give me up to them. I appeal to Caesar." ¹² Then Festus, when he had conferred with his council, answered, "To Caesar you have appealed; to Caesar you shall go" (Acts 25:1–12).

The arrival of a new procurator to govern Judea raised hopes that unresolved cases, stalled under Felix's corrupt administration, would receive closure. When he reached the province, Festus plunged into his work immediately. According to Josephus, during his brief tenure (around 59–62 AD) Festus governed fairly and controlled civil unrest. In handling Paul's case, a legacy of his predecessor, he tried to balance the competing demands of justice and political expedience.

A REQUEST GINGERLY REBUFFED

Three days after he reached Caesarea, the capital on the Mediterranean coast, Festus made the strategic move of travelling inland to meet face-to-face with the Jewish leadership in Jerusalem. Aware of Felix's hostility toward his Jewish subjects and the turbulence it had generated, the new governor was not going to repeat the previous procurator's mistake.

Despite the two-year lapse since the trial before Felix, the Jewish leaders had not forgotten the troublemaker Paul, nor abandoned their plotting to eliminate him. Paul was at the head of the list of unfinished business that they presented to the new governor. Festus could show his good will toward the Jewish people by granting them the favour of transferring Paul back to Jerusalem for further investigation or a new trial. Behind their request, unbeknown to Festus, was a new conspiracy to assassinate the apostle on the road from Caesarea to Jerusalem. This time the plot was initiated not by a band of forty zealous radicals (23:12–15), but by the priestly leadership itself.

Festus proposed an alternate plan. The prisoner was being held in the provincial capital, Caesarea, and the governor himself planned to return there in a few days. Therefore the Jewish leaders could select some of their number to accompany him to the coast and press their charges against Paul there. Why Festus refused to grant the favour requested by the chief priests we do not know for certain. There is no indication that he suspected an assassination plot. It is unlikely that he would have already reviewed the documents of Paul's case, including Claudius Lysias' letter, which reported the earlier conspiracy. He may have been sending the signal to the Jewish leaders that, although he was willing to work with them, he would not be their puppet. His report of the conversation to Agrippa implies that the Jewish leaders had asked him to condemn Paul and hand him over to them for punishment (25:15–16). Whatever his reasons, Festus' decision to keep Paul at Caesarea was part of God's invincible plan to bring Paul to Rome (23:11). To bring relief and honour to his servants our God controls even a king's insomnia (*Esther* 6). Since 'the king's heart is in the hand of the LORD', who directs it wherever he pleases (*Prov.* 21:1), why do we worry?

GROUNDLESS ACCUSATIONS REPEATED

The morning after returning to Caesarea, Festus took his seat on the imperial judgement bench and summoned Paul to face his accusers. This time they added physical to verbal intimidation by surrounding the defendant as they levelled their serious charges. Luke does not summarize their case this time, but Paul's response implies that the accusations were the same as before (25:8): Paul had attacked the Jewish law (21:21), defiled the temple (21:28–29; 24:6), and dishonoured Caesar (by fomenting civil unrest, 24:5; see also 17:7). The first two charges, as Lysias observed, concerned internal Jewish controversies over which the Sanhedrin would have claimed jurisdiction (23:29; see also 18:12–15). The last would warrant harsh punishment by the Roman court, if substantiated.

The accusers, however, could not prove their charges. The Jews from Asia who had originally raised the outcry in the temple did not appear before Felix two years earlier. Their absence again so weakened the prosecution's case that Paul apparently saw no need to expand his defence beyond a simple denial of each charge: 'Neither against the law of the Jews, nor against the temple, nor against Caesar have I committed any offence.' In the absence of witnesses to a crime, this word from a Roman citizen should have closed the case.

A 'FAVOUR' REJECTED

Festus was in a tight spot. Although he had denied the chief priests' earlier request for a change of venue, he had no wish to alienate these local power brokers in the early days of his administration. Having declined to grant that favour, if he summarily dismissed their charges and released Paul, his tenure as governor could prove as chaotic as

Felix's. On the other hand, their case against Paul was obviously baseless. Political expedience gained the upper hand. Festus asked if Paul was willing to have the trial moved to Jerusalem, giving assurance that as governor he would continue to preside and adjudicate the case there. He offered no legal or procedural rationale for this proposal, and indeed Luke indicates that his true motive was to grant a favour to the Jewish leadership – the same cowardly motive that led Felix to leave Paul in prison for two years (24:27).

Paul's reaction was immediate and adamant. As a Roman citizen, he had a right to stand before Caesar's judgement seat, to be judged by Caesar's delegate. If he were guilty of a capital crime, he would not ask to be spared from the execution he justly deserved. But since his innocence was obvious – as the governor knew very well – neither Festus nor anyone else could make Paul a political pawn, giving him as a favour to his enemies. (The Greek verb *give up* in verse 11 is related to the noun *favour* in verses 2 and 9). Since the new governor valued his own political survival above the claims of justice, Paul claimed his right as a citizen to appeal to Caesar himself to judge his cause. Governors were required to grant such appeals only in cases for which clear legal precedents did not exist. Festus consulted his circle of advisors, who agreed that Paul's was such a case. Consequently Festus issued the declaration: 'To Caesar you shall go.'

The Caesar to whom Paul appealed was Nero, whose later reign degenerated into licence, bizarre behaviour, violence (including the cruel martyrdom of Christians), and finally suicide. Nero's early reign in the 50s, however, under the guidance of the philosopher Seneca, was wise and just. Nevertheless Paul's hope for vindication lay not in Caesar's judgement seat but in the prospect that 'we must all appear before the judgement seat of Christ' (*2 Cor.* 5:10). (*Judgement seat* is the same Greek word as in 25:6, 10, rendered *tribunal*.) There, life's injustices, which frustrate and hurt us now, will be set right, and we will rejoice in Christ's righteousness, given by grace to all who believe (verse 21).

63

An Expert Consultant

Now when some days had passed, Agrippa the king and Bernice arrived at Caesarea and greeted Festus. ¹⁴ *And as they stayed there many days, Festus laid Paul's case before the king, saying, "There is a man left prisoner by Felix,* ¹⁵ *and when I was at Jerusalem, the chief priests and the elders of the Jews laid out their case against him, asking for a sentence of condemnation against him.* ¹⁶ *I answered them that it was not the custom of the Romans to give up anyone before the accused met the accusers face to face and had opportunity to make his defence concerning the charge laid against him.* ¹⁷ *So when they came together here, I made no delay, but on the next day took my seat on the tribunal and ordered the man to be brought.* ¹⁸ *When the accusers stood up, they brought no charge in his case of such evils as I supposed.* ¹⁹ *Rather they had certain points of dispute with him about their own religion and about a certain Jesus, who was dead, but whom Paul asserted to be alive.* ²⁰ *Being at a loss how to investigate these questions, I asked whether he wanted to go to Jerusalem and be tried there regarding them.* ²¹ *But when Paul had appealed to be kept in custody for the decision of the emperor, I ordered him to be held until I could send him to Caesar."* ²² *Then Agrippa said to Festus, "I would like to hear the man myself."* *"Tomorrow," said he, "you will hear him."*

²³ *So on the next day Agrippa and Bernice came with great pomp, and they entered the audience hall with the military tribunes and the prominent men of the city. Then, at the command of Festus, Paul was brought in.* ²⁴ *And Festus said, "King Agrippa and all who are present with us, you see this man about whom the whole Jewish people petitioned me, both in Jerusalem*

and here, shouting that he ought not to live any longer. [25] *But I found that he had done nothing deserving death. And as he himself appealed to the emperor, I decided to go ahead and send him.* [26] *But I have nothing definite to write to my lord about him. Therefore I have brought him before you all, and especially before you, King Agrippa, so that, after we have examined him, I may have something to write.* [27] *For it seems to me unreasonable, in sending a prisoner, not to indicate the charges against him.''* (Acts 25:13–27).

This transition to Paul's final defence speech focuses on two addresses by Festus, the first in private conversation with King Agrippa and the second to open the public hearing in which the king would hear the notorious prisoner. The procurator's purpose in both of these settings was to enhance his reputation as a competent and loyal official of the Empire, confronted with a frustratingly ambiguous case involving intractable Jewish opponents. Though better than Felix, Festus was no less a politician driven by self-interest, who could skilfully put a positive 'spin' on his actions.

Luke's purpose for recording the governor's remarks was quite different. The verdict that Festus had sidestepped earlier he now pronounced, first in private and then in public: none of the charges brought by Paul's accusers warranted the death penalty that they demanded. The gospel is not subversive of civil order, even when a judicial system is a confusing mixture of due process, political pressure, and corruption, as Rome's was.

A PRIVATE CONSULTATION WITH THE KING

A state visit from a local ruler and his sister to welcome the new governor gave Festus the opportunity to seek advice from a consultant well versed both in the pressures of imperial politics and in the puzzles of Jewish controversies. *King Agrippa* was Herod Agrippa II, a great-grandson of Herod the Great and the son of Herod Agrippa I, who had martyred James, arrested Peter, and died under God's blow of judgement (*Acts* 12). Agrippa II had been appointed by his friend, the Emperor Claudius, to rule a small kingdom in northern Palestine. Claudius later expanded his domain and gave him the right to appoint high priests for the Jerusalem temple. Nero further extended Agrippa's boundaries, including cities in northern Galilee, and the king thanked the Emperor by renaming his capital, formerly Caesarea Philippi, Neronias. Agrippa's opinion concerning Paul's case would be well informed and persuasive to the Emperor, to whom Festus needed to write a report of the charges.

Festus described his dilemma in a way that made him appear competent and conscientious, while subtly shifting blame to others. His predecessor, Felix, had negligently left this man a prisoner, whereas Festus acted with dispatch. (Interestingly, Felix was Agrippa's brother-in-law, the husband of Drusilla, sister of both Agrippa and Bernice.) According to his report, when Festus met with the chief priests and elders in Jerusalem, they demanded that he condemn Paul and hand him over to them for punishment. It is barely possible that all this was conveyed in their request that Paul be brought back to Jerusalem, but it is unlikely, since they planned to take the law into their own hands by assassinating Paul on the way.

He next blamed Paul's accusers for bringing charges that caught him off guard, inasmuch as they were utterly unrelated to serious crimes as Roman law defined them. Instead, Paul and his opponents seemed to be enmeshed in controversies about *their own religion* and a dispute over Paul's claim that a certain Jesus, who had died, was alive. The term *religion* borders on the insulting ('superstition') and probably implies Festus' contempt for the trivia that had occupied his time in this case, and now entangled him in the administrative headaches and professional risks of an appeal to the Emperor. Although Luke did not mention it in summarizing Paul's trial before Festus, obviously the debate over Jesus' resurrection had surfaced then. Paul had injected this topic into his hearing before the Sanhedrin (23:6) and his trial before Felix (24:15, 21). He must have done the same before Festus. Paul seized every opportunity to fulfil his calling, which was to bear witness to the risen Righteous One whom he had seen (22:14–15). By referring to 'some Jesus who had died' (ESV: *a certain Jesus, who was dead*) the governor showed his ignorance of even the rudiments of the gospel message, over which Paul and his accusers were so sharply divided.

Finally, Festus seemed to blame Paul. The governor had made the reasonable request that the prisoner willingly stand trial in Jerusalem, where his alleged offences, whatever they might be, apparently occurred. Instead Paul stubbornly appealed over Festus' head, demanding to be held in protective custody to await the Emperor's (literally, *the August One's*) decision. Discreetly absent from the governor's summary was Paul's rationale for lodging the appeal: despite Festus' recognition that no evidence of capital crime existed, he was ready to do Paul's influential opponents a favour by essentially placing him in their power.

Festus had presented an intriguing legal problem, and Agrippa's curiosity was piqued. What should be reported to the Emperor? The charges against this citizen were groundless in Roman law, yet his accusers demanded his death. Caught between the 'rock' of a Roman's rights and the 'hard place' of the Jewish leaders' antipathy toward Paul, Festus, like Felix, had deferred a verdict vindicating Paul for fear of the Sanhedrin's reaction. Now Paul's appeal could bring the newly appointed governor's timid indecision to the attention of the Emperor himself. Agrippa's expertise in Jewish matters could provide the insight that Festus needed to strike the right balance in summarizing the issues of the case. The king, as curious as his great–uncle Herod Antipas (*Luke* 23:8), took the bait: 'I would like to hear this man myself.' Indeed Agrippa would hear this perplexing prisoner, and as soon as possible!

A PUBLIC PAGEANT FOR THE KING

Despite the single day's notice, Festus, Agrippa, and Bernice managed to turn Paul's hearing into a lavish public event. The king and his sister entered the audience room *with great pomp*. This word (*phantasia*) sometimes refers to pageants and lavish ceremonial parades. Luke lists the dignitaries who made their entrance in the retinue of the royal couple. High-ranking officers were military tribunes, each commanding a cohort of a thousand troops. The leading men of the city were civilians of high rank and influential connections to the halls of power in the provincial government. With the exception of Agrippa and Bernice, who were Jewish, the audience would have been overwhelmingly Gentile. Finally, at

Festus' command, Paul was led in – in the sentence that sets the scene the Greek syntax places Paul's name last, as the climax of the pageant.

As the prisoner stood in chains (see also 26:29), Festus spoke with oratorical flourish, presenting the legal problem that Paul posed. On the one hand, *the whole Jewish people* had petitioned the governor both in Jerusalem and in Caesarea, demanding Paul's death. Festus may have believed that the Sadducean chief priests and elders, in their antipathy toward Paul, spoke for all Jewish people. Or by *people* he may have meant the Jewish ruling council, though the Sanhedrin itself was far from unified as to Paul's guilt or innocence (23:7–10). Perhaps the governor was embellishing his own image as a courageous defender of justice, standing alone against the violent bloodlust of the mob. In his next sentence he certainly gave himself undeserved credit for reaching a just verdict, conveniently neglecting to mention that he had lacked the courage to announce it in the presence of Paul's accusers: 'I found that he had done nothing deserving death.' If only he had said as much when Paul completed his defence! If he had, Paul would have felt no need to appeal to Caesar. Nevertheless, although Festus' declaration that Paul was not guilty of capital crime came too late to avert the apostle's arduous and life-threatening voyage to Rome, it reinforces a motif that Luke is weaving, strand by strand. Genuine Christian faith, although it recognizes that only God has ultimate authority, is submissive to the governments that God has established for society's peace and order – even when those who govern stray from their God-given mission (18:14–15; 19:37; 22:25; 23:3–5; 23:29; 26:31–32).

Festus' subtle self-justification continued with his implication that the case could have been closed with his 'not guilty' verdict, had Paul not appealed to *the August One* (ESV: *the emperor*). Luke's readers, of course, know that Festus' refusal to declare this verdict, proposing instead a change of venue to Jerusalem, had provoked Paul's appeal in the first place. The governor's political shrewdness had backfired, and now he found himself in an awkward place of his own making. It would be absurd (ESV: *unreasonable*) to send to the Emperor a case serious enough to warrant appeal by the accused citizen, unless the procurator could provide a clear statement of the alleged violations of Roman law. Festus' investigation had shown that no such charges existed, yet he had not exonerated Paul and dismissed the case. He needed something to write that would not expose his cowardly act of political expediency. For assistance he turned to Agrippa and his expertise in Jewish matters. Festus' dilemma poignantly illustrates how seemingly prudent compromises in matters of truth and justice can ensnare us in unexpected ways.

The governor's purpose in presenting Paul to King Agrippa would be frustrated. No clear statement of serious charges would emerge from the hearing (26:31–32). On the other hand, God's purpose for this convocation of Near-Eastern dignitaries would be achieved, for Paul must carry Jesus' Name before Gentiles and kings and the people of Israel (9:15). Our God is infinitely resourceful in displaying his glory and grace, even through the self–serving decisions of sinful people.

64

Paul's Defence to King Agrippa

So Agrippa said to Paul, "You have permission to speak for yourself." Then Paul stretched out his hand and made his defence:

² "I consider myself fortunate that it is before you, King Agrippa, I am going to make my defence today against all the accusations of the Jews, ³ especially because you are familiar with all the customs and controversies of the Jews. Therefore I beg you to listen to me patiently.

⁴ "My manner of life from my youth, spent from the beginning among my own nation and in Jerusalem, is known by all the Jews. ⁵ They have known for a long time, if they are willing to testify, that according to the strictest party of our religion I have lived as a Pharisee. ⁶ And now I stand here on trial because of my hope in the promise made by God to our fathers, ⁷ to which our twelve tribes hope to attain, as they earnestly worship night and day. And for this hope I am accused by Jews, O king! ⁸ Why is it thought incredible by any of you that God raises the dead?

⁹ "I myself was convinced that I ought to do many things in opposing the name of Jesus of Nazareth. ¹⁰ And I did so in Jerusalem. I not only locked up many of the saints in prison after receiving authority from the chief priests, but when they were put to death I cast my vote against them. ¹¹ And I punished them often in all the synagogues and tried to make them blaspheme, and in raging fury against them I persecuted them even to foreign cities.

¹² "In this connection I journeyed to Damascus with the authority and commission of the chief priests. ¹³ At midday, O king, I saw on the way a light from heaven, brighter than the

sun, that shone around me and those who journeyed with me.
¹⁴ And when we had all fallen to the ground, I heard a voice
saying to me in the Hebrew language, 'Saul, Saul, why are you
persecuting me? It is hard for you to kick against the goads.'
¹⁵ And I said, 'Who are you, Lord?' And the Lord said, 'I am
Jesus whom you are persecuting. ¹⁶ But rise and stand upon your
feet, for I have appeared to you for this purpose, to appoint you
as a servant and witness to the things in which you have seen me
and to those in which I will appear to you, ¹⁷ delivering you from
your people and from the Gentiles – to whom I am sending you
¹⁸ to open their eyes, so that they may turn from darkness to light
and from the power of Satan to God, that they may receive
forgiveness of sins and a place among those who are sanctified
by faith in me.'
¹⁹ "Therefore, O King Agrippa, I was not disobedient to the
heavenly vision, ²⁰ but declared first to those in Damascus, then
in Jerusalem and throughout all the region of Judea, and also
to the Gentiles, that they should repent and turn to God,
performing deeds in keeping with their repentance. ²¹ For this
reason the Jews seized me in the temple and tried to kill me.
²² To this day I have had the help that comes from God, and so
I stand here testifying both to small and great, saying nothing
but what the prophets and Moses said would come to pass: ²³ that
the Christ must suffer and that, by being the first to rise from
the dead, he would proclaim light both to our people and to the
Gentiles" (Acts 26:1–23).

P aul's address to King Agrippa is the grand finale of his defence
speeches. He had addressed the people of Israel in the temple
(22:1–21), the Jewish leaders who constituted the Sanhedrin (23:1–
6), and the Roman governor Felix (24:1–21). Finally, he would
present his witness to a king of the Jews. Moreover, the defence to
Agrippa is the last major message from Paul's lips in Acts. (Luke
will briefly summarize Paul's dialogue with the Jewish leaders in
Rome, 28:17–20, 25–28.) Although Paul calls his message a *defence*,
the venue is not a legal trial but a hearing to advise the governor as
to the contents of his report to Caesar. Because of the purpose of
this hearing and the climactic placement of this speech in Acts, the

apostle's remarks do not focus on the charges of the Sanhedrin leadership. Rather, they offer a defence of his whole life and ministry, expounding the gospel he preached as the fulfilment of God's promises, declared through Moses and the prophets, to satisfy Israel's hope and bring light to the Gentiles. Since such good news demands a response, Paul would press his case, trying to persuade King Agrippa to bow before King Jesus.

A WELL–INFORMED AUDIENCE

Although Festus had arranged the hearing and a large group of military and civilian dignitaries were present, Paul's real audience was a single individual, King Agrippa II. It was the king who granted Paul permission to speak. It was the king to whom Paul addressed his defence, not only in his introduction (26:2) but throughout his speech (verses 7, 13, 19, 27, 29). Most of those present were Gentiles, yet Paul's purpose was to persuade this Jewish ruler. Therefore Paul began his case, as he had in addressing the temple crowd, with a rehearsal of his impeccable credentials as a Jew, his persecution of the church, and his encounter with the risen Lord Jesus on the way to Damascus. Then Paul developed his case, as he had before synagogues and the Sanhedrin, by affirming that in Jesus, the suffering and risen Messiah, God kept his prophetic promises and fulfilled the resurrection hope that sustains Israel's piety.

As a skilled Hellenistic orator Paul began by winning the good will of his audience. He praised the king's competence to judge this case, inasmuch as he was well acquainted with all the Jewish customs and controversies. In contrast to Tertullus' praise of Felix (24:2–4), Paul's compliments were not insincere flattery. He really expected that the king's knowledge of the Christian movement and the Scriptures had laid a solid foundation for a vigorous attempt to persuade Agrippa to believe in Jesus (26:25–27). Without minimizing the stark reality that Jews and Gentiles are dead in sin apart from Christ's grace (*Eph.* 2:1–3), Paul never refused to recognize the beneficial fruit of God's common grace in the lives of unbelievers (see also *1 Cor.* 5:1, *Rom.* 13:1–7). When we share Paul's respect for the good evident in non-Christians' lives, we not only glorify their Creator but also open doors to tell them his great good news.

A ZEALOUS PERSECUTOR

Paul's summary of his pre-Christian life paradoxically emphasized both its continuity and its discontinuity with the man he had become since Jesus met him on the road to Damascus.

On the one hand, the message that Paul now embraced was the full flowering of the hope that he had always shared with his fellow Jews. The hope that God would keep the promise he made to the fathers not only sustained the ardent worship offered to God by *our twelve tribes* (Paul strongly identified with his people), it also stirred Paul's commitment to the strictest sect of our religion. As a Pharisee he lived a life of scrupulous observance of the commands in God's law. To sum up his record of commandment keeping, Paul could write simply: 'As to the law, a Pharisee' (*Phil.* 3:5). Paul's childhood and youth were well known to the Jewish community in general, so that even Paul's accusers could testify, if they were so inclined, regarding his commitment to the ancestral traditions that he was now accused of discarding (*Gal.* 1:13–14).

Here the significance of Paul's Pharisaic connection was the resurrection hope that fired his zealous pursuit of righteousness. This hope separated Pharisees from the Sadducees who constituted the high priestly power block of the Sanhedrin (23:6–9). In Paul's mind, both before and after he trusted in Christ, this expectation of God's future faithfulness to reverse death's grip on his saints was the engine driving the perseverance and piety of God's people. His great resurrection chapter concludes: 'Always abounding in the work of the Lord, knowing that in the Lord your labour is not in vain' (*1 Cor.* 15:58). When our stamina to serve Christ wanes, our hearts need to catch sight again of the day when Jesus will cause death to be swallowed up in victory. That hope shone so brightly for Paul that at this point he could not resist addressing all those present, expressing incredulity that they could find it incredible that the faithful and almighty Creator raises the dead.

The discontinuity between Paul's 'then' and his 'now' consisted in his previous persecution of those who confessed faith in Jesus of Nazareth. He had done everything in his power to oppose and eradicate that name, not only imprisoning Christians but even 'casting his black pebble' in support of their execution (ESV: *cast my vote against them*). Paul probably means this metaphorically, since he was then too young a man to be a voting member of the Sanhedrin. He means that he did all he could to influence the process toward condemnation of Jesus' followers. Paul now looked back on those dark days with Christian eyes, calling *saints* those he once considered apostates. In retrospect he recognized his pressure on them to renounce their faith for what it truly was, an effort to force them to blaspheme against the Christ, who is God over all, blessed forever (*Rom.* 9:5).

With a background like this, Paul's present passion to see Jesus' Name proclaimed and the Gentiles embraced in God's grace could not be explained away as the result of a lax upbringing. No one could credibly accuse Paul of compromising with the Hellenizing, pagan influences that threatened Judaism's purity and distinctiveness. There had to be some other explanation for this man's radical shift from persecutor to proclaimer of the Name of Jesus.

A SOVEREIGN COMMISSION

That explanation was found in the confrontation of Paul by the risen Jesus as the former travelled to Damascus in pursuit of Jesus' people. Luke earlier recorded this meeting for his readers, as well as preserving Paul's description of it in his defence to the Jewish people (*Acts* 9 and 22). Paul's account before Agrippa repeats the core features found in the other two narratives: the light; Jesus' rhetorical question, 'Saul, Saul, why are you persecuting me?'; Paul's bewildered response, 'Who are you, Lord?'; Jesus' answer, 'I am Jesus, whom you are persecuting'; and his commission for service in a radically new direction.

The distinctive emphases of Paul's retelling of the story for Agrippa involve the emphasis on light and the omission of any mention of Paul's blindness. The light that surrounded Paul and his travelling companions, throwing them to the ground, outshone the sun in its midday strength. The fact that all saw the overpowering light shows that this was an objective revelation from God, not a merely psychological experience for Paul (see also 9:7; 22:9). That light symbolized Paul's new calling, to fulfil the promise of the servant of the Lord who would open blind eyes and turn people from darkness toward God's light (*Isa.* 42:6–7, 16; 49:6). Paul would disseminate this light as a servant and a witness, giving testimony to Jesus' resurrection on the basis of his eyewitness experience, as the original apostles had (*Acts* 10:39; 13:30–31, *Luke* 1:2; 24:48). Moreover, Jesus would appear to Paul after the encounter on the Damascus road to reveal to him new depths of truth (*Acts* 18:9; 22:17–21; 23:11, *2 Cor.* 12:1–10). The light of God's salvation spread through Paul because he spoke of, and for, Another: the Christ who rose from the dead to *proclaim light* both to the people of Israel and to the Gentiles (26:23).

Paul's commission as servant and witness placed him in the tradition of the ancient prophets, whose writings announced the promise now fulfilled in Jesus. Not only was he called twice by name, as were Moses and Samuel (*Exod.* 3:4, *1 Sam.* 3:10), he was also commanded to stand on his feet, as was Ezekiel (*Ezek.* 2:1). God promised to rescue him from those to whom he would be sent, as the Lord had promised Jeremiah (*Jer.* 1:7–19). Summoned to such high privilege and responsibility by One who could only be called the Lord, Paul dared not disobey the heavenly vision. Jesus had quoted a famous Greek proverb to show that it would be as futile for Paul to fight his call as for a harnessed ox to kick back into the sharp goad used by its driver. Paul immediately began to preach the message of repentance and faith, first in Damascus, then in Jerusalem and all Judea, and finally among the Gentiles. As an heir of the prophets, he proclaimed nothing but what Moses and the prophets had promised: that the Christ would suffer and then shatter death's gates, blazing the trail to eternal life for those who follow him.

A COMPREHENSIVE GOSPEL

Paul deftly shifted the focus from his experience to the message that he was called to proclaim, indicating that behind the animus and accusations of the Jewish leaders lay their hostility to his gospel: 'For this reason the Jews seized me in the temple and tried to kill me' (26:21). Yet Paul was determined to go on preaching this comprehensive good news to one and all.

Paul's gospel was and is comprehensive in its *benefits*. First, it sets people free from spiritual confusion and ignorance of the true God, turning them *from darkness to light*. 'The god of this world has blinded the minds of the unbelievers, to keep them from seeing the light of the gospel of the glory of Christ, who is the image of God . . . For God, who said, "Let light shine out of darkness," has shone in our hearts to give the light of the knowledge of the glory of God in the face of Jesus Christ' (*2 Cor.* 4:4, 6).

Secondly, it sets us free from the oppressive tyranny of our souls' Enemy, turning us *from the power of Satan to God*. Israel, the people of God's covenant, had been under Satan's sway no less than their pagan neighbours, deluded and doomed to self-destruction (*Eph.* 2:1–3). But God 'delivered us from the domain of darkness and transferred us to the kingdom of his beloved Son' (*Col.* 1:13).

Thirdly, the gospel sets believers free from guilt, condemnation, and eternal punishment, for by it we receive *forgiveness of sins*. Christ 'was delivered up for our trespasses and raised for our justification. Therefore, since we have been justified by faith, we have peace with God through our Lord Jesus Christ' (*Rom.* 4:25 – 5:1).

Fourthly, through the gospel God gives to disinherited drifters, who deserve their exile, *a place among those who are sanctified*, a home of unimaginable comfort and impregnable security. We who have been turned from strangers into sons give 'thanks to the Father, who has qualified [us] to share in the inheritance of the saints in light' (*Col.* 1:12, see also *Acts* 20:32). The heirs of God are sanctified, set apart as his holy treasure, not by their own strenuous efforts at obedience but through faith in Christ.

The gospel is also comprehensive in its *beneficiaries*. As our human need for redemption and reconciliation with God is universal, so God's provision in Christ knows no bounds of nationality or social class. Through God's help Paul stood ready to testify *both to small and great*, and particularly to preach, not only to his own people but also to the Gentiles. None can boast of being so close to God that he does not need Christ's grace. None need despair of being so far from God as to be beyond the reach of Christ's grace.

Finally, Paul focused on the *Source* from whom these comprehensive benefits flow to these comprehensive beneficiaries. That Source is the Christ who suffered, was the first to rise from the dead, and now proclaims light to Israel and the nations. Jesus showed his disciples these truths in the Scriptures after he rose from the dead (*Luke* 24:26–27, 44–47). This was the core of Paul's preaching in every synagogue (*Acts* 17:2–3). As *the first to rise from the dead,* Christ inaugurated a new creation. He was the first-fruits of the resurrection, guaranteeing that everyone who believes in him will be harvested from the grave into eternal life (*1 Cor.* 15:20–23). As 'the firstborn from the dead', Christ is the pre-eminent heir, who rules the new creation just as he did the original creation (*Col.* 1:18; see also verses 15–17). Jesus' ministry in Galilee of the Gentiles gave a preview of how he would fulfil God's ancient promise: 'The people walking in darkness have seen a great light; on those living in the land of the shadow of death a light has dawned' (*Isa.* 9:2, *Matt.* 4:16). Now through his servant Paul the risen Messiah was radiating his light to the nations, his salvation to the ends of the earth.

Jesus had promised to give his witnesses words to speak when summoned before kings and governors (*Luke* 21:12–15). He kept his promise as Paul addressed King Agrippa, Governor Festus, and the other assembled dignitaries. When you encounter the unexpected opportunity to give 'a reason for the hope that is in you' (*1 Pet.* 3:15), what you say will reveal what you know by heart. What Paul knew by heart was Jesus, the suffering and risen Messiah.

65

The King's Verdict

And as he was saying these things in his defence, Festus said with a loud voice, "Paul, you are out of your mind; your great learning is driving you out of your mind." 25 But Paul said, "I am not out of my mind, most excellent Festus, but I am speaking true and rational words. 26 For the king knows about these things, and to him I speak boldly. For I am persuaded that none of these things has escaped his notice, for this has not been done in a corner. 27 King Agrippa, do you believe the prophets? I know that you believe." 28 And Agrippa said to Paul, "In a short time would you persuade me to be a Christian?" 29 And Paul said, "Whether short or long, I would to God that not only you but also all who hear me this day might become such as I am – except for these chains."

30 Then the king rose, and the governor and Bernice and those who were sitting with them. 31 And when they had withdrawn, they said to one another, "This man is doing nothing to deserve death or imprisonment." 32 And Agrippa said to Festus, "This man could have been set free if he had not appealed to Caesar" (Acts 26:24–32).

As he closed his defence, Paul pressed King Agrippa for a verdict. It was not a verdict on Paul's innocence, although the king would privately express his opinion on that after adjourning the inquest. Paul himself had a bigger concern than his own legal standing. As the Lord's witness to kings and governors, Jews and Gentiles, small and great, Paul's goal had been to persuade the king and all those present to turn from sin and put their faith in Jesus the Messiah.

A VERDICT ABOUT JESUS

As Paul appealed to ancient writings to support his claim that the Christ would rise from the dead, Governor Festus, a practical politician impatient with theoretical discussion, became frustrated. The prisoner had diverted the hearing from its concrete objective, to produce a statement of charges to accompany Paul's appeal. In Festus' estimation Paul's defence had wandered off into confusing, irrelevant theological terrain, and was revealing an addled brain so absorbed in books that it had lost touch with reality. Suddenly the governor exploded, shouting his own verdict on Paul's mental state, literally: 'You are mad! Your great learning has turned you to mania.' (English later borrowed the Greek word *mania*, with no change in meaning.)

Paul had been addressing not the Roman governor but the Jewish king, whose expert knowledge qualified him to render an informed verdict on Paul's case. Calmly denying the charge of insanity, Paul turned back to Agrippa as a witness not only to the soundness of his mind but also to the soundness of his biblical rationale for believing in Jesus. Thus Paul turned the governor's rude interruption into an opportunity to put to Agrippa directly the question on which the king's eternity hung. Agrippa could attest to the truth and sobriety of Paul's argument, inasmuch as the king knew well not only the prophetic Scriptures but also the public events of Jesus' life and the movement he had founded. *This has not been done in a corner*, Paul insisted. Greek writers were critical of 'ivory tower' academics who withdrew from public life 'into a corner' to generate theories irrelevant to society's welfare and untested by others' critiques. Paul was no such armchair philosopher, nor was his message the fruit of introverted speculation. Confident that nothing had escaped the king's attention, Paul had spoken openly and boldly. In fact, Paul suddenly became bolder still, asking the king directly, 'King Agrippa, do you believe the prophets?' and immediately answering his own question, 'I know that you believe!'

The defendant had placed the king in a trap. What could he say? If he confessed belief in the prophetic writings, Paul would keep pressing for agreement that Jesus fulfilled the prophets' promises. But if Agrippa denied faith in the prophets, his reputation as king of the Jews would suffer serious harm. Like the leaders whom Jesus had challenged to identify the authority behind John's baptism (*Luke* 20:3–8), Agrippa sensed that neither answer could extricate him from the dilemma. Therefore he sidestepped it with urbane, non-committal humour. It was either a question (ESV: *In a short time would you persuade me to be a Christian?*) or an ironic observation: 'In so short a time you are trying to persuade me, to make me a Christian!' He was not hostile to Paul, but he would reserve judgement on Paul's gospel. He needed more time before committing himself to the connection that Paul drew between the biblical promises and Jesus.

Paul's response, which apparently brought the hearing to a close, exuded confidence in God's power, joy in Christ's grace, and compassion for the king and all those present. Whether sooner or later, Paul prayed that God would bring his hearers to faith. That Jesus was the fulfilment of God's promises was obvious, yet Paul knew that even those who thought they knew Scripture would not see this link unless God himself intervened. Paul longed for all to be as he was, except for the shackles on his hands – to share his privilege as a forgiven, beloved child of God. If that is not your longing for family, friends, co-workers, and neighbours, you have misunderstood or forgotten how good the good news of God's grace really is. Listen to Paul – the letters to the Galatians and the Romans are good starting points – and ask God to 'infect' you with Paul's contagious joy in Christ.

A VERDICT ABOUT PAUL

When the king stood, the hearing was over. As he and the governor exited the auditorium, they discussed what they had heard, agreeing that Paul had not violated any Roman law that would justify his execution or exile in chains. The tribune Lysias had said as much two years before (23:29), and it was already Festus' tentative conclusion (25:25). Agrippa, in fact, concluded that Paul could have been released, had his appeal to Caesar not carried his case beyond the governor's authority. Just as a Roman procurator and a Jewish king had concurred that Jesus had done nothing deserving of death (*Luke* 23:14–15), so now a Jewish king and a Roman procurator reached the same verdict about Paul, Jesus' servant. Despite the verdict of Pilate and Herod, Jesus was handed over to his enemies to be killed. Despite the verdict of Festus and Agrippa, Paul would travel in chains to Rome. Yet his joy overflowed, for his travels and trials contributed to his defence of the gospel (*Phil.* 1:16).

66

Good Advice Ignored

And when it was decided that we should sail for Italy, they delivered Paul and some other prisoners to a centurion of the Augustan Cohort named Julius. [2] And embarking in a ship of Adramyttium, which was about to sail to the ports along the coast of Asia, we put to sea, accompanied by Aristarchus, a Macedonian from Thessalonica. [3] The next day we put in at Sidon. And Julius treated Paul kindly and gave him leave to go to his friends and be cared for. [4] And putting out to sea from there we sailed under the lee of Cyprus, because the winds were against us. [5] And when we had sailed across the open sea along the coast of Cilicia and Pamphylia, we came to Myra in Lycia. [6] There the centurion found a ship of Alexandria sailing for Italy and put us on board. [7] We sailed slowly for a number of days and arrived with difficulty off Cnidus, and as the wind did not allow us to go farther, we sailed under the lee of Crete off Salmone. [8] Coasting along it with difficulty, we came to a place called Fair Havens, near which was the city of Lasea.

[9] Since much time had passed, and the voyage was now dangerous because even the Fast was already over, Paul advised them, [10] saying, "Sirs, I perceive that the voyage will be with injury and much loss, not only of the cargo and the ship, but also of our lives." [11] But the centurion paid more attention to the pilot and to the owner of the ship than to what Paul said. [12] And because the harbour was not suitable to spend the winter in, the majority decided to put out to sea from there, on the chance that somehow they could reach Phoenix, a harbor of Crete, facing both southwest and northwest, and spend the winter there (Acts 27: 1–12).

Festus now had King Agrippa's agreement that there was no evidence to show that Paul was guilty of a serious violation of imperial law, and that Paul's appeal to Caesar required that the case be transferred to Rome for disposition. No doubt the governor wrote his report in such a way as to blame Paul's accusers for the insubstantial charges and to blame Paul's stubbornness for troubling the emperor with his appeal. He could thereby portray himself as a conscientious public servant who would have freed Paul but did not want to trespass on Caesar's authority. Festus entrusted Paul and other prisoners bound for Rome to the custody of a centurion for safe conduct to the capital.

Luke honours this centurion by recording his name, Julius. This officer would distinguish himself by his courtesy toward Paul and his decisive action during the storm at sea. His Roman name suggests that his family received citizenship under Julius Caesar or Augustus, so perhaps his concern for Paul's comfort and safety is explained by their shared citizenship. The Imperial Regiment to which Julius belonged was the *Augustan Cohort*, composed of six hundred Syrian soldiers under the governor's command. Some time during Paul's two-year imprisonment in Caesarea, Luke had made his way from Jerusalem to the capital on the coast. Now our narrator resumes his use of the pronoun *we* to indicate that he also was among the group who shared Paul's harrowing journey to Rome. This gripping tale of adventure on the high seas – storm, shipwreck, and (in Paul's case) snakebite – is not fiction or hearsay. Luke was there. Aristarchus, a faithful co-worker from Thessalonica who had been beaten up at Ephesus and had accompanied Paul to Jerusalem (19:29; 20:4), also travelled to Rome and even shared the apostle's imprisonment (*Col.* 4:10, *Philem.* 24). Although the spotlight is on Paul, the apostle is not a solitary super-hero. Even in his life-threatening trials Paul was surrounded and supported by Christian friends, as well as by compassionate unbelievers.

SLOW SAILING

Julius booked passage for his prisoners, his soldiers, and himself on a small privately-owned ship that was to skirt the west coast of Syria and the south coast of Asia Minor before turning north into the

Aegean Sea on its return to Adramyttium, not far from Troas. At a port where the Aegean meets the Mediterranean they would transfer to a larger westbound vessel sailing to Italy.

On the first day at sea they covered close to seventy nautical miles, putting in at Sidon in Phoenicia. Believers scattered after Stephen's death had evangelized this region (11:19). Paul and Barnabas encouraged these Phoenician churches on their way to the council in Jerusalem (15:3), and Paul later enjoyed a week of fellowship with believers in Tyre, near Sidon (21:3–6). From these contacts Paul had *friends* at Sidon, and the centurion Julius showed Paul both kindness and trust in allowing him to leave the ship so that these Christian friends could care for his needs. Long ago a princess from Sidon, Jezebel, had forced Baal-worship on Israel through her husband, King Ahab (*1 Kings* 16:31). Now in the same city Paul found friends who helped him because they loved his Master, King Jesus.

As they sailed north and west from Sidon, the crew steered east of Cyprus so that the island could shield the sails from the westerly winds. Passing north of Cyprus along the coast of Cilicia and Pamphylia in Asia Minor, the ship reached Myra, a good-sized port in south-western Asia Minor. Cargo vessels bearing Egyptian grain regularly docked at Myra before sailing west to Italy, and on one of these, an Alexandrian ship, Julius and the group under his charge found accommodation.

Contrary winds out of the west slowed their progress and after docking at Cnidus, at the south–western tip of Asia Minor, the ship was blown off course and forced to sail almost due south. They passed to lee of Crete, rounding the island's eastern tip and hugging its southern coast until they arrived at last, with difficulty, at a small natural harbour named Fair Havens. Luke expected Theophilus to recognize most of the sites in his story by name, but this tiny bay he introduced as a place called Fair Havens, knowing that even well–travelled Hellenistic readers may not have heard of it. Despite the local pride implied in its name, the harbour's small size and its exposure to high winds from the south prompted experienced seamen to look elsewhere for a safer haven from the stormy winter months to come.

THE VOICE OF EXPERIENCE

There was considerable debate on-board about whether or not to try to move on from Fair Havens before heavier weather hit them. It was after the Fast, that is, Yom Kippur, the Day of Atonement (the only annual observance on which Israelites fasted). Yom Kippur falls in late September or October, and in mid-autumn the unpredictability of the weather made travel on the Mediterranean risky, though not impossible. The ship owner, who probably acted as captain, and the pilot who handled the helm, favoured pressing on, at least as far as Phoenix in western Crete.

This larger harbour, facing both south-west and north-west, would provide shelter from the fierce southerly winds throughout the winter. If this was a grain ship, their motive might have been not only to protect the owner's investment, cargo, and passengers, but also to try to reach their Italian destination quickly. To satisfy the Roman capital's voracious masses, the Emperor Claudius had generously rewarded Egyptian grain merchants who dared the elements to deliver in winter, and such financial bonuses may have continued under Nero. Perhaps by the time they reached Phoenix the heavy weather would let up enough to permit an attempt to make the long run west to Sicily or north-west into the Adriatic Sea.

On the other hand, another voice of experience advised caution. Paul was no sailor, but he was a seasoned traveller who had seen mishap and misery in his many journeys by sea. Several years earlier he had written to the Christians at Corinth, listing among his sufferings the three shipwrecks he had already undergone, and the night and day he had spent in the open sea (*2 Cor.* 11:25–26). It may seem odd that a tent maker and landlubber, who was a prisoner besides, would presume to disagree with the professionals, especially since Paul was not citing divine revelation to support his advice. Nevertheless common sense and experience's hard school had taught him that the sea's power deserved respect. Anticipating the loss of the ship, its precious cargo, and its passengers, he recommended discretion over impatient valour.

REASON OUTVOTED

Although the ship was privately owned, the centurion, as an imperial officer, had the authority to decide whether or not they would leave Fair Havens. When all had had their say it was evident that the majority sided with the captain and the pilot and against the prisoner, and Julius approved their setting sail, his respect for Paul notwithstanding.

Paul's foreboding was not completely fulfilled. The ship and its cargo would be lost, but neither crew nor passengers – even those in chains – would lose their lives in the coming storm. Yet his prudent counsel would be vindicated by that catastrophe (27:21). He had no doubt that he himself would reach Rome, for neither high winds nor ocean depths could thwart Jesus' purpose (23:11). But he also wanted to spare those around him harm and loss, and to that end offered his best wisdom to the shipboard community to which he now belonged. Like Joseph in Egypt, he offered God-given wisdom for the benefit of his neighbours, whether Christian, Jewish, or pagan, as we are called to do even in our spiritually-compromised culture today (*Gen.* 41:33–40).

67

Hope Amid the Storm

Now when the south wind blew gently, supposing that they had obtained their purpose, they weighed anchor and sailed along Crete, close to the shore. ¹⁴ But soon a tempestuous wind, called the northeaster, struck down from the land. ¹⁵ And when the ship was caught and could not face the wind, we gave way to it and were driven along. ¹⁶ Running under the lee of a small island called Cauda, we managed with difficulty to secure the ship's boat. ¹⁷ After hoisting it up, they used supports to undergird the ship. Then, fearing that they would run aground on the Syrtis, they lowered the gear, and thus they were driven along. ¹⁸ Since we were violently storm-tossed, they began the next day to jettison the cargo. ¹⁹ And on the third day they threw the ship's tackle overboard with their own hands. ²⁰ When neither sun nor stars appeared for many days, and no small tempest lay on us, all hope of our being saved was at last abandoned.

²¹ Since they had been without food for a long time, Paul stood up among them and said, "Men, you should have listened to me and not have set sail from Crete and incurred this injury and loss. ²² Yet now I urge you to take heart, for there will be no loss of life among you, but only of the ship. ²³ For this very night there stood before me an angel of the God to whom I belong and whom I worship, ²⁴ and he said, 'Do not be afraid, Paul; you must stand before Caesar. And behold, God has granted you all those who sail with you.' ²⁵ So take heart, men, for I have faith in God that it will be exactly as I have been told. ²⁶ But we must run aground on some island" (Acts 27:13–26).

Against Paul's advice the ship set sail – and almost immediately met the storm that he had anticipated. Infinitely more reliable than Paul's prior experience at sea, however, was the promise of the God to whom Paul belonged, and a new revelation brought by God's angel enabled Paul to bring courage and hope to his despairing shipmates.

WEATHER-BEATEN TO DESPAIR

Now that the decision had been made to seek a fairer haven than Fair Havens before the winter storm season, virtually everyone on board waited anxiously for a change in the weather that would enable them to sail west, around Cape Matala, and north to the harbour at Phoenix. With favourable breezes, this short voyage would take less than a day, but if the ship had to head into the north or west winds that had already driven them so far off course, the last leg would be impossible. Mid-November was approaching, when the Mediterranean became a 'closed sea' (as the Romans called it) to shipping until spring. As they waited, the strong north wind gave way to a gentle breeze from the south, belying (it seemed) Paul's dire expectation of disaster. The seamen welcomed this window of opportunity as confirmation of their plan. They weighed anchor and set sail for Phoenix, skirting as close to the shoreline as possible.

Suddenly, as they rounded the cape, the ship was hit with a hurricane-force wind driving over the mountains of Crete from the north. Luke describes its power with a Greek word that is the source of our 'typhoon'. Sailors had a name for this nemesis, the 'north-easter', and they dreaded its irresistible might. Ancient ships were not designed for tacking in general, much less for advancing when facing into a north-easter; so all they could do was to turn tail to the wind as it drove them south-west.

The ship had drifted over twenty miles when they found a brief respite from the gale in the lee of the island of Cauda (today called Gozzo). The crew and passengers pitched in to batten down the ship for the storm's fury, since its sudden onslaught had given no time for such preparations. With great difficulty they heaved the waterlogged lifeboat, which had been towed behind, up to the ship's deck and secured it. The sailors used ropes to hold together the ship's hull, as in a tight girdle, against the battering of the waves. The northeaster was driving the ship toward north Africa, four hundred miles from Cauda. Ahead of them somewhere in the darkness lay the Syrtis, a broad gulf off the Libyan coastline that was notorious for shallows and shifting sandbars, on which ships often ran aground. Terrified that the keel would suddenly strike one of these hidden hazards while waves pounded it to pieces, the crew tried to slow their pace by lowering a sea anchor or drag anchor.

Despite their precautions, when the ship was blown back into the open sea, it began to take on water. The next day, in order to raise it in the water, the cargo was jettisoned. The day after that, the crew threw the ship's equipment overboard with their own hands – Luke's detail implies the poignant desperation he observed as seasoned seamen parted with the tools of their trade. Though essential under normal circumstances, this tackle would help no one if the ship went down, as seemed its likely end.

Although they knew that the storm was driving them south, they could not calculate their location or speed. Heavy storm clouds obscured sun and stars from view day and night, so navigation was out of the question. Soldiers, sailors, prisoners, passengers – apparently even Luke himself (*we* in 27:20) – gradually abandoned hope of being saved. But Paul had not given up, for he knew God to be true to his Word.

GOD'S WORD OF HOPE

Luke the physician had observed another factor contributing to the group's low spirits. They had not eaten for days. Not only had they gone without food, but because of seasickness and anxiety they could not stomach any. The Greek word means not just fasting but lack of appetite. In this hopeless situation, with winds howling, waves breaking, and strength depleted, Paul stood to encourage his fellow travellers.

He first reminded them that he had urged them to stay the winter in Fair Havens, anticipating the damage and loss that was now imminent. Many commentators hear in this reminder a touch of smug self-vindication, 'I told you so!' Paul was not above such an attitude, since he had not yet reached the goal of complete

Christ-likeness. It is also possible, though, that he hoped that his hearers would believe his present word of hope when reminded that his past warning had been accurate.

In contrast to that warning based on his own travelling experiences, Paul now had a clear word from God, and it was good news. At Fair Havens Paul had foreseen the loss not only of ship and cargo, but also of life. God's angel had now revealed that no human life would be lost, although the ship would run aground and be destroyed. The key to their salvation from a watery death was simple: Paul belonged to the God who ruled the storm; this God had a task for Paul to do in Rome; and as a token of his favour God had given Paul the lives of all those travelling with him.

Paul's security lay in the fact that he was God's property: 'There stood before me an angel of the God to whom I belong and whom I worship.' Believers belong to God not only by creation but also by redemption (*Psa.* 100:3, *1 Cor.* 6:19–20), but we do not always take the comfort we should from being his property, under his protection. Having purchased Paul with his own blood, Christ would let nothing separate Paul from God's love or stand between Paul and God's purpose (*Acts* 20:28, *Rom.* 8:31–39). Tucked into Paul's concise reference to the God whose I am, is the comfort for all seasons summarized in the *Heidelberg Catechism*: 'I am not my own, but belong – body and soul, in life and in death – to my faithful Saviour Jesus Christ. He has fully paid for all my sins with his precious blood and has set me free from the tyranny of the devil. He also watches over me in such a way that not a hair can fall from my head without the will of my Father in heaven: in fact, all things must work together for my salvation.'

The angel had repeated what the Lord himself had told Paul in more general terms (23:11), that Paul must not only testify in Rome but also do so before Caesar himself. This 'divine must' expresses God's invincible plan, which every storm at sea and human conspiracy must ultimately serve. Moreover, as a bonus, God's grace *granted* Paul the lives of his shipmates: sailors, soldiers, fellow prisoners, and other passengers. The verb *granted* or *graciously given* last appeared when Festus tried to show favour to the Jewish leaders by taking Paul to Jerusalem, giving him into his opponents' power (25:3, 11, 16). The governor's 'grace' would have meant death for Paul, but God's grace meant life for those given to Paul.

Paul's calm ability to encourage others sprang from his faith in God, his calm confidence that the divine Word would never fail. The depth of your trust in God's promises is shown not when you enjoy smooth sailing on calm seas, but when the hurricane howls, the breakers crash, and those around you lose all hope. Faith grows strong as you lean on God in tough times, and find him faithful (*James* 1:2–3).

68

Shipwreck and Salvation

When the fourteenth night had come, as we were being driven across the Adriatic Sea, about midnight the sailors suspected that they were nearing land. ²⁸ So they took a sounding and found twenty fathoms. A little farther on they took a sounding again and found fifteen fathoms. ²⁹ And fearing that we might run on the rocks, they let down four anchors from the stern and prayed for day to come. ³⁰ And as the sailors were seeking to escape from the ship, and had lowered the ship's boat into the sea under pretence of laying out anchors from the bow, ³¹ Paul said to the centurion and the soldiers, "Unless these men stay in the ship, you cannot be saved." ³² Then the soldiers cut away the ropes of the ship's boat and let it go.

³³ As day was about to dawn, Paul urged them all to take some food, saying, "Today is the fourteenth day that you have continued in suspense and without food, having taken nothing. ³⁴ Therefore I urge you to take some food. It will give you strength, for not a hair is to perish from the head of any of you." ³⁵ And when he had said these things, he took bread, and giving thanks to God in the presence of all he broke it and began to eat. ³⁶ Then they all were encouraged and ate some food themselves. ³⁷ (We were in all 276 persons in the ship.) ³⁸ And when they had eaten enough, they lightened the ship, throwing out the wheat into the sea.

³⁹ Now when it was day, they did not recognize the land, but they noticed a bay with a beach, on which they planned if possible to run the ship ashore. ⁴⁰ So they cast off the anchors and left them in the sea, at the same time loosening the ropes that tied the rudders. Then hoisting the foresail to the wind they made for

the beach. *⁴¹ But striking a reef, they ran the vessel aground. The bow stuck and remained immovable, and the stern was being broken up by the surf. ⁴² The soldiers' plan was to kill the prisoners, lest any should swim away and escape. ⁴³ But the centurion, wishing to save Paul, kept them from carrying out their plan. He ordered those who could swim to jump overboard first and make for the land, ⁴⁴ and the rest on planks or on pieces of the ship. And so it was that all were brought safely to land* (Acts 27:27–44).

The account of the events leading up to the ship's loss reads like a 'cliffhanger' novel, or, for our visually-oriented age, it plays out like a suspense-filled adventure film. One moment we feel relief as a crisis passes, the next, a new threat looms and all seems lost. Yet through dangers from the sea, sailors, soldiers, and shipwreck, Paul's faithful God carried him and every one of his two hundred and seventy-six fellow-travellers to safety on an unknown shore. Paul's confidence that God would prove true to his Word was fully vindicated.

SELF-SERVING SAILORS

Although the crew and passengers would not realize it until they were washed ashore and learned the name of the island, the 'north-easter' had shifted direction and was driving them due west across the Adriatic Sea. (The body of water between Italy and the Balkans that we now call by this name was a 'gulf' to the ancients, for whom the name Adriatic Sea referred to the north-central Mediterranean, reaching as far south as Crete and Malta.) The ship had been driven before the storm for two weeks when, in the darkness of night, sailors heard the crash of waves on a shore and realized that they were approaching land. Their first sounding showed the water's depth to be twenty fathoms. Since a fathom is roughly six feet, the breadth of a man's outstretched arms, the seabed was 120 feet below the surface. A second sounding not long after showed that the floor had risen five fathoms (30 feet), confirming their suspicion that land lay ahead.

Although the proximity of land was a hopeful development, the dark night now posed danger. The roar of the surf suggested a rocky coast beaten by breakers. Daylight was needed to navigate the ship's approach to whatever shoreline lay ahead. The crew dropped four anchors from the stern to catch the seabed 90 feet below and stall the ship's movement until morning. Dropping anchors from the stern kept the bow pointed toward the land, making it possible to use rudders to steer the ship toward shore when day broke.

Instead of waiting until morning to assess the situation, some sailors panicked and attempted a desperate plan to save themselves at the expense of everyone else. They unlashed the small lifeboat or skiff from the deck and let it down, claiming that they needed to row out to drop anchors tethered to the ship's bow. Paul sensed something amiss, realizing that the sailors were using this pretext to abandon ship altogether and make for the shore in the skiff. He discreetly warned the centurion and his soldiers, 'Unless these men stay in the ship, you cannot be saved.' They acted immediately, closing the escape route by cutting the skiff loose to float, empty, to shore.

This is among the clearest examples in Scripture of the interplay and harmony between God's sovereignty and our responsibility. Paul was no passive fatalist. He knew beyond the shadow of a doubt that he and all those travelling with him would be preserved from drowning, for God had said so and God's purpose could not fail (27:24–26). On the other hand, the decisions of the sailors, the centurion, and his soldiers were integral parts of that divine purpose. Julius and his men had to stop the sailors from abandoning ship. Their action was an indispensable means to the achievement of God's saving plan (see also *Gen.* 50:20, *Acts* 2:23; 4:25–28).

NEEDED NOURISHMENT

As they waited through the night, praying for the dawn, Paul encouraged his shipmates to replenish their strength for the ordeal ahead. Held in constant suspense by the danger of the storm for the last fourteen days, they had been unable to eat. Now that the challenge of reaching land somehow would be upon them in a few hours, they needed the strength that food would supply. Their salvation from the sea depended on it. Again Paul reassured them of the protection promised by the living God whom he served, using a common biblical metaphor: 'Not a hair is to perish from the head of any of you' (see also *1 Sam.* 14:45, *2 Sam.* 14:11, *Luke* 12:7; 21:18).

Then Paul set his companions an example by following his own advice. Taking the role of the father or host at a Jewish meal, he took bread, gave thanks to God for all to hear, broke it and began to eat. Luke's methodical description of each step reminds Christians of Jesus' institution of the Lord's Supper (*Luke* 22:19; see also 9:16; 24:30, *Acts* 2:42). This shipboard meal was not the sacrament, for Paul urged all his fellow-travellers, most of whom were pagans, to partake for the sake of their physical strength and stamina. Nevertheless Paul's calm consumption, and especially his public thanksgiving to the God of grace, bears witness to the peace amid life's storms that Jesus gives through the new covenant.

Well fed, the crew and passengers jettisoned the rest of the grain that had been left in the hold as ballast. They hoped to lift the ship in the water, to clear as many shoals and shallows as possible and drive close to the shoreline.

A HIDDEN SANDBAR AND CRUSHING BREAKERS

Daybreak brought the first visible ray of hope that they had seen for weeks. There was at least one break in the rocky coastline, a sandy beach at the back of a bay. With the skiff gone, their best chance of survival would be to beach the ship itself there. They cut loose the anchors, untied the ropes that had secured the rudders and dropped them back into the water, and hoisted the foresail. With rudders and foresail they should be able to steer directly toward the beach ahead.

Suddenly the ship shuddered and stopped with a grinding groan. It had struck a sandbar or reef beneath the surface. The Greek says 'a place of two seas', apparently describing a shallow outcropping between two expanses of deeper water. The bow was immovably hung up on the sandbar, while the stern, exposed to the pounding of the waves, began to disintegrate. Obviously the vessel could do no more to carry its occupants to land. It would soon be shattered, as Paul had predicted (27:22), and those aboard cast into the churning waters.

CONSCIENTIOUS SOLDIERS

Julius' troops saw immediately that they confronted a double threat. To stay alive, they would first have to swim or float ashore. But, having reached land, if they then found that any of their imperial prisoners had escaped, they would have cheated death only briefly. Execution awaited guards who let inmates escape (12:19), and it was accompanied by such torture and shame that suicide seemed preferable (16:27). Prudence and duty dictated, therefore, that the appropriate step be taken to ensure that none of the prisoners seize the opportunity afforded by the chaos of the shipwreck to escape. Wielding their swords, the soldiers prepared to slay each of those in their custody before jumping overboard.

Just in time their commander, the centurion Julius, stopped them. He had shown Paul kindness at the start of the trip, releasing him from the ship at Sidon to receive care from his friends. He had been swayed from Paul's advice at Fair Havens, only to find himself in the very catastrophe that Paul had foretold. He had acted immediately on Paul's warning during the night that sailors were about to abandon the ship. His respect for Paul must have grown throughout the journey, and quite probably he took seriously the message that Paul's God planned to save him from the sea to stand before Caesar – and to deliver all his shipmates with him. Therefore, instead of 'protecting' himself by allowing the prisoners to be slain, Julius protected Paul by ordering everyone to make for land as best he could, swimmers jumping overboard first while others caught planks or other flotsam from the ship. In this way, Luke concludes, everyone was saved on land. All two hundred and seventy-six were accounted for (which is why he gave us the total in 27:37).

Our daily experience of life is so full of contingencies, of decisions large or small, and circumstances beyond our control, that, from our perspective, these all have unpredictable outcomes. Paul lived in the same world that we inhabit, and we might ask all sorts of 'what if?' questions about his experience in the storm and shipwreck: What if the night look-outs had not heard the breakers and ordered the soundings? What if the sailors had got away in the skiff? What if Julius had ignored Paul's word of warning about their plan to escape? What if some, paralysed in terror, had clung to their fears and refused to eat, later plunging into the sea without strength to swim or clutch a board? What if the soldiers had secured their careers and their lives by 'making sure' no prisoner escaped? These are real people, making real decisions with real outcomes. Yet through them all – and through all the contingencies of our lives, too – our sovereign God quietly, inexorably, works everything together for good for those who love him, who are called according to his purpose, to be conformed to the likeness of his Son (*Rom.* 8:28–29).

69

Snakebite and Hospitality

After we were brought safely through, we then learned that the island was called Malta. ² The native people showed us unusual kindness, for they kindled a fire and welcomed us all, because it had begun to rain and was cold. ³ When Paul had gathered a bundle of sticks and put them on the fire, a viper came out because of the heat and fastened on his hand. ⁴ When the native people saw the creature hanging from his hand, they said to one another, "No doubt this man is a murderer. Though he has escaped from the sea, Justice has not allowed him to live." ⁵ He, however, shook off the creature into the fire and suffered no harm. ⁶ They were waiting for him to swell up or suddenly fall down dead. But when they had waited a long time and saw no misfortune come to him, they changed their minds and said that he was a god.

⁷ Now in the neighbourhood of that place were lands belonging to the chief man of the island, named Publius, who received us and entertained us hospitably for three days. ⁸ It happened that the father of Publius lay sick with fever and dysentery. And Paul visited him and prayed, and putting his hands on him healed him. ⁹ And when this had taken place, the rest of the people on the island who had diseases also came and were cured. ¹⁰ They also honoured us greatly, and when we were about to sail, they put on board whatever we needed (Acts 28:1–10).

When Paul wrote to the church at Rome some years earlier, expressing his hope to bring the joy of the gospel to the capital of the Empire, he spoke of a sense of obligation, even indebtedness, to all sorts of people: 'I am under obligation both to Greeks and to barbarians, both to the wise and to the foolish. So I am eager to preach the gospel to you also who are at Rome' (*Rom.* 1:14–15). Just as Abraham's descendants divided the human race into two camps, Jews and Gentiles, so also the cultured Greco–Roman population distinguished themselves, the civilized people who spoke Greek, from non-Greek speakers, whom they labelled 'barbarians', in mocking imitation of their foreign tongue, which to Greek ears sounded like a toddler's gibberish ('bar, bar, bar'). Greek-speaking Luke here applies the term 'barbarians' (ESV, *native people*) to the inhabitants of Malta, since they preferred their own Phoenician-based language to Greek, and seemed rustic. Yet the Maltese were anything but barbaric, for they welcomed the castaways with gracious hospitality. Paul, in turn, was able to 'repay' a little of his 'debt' to the barbarians by extending the healing power of Christ to those in need.

JUSTICE RENDERS HER VERDICT

The ruthless 'north-easter' had actually pushed them toward their destination, for Malta was only sixty miles from Sicily, perhaps one hundred and fifty miles south of Italy itself. Apparently the residents of Malta had aided many shiploads of traumatized, half-drowned seafarers, for they moved with dispatch, skill, and compassion to meet the needs of the unexpected guests who lay panting and shivering on their beach. They built a bonfire and kindly welcomed the soggy castaways to warm themselves from the chill and rain. Paul, whose faith had buoyed the spirits of the others at sea, now pitched in by gathering fuel to feed the blaze. One of the 'branches' in a bundle he tossed on the fire turned out to be a viper, semi-dormant in the cold but suddenly awakened by the fire's heat. The snake lashed out, fastening itself on Paul's hand.

Their gracious hosts were shocked. Though considered uncivilized by some, the Maltese knew well that evil-doers could not mock justice and evade the gods' vengeance for past crimes. Obviously the gods were trying to kill this man; he must be a murderer. He had escaped King Neptune's sea, but now the goddess *Diké* (Justice) had caught up with him. In minutes the viper's venom would cause him to swell up or drop dead. Long after Paul had calmly shaken the snake into the fire, the islanders watched him, waiting for Justice to impose her sentence. When nothing untoward happened to Paul, they reversed their opinion completely. Invincible against storm and snake, he must be a god in human disguise! Paul had suffered this 'case of mistaken identity' before, among the Lystrans who also spoke an alien dialect (14:11). There, because the confused pagans were about to commit the blasphemy of worshipping Paul and Barnabas, the apostles protested strongly (14:14–18). Since the Maltese pagans attempted no such sacrilege, their mistaken conclusion about Paul's divinity is recorded without correction (although Luke's readers know better). Paul was no more a god than a murderer, but in one sense the islanders' second opinion was closer to the truth: Paul had done nothing deserving death, and through Paul the power of the God who rules heaven, earth, and sea had visited them.

Jesus had used an ancient biblical metaphor (*Gen.* 3:15) to assure his messengers that they shared in his victory over Satan: 'Behold, I have given you authority to tread on serpents and scorpions, and over all the power of the enemy, and nothing will hurt you' (*Luke* 10:19, see also *Rom.* 16:20). That spiritual authority received visible expression in Paul's victory over the viper.

A HEALER VISITS MALTA

Paul was an instant celebrity. He was invited with others – either the whole ship's company or a smaller group including Aristarchus, Luke and probably Julius – to enjoy the hospitality of Publius, the island's *chief man* (Greek, 'the first man'). When they arrived at his estate, the official's father was bedridden with fever and dysentery. Paul went in and prayed, making clear that the healing power was not his own (see also 3:12; 9:34, 40). Then he laid his hands on the aged man, and healed him. Jesus, who had banished the fever from Peter's mother-in-law, immediately restoring her strength, now extended his healing hand through his servant to heal Publius' father (see also *Luke* 4:38–39).

As the word got out that Paul had not only defied death for himself but defeated disease for the chief official's father, crowds of sick folk from all over the island flocked to Paul. They too experienced the healing power of the Jesus whom Paul served (see also *Luke* 4:40–41). They, in turn, expressed their gratitude in respectful gifts brought for Paul and his colleagues. Luke recalls, 'They honoured us with many honours' (ESV, *honoured us greatly*), using a term that often refers to financial honoraria (see also '*the proceeds*' in Acts 4:34; 5:2). Thus the Maltese supplied the provisions for the voyage to Rome.

Luke's account of the castaways' stay at Malta highlights unexpected kindness flowing in two directions, as radically different people were thrust together by human need and God's sovereign mercy. When Christians gratefully receive the extraordinary hospitality of unbelievers, we may have opportunity to invite them into the extraordinary hospitality of God, who welcomes all sorts of people to his banquet, where 'there is not Greek and Jew, circumcised and uncircumcised, barbarian, Scythian, slave, free, but Christ is all, and in all' (*Col.* 3:11; see also *Luke* 14:21–24).

70

Paul's Unhindered Witness
in Caesar's City

After three months we set sail in a ship that had wintered in the island, a ship of Alexandria, with the twin gods as a figurehead. ¹² Putting in at Syracuse, we stayed there for three days. ¹³ And from there we made a circuit and arrived at Rhegium. And after one day a south wind sprang up, and on the second day we came to Puteoli. ¹⁴ There we found brothers and were invited to stay with them for seven days. And so we came to Rome. ¹⁵ And the brothers there, when they heard about us, came as far as the Forum of Appius and Three Taverns to meet us. On seeing them, Paul thanked God and took courage. ¹⁶ And when we came into Rome, Paul was allowed to stay by himself, with the soldier that guarded him.

¹⁷ After three days he called together the local leaders of the Jews, and when they had gathered, he said to them, "Brothers, though I had done nothing against our people or the customs of our fathers, yet I was delivered as a prisoner from Jerusalem into the hands of the Romans. ¹⁸ When they had examined me, they wished to set me at liberty, because there was no reason for the death penalty in my case. ¹⁹ But because the Jews objected, I was compelled to appeal to Caesar – though I had no charge to bring against my nation. ²⁰ For this reason, therefore, I have asked to see you and speak with you, since it is because of the hope of Israel that I am wearing this chain." ²¹ And they said to him, "We have received no letters from Judea about you, and none of the brothers coming here has reported or spoken any evil about you. ²² But we desire to hear from you what your views are, for with regard to this sect we know that everywhere it is spoken against."

²³ *When they had appointed a day for him, they came to him at his lodging in greater numbers. From morning till evening he expounded to them, testifying to the kingdom of God and trying to convince them about Jesus both from the Law of Moses and from the Prophets.* ²⁴ *And some were convinced by what he said, but others disbelieved.* ²⁵ *And disagreeing among themselves, they departed after Paul had made one statement: "The Holy Spirit was right in saying to your fathers through Isaiah the prophet:*

²⁶ *" 'Go to this people, and say,*
  You will indeed hear but never understand,
    and you will indeed see but never perceive.
²⁷ *For this people's heart has grown dull,*
    and with their ears they can barely hear,
    and their eyes they have closed;
    lest they should see with their eyes
    and hear with their ears
    and understand with their heart
    and turn, and I would heal them.'

²⁸ *Therefore let it be known to you that this salvation of God has been sent to the Gentiles; they will listen."*

²⁹⁻³⁰ *He lived there two whole years at his own expense, and welcomed all who came to him,* ³¹ *proclaiming the kingdom of God and teaching about the Lord Jesus Christ with all boldness and without hindrance* (Acts 28:11–31).

P aul's arrival at Rome brings Luke's narrative to its conclusion. Luke has traced the movement of Jesus' witnesses from Jerusalem, the city of David, to Rome, the city of Caesar (although the gospel had reached Rome before Paul did, *Acts* 28:15, *Rom.* 1:7–8). Appropriate to a conclusion is the way that this account echoes themes introduced at earlier turning points in Luke's two volumes. Paul's first recorded preaching to the Dispersion contained a prophetic warning to unbelieving Jews and an announcement that God's salvation was now extended to Gentiles (13:46–48). His witness to fellow-Jews in Rome closed with a similar warning and announcement (28:26–28). At Rome, Paul expounded the kingdom of God and the Lord Jesus Christ from Moses and the prophets (28:23, 31), just as Jesus taught his disciples about himself and God's kingdom after his resurrection (*Luke* 24:26–27, 44–49; *Acts* 1:3). As Luke's Gospel opened, Simeon predicted that Jesus, God's salvation in Person, would divide people as 'a sign that is opposed' (*Luke* 2:34). Likewise, the Jewish leaders in Rome perceived the Jesus movement as a sect 'everywhere . . . spoken against' and found themselves divided over its message (*Acts* 28:22, 24–25).

COURAGE FROM THE BROTHERS

The survivors from the shipwreck spent the three months of winter, when storms 'closed' the Mediterranean, on Malta. Another Alexandrian ship had wintered there after failing to reach Italy with its precious cargo of Egyptian wheat. It had space for Julius, his soldiers and prisoners, and other passengers. It was ready to set off by mid-February, early in the shipping season. This ship bore the name and figurehead of the twin sons of Zeus, the Gemini (twins) Castor and Pollux, the patron deities of seafarers.

The ship first sailed from Malta to Syracuse on the east coast of Sicily. After three days of transferring cargo or awaiting favourable winds, it sailed for Rhegium, on the Italian side of the strait between Sicily and Italy. The southerly wind that blew as they left Rhegium was strong, propelling them over two hundred miles north to Puteoli in less than two days.

Puteoli, a major port on the Bay of Naples, marked the welcome end of the sea leg of their journey – welcome not only because of the dangers that lay behind them, but even more so because Paul, Aristarchus, and Luke found brothers in Christ there. At these brothers' insistence Paul and his group enjoyed their hospitality for seven days. This may seem odd, since Paul was in the custody of a Roman centurion. It was one thing for Paul to stay a week with believers at Troas and Tyre, when he was free to set his own itinerary (20:6; 21:4), and quite another now that his schedule was subject to the power of Rome. Yet several factors can explain Julius' decision to have the group linger at Puteoli. When they set out from Caesarea, the centurion already respected Paul enough to grant him 'shore leave' at Sidon with Christian friends (27:3). Over the course of the voyage, as Paul's warning about the weather proved right, as his warning about the sailors' cowardly plan saved lives, as his encouragement moved all to gather strength for the swim to land, and as Paul survived snakebite and healed many on Malta, Julius' respect for Paul must have grown into awe, and with it his desire to accommodate Paul's comfort. Besides, they were many days ahead of the time they would have reached Italy, if they had wintered in Crete. An overland trek of one hundred and thirty miles lay before them on the Via Compania and then the well-paved Via Appia. Perhaps a few days' rest for Julius' soldiers and their captives – at the expense of these hospitable people who shared Paul's religion – was a welcome 'breather' before the long march. This week of fellowship with Italian believers must have given Paul, Aristarchus, and Luke sweet spiritual refreshment.

During the week messengers apparently notified congregations at Rome that the apostle to the Gentiles, whose magisterial epistle had reached them three years earlier, was about to satisfy his long-held desire to minister in person to Christians living in the Empire's capital (*Rom.* 1:11–13; 15:23). Two delegations of Roman Christians, perhaps from different house-churches, set out to meet Paul and his company on their way. The first group reached him at the Forum of Appius, forty-three miles from Rome, and the second at the Three Taverns, ten miles closer to the capital. Their appearance moved Paul to thanksgiving and steeled his courage to face the threats ahead. Over two years earlier the Lord had stood by Paul at night, calling him to '*take courage*' and assuring him that he '*must testify also in Rome*' (23:11). Now Christ used fellow-believers to encourage Paul, who always knew his need for God-given boldness (*Col.* 4:4, *Eph.* 6:19–20).

CONSULTATIONS WITH JEWISH LEADERS

Julius' report to the authorities when he handed Paul over no doubt made clear that the prisoner, a Roman citizen, posed no risk of flight or violence. Therefore Paul was permitted to rent his own quarters. This 'minimum security' arrangement allowed him to receive guests freely, although he remained chained to a Roman soldier. With six soldiers daily serving four-hour watches at Paul's side, it is no wonder that Paul could soon report that the whole Praetorian Guard, Caesar's personal army, knew that Paul was in chains for Christ (*Phil.* 1:13).

Paul moved proactively to clear his name with the leaders of the Jewish community in Rome. He invited them to his lodgings to hear the facts of his appeal directly. He had no idea what they might have heard, or whether the Jerusalem Sanhedrin had sent letters or representatives to enlist their support in prosecuting Paul before the Emperor. He addressed them as brothers, for he gladly remained a Jew and saw in Jesus the fulfilment of the promises in which he had always hoped. He insisted that he had committed no offence either against 'the people' (ESV supplies *our*, but Paul's 'the people' was shorthand for 'the people of God') or against their ancestral customs, the Mosaic laws entrusted to Israel. These, along with temple desecration, were the accusations that the Asian Jews first made against Paul in the temple courts, but Paul had come to the temple that day to prove such rumours false.

Paul's abbreviated summary of his arrest in Jerusalem and being 'delivered . . . into the hands of the Romans' omits the details of Lysias' intervention to rescue him from the mob. Its wording reminds Luke's readers that Paul followed in the footsteps of his Master, who was likewise 'delivered' by Jewish leaders into the hands of Gentiles (*Luke* 18:32; 24:7). Having interrogated Paul, Roman provincial authorities found him not guilty of capital crime and wanted to release him (see also *Acts* 26:32) but objections from the Jewish leaders prevented them from doing so, just as Pontius Pilate had wanted to release Jesus but did not dare do so (*Luke* 23:13–24).

Paul's appeal had been forced by the Sanhedrin's relentless pressure on the Roman procurators of Judea (specifically, Festus). In bringing this internal controversy to the Emperor's attention, Paul had no desire to cast his own people in a negative light, nor was he filing a countersuit against them for frivolous and false accusation (as was his right). Finally, as he had insisted before the Sanhedrin and King Agrippa, Paul closed his 'brief' with the declaration that his fidelity to the hope of Israel – the resurrection of the dead – was the reason for the chain he now wore (*Acts* 23:6; 26:6–8).

The Jewish elders' answer not only relieved Paul's legal concerns but also, more importantly, opened another door for his life's mission, to bear witness on behalf of Jesus. They had received no communication from Judea, either by letter or in person, about Paul's case. Therefore their minds were not poisoned against Paul's person or message. Although they were aware that the Jesus '*sect*' was spoken against throughout the Empire, they were nevertheless prepared to give Paul's views an honest hearing, as other Jewish communities had done (17:11–12; 18:4–5, 8). They made an appointment to return to hear Paul's case for Jesus as the fulfilment of Israel's hope, and when that day arrived, an even larger group gathered.

When Paul launched into his favourite topic, his stamina was astonishing. He had preached through the night to Christian brothers at Troas (20:7, 11), and now he went from dawn to dusk in dialogue with his Jewish brothers, trying to persuade them from Moses and the prophets that Jesus is the promised Messiah who establishes the kingdom of God (see also 17:1–4; 19:8; 26:22–23). As always happened, the gospel proved to be a 'fragrance from life to life' and a 'fragrance from death to death', with some of Paul's hearers persuaded while others remained unbelieving (*2 Cor.* 2:16; see also, in addition to texts cited above, *Acts* 13:43; 14:1–2). Although carrying a message with such momentous, life-or-death consequences is a sobering responsibility, the opposite outcomes that it elicits should not surprise us, nor discourage us from faithfully declaring it.

Their disagreement among themselves prompted Paul to issue a prophetic warning to those who refused to believe. It was the Holy Spirit himself, speaking through the prophet Isaiah, who rightly described Israel as a people of calloused heart, deaf ears, and eyes shut tight, unwilling to see, hear, understand, and turn to the Lord for healing (*Isa.* 6:9–10). Jesus had spoken in parables to conceal kingdom truths from people who matched Isaiah's description (*Matt.* 13:13–15). Now many of Paul's contemporary kinsmen were showing that they had inherited their fathers' spiritual blindness, deafness, and dullness (*Rom.* 11:8, citing *Deut.* 29:4 with wording drawn from *Isa.* 6:9–10; 29:10). Although only a remnant trusts Jesus the Messiah, God was still calling to his ancient people. They needed to know, however, that God was also calling Gentiles to experience his salvation, and the Gentiles were responding. The psalmists' hopes were and are being fulfilled: '...that your ways may be known on the earth, your salvation among all nations' (*Psa.* 67:2). 'All the ends of the earth have seen the salvation of our God' (*Psa.* 98:3).

THE WORD OF GOD UNLEASHED

The close of the book of Acts seems a strange sort of conclusion. Luke implies that Paul's circumstances changed after he had spent 'an entire two-year period' (ESV, *two whole years*) in house arrest, awaiting a hearing, but the change is not revealed. Although the Lord's promise guaranteed that Paul's appeal would be heard by Caesar (27:24), we read nothing of Paul being called before the Emperor, nor of the outcome of the process. Was Paul vindicated and released? Or condemned and executed? Luke leaves these tantalizing questions unanswered, although the several 'not guilty' verdicts pronounced informally at earlier points (23:29; 25:18–19, 25; 26:31–32) suggest that Paul's case was dismissed – perhaps because the Sanhedrin failed to send delegates to prosecute their charges. This theory also best explains the activities in Ephesus and Crete referred to in Paul's epistles to Timothy and Titus, and the fact that when he wrote Philippians he expected release (*Phil.* 1:25–26), whereas when he wrote 2 Timothy, presumably from a second imprisonment, he expected execution (*2 Tim.* 4:6).

Luke, however, is not writing a biography of Paul but a history of the spread of God's Word from Jerusalem to the ends of the earth. Therefore he does not close with legal vindication nor with martyrdom, but with the image of Paul chained to a soldier but continuously, boldly, and freely, proclaiming God's kingdom and the Lord Jesus Christ. From the perspective of the first disciples, at the time when the Lord Jesus commissioned them as witnesses, Rome seemed to be 'the end of the earth' (*Acts* 1:8). To Luke's audience, however, Rome was the world's centre, and the ends of the earth were beyond the borders of the Empire. Paul himself had a restless desire to press beyond Rome to Spain (*Rom.* 15:23–24). Because the Lord's commission to carry salvation to the earth's ends was far from complete when Paul reached Rome, Luke's open-ended 'conclusion' implies a 'To Be Continued' that embraces the whole history and mission of the church until the return of Jesus from heaven (*Acts* 1:11). The invincible power of the Word, however fragile its messengers, is shown in the final word of the Greek text of Acts, a single adverb rendered *without hindrance* by the ESV. The gospel's unhindered, irresistible victory is the note that Luke leaves ringing in our ears. Even from the chains that would lead him to his death, Paul declared, 'But the word of God is not bound!' (*2 Tim.* 2:9). That confidence must steel our own commitment to advance, by the Spirit's power, the church's mission of proclaiming Christ's salvation to the very ends of the earth.

Group Study Guide

This Study Guide has been prepared for group Bible study, but it can also be used individually. Those who use it on their own may find it helpful to keep a note of their responses in a notebook.

The way in which group Bible studies are led can greatly enhance their value. A well-conducted study will appear as though it has been easy to lead, but that is usually because the leader has worked hard and planned well. Clear aims are essential.

AIMS

In all Bible study, individual or corporate, we have several aims:

1. To gain an understanding of the original meaning of the particular passage of Scripture;
2. To apply this to ourselves and our own situation;
3. To develop some specific ways of putting the biblical teaching into practice.

2 Timothy 3:16–17 provides a helpful structure. Paul says that Scripture is useful for:

(i)   teaching us;
(ii) rebuking us;
(iii) correcting, or changing us;
(iv) training us in righteousness.

Consequently, in studying any passage of Scripture, we should always have in mind these questions:

What does this passage teach us (about God, ourselves, etc.)?

Does it rebuke us in some way?

How can its teaching transform us?

What equipment does it give us for serving Christ?

In fact, these four questions alone would provide a safe guide in any Bible study.

PRINCIPLES

In group Bible study we meet in order to learn about God's Word and ways 'with all the saints' (*Eph.* 3:18). But our own experience, as well as Scripture, tells us that the saints are not always what they *are* called to be in every situation – including group Bible study! Leaders ordinarily have to work hard and prepare well if the work of the group is to be spiritually profitable. The following guidelines for leaders may help to make this a reality.

Preparation:

1. Study and understand the passage yourself. The better prepared and more sure of the direction of the study you are, the more likely it is that the group will have a beneficial and enjoyable study.

Ask: What are the main things this passage is saying? How can this be made clear? This is not the same question as the more common 'What does this passage "say to you"?', which expects a reaction rather than an exposition of the passage. Be clear about that distinction yourself, and work at making it clear in the group study.

2. On the basis of your own study form a clear idea *before* the group meets of (i) the main theme(s) of the passage which should be opened out for discussion, and (ii) some general conclusions the group ought to reach as a result of the study. Here the questions which arise from 2 Timothy 3:16–17 should act as our guide.

3. The guidelines and questions which follow may help to provide a general framework for each discussion; leaders should use them as starting places which can be further developed. It is usually helpful to have a specific goal or theme in mind for group discussion, and one is suggested for each study. But even more important than tracing a single theme is understanding the teaching and the implications of the passage.

Leading the Group:

1. Announce the passage and theme for the study, and begin with prayer. In group studies it may be helpful to invite a different person to lead in prayer each time you meet.

2. Introduce the passage and theme, briefly reminding people of its outline and highlighting the content of each subsidiary section.

3. Lead the group through the discussion questions. Use your own if you are comfortable in doing so; those provided may be used, developing them with your own points. As discussion proceeds, continue to encourage the group first of all to discuss the significance of the passage (teaching) and only then its application (meaning for us). It may be helpful to write important points and applications on a board by way of summary as well as visual aid.

4. At the end of each meeting, remind members of the group of their assignments for the next meeting, and encourage them to come prepared. Be sufficiently prepared as the leader to give specific assignments to individuals, or even couples or groups, to come with specific contributions.

5. Remember that you are the leader of the group! Encourage clear contributions, and do not be embarrassed to ask someone to explain what they have said more fully or to help them to do so ('Do you mean . . . ?').

Most groups include the 'over-talkative', the 'over-silent' and the 'red-herring raisers'! Leaders must control the first, encourage the second and redirect the third! Each leader will develop his or her own most natural way of doing that; but it will be helpful to think out what that is before the occasion arises! The first two groups can be helped by some judicious direction of questions to specific individuals or even groups (*e.g.* 'Jane, you know something about this from personal experience . . .'); the third by redirecting the discussion to the passage itself ('That is an interesting point, but isn't it true that this passage really concentrates on . . . ?'). It may be helpful to break the group up into smaller groups sometimes, giving each subgroup specific points to discuss and to report back on. A wise arranging of these smaller groups may also help each member to participate.

More important than any techniques we may develop is the help of the Spirit enabling us to understand and to apply the Scriptures. Have and encourage a humble, prayerful spirit.

6. Keep faith with the schedule; it is better that some of the group wished the study could have been longer than that others are inconvenienced by it stretching beyond the time limits set.

7. Close in prayer. As time permits, spend the closing minutes in corporate prayer, encouraging the group to apply what they have learned in praise and thanks, intercession and petition.

NOTE: Though the Study Guide which follows is arranged in thirteen studies, each contains enough material for it to be divided into two studies, making a programme of twenty-six studies in all.

Group Study Guide

STUDY 1: Acts 1–2

AIM: To understand the significance of the Holy Spirit's descent at Pentecost for the identity, fellowship, and mission of the church.

1. What do you already know about the Book of Acts from your previous study or contact with it? What is its purpose? What are its main themes? How should it guide the faith and life of the church today? List your responses and keep your list to compare it with what you will have learned when you have completed this study.

2. Why did the disciples believe that, since Jesus had risen from the dead, 'the kingdom' was about to be restored to Israel? Are there parallels with the longings of Christians today? How did Jesus correct their understanding of the timing, dimensions, and power of the kingdom? How can his correction refocus our own perspective regarding his kingdom?

3. How did the disciples and the women prepare for the outpouring of the Holy Spirit? Why is prayer, rather than some more obviously 'productive' activity, the appropriate way to receive the Spirit's enabling for witness and service?

4. What does Peter's speech about Judas reveal of Peter's growth of understanding since Caesarea Philippi (*Matt.* 16:21–23), especially of: (1) the work of the Messiah, (2) the interpretation of the Old Testament? How did Peter learn to read the Old Testament in this way?

5. What are the Old Testament backgrounds for the signs of the Spirit's coming at Pentecost (wind, tongues of fire, foreign 'tongues')? What does each sign reveal about the Spirit's present activity in the church and in the lives of believers?

6. Although the crowd gathered in amazement because of the gift of tongues, Peter immediately 'changed the subject' to Jesus – or was it a change of subject? Why did he answer their questions about the Spirit in terms of Jesus' suffering and exaltation?

7. What four activities constantly characterized the greatly-expanded church in the weeks after Pentecost? In which of these is your church strong or weak?

FOR STUDY 2: Read Acts 3–5 and chapters 6–14 of the text.

STUDY 2: Acts 3–5

AIM: To see and gladly embrace Christ's purpose for subjecting his church to both external suffering and internal discipline.

1. References to the power of Jesus' Name appear throughout the account of the healing of the lame man and its sequel (*Acts* 3–4). What is the significance of God's Name in Scripture? How does the apostles' use of Jesus' Name differ from ancient and modern magic?

2. Which Old Testament texts form the background for Peter's sermon in Acts 3? What do these passages reveal about Jesus' Person and redemptive work?

3. Peter's sermon opens with the affirmation that Jesus, not Peter, has brought healing. It closes with the promise that Jesus turns people from their wickedness. Why should the truth that Jesus alone saves humble us? Why should it encourage us?

4. In our day of religious pluralism Christians are accused of being intolerant and arrogant when they echo Peter's confession in Acts 4:12. Is this criticism justified? Why or why not?

5. As you read the prayer of these early believers (*Acts* 4:24–30) in the light of the crisis they faced, what impresses you about their priorities? How do your priorities in prayer compare with theirs?

6. Was the punishment of Ananias and Sapphira too harsh? Why, or why not? What does your answer reveal about your perception of the holiness and presence of God's Spirit?

7. During their second arrest the apostles were not only threatened but also beaten. Why did they consider it an *honour* to suffer *dishonour* for the sake of Jesus?

FOR STUDY 3: Read Acts 6–7 and chapters 15–20 of the text.

STUDY 3: Acts 6–7

AIM: To appreciate the variety of needs and ministries in Christ's church, and to see how God used suffering leaders throughout biblical history to deliver his rebellious people.

1. What differences between members in the Jerusalem church provoked the discontent of Greek-speaking believers? What differences between Christians today may threaten the unity of a congregation? What features of the apostles' attitude, as well as the solution they proposed, defused the tension and restored harmony?

2. Why did the apostles refuse to neglect their preaching ministry in order to care for widows? How do the qualifications they lay down for the leaders of mercy ministry show the importance, difficulty, and dignity of that ministry?

3. Why did the developing leadership structure, with the Seven charged to care for widows in need, further the evangelistic expansion of the church? Does the 'division of labour' between leaders who care for spiritual needs with the Word, and those who care for material needs with compassion and competence, operate well in your church? How could it be improved?

4. Why did Stephen's preaching about Jesus provoke such strong opposition from the Hellenistic Jews who belonged to the Synagogue of the Freedmen? If the message about Jesus is good news, why do people find it threatening?

5. How did Stephen's 'defence' speech answer the charge that he was attacking God by speaking of the destruction of the temple?

How may we be tempted to place more value on majestic buildings than on the reality of God's presence?

6. What threads woven through redemptive history link Joseph, Moses, the prophets, and Jesus, 'the Righteous One'?

7. How did Stephen follow the footsteps of his Master to death? How did Jesus respond to his servant Stephen's faithfulness?

FOR STUDY 4: Read Acts 8–9 and chapters 21–26 of the text.

STUDY 4: Acts 8–9

AIM: To grasp how God used the painful dispersion of his church to spread his Word to religious 'half-breeds' (Samaritans), to the marginalized (Ethiopian eunuch), and even to a violent enemy (Saul).

1. Why might the report that 'Samaria had received the word of God' raise eyebrows in the Jerusalem church and call for investigation? What was the history of the relationship between Jews and Samaritans?

2. Why did the Holy Spirit come upon the Samaritans at a later point, some time *after* they had believed the gospel that Philip preached? Should we expect this two-step process as the normal pattern for Christians today? Why, or why not?

3. In the light of Peter's words to Simon the magician in 8:20–23, what does Luke mean when he says that Simon had 'believed' (verse 13)? Can Christians lose their salvation? Why, or why not?

4. In his own country, the Ethiopian eunuch had power, wealth, and respect, yet two obstacles kept him on the margins of the people of God, despite his devotion. What were those obstacles? What types of people today, like the Ethiopian, enjoy affluence and influence in the present culture but would have difficulty gaining acceptance in the church?

5. Saul was outside the new people of God, the church, of his own choice: he regarded believers in Jesus as dangerous apostates, deserving death. Was anyone praying for Saul's conversion (see Acts 7:60–8:1)? Does someone come to your mind whose conversion would be as 'impossible' as Saul's? Will you pray consistently for that person?

6. What did Jesus imply about his church when he accused Saul, 'Why are you persecuting *me*?' How did Paul bring out these implications in his epistles?

7. How did Peter reveal his dependence on the Lord Jesus in raising Aeneas from his mat? In raising Tabitha from the dead? How can we practise genuine dependence on Christ's power as we serve others?

FOR STUDY 5: read Acts 10–11 and chapters 27–32 of the text.

STUDY 5: Acts 10–11

AIM: To discover that God welcomes and cleanses all sorts of people through faith alone in Christ alone.

1. What qualities and practices set Cornelius apart from most Roman soldiers and other Gentiles? Did these things give Cornelius a right to God's favour? Why, or why not?

2. Why was Peter shocked at God's command during the vision on the rooftop? What was the religious significance of the dietary restrictions in Leviticus? How did Peter's response show that he had not fully grasped Jesus' teaching in Mark 7? In what ways are we tempted to blame outside influences for being the source of defilement?

3. In his sermon to Cornelius and his friends Peter referred to Jesus' crucifixion in words drawn from Deuteronomy 21:23. Paul used these words in Galatians 3:13 to explain how Gentiles, as well as Jews, can receive forgiveness and the Holy Spirit of God. What is

[359]

the connection between Jesus' death as one 'hanged on a tree' and the blessings that we receive by faith?

4. Why is it important for your faith that the apostles, like Peter here with Cornelius, continually stress their calling as witnesses to Jesus' resurrection, having eaten and drunk with him after he rose from the dead?

5. Who made the decision that circumcision was no longer required in order to join the people of God? How did he indicate his decision?

6. Why was Barnabas sent to Antioch when news of the Lord's blessing on the multi-ethnic church there reached Jerusalem? What features of his background and personality made him the ideal choice to encourage and guide this church? What qualities in Barnabas reflect the beauty of Jesus and deserve to be cultivated in your own life?

7. How did the church at Jerusalem minister to the church at Antioch? How did the church at Antioch minister to the church at Jerusalem? How should different congregations, even in different locations, serve each other through the gifts God has given to each?

FOR STUDY 6: Read Acts 12 and chapters 33–34 of the text.

STUDY 6: Acts 12

AIM: To recognize that Christ triumphs over his enemies through us, whether he calls us to die for the faith or to be released for further service.

1. James, son of Zebedee, became the first apostle to be martyred. Where are Christians answering Christ's call to be 'faithful unto death' today (*Rev.* 2:10)? How can we help them?

2. What does the soundness of Peter's sleep tell us about his confidence in God's care? Compare or contrast the sleep described in Mark 4:38 and Luke 22:45. How should we respond to anxiety-produced insomnia?

3. The Christians who were praying for Peter's release had trouble believing that God had answered their prayers. What recent event might have led them to doubt? Do you also offer 'double–minded' requests to God, doubting that your Father is willing or able to provide for you (*James* 1:6–8)? Why do we struggle to pray in confident faith?

4. We see Luke's gentle humour in the description of Peter's dreamy sleepwalk (as he thought) and in his being left locked outside by Rhoda in her excitement. How can the gospel's realism about our sin and weakness and its assurance of God's amazing grace keep us from taking ourselves too seriously?

5. Politicians, business leaders, pastors – all of us – can succumb, as King Herod did, to the temptation to divert glory from God to ourselves (although usually we are subtler than he was). How are you tempted to steal God's glory, even in little things? Why does God take such offence at this sin?

6. Acts 12:24 is the second summary that speaks of the growth and spread of God's Word. How are you participating in that growth of the Word today through witness, teaching, service, prayer, giving, or in other ways? What fruit do you see developing in your own life as a result of the Word's organic power?

7. This week's group study, which is shorter than others, brings us to the close of the second section of Acts. Think back over the last six weeks and share how your perspective on the church and your calling as a Christian is changing. How is this growth in your convictions being worked out in your priorities and behaviour?

FOR STUDY 7: Read Acts 13–14 and chapters 35–40 of the text.

STUDY 7: Acts 13–14

AIM: To discover how the good news of Christ can be communicated both to those who know the Bible well and to those who do not know it at all.

1. 'World missions begin in worship.' Is this more than a mere historical observation upon the time of prayer and fasting at Antioch when the Holy Spirit called Barnabas and Saul to bring God's Word to other lands? Is there something about true worship that should propel us to witness and to support the advance of the gospel? What is it?

2. What is the symbolism of the judgement imposed on Elymas Bar-Jesus, the sorcerer? Is it possible for someone to have perfect eyesight and still be blind? How can such blindness be healed?

3. In the synagogue of Pisidian Antioch, what theological and pastoral points did Paul make in his selective survey of Israel's history? Where was it all leading?

4. What can Jesus do for us that the Law cannot (13:38–39)? Where does Paul teach this same point in his letters? How does this truth calm your guilty conscience? How does this truth open up salvation to the Gentiles?

5. Why does the gospel divide people wherever it is taken seriously?

6. What are the similarities between the healing of the crippled man in Lystra and the healing of the crippled man at the temple gate in Jerusalem (*Acts* 3)? How does the attitude of Paul here, and Peter there, differ from the attitude of King Herod (*Acts* 12:21–23)? What made them different?

7. How does Paul's speech in Lystra differ from his sermon in the synagogue at Antioch? Why does it differ in this way? Discuss how the previous experience and belief system of those to whom we

witness should influence our approach in communicating God's truth to them.

FOR STUDY 8: Read Acts 15 and chapters 41–44 of the text.

STUDY 8: Acts 15

AIM: To observe how God used the wisdom of the church's leaders to protect the liberty of believers in the gospel of grace.

1. What do the controversy over Gentile circumcision at Antioch and its resolution teach us about the relationship between congregations in the apostolic church? What are the strengths and safeguards of this type of relationship?

2. Peter reminded the apostolic council that, when he brought the gospel to the Gentiles, God 'made no distinction' between Gentiles and Jews. How are we all alike in relation to the Law of God? In relation to the grace of God? What does the gospel have to say about our tendency to draw distinctions between ourselves and others?

3. What were the factors raised in the discussion that informed the council's final decision? That is, what did Peter's speech, Paul's and Barnabas' report, and James' speech each contribute to the process? What can we learn from this process for our own decision-making, whether as individuals or in concert with fellow believers in the church?

4. What were the four prohibitions that the council gave to Gentile believers? What was the foundational rationale behind these restrictions? How should this rationale be applied in our culture? Why did the council supplement their encouraging letter to the Gentiles by sending it with encouraging leaders, Judas and Silas? What can 'in person' conversation accomplish that written communication (including e-mail) cannot?

6. If Paul had commended the churches of Asia Minor to the care of the Lord (14:23), why did Paul feel a need to visit them again and strengthen them (15:36, 41)? How does Paul exemplify a sound grasp of the relationship between God's sovereignty and our responsibility?

7. Why does Luke record the conflict between Paul and Barnabas? What does it reveal about even the most godly church leaders? How should this affect our attitude toward our pastors and our ministry to them?

FOR STUDY 9: Read Acts 16–17 and chapters 45–48 of the text.

STUDY 9: Acts 16–17

AIM: To note how the gospel speaks to all sorts of people – businesswoman, slave, jailer, Jewish students of Scripture, and Greek philosophers – giving life to all who believe.

1. In circumcising Timothy, was Paul betraying what he had defended so strongly at Antioch and in the apostolic council? Why, or why not? What principle drove his decision to circumcise Timothy?

2. Have you experienced 'closed doors', as Paul's team did when trying to enter Asia and Bithynia, only to learn later the unexpected direction that the Lord intended to take you? Share your experience with others, for their encouragement.

3. Why did Lydia believe the gospel when Paul preached it by the river side?

4. How could Paul and Silas sing in the Philippian jail, with welts on their backs and stocks on their ankles? Paul's letter to the Christians of Philippi often mentions joy. Where does such joy – utterly independent of circumstances – come from?

5. At Thessalonica, jealous Jews accused Paul of defying Caesar's decrees and proclaiming another king, Jesus. Was their charge true or false – or partly true? What should our non-Christian neighbours notice about our relationship to the local and national government?

6. In speaking to the philosophers at the Areopagus of Athens, why did Paul begin as he did? Why did he develop his argument as he did, even quoting pagan poets? How does his strategy inform our strategy for presenting the message of Christ in our secularized, post-modern culture?

7. Paul returned to the theme of Jesus' resurrection by mentioning the last judgement. Why is the reality of judgement to come an important truth for people to understand and believe, in order for them to understand Christ's cross and resurrection?

FOR STUDY 10: Read Acts 18–20 and chapters 49–54 of the text.

STUDY 10: Acts 18–20

AIM: To see the power of the gospel changing lives in major cities on both sides of the Aegean Sea, Corinth and Ephesus, in the midst of opposition from Jewish and pagan sources.

1. Why was Paul willing to work as a tentmaker, when other Hellenistic teachers demanded payment for their wisdom? What fundamental principle of the gospel was he trying to express in this aspect of his life? (See *1 Cor. 9*.)

2. Do you think of Paul as needing special encouragement from the Lord when facing opposition (18:9–11)? When we take seriously his weakness and fear, how does this encourage us to expect the Lord to use us for his glory?

3. What are the differences and similarities between Apollos, who knew only John's baptism, and the twelve 'disciples' at Ephesus, who had only received John's baptism? In our day there are varying

types and degrees of misunderstanding of biblical doctrine among groups claiming to be Christian. What are the essentials that a group must believe to claim legitimately the Name of Christ?

4. In Corinth and Ephesus, as elsewhere, Paul began his ministry in the city's Jewish synagogue. Why did he do this over and over again? (see *Rom.* 1:16–17; chapters 9–11). Should the church still place a high priority on evangelizing the Jewish people? If so, how should this be done in light, not only of the spiritual dynamics but also, of the legacy of twenty centuries of Jewish-Christian interaction?

5. The Ephesian silversmiths resented Paul's preaching because it cut into their profits, but they recruited the angry mob by appealing to civic pride. Do you know people who reject Christ because his Lordship could jeopardize their income or their place in the community? What are they failing to see when they choose money or social standing over Jesus?

6. What should the Ephesian elders learn from remembering the example of Paul's ministry among them? How should Paul's example not only guide our elders but motivate us all to communicate God's whole message at every opportunity?

7. How can the church be protected from dangers within its own leadership?

FOR STUDY 11: Read Acts 21–23 and chapters 55–60 of the text.

STUDY 11: Acts 21–23

AIM: To watch Paul seize every opportunity, even when he is falsely accused and his life is threatened, to bear witness for Jesus Christ.

1. When Agabus predicted that Paul would be bound and handed over to the Gentiles in Jerusalem, other Christians immediately concluded that Paul should not go there. Why did Paul travel to

Jerusalem anyway? What was more important to him than his personal safety? Which is more important to you, really?

2. James advised Paul to participate in the ritual for brothers who had taken a Nazirite vow, forfeiting some of his personal freedom for the church's peace and its testimony to other Jews. Is this always the right thing to do? (Remember Paul's stubbornness at the apostolic council, or when demanding an apology from the magistrates of Philippi.) How do we decide when and why to give up our rights, and when to stand up for them?

3. In Paul's defence before the Jewish people in the temple courts, he described his 'Jewish credentials'. What were they? Compare this list with those in Paul's letters: Galatians 1:13–14 and Philippians 3:4–11. What was Paul's evaluation of these achievements after he met Jesus? Why? Of what abilities, virtues, or achievements are you inclined to boast?

4. According to Ananias, for what purpose did God choose Paul? Apart from receiving a direct revelation as Paul did, how can you discern God's purpose for your life? While Paul's calling was unique, are there aspects of his calling that apply to you too?

5. Was Paul being unsubmissive toward the government's authority (*Rom.* 13:1–5) when he mentioned his Roman citizenship as the soldiers were about to flog him? Why or why not? When and how is it appropriate for Christians to defend their rights under civil law?

6. Was Paul sincerely apologetic for having called the high priest a 'whitewashed wall'? What leads you to believe that he was or was not? What should our attitude be toward a leader whose evil conduct dishonours his office?

7. Since the Lord had told Paul that he 'must' testify in Rome, did the actions of Paul's nephew, the centurion, and the commander

Claudius Lysias really make any difference in averting Paul's assassination? Explain your answer. We cannot always discern God's guiding hand of providence as we observe our daily lives, but sometimes we can. Share with the group an experience in which you have seen God's good plan worked out through the decisions of other people.

FOR STUDY 12: Read Acts 24–26 and chapters 61–65 of the text.

STUDY 12: Acts 24–26

AIM: To observe in Paul the calm confidence and integrity that Christ gives, winning the respect even of governors and kings.

1. What are the similarities and the differences of style between Tertullus' prosecution speech and Paul's defence speech? Christians engaged in society (work, politics, academics, etc.) often wrestle with the issue of how different Christ calls us to be from unbelieving co-workers, colleagues, or competitors. Discuss some of the dilemmas you have faced in your engagement with the broader culture.

2. Why does Paul's hope in the resurrection motivate him to keep his conscience clear before God and man? Compare the conclusion of Paul's great resurrection chapter, 1 Corinthians 15:58. Does your resurrection hope actually function as a motivation in your daily decisions? If not, why do you think it does not?

3. What strengths and weaknesses of Governor Felix's character are exposed by his treatment of Paul? What opportunity of eternal significance confronted the governor? How and why did he miss this opportunity?

4. Why did Felix's successor, Festus, not simply release Paul, in view of his belief in Paul's innocence? How did his attempt to please his 'constituency' backfire? Have you seen an effort to avoid conflict breed bigger problems in the long run?

5. The third retelling of Paul's conversion, which is in his defence before King Agrippa, parallels the first two (*Acts* 9 and 22) in many respects. What themes and emphases make it unique? Why did Paul stress these points in addressing the king?

6. In Paul's speech before Agrippa, what four benefits of the gospel does he mention? What universal human needs do these benefits meet? From what does the gospel set us free?

7. The king had entered the auditorium with pageantry. Paul had entered in chains. Yet Paul saw himself as the happiest, most privileged person in the room, longing for everyone else to enjoy what he had (except for the chains). What did Paul have that Festus, Agrippa, and Bernice lacked? Why was it sweeter to him than his freedom, or even life itself?

FOR STUDY 13: Read Acts 27–28 and chapters 66–70 of the text.

STUDY 13: Acts 27–28

AIM: To watch the Lord subdue the forces of nature and the self-serving decisions of men, in order to bring his servant to the heart of the City of Man, so that he could freely announce the Kingdom of God.

1. Do you draw the comfort that Paul did in the storm from the truth that you are not your own but belong, body and soul, to your faithful Saviour Jesus Christ? If that truth does not put our worries and fears to rest, why is our emotional response to stress or crisis sometimes 'disconnected' from the doctrines we say we believe? How can we become integrated people, whose feelings, affections, and values correspond to our convictions?

2. As the ship neared Malta at least four obstacles stood in the way of the fulfilment of God's promise that no one on board would die. What were they? How did Paul's and the Centurion Julius' exercise of human responsibility contribute to the fulfilment of God's sovereign purpose?

3. If the natives of Malta were pagans, dead in trespasses and sins (as their belief that Paul was a god suggests), how could they extend such compassionate hospitality to the castaways? How should we think about the integrity and kindness of unbelievers such as the Maltese or Julius the centurion?

4. What do we learn about Paul as a person through his contacts with the Christians of Sidon, Puteoli, and Rome, at either end of his long voyage? His letters also reveal a man who relied on his brothers and sisters in Christ for comfort and refreshment of heart (*2 Cor.* 2:1–4; 6:11–13; *Gal.* 4:12–20, *Phil.* 4:1). Is it a sign of shameful weakness to need others so much? Why, or why not?

5. Paul had two motives, one legal and one pastoral, for wanting to meet with the leaders of the Jewish synagogues in Rome. What were these motives for initiating contact? Review together the variety of circumstances throughout Acts in which Paul creatively brought the conversation around to Jesus. What interactions with others have you been able to convert into openings for the gospel?

6. Repeatedly throughout Acts we have heard that Paul proclaimed Jesus as Messiah from the Law of Moses and the prophets, as he did in dialogue with the synagogue leaders at Rome. What texts might he have used? Can you show where the Old Testament Scriptures teach that the Messiah must suffer and then rise from the dead to bring forgiveness of sins to those who trust him?

7. Review the answers that were given in response to question 1 of the first study (What did you already know or believe about the Book of Acts from your previous study or contact with it? What is its purpose? What are its main themes? How should it guide the faith and life of the church today?).

What new insights have you gained from working through this study of Acts? How have these insights affected your convictions, attitudes, and patterns of behaviour in relation to Christ, his church, and its mission in the world?

FOR FURTHER READING

The following books are recommended for study of the Acts of the Apostles:

F. F. BRUCE, *Commentary on the Book of Acts* (*New International Commentary on the New Testament* series), Grand Rapids: Eerdmans Publishing Company, 1954.

SIMON J. KISTEMAKER, *New Testament Commentary: Exposition of the Acts of the Apostles,* Grand Rapids: Baker Book House, 1990.

JOHN B. POLHILL, *Acts* (*The New American Commentary*), Nashville: Broadman Press, 1992).

A thematic study:

DENNIS E. JOHNSON, *The Message of Acts in the History of Redemption,* Phillipsburg, New Jersey: P & R Publishing Company, 1997.

SOME OTHER
BANNER OF TRUTH
TITLES

AUTHENTIC CHRISTIANITY

VOLS. 1–3

SERMONS ON THE
ACTS OF THE APOSTLES

D. Martyn Lloyd-Jones

These volumes bring together much of Dr Lloyd-Jones' evangelistic preaching on the Acts of Apostles originally given in Westminster Chapel in the mid-1960s. The first three volumes deal with chapters 1–6 of Acts, bringing the message of these chapters powerfully to bear on the heart and conscience of the reader.

'The style is crystal clear. The content is thoroughly evangelistic. The glory of the gospel shines forth on every page. I thoroughly commend it – truly Dr Lloyd-Jones at his best.'

EVANGELICAL TIMES

'Get it – Read it – Promote it – Re-read it – Pray in the light of it.'

MONTHLY RECORD

ISBNs
0 85151 776 5 (VOL. 1)
0 85151 807 9 (VOL. 2)
0 85151 832 X (VOL. 3)
Approximately 336 pp. per volume
clothbound

ACTS
A COMMENTARY IN
THE GENEVA SERIES

J. A. Alexander

C. H. Spurgeon's verdict on this commentary was: 'In all respects a work of the highest merit.'

J. H. Thornwell wrote: 'Alexander's commentaries on Acts and Mark [are] as near perfection in their kind as human skill could make them, and I have been in the habit, not only of recommending them, but of insisting on my classes procuring and studying them.'

'So forceful are some of the thoughts suggested that the reader is compelled to stop reading in order to think out the application . . . This is the hallmark of the true commentator. He is to the reader what the bucket of water is to the pump. His thought poured into the reader's heart and mind enables him to bring forth his own thoughts.'

IRISH EVANGELICAL

'One of the best, most powerful, expositions of Acts now extant. More than worth its price.'

CRUSADE

ISBN 0 85151 309 3,
984 pp., clothbound

The LET'S STUDY Series

If you have enjoyed *Let's Study Acts* and found it helpful, you will be interested in other titles from this series of books for personal and group Bible Study from the Banner of Truth Trust:

- **LET'S STUDY MARK** by Sinclair B. Ferguson
- **LET'S STUDY JOHN** by Mark Johnston
- **LET'S STUDY 2 CORINTHIANS**
  by Derek Prime
- **LET'S STUDY PHILIPPIANS**
  by Sinclair B. Ferguson
- **LET'S STUDY 1 & 2 THESSALONIANS**
  by Andrew W. Young
- **LET'S STUDY HEBREWS** by Hywel R. Jones
- **LET'S STUDY REVELATION** by Derek Thomas

The books in this series are written in a straightforward way to help ordinary Christians to understand and apply Scripture. They are ideal for personal use or for families and feature additional material for Bible study groups. Please order from your local Christian bookshop, or in case of difficulty from:

THE BANNER OF TRUTH TRUST

3 Murrayfield Road,
Edinburgh EH12 6EL
UK

P O Box 621, Carlisle,
Philadelphia 17013,
USA